Professional Communication Skills
Fifth Edition

Edited by:

Adria Battaglia

John A. Daly & Anna M. Young

Learning Solutions

New York   Boston   San Francisco
London   Toronto   Sydney   Tokyo   Singapore   Madrid
Mexico City   Munich   Paris   Cape Town   Hong Kong   Montreal

**Pearson
Custom Publishing**
is a division of

www.pearsonhighered.com

ISBN 10: 0-558-41954-2
ISBN 13: 978-0-558-41954-7

Contents at a Glance

Part 4   Informative and Persuasive Speaking

Table of Contents

Part 2   Interpersonal and Group Communication

Part 3   Preparing Public Presentations

CMS 306M
Professional Communication Skills
Course Packet

Professional Communication Skills
CMS 306M

Course: CMS 306M

Day & Time:

Instructor:

Office:

Section :

Location:

E-mail:

Office Hours:

COURSE GOALS

The major aims of this course are to make you a more effective professional communicator, analytical thinker and critical listener. Throughout the session you will study the theories and principles of effective communication, practice applying these principles in a variety of assignments, and critique the performances of other speakers. By the end of the semester, you should be able to plan and prepare professional meetings and presentations; deliver a good speech; analyze and adapt to various audiences; and adjust to different speaking situations, purposes, and contexts. **NOTE:** ONLY 1 OF THE FOLLOWING COURSES MAY BE COUNTED FOR YOUR DEGREE: CMS 305, 306M, 319, SPE 305, 319.

REQUIRED COURSE MATERIALS

❑ *Professional Communication Skills,* 4th edition (2008). Anna M. Young, John A. Daly, & Adria Battaglia (Eds). Indianapolis, IN: Pearson. This book will serve as both a textbook and a workbook. Inside it you will find instructions for assignments, pages that you will tear out and hand in, and blank leaflets for taking notes. With a new media component (access code included in the workbook), you will utilize a wide array of resources such as sample student speeches, interviews with UT faculty on communication issues in our world, researching and outlining tools, and chapter quizzes to help familiarize you with important communication concepts before course exams.

❑ A CD or memory stick for PowerPoint presentations and other electronic documents

IMPORTANT WEBSITES

❑ Blackboard is the course management software for CMS 306M and can be accessed at: **http://courses.utexas.edu**.

❑ Although extra credit opportunities will be announced in class, they also may be found online at: **http://commstudies.utexas.edu/undergraduate/prod_002396.html**.

ASSIGNMENTS

We will explore the various contexts of professional communication through the following assignments. Additional instructions (including the length of presentations, required visual aids, outlines to turn in, etc) are found in your workbook, along with worksheets that your instructor may ask you to turn in to accompany lessons and assignments.

Group Presentation: For this assignment you will acquire the skills necessary for decision making and problem solving processes; interaction with audiences; planning, organizing, and facilitating meetings; anticipating and utilizing audience feedback; and working effectively in group contexts. NOTE: all group members will receive the same grade for the presentation. Because group members must count upon one another for success, you are expected to contribute and participate to the highest of your ability in your group project. While your participation during preparation of this assignment will not be monitored by your instructor, if allegations are raised and subsequent investigation reveals that a member habitually missed meetings, arrived unprepared, and/or failed to complete work, then a substantial penalty will be imposed. Worth a **total of *35 points***, this assignment is graded in two sections: the group grade worth 30 points and an individual grade based on a written assessment of your group interaction worth 5 points. On your presentation day, please tear out and bring to class the instructor evaluation sheet and the peer evaluations from your textbook/workbook.

Informative Presentation: For this assignment you will learn to organize, clarify, refine, and deliver informative messages. Following the presentation, you will be required to watch a videotape of your presentation and complete a self-assessment of your performance. This assignment is worth **a total of *65 points***: 60 points for the presentation and 5 points for the self-assessment. On your presentation day, please tear out and bring to class the instructor evaluation sheet and the peer evaluations from your textbook/workbook.

Persuasive Speech: For this assignment you will learn to critically construct, evaluate, and deliver persuasive arguments through various appeals and reasoning. Following the presentation, you will again be required to watch a videotape of your presentation and complete a self-assessment of your performance. This assignment is worth **a total of *65 points***: 60 points for the presentation and 5 points for the self-assessment. On your presentation day, please tear out and bring to class the instructor evaluation sheet and the peer evaluations from your textbook/workbook.

Impromptu Speech: For this assignment, you will use what you have learned about audience analysis, language use and organization to construct and deliver an impromptu speech. This assignment is worth ***30 points***. On your presentation day, please tear out and bring to class the instructor evaluation sheet.

Exams 1 & 2: There will be two exams during the course of the semester. Refer to the course schedule for exam times and material covered. Your instructor will provide a review sheet prior to each exam. Each exam is worth ***60 points***.

Written Self-Evaluations & Video-Taped Presentations: All assignments will be taped for your benefit. You are required to watch the videotapes of your first (Group), second (Informative) and third presentations (Persuasive) and provide written critiques based upon your observations and recollections of the assignments. **[NOTE: If you do not view the videotape prior to completing the Informative and Persuasive Self-Assessment, you will receive ZERO points on that assignment.]** You also have the option of scheduling a time to watch your taped presentation with your instructor. **The video will be available in the CMA Instructional Media Center (IMC) playback room, located in CMA 5.110 and is open Monday–Thursday from 7:45 a.m. until 6:30 p.m., Friday from 7:45 a.m. until 5 p.m., and weekends from 12:00 until 6 p.m.** Your assessment papers will be worth 5 points each for **a total of *15 points***.

Participation Points: In class, you are expected to participate in discussion, oral/written critiques of speeches, practice/impromptu speeches, and other activities. Your instructor may also ask you to complete additional written work, video viewings, and other related exercises outside of class. **No make-ups will be granted for participation activities.** Participation is worth **a total of *30 points*.**

Peer Evaluations: All assignments will be evaluated and critiqued by the audience. You are expected to share both positive and negative feedback in the form of constructive comments. Written evaluations will be assigned on presentation days and are **due at the end of the speech day (late critiques will not be accepted).** You must put your name on the peer evaluations to receive credit. You will find peer evaluations in your textbook/workbook that you should tear out and bring with you to class on presentation days.

Chapter Quizzes

Your instructor will ask you to complete chapter quizzes for homework. These quizzes are an opportunity for you to both keep up with your readings and familiarize yourself with the testing format of this course. The quizzes are accessible through Blackboard (you have an access code in your workbook). After you enter your access code in CMS 306M course on Blackboard, select "Chapter Quizzes and Media Content" from the menu. Then select the folder of the chapter you wish to access. Click on the "Quiz" link. Questions are randomized, and quizzes are timed. If you do not complete the quiz within the time allotted to you by your instructor, you will receive ZERO points. No make-ups will be granted. Quizzes are worth a total of *30 points*: There are 15 quizzes, two questions per quiz, and 1 point per question.

Extra Credit

Extra credit will be offered for your participation in departmental research projects, **up to four points.** Participation in extra credit projects beyond the allotted maximum of four points will not be considered. Extra credit is to encourage student involvement in communication issues, not simply bolster grades. If your primary goal is to raise your grade in this course, do not rely on extra credit. Your time will be better invested in studying the material from lecture and the reading assignments. Late requests for extra credit, like late assignments, will not be considered.

These opportunities will be posted on the participant pool board in the CMA building (where you will sign up), and/or can be viewed online through the Current Extra Credit & Research-related Opportunities at **http://commstudies.utexas.edu/undergraduate/prod_002396.html**.

NOTE: You should check these postings regularly to sign up for different research opportunities. These research opportunities will occur throughout the semester and are not guaranteed at any specific time (thus, don't wait until the last minute!). They are on a first-come first-served basis. Written confirmation from the researcher will be sent to your instructor to guarantee you receive your points. Typically, researchers wait until they have gathered all their data before contacting instructors, so please calculate extra credit points at the end of the semester (the week before the second exam, check to make sure you have your extra credit points).

GRADING

Grades are determined on a straight percentage scale based on the number of points earned out of a **maximum of 375 points. <u>There will be no further rounding or curving of grades.</u>** Final grades are calculated as follows:

A	=	89.5%–100%	(336–375)
B	=	79.5%–89.49%	(298–335)
C	=	69.5%–79.49%	(261–297)
D	=	59.5%–69.49%	(223–260)
F	=	below 59.5%	(0–222)

Assignment	Maximum Points Possible	My Points
Group Meeting	30 points	
Informative Presentation	60 points	
Persuasive Presentation	60 points	
Impromptu Presentation	30 points	
Midterm Exam	60 points	
Final Exam	60 points	
Participation	30 points	
Chapter Quizzes	30 points (15 quizzes, two question per quiz, 1 point per question)	
Three Written Evaluations	15 points (5 points each)	
Optional Extra Credit (no more than 2)	*2 points each, 4 points max*	
TOTAL COURSE POINTS	375 points	

A Note about Grading: The Communication Studies Department holds the same set of standards for all students in this course. Instructors are trained to help you aim for (and ideally reach) a certain level of presentation skill. Some students will develop the skills taught in this class sooner than others (just like some students are stronger in math, and others in history, so some are stronger in communication studies). The final grade in this class is cumulative, not merely reflective of a student's work during the latter portion of the semester. Just like in any other course, sometimes a student may struggle at the beginning, develop stronger skills throughout the course of the semester, and still earn an overall grade of a 'D,' 'C' or 'B.' It is important to remember that hard work does not always result in a student's desired grade.

Discussion of Graded Assignments: University procedure for a grade contestation begins with a student and the instructor. Success in this course requires thoughtful self-evaluation of your performance. A student wishing to contest a grade **must** present his or her instructor with a **typed** (either e-mail or paper), well thought out case regarding the evaluation **within one week of having received the evaluation** of the assignment in question. The argument must be related to the assignment as presented, and based on how it compares with the criteria for the assignment (not how it compares with someone else's work or how it will affect a student's GPA). Once the student has submitted his or her argument to the instructor, the instructor will respond in writing within 7 days. Student and instructor then may meet face-to-face to view the speech in question, and discuss ways to improve future papers/presentations. Instructors are available for questions or if you need extra assistance outside of class. Please schedule an appointment during an instructor's office hours.

COURSE POLICIES

Instructional Methods: You should expect this class to be different from other courses you have taken because there is a large experiential element. Therefore, a significant amount of the teaching in this course is done by you through the presentation, observation, and evaluation of in-class exercises and performances. You will learn communication skills by practicing them.

Attendance: Attendance is required. You cannot do public speaking without a public. Because of the unique nature of this class, grades and classroom attendance are closely related. Much of what you will learn will be through experimentation as well as observation. Given this, attendance as well as participation, (exercises and discussions) becomes an essential part of professional communication. You are expected to attend every class period. A **roll sheet** will be passed around each day. It is your responsibility to sign in (**being present but not signing the roll is the same as being absent**). The following policy will be enforced in this class:

(1) Your first THREE unexcused absences are without penalty. If you do miss a class, it is your responsibility to get the information that was covered from one of your classmates.

(2) Your fourth absence will lower your final course average by 4 points. (ex: If you have 296 points, you will be reduced to 292 points).

(3) Each subsequent unexcused absence will lower your final course average by 4 points.

(4) An unexcused tardy (ten minutes late in a 50 minute class, fifteen minutes late in a 75 minute class) is considered an absence.

The only absences recognized as excused are those noted by the University.
For a listing of University approved absences, please visit:
http://www.utexas.edu/student/registrar/catalogs/gi06-07/ch4/ch4g.html#page.top.

Just so that we are clear, work conflicts, being delayed by traffic, trips that you had planned before/during/after signing-up for this class, being tired from previous evening activities, and faulty alarm clocks are **not** the type of events that fall into the category of excused absences. Use your three free absences for such events.

If you have an unexcused absence on an exam day or the day you are assigned to present, you will receive a zero on that exam/assignment.

A student wishing to observe a religious holy day must notify the instructor in writing at least 14 days prior to the classes scheduled on dates the student will be absent. For religious holy days that fall within the first two weeks of the semester, notice should be given on the first day of the semester. Other absences may be excused according to University policy.

Given the importance of participation in this course, should you begin to struggle at any point during the semester due to personal reasons (unforeseen events like family emergences, a significant illness, etc), please speak with your academic advisor. The University has many options to help students, ranging from Q-drops and reduced workloads (reducing the number of hours you are enrolled in) to incompletes (this option is NOT available if you are failing a course) and withdraws. The sooner you let your advisor know when something is wrong, the sooner (and better) the University can help you.

The Americans with Disabilities Act (ADA) is a federal anti-discrimination statute that provides comprehensive civil rights protection for persons with disabilities. Among other things, this legislation requires that all students with disabilities be guaranteed a learning environment that provides for reasonable accommodation. The University of Texas at Austin offers support services for students with documented physical or psychological disabilities. A students with a disability should visit with her instructor after requesting reasonable accommodations through the Service for Students with Disabilities: http://www.utexas.edu/diversity/ddce/ssd/.

Readings must be completed **on the day they are assigned** on the course schedule. Be sure to read the book and take notes while reading. In your textbook/workbook, there are blank leaflet pages for you to take notes from your readings as well as from lecture. Lectures are intended to *complement* (not duplicate) that information.

Written Work (presentation preparation, self-evaluations, etc.) must be typed. Failure to type any written portion of an assignment results in a 10% point deduction off the whole point value of that assignment. Since peer evaluations are due at the end of class they may be hand written. Any assignments completed in class as part of class participation may also be hand written.

Deadlines will be announced by your instructor. Assignments must be turned in at the beginning of class on the day they are due. **Assignments turned in after class on the due date are considered late. Late assignments will be penalized. No assignments will be accepted after one week beyond the due date.** In addition, the tentative course schedule does not allow flexibility in rescheduling presentations. Don't miss class on a day you are scheduled to speak. Unexcused absences on presentation or exam days and will be earn a grade of zero; **no make-ups will be granted.** If you miss an in-class activity for participation points, you will earn a zero for that assignment (unless you have a university excused absence).

Changes to the schedule may be made at your instructor's discretion and if circumstances require. It is your responsibility to note these changes when announced.

Visual Aid Backups: You will often be required to design and deliver presentations using Power Point software and computer projection systems. While every effort is made to keep the equipment in working condition, on occasion the equipment may not work properly. You are therefore required to bring backup overhead slides to <u>all</u> of your presentations. In the event of problems, these backups will allow you to complete the assignment.

Classroom Civility: People and ideas must be treated with respect. Please avoid disruptive behavior that makes it difficult to accomplish our mutual objectives. ★★★**Please remember to turn off all cell phones or other noisy devices before entering the classroom each day. Needless to say, they are highly disruptive during lectures and presentations.** Distracting behavior during speech days (i.e., working on laptops, or talking) may result in a reduction of points on your own speech. On presentation days, please arrive on time or early and, if you're late, please wait outside until the first presentation is completed.

Academic Integrity: University standards regulating academic integrity (e.g., cheating, plagiarism, etc.) are strictly enforced. Infractions may result in a zero for the assignment or a failing grade in the course.

Plagiarism is a serious offense in this course. Using the words and ideas of others is borrowing something from those individuals. It is always necessary to identify the original source of supporting information; you must cite the source of any material, quoted or paraphrased, used in your presentation. The absence of this documentation constitutes *plagiarism*—a serious academic and professional offense. Proper documentation requires a bibliography of any outside texts you have consulted including both traditional sources and on-line sources.

Your responsibility as a speaker is to distinguish between what are *your* thoughts and ideas and what is not, and to credit those who have contributed to your presentation. Putting your name on a piece of work indicates that the work is *yours* and that the praise or criticism is due to *you* and no one else. Putting your name on a piece of work in which any part is not yours, is *plagiarism*—unless the borrowed thought or wording is clearly marked and the work is fully identified. Keep in mind that plagiarism is a form of theft. Taking words, phrasing, or sentence structure, or any other element of another person's ideas, and using them as if they were your own, is stealing. Simply paraphrasing the work of another without acknowledging the information source is also plagiarism. Merely restating another individual's ideas in different words does not make the ideas yours. ALL presentations are to be your original work. **Using speeches or presentations from previous semesters or other classes is still considered plagiarism. Unauthorized collaboration on presentations (with a student in your section or another student in a different section) is not allowed without prior approval from your instructor.**

If you are caught being dishonest, you will be given an "F" for the assignment and/or the course depending on the severity of the offense. To avoid getting into trouble for academic dishonesty, please visit the following websites and read-up:

http://deanofstudents.utexas.edu/sjs/acint_student.php
http://uts.cc.utexas.edu/~rhart/courses/materials/plagiarism/

Please understand that instructors do not tolerate plagiarism and will fail you for it, even if your plagiarism is unintentional. As a professor in our department often reminds students, "When you started at UT you signed a document that said you would uphold the UT Honor Code. Inclusive of that code is an understanding of plagiarism and what is and is not permissible. Hence, even if you cheat without full knowledge of doing so, you can still receive a failing grade." These standards may seem subtle, so feel free to ask if you have questions or concerns.

CMS 306M Media Component
What is this thing?

The Department of Communication Studies at the University of Texas at Austin has joined hundreds of other universities and colleges across the nation in the move towards integrating media technology into the classroom. The CMS 306M media component is customized to reflect and adapt to the changing needs of our instructors and students.

Our media component includes tools to help engage you in the course material. Through interviews with UT faculty members and graduate students, as well as links to historical and contemporary speeches by social and political leaders, the media component helps you see abstract communication concepts in the real world. Chapter quizzes will help familiarize you with the style of exam questions in this course. The UT Speech Team provided sample student presentations (both "professional" and "unprofessional" versions) to help you see which type of organizational and delivery strategies can make you a more successful public presenter. Links to current news stories and Hollywood movies help you find communication principles at work all around you. And of course, you have access to a range of research tools to help you generate thoughtful topics and write effective outlines.

How do I install it?

1) Log in to Blackboard using your UTEID. Select your CMS 306M section.

2) In the announcements section, click "Start Here." You will need your **student access code.** Key in the code provided to you in the workbook you purchased, *Professional Communication Skills*. A window will open thanking you for registering and instructing you to close the window. This will return you to your home page within your course on Blackboard. The menu on the left side of the screen is now longer, as the code provides you access to the Media Component. You should see a screen like this:

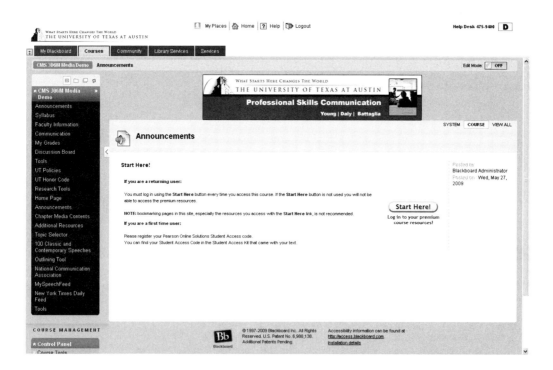

Each time you log into Blackboard and select your CMS section, you will have to **click on the "Start Here" button** and key in your password to access the media component. Because your quizzes are graded through the media component, it is important to remember that you will need your own access code. Do not lose your code.

Okay. I'm in. Now what?

On the left side of the screen, you will see the traditional Blackboard menu. You will see links for "Announcements," "Syllabus," "Faculty Information," "Communication," "My Grades," "Discussion Board," "Tools," "UT Policies," "UT Honor Code," etc. These links appear in the menu for all of your UT courses.

You will see additional links for "Chapter Quizzes and Media Contents," "Additional Resources," "Topic Selector," "100 Classical and Contemporary Speeches," "Outlining Tool," "National Communication Association," "MySpeechFeed," and the "New York Times Daily News Feed." **Remember, to access these links, you will need to log in using your access code each time you log into your CMS 306M section.**

Let's walk through the benefits of each link so that you know where to go to access resources, take quizzes, or complete assignments.

1) **Chapter Quizzes and Media Contents.** This is the main tool in the media component. This is where you will access chapter folders and quizzes. If you click on the Chapter Quizzes and Media Contents link, you will see an ABC News Feed and then chapter folders. It should look something like this:

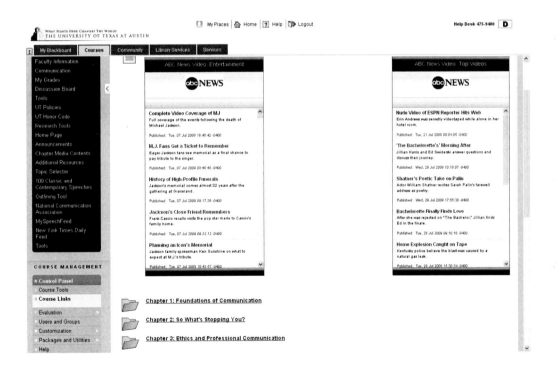

Each chapter folder contains links to helpful resources. In some folders, you will find sample student speeches, YouTube clips, links to Hollywood movie scenes, interviews with UT faculty or graduate students, and more. You will also find a chapter quiz. We'll talk more about the quizzes a little later on.

Throughout your workbook, look for "media boxes" in each chapter. These boxes will direct you to particular resources within the Chapter Quizzes and Media Contents folder online.

2) **Additional Resources**. This includes a link to the workbook's publisher's webpage, should you have any concerns or questions. It also includes a link to the National Communication Association's credo for ethical communication. You will read more about the importance of this credo in the chapter on ethics.

3) **Topic Selector**. Selecting this link will open a new window. Click "Begin!" You can select topic "genres" and see sample central ideas for both an informative and a persuasive speech on a given topic. This tool is not intended to supply you with central ideas verbatim, but is to help you understand how to narrow down ideas and develop a strong central idea.

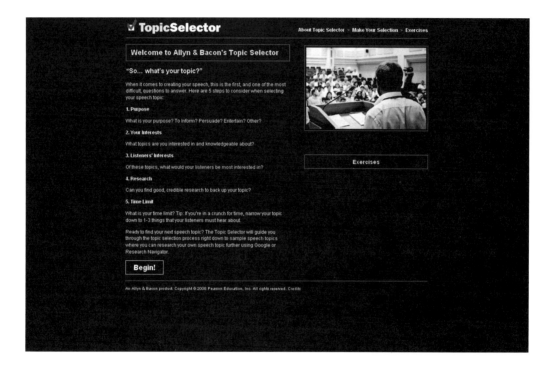

4) **100 Classical and Contemporary Speeches**. Selecting this link will open up a new window. You will see a list of speeches. Each speech link will take you to American Rhetoric, a site dedicated to collecting historical and contemporary speeches, as well as speeches from movies, that help illustrate rhetorical strategies.

5) **Outlining Tool**. This tool will help you think through the development of a speech. It walks you through writing a speech in sections: introduction, body and conclusion. The introduction section will prompt you for a general and specific purpose, a central idea, etc. After reading your workbook on organization, you should be able to move through this outlining tool with ease, developing the key parts of a speech: an introduction, body, transitions, main ideas, supporting ideas, and a conclusion. This tool is not intended to write your preparation outline for you verbatim. You should always defer to your instructor's guidelines and requirements.

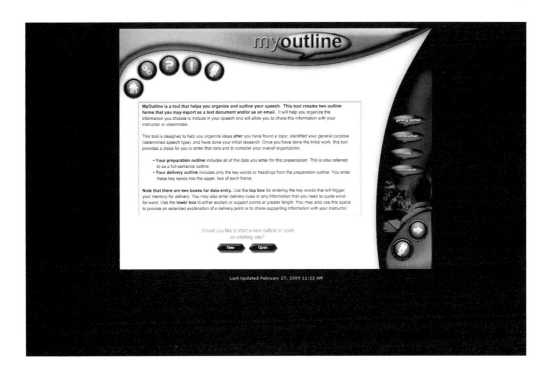

6) **National Communication Association**. This link takes you to the main home page for NCA, which is the national organization for communication scholars.

7) **MySpeechFeed**. Selecting this tool will open up a new window in which you can see selected speeches from the news that week. So for instance, let's say it is July 23, 2009 (when this is being written). Here is what comes up for today:

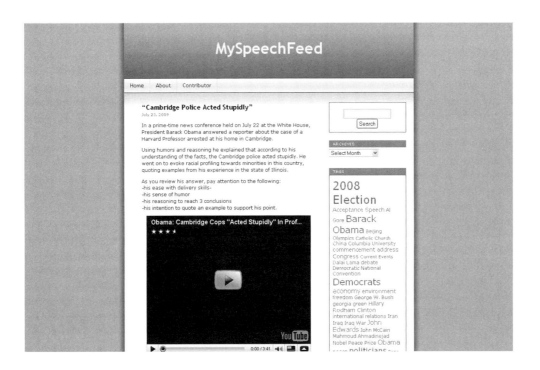

The news for July 23, 2009 is covering Barack Obama's address regarding the arrest of Henry Louis Gates, Jr. If you check in with MySpeechFeed once a week, you will stay up-to-date on current public address issues. This can help you understand communication concepts being discussed in class (and will impress your instructor for sure!).

8) **New York Times Daily News Feed**. This tool encourages participation in civic engagement, and has the potential to help you as you begin to research sources for your presentations.

Chapter Quizzes and Media Contents: Accessing and Completing Quizzes

Ever wonder how an instructor tests? What kinds of questions will he/she ask? What sort of content is covered? Quizzes are part of your grade in this course. However, they also provide an opportunity for you to familiarize yourself with our course's testing procedures.

How many quizzes do I have to take? There are **15 Chapter Quizzes** with two questions each. Each question is worth one point. That means you can earn a total of *30 points*. Questions are randomized, so you may not have the same questions as one of your colleagues in the class.

When do I take a quiz? Your instructor will notify you when you need to take a quiz. Typically, quizzes will be assigned for homework after you have covered a given chapter in class. This means that you can use your workbook when you take the quiz at home. Remember, the quizzes are not meant to trick you, but to help you keep up with the readings and practice sample exam questions.

How do I take a quiz? Your instructor will assign you a quiz on a given chapter. When your instructor wants you to take the quiz, he/she will make the quiz link available for you, and you will see it in the Chapter folder. If you do not see a link, your instructor has not yet made the quiz available.

Your instructor will set a start and end time. This means that you will not be able to access the quiz until your instructor's "start" day and time. Similarly, you will not be able to access the quiz after your instructor's "end" day and time. If you do not take the quiz in the hours provided by your instructor, you will not receive credit for that quiz. Don't worry about conflicting obligations: you will be given at least 48 hours to complete the quiz.

Accessing the Quizzes

1) Log into Blackboard using your UTEID.
2) Select your CMS 306M section.
3) Click on the "Start Here" button and log into the Media component using your access code.
4) Return to your course's page in Blackboard.
5) From the menu on the left side of the screen, click on "Chapter Quizzes and Media Contents."
6) Select the Chapter you wish to access. For example, let's select "Chapter One." You should see something like this:

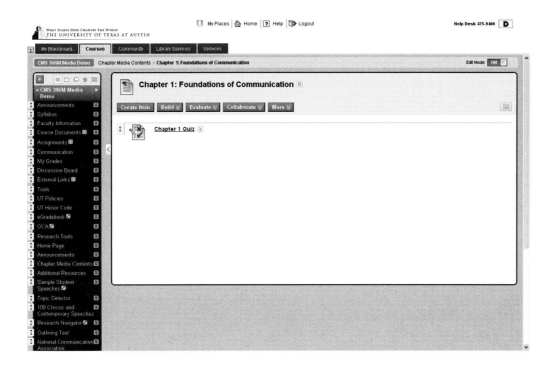

7) Click on the link for "Chapter 1 Quiz."

8) Click "Begin!"

9) A new window will open where you will see a link that reads, "Click Here to View the Quiz Question"

10) Click on that link to read the quiz question and then close out of that window to return to your Blackboard course where you will select your answer.

11) Follow instructions for selecting the best answer. You should be able to narrow down most questions to two answers: your job is to chose the *best* answer.

12) Submit your answer by selecting one of the answer choices 'A' through 'E' on your Blackboard page.

Remember: You may not "backtrack," so don't submit an answer unless you're sure it's the one you believe is correct! Once you have completed the quiz, your grade will be transferred automatically to your grade book on Blackboard. If you missed a question, you will be given the chance to see the correct answer.

Classroom Contacts

Write your name on this sheet. Then collect the names, e-mail address, and phone numbers of at least four of your classmates. Should you miss a class or need help with an assignment, you now have some contacts!

Your Name: _____

1. Classroom Contact One

    a. Name: _____

    b. E-Mail: _____

    c. Phone: _____

2. Classroom Contact Two

    a. Name: _____

    b. E-Mail: _____

    c. Phone: _____

3. Classroom Contact Three

    a. Name: _____

    b. E-Mail: _____

    c. Phone: _____

4. Classroom Contact One

    a. Name: _____

    b. E-Mail: _____

    c. Phone: _____

PREFACE

Why Communicate?

by Roderick P. Hart[1]

Objectives

After studying this Preface, you should be able to do the following:

- ☐ List and discuss several reasons why human beings talk.
- ☐ Explain the connection between public and professional communication.
- ☐ List some unique features of public speaking.
- ☐ Know the risks of speaking in public.

Introduction

It's often hard to find the right thing to say. What do you say, for example, to the interviewer who wants you to describe your most significant weakness? To the co-worker who wants your opinion on a poorly written proposal? To the supervisor who wants you to work overtime this weekend—again? Such moments test people's communication skills. If given the choice, most of us would decline to take the test. Life does not allow that, however, and so we usually muster our courage and find something to say. How do we do it? And why?

The Nature of Human Talk

Consider the old saw about the boy who, by age five, had not yet uttered a single syllable. His parents were beside themselves with worry. Where had they gone wrong in producing a speechless child? One morning at the breakfast table the boy suddenly spoke: "This oatmeal is damned lumpy." Uncontrollably excited, his parents ignored the vulgarity and posed the obvious question: "For five years you've said nothing, not even baby talk? And now this! Why?" The answer: "Until now, everything was all right."

We humans speak when we have to. We speak because it is one of the few nonviolent ways of changing the world around us. We speak because we are naturally attracted to others and because we want to know them better. We speak because we need to impress the boss or because we want a better job. There are a thousand reasons to speak. Here are some of them.

To talk is human.

Researchers have yet to find a group of animals that "talks" in a clear way save one—humankind. By some method of intellectual and physiological happenstance, human beings are unique in their ability to produce meaningful speech: Not only can A produce verbal sounds, but B can comprehend those utterances and react to them. Although this system sometimes breaks down, we humans are distinctive in our ability to create and use language systems—for pleasure, for profit, and sometimes for pain. We talk because we are human and we are human because we talk. We talk because we have no other choice. We talk to cats who cannot return the compliment and we yell our lungs out at high-definition pictures of basketball players a thousand miles away. We do so because talking somehow soothes us.

We also take our talking seriously. Our governments institutionalize people who continually talk to lamp posts and incarcerate those who incite riots with their talk or make obscene phone calls. Yet before sending these latter unfortunates off to jail, our judges ask them if they have anything to *say* before sentence is passed.

Even when humans are alone, we talk in order to simulate social connectedness. After watching Tom Hanks in *Cast Away*, who can doubt that Robinson Crusoe spent much of his solitude talking to himself or that, as he constructed one of his endless contraptions, he sang—that is, he used rhythmic, melodious *speech* to entertain himself? Human speech is the tool we use to describe our worlds, to define and change our acquaintances. While we can function without speech and still remain human, all reports indicate that a speechless existence is far from pleasurable. An intriguing claim that remains to be substantiated is that the suicide rate among servicemen who went deaf during World War II was higher than the rate among those who were blinded. Even if untrue, the fact that such a proposition seems plausible demonstrates how our most human gift penetrates and shapes our existences.

To talk is to define ourselves.

You ask a friend, "How's your sprained ankle today?" Your friend replies: "The extremities are salubrious." What an odd response, using such formal language for an informal friend—such distanced language for one so close. It's as if she had stepped outside of her skin and somehow detached herself from her feelings. There is no "me" in her speech pattern, no "I" or "myself." This, combined with her inflated vocabulary, makes her seem detached, alien.

If asked, "Who are you?" how would you respond? Most likely your reply would include your name, occupation, personality characteristics, place in your family, political affiliation, or some such objective description. This question is not an idle one. With the number of social roles humans play each day in a world of rapidly changing ideas and values, "Who am I?" becomes perhaps the only question worth asking. And we ask that question over and over again, always veiling it in some sort of conversational guise ("Everybody else gave a much better presentation than I did, don't you think?" or burying it beneath the cloak and dagger of courtship ("I hope you don't think I'm just another undereducated Aggie."). To put it simply, we are fascinated by ourselves.

We humans enjoy listening to our own words. We are all egocentric even though only some of us are egotistical. If this statement weren't true, why would 40-80 percent of all our spoken statements contain the pronoun "I"? As communication scholars Charles Brown and Charles Van Riper say, "Listen, if you will, to the staccato of the perpendicular pronoun in the speech about you: 'And I said to him, I said . . .' 'I'm the kind of person who . . .' 'I think that . . .' The "I"s explode like popcorn in the conversational pan."[2] Could there be a more natural way for finding out about ourselves than by listening to our very own speech or to the spoken remarks made about us by others?

To talk is to share ourselves.

It's hardly an accident that communication is the stock-in-trade of psychiatrists, school counselors, politicians, preachers, and teachers. When people share their feelings in the psychiatrist's office, they are essentially trying to make their problem the psychiatrist's problem. Imagine that you've just received a B in a course you were sure you would fail. What do you do? You jabber to your roommate, your parents, and your pals. And if they are not available, you corner the poor fellow across the hall, the very person you've ignored all semester. Some experiences, some feelings, *demand* to be shared.

Who can ride a crowded elevator from the 23rd floor to street level without feeling the tension generated by a dozen non-talkers staring mindlessly at the elevator door? But should some brave soul make a statement, no matter how foolish, there's an almost audible sigh or relief from the otherwise reticent multitude—as long as it's just that one statement. People make us talk. Who can endure more than five minutes in a small room with a stranger without muttering some inane pleasantry? Again, just uttering that one statement, which is enough to acknowledge that person's humanity and our own social responsibility. Perhaps the most vivid manifestation of the social import of speaking is the decision not to talk. Angry spouses give their unfaithful partners the "silent treatment;" modern prisons cast the most heinous felons into solitary confinement. We are somehow diminished as people when we cannot share who we are with others.

Humans also talk just because talking is fun. We engage in bull sessions, talk dates, all-nighters, and gossip parties simply because we must. Psychiatrist Eric Berne observes that the ultimate function of speech is to structure time, to give us something to do.[3] We spend much of our day "just talking" even as our cousins in the animal kingdom devote their days to satisfying their bodily needs. To be human is to have more time, and to have more time is to talk.

To talk is to think.

"How can I tell what I think until I see what I say?" asked novelist E.M. Forster. Scholars observe that we never really "know" something until we can say it clearly, lucidly, and articulately. For example, even though you may have traversed the 40 acres hundreds of times, can you give strangers precise, well-phrased directions to the Cactus Café? And how many times have you found yourself confidently beginning to explain a homework problem to a friend, only to discover that you did not know the material as well as you had presumed?

Speech-for-thought also has more serious consequences. For many years, Russian psychologists have studied the relationships between thinking and speech. Roughly stated, their conclusions are twofold: Speech is a fairly good indicator of mental development, and the ability to verbalize can help individuals grow intellectually. They have found, for example, that patients whose mental disorders have impaired their motor abilities can move around better by saying out loud what they are trying to get their bodies to do. This same principle of transference operates in the counselor's office. Sometimes by putting their feelings into words (which can be painful), clients are better able to understand the root of their problems. Anyone who has ever read an essay out loud to see if it "sounds like I know what I'm talking about" knows about the speech-for-thought phenomenon.

To talk is to communicate.

Ethnologist Desmond Morris has studied why infants cry. According to him, they cry because they are in pain, hungry, or alone; because they're in unfamiliar territory; want to change their physical surroundings; or because they are frustrated. These conditions end up being a good list for beginners as to why we communicate. And, what a way for infants to begin to learn that they'll need the help of others to cope with the world's demands.

Communication puts speech to work—preaching the Good News, constructing a Third Reich, cleaning up the local polluter, or putting pressure on politicians. Communication is the speech of saviors and demagogues, kings and paupers, courtiers and those they court. A practical use of talk is to change existing conditions, right wrongs, or create new ones in their stead. Because we humans are so in love with ourselves, speech for communication—speech for others—must fight for its place in the sun.

To talk is to be multidimensional.

The foregoing functions of human talk are hardly mutually exclusive. We do all of them all the time, and we do many of them at the same time. For example, besides keeping us from studying, small talk can give us insight into ourselves and help us to understand something we have never really grasped before. Or we may sit down for a pleasant meal only to wind up exhorting our dinner companions to join a peace march. Sometimes we misjudge the appropriate speech function and that creates problems—as is the case, for example, with the businessperson who cannot suppress the impulse to "talk shop" during a golf match. Maturity is often measured by our ability to choose the speech function best suited to the occasion at hand.

To understand talk is to be able to control it intelligently. Speech makes us unique. It makes us happy and sad. It terrifies us. It comforts us. And it gives us social power. It both says things and does things. ("I do" is a good example of the Unitarian power of speech.)

And all of these complexities become especially important when talk goes public.

The Nature of Public Talk

All professional talk is, in essence, public talk. When you speak professionally—whether you're participating in a one-on-one discussion, a small-group meeting, or a formal presentation to an audience—you engage others first as representatives of the organization and, therefore, are using a form of public speech. To learn to speak in public is to be made aware (sometimes painfully) of the amount of personal investment which public talk demands. However, learning to speak in public also amplifies your ability to control your environment . . . and your own future.

Speaking in public is not something most people do lightly. Because of this fact, the very act of public speech sends a number of implicit messages:

- ❑ *Some sort of problem exists.* Here "problem" means any set of conditions that should be changed. The problem can be as mundane as the need to meet departmental milestones or as radical as a plan to nationalize the oil industry.
- ❑ *The problem can be overcome . . . with the help of others.* Resorting to public communication implies that some sort of collective effort will be needed if a problem is to be fixed.
- ❑ *The topic is important enough for you to risk public exposure.* That a speaker chooses to speak implies that the costs associated with nervousness are outweighed by the cost of not being heard.

❑ *You're willing to be changed personally.* Public communication is not a one-way street. To talk in public is to open yourself to the social environment: You may be shouted down. You may be promoted. Because communication outcomes are never completely predicted, a speaker is as open to change as an audience member.

❑ *Your audience is willing to be changed, too.* This proposition is so subtle that it is frequently overlooked. When a group gathers to hear a public talk, they are making an implicit bargain with the speaker that goes something like this: "I'm listening; so go ahead and try to change me—but you'd better make it good!"

This list of the "implicit messages" surrounding public speech is quintessentially optimistic. It asks you to emerge from the background and share yourself with other people. In recompense, it gives you the feeling of empowerment and the opportunity to influence others.

Unique Features of Public Talk

Unlike the everyday conversationalist, the public speaker operates in a special sphere of influence—a sphere that presents problems as well as opportunities. Compared to private talk, public speech taxes us with the following demands:

❑ Your message must be relevant to the group as a whole, not merely to one or two individuals in that group. In public communication, the "common denominator" must be the bottom line.

❑ The language you can use is more restricted and less flexible. It uses a more common code, is less personal in phrasing, and is filled with fewer individual connotations.

❑ Your audience is likely to be more diverse, requiring you to enter many perceptual worlds simultaneously.

❑ As the size of your audience increases, you have a greater chance of misinterpreting feedback.

❑ You must do a more complete job of preparing for the communication event in order to have the capacity to make needed moment-to-moment changes during the speech event.

❑ You may find it difficult to focus listeners' attention on your message because of the great number of distractions a public situation can entail.

❑ You have the potential to accomplish much more attitudinal change because your message reaches so many more people simultaneously.

Although public talk has special features, it is not fundamentally different from private talk. Both forms let us make a difference in the world, drawing us out of our shells and giving us an opportunity to see ourselves as others see us. More than anything, speaking in public gives you a unique kind of self-knowledge, a kind of knowledge that can stay with you for life. However, self-knowledge has its hazards, which can be minimized considerably once you know why they exist in the first place.

The Risks of Public Talk

Why does public speech seem so unsettling to people who have not done it before? It's a simple question, with answers that are anything but simple. Still, the more you know about something you fear, the better you can cope with it. The prospect of death frightens us, after all, in part because no one has yet been able to tell us what "becoming dead" involves. However, a great many people have experienced the rigors of public talk and have lived to tell about it. So let's examine what they've learned.

Speech expresses personality.

When you talk, *you* talk. There is no way for you to escape your public words, since it is your body that has produced them and your eyes that have registered their impact on others. As a result, speech behavior is an especially good mirror of people's personalities, attitudes, and feelings. You can easily document the interconnectedness of speech and personhood by trying to carry on a conversation in the third person for five minutes. ("Bob thinks he'll go to the refrigerator to get some leftover pizza. Bob thinks he'll also have a beer.") It seems funny, as if someone else were speaking for you, as if your body were being used to convey a message that someone else had created. While con artists, espionage agents, and professional actors can step away from their own messages and speak someone else's part, they no doubt feel some tension, at least initially, when choking off their feelings in such ways.

As speech scholar Carroll Arnold points out, a presentation is an action, not a product.[4] We do not "make" a presentation as we do an essay. We are what we say, much more than we are what we write. Business executives attest to the fact that the easiest way to dismiss a troublesome subordinate is to tell the employee, "Send me an email on that, Johnson." This allows the executive, when responding, to think through the available options carefully and to criticize a disembodied product rather than engage in the personal, human activity that spoken confrontations necessarily entail. It is for this reason that the late psychologist Haim Ginott used to advise parents who have "had it" with their kids to write them but not show them "hate letters," rather than display those resentments in person.[5] Because we are our talk, talking is the warmest way of saying "I love you" and the cruelest way of saying "Get lost."

Speaking in public invites evaluation.

When we recognize how very personal the act of speaking is, it becomes easier to understand why public talk can be scary. Some of our most common daily experiences center around the mild (sometimes not so mild) fear associated with the speech act: "I've never had a job interview before; how will I know what to say?" or "Why did I agree to give that presentation? I just know I'll freeze up."

Most people grit their teeth and get through such experiences, eventually coming to understand that anything important introduces an element of risk. Only those who do nothing risk nothing. While all communication involves some element of tension, the ability to deal with those tensions varies from person to person. Consider, for example, an employee's request for a promotion, a situation that generally involves risk. In asking for a better job, the employee risks not only rejection but also being thought presumptuous. And because the employee cannot totally predict the boss's response, fear of the unknown looms large. In other words, fear is high when you become acutely aware that you are being evaluated. What increases your awareness of the evaluation process? Three factors seem especially important:

❑ *Your audience is composed of people who are important to you.* This factor is one way of explaining the tension some students feel when speaking in front of their class: Your teacher is grading you, your peer group is sizing you up, so you become especially conscious of the words you are using.

❑ *The size of your audience is larger than usual.* This factor, too, applies to speaking in class, where many people are evaluating you simultaneously and monitoring such a number of judgments can be daunting. (Remember, though, that the composition of an audience is as important as its size. Who would you rather speak to—a roomful of friends or one irate employer?)

❑ *There is an imbalance in the status of the interactions.* This factor probably explains why it takes some people so long to "warm up" when talking to a teacher. Because your teachers have a certain amount of power over you, you can't help but feel that they are judging everything you say.

All these situations have one thing in common—a sudden consciousness of the evaluation process. The "risk" involved is that the judgment will be negative. That is perhaps why lulls in conversations—those awful "dead" spots during an otherwise convivial evening—are especially painful. Suddenly, we become aware that people have been judging us as we have been judging them.

Speaking produces unpredictable consequences.

When you speak in public, you can't predict the outcome of the interaction. This fact increases your sense of risk because of the very nature of fear itself. "When in doubt, fear!" is a reasonable reaction for most people in most circumstances, since maintaining the status quo will generally suffice—especially if your only other option involves embracing a hazy future. The unknowns in the speaking situation, of course, are many. In addition to the sometimes tortuous search for things to say and ways to say them, you also have to decide what your feelings are on the subject and how your listeners will react. You can try to control as many factors as possible, but the tensions connected with speaking seem especially high when the following occurs:

- ❑ *You don't know (or are unsure of) how you feel about yourself.* This may seem like a strange proposition, but one of the most unnerving human prospects is to find out something about ourselves that others have known for a long time. It's probably for some such reason that many persons fear counseling or advising sessions, situations that present two risks: "I'll find out something about me I'd rather not deal with," or "You'll find out something about me that I'd rather we didn't discover simultaneously."

- ❑ *You don't know (or are unsure of) how you feel about your audience.* The archetypal unpredictable situation involves conversing with strangers. Because each of us lives in our own unique world, we engage an "unknown quantity" when we talk with someone else. Strangers are sometimes awkward because we are unsure what we might be risking by talking to this new addition to our lives.

- ❑ *We are unsure of the dynamics of the speaking situation.* Life is filled with examples of this type of unpredictability. How do you behave when meeting a potential employer for the first time? What do you say to your professor when you meet in the vegetable aisle of the grocery store? The unknowns presented by such unfamiliar settings can wither the hardiest of us.

At this point two questions might puzzle you: "With all these risks and tensions, why should I ever open my mouth?" and, "How do I cope with my fears?" The answer to the first question is obvious from our initial discussion in this chapter. As humans, we have no other choice but to speak. The second question is a bit more difficult to answer. You could, of course, simply avoid talking to people who are important to us, whose status is higher than yours, who you do not know, or who appear before you in numbers larger than one. Obviously, such a solution is impractical.

As is the case in all human problems, the antidotes to fear are knowledge and experience. Reduce the unknowns in the speaking situation, and you increase your chances of having a decent interchange. Become aware of your uncertainties and limitations, and you can get better at coping with them. People get a feeling for the range of human behavior only by meeting new people. By thrusting yourself into new situations, you challenge yourself, and by challenging yourself you inevitably grow. By dealing with the risks of speech head-on, you can put the tensions of speech in their proper perspective—as necessary but conquerable aspects of your life.

Thus, the psychology of the communication classroom is not very different from the psychology your parents used when, as a four-year-old, you felt sure that goblins laid in wait in your closet, ready to spring out when the shadows lengthened. If they were sensible, your parents invited you to come with them, hand in hand, and investigate the nature of dark closets. While the closets can be just as dark in spoken interactions, experience (in the form of sensitive classroom exercises) is the very best guide available.

Conclusion

Life is a gamble. It has always been thus. Speaking to other people reminds us of that. Although human speech is the most normal, the most natural, thing we do, it is also one of the most complicated. Talking to strangers force that fact upon you, but talking to your friends is often no picnic either. Speaking requires you to make choices—who to address, what to talk about, how to phrase what you want to say—and you must often make these choices in a situation not of your own making.

But talk is also a gift. It lets us touch the lives of the other creatures with whom we share this planet. It tells us, better than anything else can tell us, who we are and what we might become. It is possible to get very good at speech—articulate, savvy, charming, and filled with wisdom. However, even the best among us will make mistakes when talking. We will do so because speaking is a complicated business and because we want others to like and admire us so much. For all of these reasons, it behooves us to study the mysteries and possibilities of human communication. This book is not the last word on such matters but it is a serviceable first word. Your world awaits.

Endnotes

1 Portions of thi_ chapter have been adapted from Roderick P. Hart, Gustav W. Friedrich, and Barry Brummett, *Public Communication* (New York: Harper, 1983).

2 Charles Brown and Charles Van Riper, *Speech and Man* (Englewood Cliffs, NJ: Prentice-Hall, 1966), 36.

3 Eric. Berne, *Games People Play* (New York: Grove Press, 1964).

4 Carroll. C. Arnold, "Speech as Action," The English Record, 20 (1970): 36–53.

5 H. Ginott, *Between Parent and Child* (New York: McGraw-Hill, 1965).

PART 1

Introduction to Professional Communication

CHAPTER 1

Foundations of Communication

by John A. Daly

Objectives

After studying Chapter 1, you should be able to do the following:

- ☐ Define human communication.
- ☐ Construct a communication model and explain its components.
- ☐ Identify and provide examples of the eight human communication propositions.

Key Terms

TERM	DEFINITION
channel	The medium through which a message passes on its way from source to receiver.
communication	The process whereby one person stimulates meaning in the mind of another through verbal and/or nonverbal means.
content	The substantive aspect of a message.
decoding	The receiver's act of attaching meaning to a message sent by a source.
encoding	The source's act of transforming an idea into a message to transmit to a receiver.
feedback	The interplay between encoding and decoding messages.
fidelity	The extent to which the message after transmission is similar to the message originally transmitted.
labeling	The act of interpreting a situation and treating the interpretation as real.
message	The result of an act of encoding.
noise	Any condition that affects the fidelity of the message being sent.
punctuation	The way in which people segment a sequence of words or behaviors.
receiver	The recipient of a message.
relationship	The affective aspect of a message.
source	The originator of a message.

Introduction

Communication is central to people's lives. Our successes and failures, both personal and professional, are tied directly to our skills as communicators. In the working world, successful people are, in virtually every case, excellent communicators. The corollary is also true: Less capable communicators often achieve less professional success.

A major task in professional settings is communication. This chapter provides an introduction to the fundamentals of human communication that underlie professional communication. We begin with a formal definition of communication, continue with a model of the communicative process, and then present a summary of its critical components. We conclude by offering eight propositions that highlight key concepts about communication.

Our emphasis in this chapter is on interpersonal communication, which is the foundation of other types of communication. Not surprisingly, you will find that many of the points we make about interpersonal communication pertain to group, public, and professional communication too.

Defining Communication

What is communication? Communication is the process whereby one individual stimulates meaning in the mind of another through verbal and/or nonverbal means. In this definition, three ideas are critical:

- ❑ Communication is a *process*. It is ongoing, irreversible, and systematic.
- ❑ Communication is the *stimulation* of meaning (not the transfer of meaning). When people communicate, we do not put meanings into another person's mind, like dropping a letter into a post-office box. Instead, our communication stimulates the other person to create meaning.
- ❑ Communication is both *verbal* and *nonverbal*. In face-to-face encounters, the verbal and nonverbal components are inherently intertwined.

Although this definition seems pretty straightforward, things do get a bit more complicated. . . .

Modeling Communication

A good way to understand communication is to build a model of the communication process. Figure 1.1 shows a basic model that divides communication into eight major components (source and receiver, encoding and decoding, message, channel, feedback, and noise). The originators of this model were telecommunication theorists Claude Shannon and Warren Weaver, who explained its emphasis on transmission, and its somewhat mechanistic flavor.[1]

The first component of this model is the source, a person who has an idea to communicate to another person. The source encodes the idea into a form suitable for communication—words and/or nonverbal behaviors. People often encounter problems in communication as they encode messages. Have you ever been at a loss for words? Have you ever felt frustrated, knowing what you mean but finding that you simply cannot come up with the right thing to say? Have you ever said something and later thought ruefully that the conversation could have gone better had you used your words differently? Each of these cases represents an encoding problem.

In many cases, problems with communication arise because of sloppy encoding, especially when people assume that their own meanings for particular words and behaviors are necessarily their listeners' meanings too. When you do not pay attention to the way you encode a message, you may end up with a message that is not optimally encoded for understanding by others. This can lead to misunderstandings. Carefully encoding your ideas means thoroughly thinking out—*before you start talking*—both what you want to say, and how you want what you say to be understood by the other person. Further, it means considering what your listeners bring with them to the conversation. Do they understand the topic? Are they familiar with current slang or would more formal speech be more fitting? These questions will be addressed in greater detail in our chapter on audience analysis but they are important to begin thinking about early in the course. Working hard to effectively encode your messages so that others share your meanings leads to more successful communication.

Figure 1.1. A Model of Interpersonal Communication.

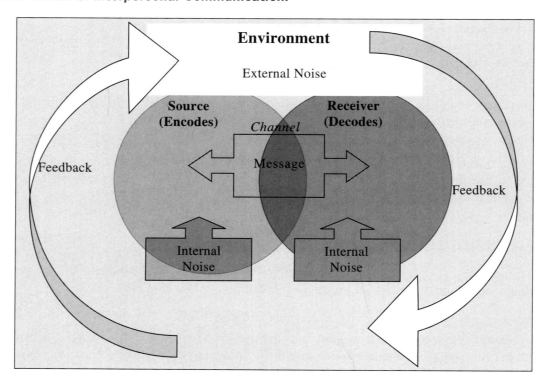

The result of an act of encoding is a <u>message</u>, which can be both verbal and nonverbal. A message consists of both what you say and the way you say it—the tone of your voice, the line of your posture, the expression on your face, the smiley-face emoticon you add to the end of an IM sentence to take the sting out of sarcasm. (After all, as simple a statement as "Dude: Nice shirt." can mean anything from "I like your shirt" to "I hate your shirt," with stops in between for "Do you know your shirt's buttoned incorrectly?" and "What on earth did you spill on your shirt?)

> "Communication is a process. It is ongoing, irreversible, and systematic."

When the source sends an encoded message, the message passes through some kind of <u>channel</u>. When you send a text e-mail, the single channel is the written word electronically transferred. When you talk over the telephone, the single channel is vocal signals electronically transferred. Face-to-face encounters always involve at least two major channels: One is the sensory channel; you experience expressions and behaviors as someone communicates a message to you. The other is the air through which the sound waves travel to reach you. The more channels involved in communication, the richer its texture. Because of its richness, people tend to prefer face-to face conversations to phone conversations and phone conversations to letters: With face-to-face interactions, you get to hear the words *and* experience the nonverbal behaviors that accompany them. And with phone conversations, at least you get to hear the voice along with the words.

After the encoded message travels through one or more channels, it reaches one or more <u>receivers</u>, who <u>decode</u> the words and nonverbal behaviors sent by the source of the message. Because errors occur not only in the encoding of a message, but also in the decoding of the message, misunderstandings arise: The meanings intended by the source are not always the meanings stimulated in the receiver(s), as a receiver can easily interpret a message differently than what the source intended. Further, the different receivers that make up an audience can interpret the same stimuli in different ways. Just as encoders have the responsibility to consider their audiences when encoding their messages, receivers who want to accurately decode a message have the responsibility to listen carefully, ask relevant questions, and avoid prejudging content or person.

To minimize the opportunity for errors in decoding, most effective communicators adapt their messages to the specific receivers they expect to encounter. For example, good teachers know how to present lecture material in a variety of ways, even though the content of the material may stay the same. They make their encoding decisions based on the age, maturity, capability, and level of interest they expect to find in their students, so that individual students can more adequately decode their messages. If teachers of communication had to select the biggest single problem people experience in face-to-face communication, a very likely candidate would be the degree of mismatch between what is encoded by the source and what is decoded by the receiver. Enhancing the match between what the source encodes and receiver decodes is one of the major goals of conscientious communicators.

So far we have considered communication as a one-way event that travels from source to receiver, and then stops. But is this actually correct? Not really. In face-to-face encounters, each person involved encodes messages to send at the same time as decoding the messages received, and is thus simultaneously both source and receiver. This interplay between encoding and decoding messages is referred to as <u>feedback</u>. The recursive quality of feedback is a critical component of any model of interpersonal communication; indeed, as is the extent to which people control each other's communication by providing feedback.

When you talk to other people in a face-to-face situation, you observe their responses, and modify your communication accordingly. If, for example, a friend smiles and nods as you speak, you respond differently than if you provoke a scowl. When you do get that scowl—especially if you do not expect it—you probably review what you have just said and try to figure out what went wrong. To repair the problem, you may then back up and say the same thing again, paraphrase it, give more evidence, expand on the concept, come up with a whole new illustration—or change tactics entirely, or you may just stop and ask what is wrong. In this exchange, although you are doing most of the talking, your friend has shaped your communication through feedback.

> "... problems with communication arise ... when people assume that their own meanings for particular words or behaviors are ... their listeners' meanings, too."

You can easily see the impact of feedback in classroom settings. Very early in a course, teachers typically discover a few students who are extremely responsive in a positive way—they pay rapt attention, nod their heads regularly, and smile at even the teacher's lamest attempts at humor. These students are experts at giving positive feedback. Since most teachers appreciate this sort of feedback, they quickly identify these students and engage them for the remainder of the semester as focal points for their teaching. If, during a given lecture, any of these students stops giving positive feedback, the teacher is likely to quickly react and adjust the lecture to regain positive responses. In essence, these students control their teachers through their feedback.

Surrounding the entire model is <u>noise</u>, which is any condition that affects the <u>fidelity</u> of the message being sent. There are two types of noise: external and internal. External noise, for you, includes any distracting condition outside of yourself. Look around your current environment. What is distracting you from reading this book? If you were talking with another person in this location, what might distract the two of you from your conversation? You might experience external noise from the other person (e.g., an unfamiliar accent, a striking appearance, an annoying personal habit), external noise in the channel (e.g., a bad connection, poor volume, competing sounds such as traffic, music, and other voices), external noise in the environment (e.g., heat, cold, messy surroundings, uncomfortable seating), or even external noise in the message (e.g., jargon, disorganization, offensive language). The presence of any or all of these types of external noise reduces the fidelity of a message.

In classrooms where communication is central to effective instruction, think of all the potential external distractions. How many times have you found yourself staring out the classroom window at the Tower rather than listening to your teacher? Watching the hands of the clock on the wall oh-so-slowly move? Listening to the murmur of the seminar in the next room? Or just noticing every little physical characteristic of the back of the person who sits in front of you? All of these are examples of external noise.

Internal noise, on the other hand, includes all the barriers to communication that come from *within* yourself—your own physiological and psychological distractions. Are you taking a class just before lunchtime (or even instead of lunch)? The mumblings outside you may seem far less significant than the rumblings within. Have you ever tried to study for a test after having a fight with your roommate or significant other? Although you try to concentrate on your reading, you may find your mind constantly wandering back to the fight. In both cases, what you are experiencing is internal noise. The presence of internal noise can reduce your effectiveness in both encoding and decoding messages. It is particularly problematic because—unlike external noise—its existence is often invisible to the person who is communicating who may not know why (or even that) the message is not getting through.

One task participants have in any communicative encounter is to reduce, as much as possible, both the external and internal noise that surrounds their interaction. That may mean moving to a different channel or environment, altering your message, disciplining yourself to ignore physiological symptoms and psychological distractions, or even deciding not to communicate in a given situation because the noise is too great.

This model of the communicative process is only one of many models that have been developed over the years; you will encounter others as you take more advanced courses in communication. Still, this simple model anchors a wealth of information about communication in general—and the ways you can improve your own communication in particular.

Eight Propositions about Interpersonal Communication

Now that we have provided you with a brief definition of communication and introduced you to a simple model of the communicative process, let's branch out a little and discuss some general propositions that summarize important concepts about interpersonal communication. When you understand these propositions, you will have a solid introductory grounding in the study of interpersonal communication and just what it is that happens when people talk with one another.

1. Communication has both verbal and nonverbal components.

As already noted, communication has both verbal and nonverbal components. The verbal component consists of the words people speak when communicating with others. The nonverbal component is everything other than words people use when communicating. In a face-to-face encounter, the nonverbal component may include such things as gestures, eye contact, facial expressions, body positions, tones of voice, and all the environmental variables that surround people when we talk.

This proposition may seem patently obvious. Of course, you might say, everyone knows that when you communicate with another person you use both words and actions. But do people really believe it? If behavior is any guide, probably not. When you are asked to prepare a presentation, or plan to engage in a difficult conversation, you probably spend the bulk of the available time working on the verbal portion of the message, leaving the nonverbal portion to "just happen."

Our society as a whole demonstrates this bias towards the verbal component. Consider our society's dependence on written transcripts. Legislators, jurists, scholars, journalists, and politicians, to name just a few, put great faith in written records of verbal interchanges. But can a transcript adequately convey the experience of a conversation, a speech, a press conference, or any other oral message? In everyday interactions the same bias is present. How many times have you consciously considered your choice of words prior to an employment interview, a talk with your parents, a meeting with your professor, or any other special conversational event? Have you just as consciously thought through your nonverbal behaviors? If you are like most people, you will probably answer the latter question in the negative. Very simply, people behave as if they communicate solely through words.

> "people typically depend more on what someone does (the nonverbal component) than on what the person says."

Thoughtful observation, however, as well as research, suggests the opposite better represents reality. In social exchanges, people typically depend more on what someone does (the nonverbal component) than on what the person says. If you took two speakers and had each read the same passage, you could, by manipulating the speakers' voices, gestures, and other nonverbal behaviors, easily engender two very different messages. When social scientists isolate what contributes to listeners' understanding of what speakers mean, especially in terms of feelings, they find that the speakers' nonverbal behaviors generally count more than their words. They also note, not surprisingly, that when people's verbal messages conflict with their nonverbal displays, observers are more likely to trust the meanings they infer from the nonverbal behaviors than those they draw from the verbal message. For example, frustrated instructors often complain that even though they "clearly tell" students to do something, the students do not comply. When questioned, the students often retort that their instructors "did not act like they really meant it," and, as a consequence, they felt they need not pay much attention to the instructors' requests. Actions, as that piece of folk wisdom suggests, do speak louder than words.

There are exceptions to this observation. One is that children, as they are learning language, appear to rely more on the verbal than the nonverbal. When a speaker's nonverbal behavior contradicts the verbal behavior, young children believe the verbal. For adults, it's exactly the opposite: They believe the nonverbal. Why? Perhaps an analogy may help explain this phenomenon. Suppose you are just beginning to learn German. Further, imagine that you meet a German speaker who starts *sprechen mit*

> "... verbal communication consists of the words people use when communicating with another person. The nonverbal component is everything other than words that people use when communicating."

Ihnen auf Deutsch. What do you focus on? Most likely, it is the words. You listen carefully and then try to reference each word to some vocabulary list you have in your mind. You pay little, if any, attention to the speaker's nonverbal messages because your attention is narrowly focused on the words. Later, suppose you have become more fluent and confident speaking German. Now when you meet a German speaker, you are free to pay more attention to nuances of voice, gestures, and so on. In short, you now have the ability to focus more on the nonverbal. For children and others who are learning language for the first time, the task requires incredible effort—effort that needs a singular focus on what is being said.

A second explanation may lay in the different amounts of experience a child and an adult have with nonverbal behavior. Compared to nearly any adult, children have very little understanding of what behavior means. As they get older, their experience grows. Consequently, adults, who have developed a wealth of experience about nonverbal behavior, depend more on nonverbal than verbal behavior. Just learning that nonverbal behaviors may contradict verbal ones is a task that requires experience and consciousness of meaning. The more aware we become of what communication can do, the more proficient we are likely to become in distinguishing meaning.

All this is not to imply that the verbal and nonverbal components of a message are independent of one another—just the opposite, in fact: They are intricately intertwined. Paul Ekman, a psychologist who studies the relationship between the verbal and nonverbal components of communication, has specified six ways in which nonverbal behavior interacts with verbal behavior to produce meaning: repeating, accenting, substituting, complementing, regulating, and contradicting.[2] Some nonverbal behavior functions by simply *repeating* what you say verbally. "How do I get to CMA?" someone asks you. "Walk two blocks up Guadalupe," you reply, pointing up Guadalupe as you say it. You are using nonverbal gestures to "second" or "repeat" your words.

Other nonverbal behavior emphasizes particular parts of your verbal statements by *accenting* them. "I've just *got* to get to South Padre for spring break this year," you tell your roommate, clenching your fists, scrunching up your face, and closing your eyes on the "got." You are using nonverbal gestures to highlight or "accent" a portion of your verbal message.

Substituting is nonverbal behavior that uses gestures to replace the words you normally use. Suppose you are sitting with a friend at Trudy's eating chips and salsa. The waiter comes by with a carafe of green sauce and points to your nearly empty bowl. Caught while chewing, you swallow hard and look to your friend to answer, only to see her shaking her head with wide eyes and her own mouth obviously full. You glance back to the waiter, roll your eyes, smile, look pointedly at the bowl, and nod vigorously in answer. The waiter grins, pours, leaves. The entire communicative transaction occurs without a word being uttered. All three of you are using nonverbal behavior instead of verbal messages.

People often use *complementing* nonverbal behavior to add depth or detail to the meanings of their verbal messages—to modify or expand what they say and to make it more vivid and interesting. Complementing behaviors often express how people feel. When you tell a story about your last all-nighter and you slump over, prop up your chin with your fist, lower your eyelids to half-mast, and simulate an exhausted caffeine buzz, you use your nonverbal behavior intentionally to help communicate what you felt in the past; when you exhibit those same behaviors because you are in fact sleep-deprived, you unintentionally communicate how you feel right now. In either case, your nonverbal behaviors bring depth to your verbal messages by complementing them.

Another major function of nonverbal behavior is *regulating* the pace and flow of the verbal messages in a conversation. Together the participants in the conversation "read" and react to each other's regulating behaviors by providing their own to shape what is said. Say, for example, that you are in a compelling conversation and your friend is currently speaking. To show that you are eager for your own turn, you lean forward with your lips slightly apart and your hands open as if about to catch a ball. Finally—*finally!*—he pauses, but as he hurriedly lifts his glass to take a drink of water, he raises his other hand in the "stop" position to signal that he is not yet finished. You grimace in annoyance, and throw yourself back in the chair to signal your reluctant willingness to let your friend keep hold of the conversational "ball." Each of you is using nonverbal behavior to regulate the conversation's flow.

These first five types of nonverbal behavior *agree* with the verbal behaviors they repeat, accent, replace, complement, or regulate. *Contradicting,* the final type of nonverbal behavior, disagrees with the verbal behavior it modifies. Sarcasm and irony are good examples of intentional contradicting—as people say one thing with the words they use and another with the tone of voice that accompanies those words. ("I live for drop/add," you say dryly, as your connection to the registrar is dropped for the 10th time for a place in a class you do not even want to take.) Unconscious contradicting takes place when people's nonverbal behavior betrays a feeling that they verbally deny. ("Who cares?" you say—as a hurt look crosses your face—when you find you received a poor grade.)

Verbal and nonverbal behaviors combine to form complex meanings. You must understand both to understand what's being communicated.

> **"People . . . assume that if they are not talking they are not communicating. This is not a very accurate assumption."**

2. You cannot *not* communicate.

In general, communication occurs whenever people are together. To put this proposition more succinctly: In the presence of others, you cannot not communicate.[3] "Sure I can," you may be thinking. But because communication has both verbal and nonverbal aspects, and it occurs with or without you intending it, you communicate even when you do not think you are.

First, the nonverbal aspect of communication is ubiquitous and powerful. Try a little thought experiment to demonstrate the point. (Do not try this in real life unless you want to spend some time repairing damage to a friendship.) "I can, too, not communicate," you think, and decide to prove it. Just at the moment, imagine you are driving with a friend and you suddenly begin to try to avoid all communication. You stop speaking, and you stop responding to your friend's attempts to engage you in conversation. You keep to your side of the car to avoid accidental touch; you look anywhere but at your friend to avoid trading expressions. As your behavior begins to feel odd, you turn up the radio enough to make it impossible to talk. Now visualize the scene: You are sitting far away from your friend, staring out the window, ignoring her comments, and keeping silent. Suddenly you reach over and blatantly turn up the radio. Have you succeeded in your attempt to avoid communication? Hardly. In fact, your friend is reading your abrupt behavior loud and clear and wondering "What's wrong?" or "What did I do?" or "Why are you being such a jerk?"

People often seem to assume that if they are not talking they are not communicating. This is not a very accurate assumption. Absence of talk can clearly communicate a message. Think of the person who does not call, or return a call, after a first date. Think of a dozen silent people jammed into an elevator, all looking up. Think of the roommate stomping out of the apartment after an argument, pausing only to slam the door. Think of the potential employer who does not respond to your cover letter and resume. A variety of nonverbal behaviors are always present when two or more people are in contact. It is nearly impossible to imagine a case where people in one another's presence lack

> **"Every message we communicate has two aspects: content and relationship."**

the ability to communicate in some way. Experienced communicators know that their every move has the potential for communication. As a consequence, they are always conscious of the possible impact of their behaviors on others around them.

Second, communication occurs whether you intend to send messages or not—and whether the person receiving the message believes you sent the message intentionally or unintentionally. Recall that communication is the *stimulation* of meaning and *not the transfer* of meaning. Figure 1.2 shows four possible cases for meaning stimulation. In the first two cases (Boxes 1 and 2), the receiver interprets the communication as intentional—whether the source intends it or not. In the second two cases (Boxes 3 and 4), the receiver interprets the communication as *unintentional*—again, whether the source intends it or not.

In the case of Box 1, the source *intentionally* communicates a message to the receiver, who perceives the message to be intentionally sent. Suppose I walk into a room where you sit, reading. I begin to speak. You sigh theatrically, turn a page, and keep your eyes riveted on your book. I "get the message:" You do not want to talk. You intend to send me a message and I understand that you intend to do so.

In the case of Box 2, the receiver attaches intention to a message the source *unintentionally* sends. Again I walk into a room where you sit, reading, and again I begin to speak. This time you are so engrossed in your book that you do not even notice me. There is, on your part, no intentional message sent. Observing you sigh and turn a page, I decide that you are in "one of those moods" and that you do not want to talk to me. I infer an intentional message where none was sent. In Box 3, the situation is just the opposite. This time the source intentionally sends a message, but the receiver does not perceive the message as intentional. When you sigh theatrically, as in the first scenario, I just think "poor dear must be tired" and keep talking. In this case, although you intend a meaning, I do not see your communication as intentional. Finally, in the case of Box 4, no message is intentionally sent and none inferred. You sit, reading. I enter the room, I speak, you unconsciously sigh, I interpret the sigh as unintentional and I pay it no mind, and you never notice it in the first place.

Figure 1.2. Intentional and unintentional results of communication.

		Source	
		Intentional	**Unintentional**
Receiver	**Intentional**	1	2
	Unintentional	3	4

Where does effective communication occur? It occurs in the first and fourth boxes where intention or lack thereof is accurately perceived. When you improve your communication skills, you move more of your exchanges from the second and third boxes into the first and fourth, where the meaning intended is the meaning stimulated.

A corollary to the idea that you cannot not communicate is that communication among people in contact does not ever truly "break down" or stop—it may not bring the results you want, but it still occurs. When people complain that they have experienced a communication breakdown, what they typically mean is that they have encountered a misunderstanding or a seemingly unresolvable disagreement with another person. But is disagreement really a breakdown of communication? Not really. After all, the facts of the disagreement are very clearly communicated.

3. Communication expresses both content and relationship.

Every message we communicate has two aspects: content and relationship. The <u>content</u> aspect of a message is the substantive information it conveys to the listeners. When, for example, an instructor enters the classroom and tells your class to take your seats and settle down, the content message is that she is ready to begin class. The <u>relationship</u> aspect of a message conveys affective, emotional information—information that leads listeners to think that the speaker likes or dislikes them and that the speaker is interested or uninterested in them or their relationship. It communicates simplistically the speaker's emotional state and/or the speaker's view of the relationship between speaker and listeners. Look again, for example, at the instructor's statement about settling in for class. Suppose she says it in a sarcastic, somewhat cynical way. What would you think? Probably that she does not like you, or is in a bad mood, or perhaps feels that you are not interested in starting class (which may be true!).

On the other hand, suppose she gives the same instruction in an enthusiastic, sociable, and friendly tone. In this case you might think that the instructor likes you, or is in a good mood, or perhaps believes you to be looking forward to the class (which may also be true!). Note that the same content—settle in for class—is offered in both cases; how you understand the content is framed by the relationship information that occurs with the content information.

Another example: When you get together with friends you may exchange a lot of "small talk"—seemingly meaningless chatter that lacks much content and thus may appear dispensable. But small talk is not dispensable; to the contrary, it is very meaningful for its relational aspect. Without small talk, relationships begin to fray; small talk is the glue that binds relationships together. Even when small talk is nothing but a greeting it is still important as relationship information. Suppose you are walking down a street and spy a friend coming the other way. You expect your friend to greet you as he walks by and maybe ask how you are doing.

"Hey," he says.

"Hi," you answer.

"How you doing?"

"Fine. You?"

Such a basic exchange, itself, offers very little content information. What is offered in this greeting is relationship information. You learn that your friend recognizes you, is interested in you socially, and wants to continue your acquaintance. Are we putting too much emphasis on such a brief encounter? Change the scenario just slightly. Suppose your friend, instead of pausing to chat, seems not to notice you. Would you wonder if the inattention was intentional? Would you fret over this seeming snub? Are content and relationship information communicated in the same way? Not entirely.

What Figure 1.3 suggests is that most messages contain both verbal and nonverbal information and communicate both content and relationship. But the content aspect of a message is closely associated with its verbal component, while the nonverbal component provides mostly relationship information. Only a tiny proportion of messages combine mostly content and nonverbal communication; only a tiny proportion of messages use verbal means to communicate relationship information. For example, you are unlikely to attempt to deliver a formal presentation,

Figure 1.3. Interaction between verbal/nonverbal behaviors and the content/relationship aspects of a message.

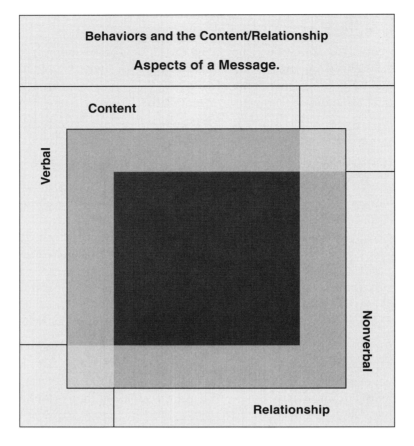

which has a high content level, using mostly nonverbal means. You are just as unlikely to try to communicate how you feel about someone only verbally. Still, remember that both verbal and nonverbal components play a role in nearly every interpersonal encounter and that every message contains both content and relational aspects.

"The safest assumption you can make in communicating a message is that the people listening to your words or observing your behaviors will take away meanings that are different than those you intend."

4. Meanings are in people.

We have already noted that meaning is not transmitted from one person to another; rather, it is stimulated by one person in another. It follows from this concept that, as communication theorist David Berlo posited, meanings are in people, not in words.[4] What does this proposition mean in practical terms? If you want to communicate effectively, you must lose your assumption that everyone else has the same meanings as you do for every word and behavior.

Most people are aware that people sometimes need to carefully craft their language and behavior to make sure that their meanings are clearly conveyed. This need for care is evident in law and diplomacy where communicators painfully consider potential misinterpretations that could be created out of even the simplest and clearest messages. It is also true in high-stakes interpersonal encounters where participants want to guard against making wrong impressions. But people quite often take little care in their everyday communications, even though opportunities for miscommunication abound. The safest assumption you can make in communicating a message is that the people listening to your words or observing your behaviors will take away meanings that are different than those you intend. At the very best, their inferences will approximate your intended meaning; at worst, what they come up with will in no way resemble what you meant.

For just one example, think of how many words in English have multiple meanings. The tendency for people to believe that everyone has the same meaning for words was a constant problem during World War II as American soldiers flooded England in anticipation of the invasion of Europe. Both the British and Americans spoke, in their minds, English, and yet they kept running into each other's "eccentric" use of the same words. To help solve this problem, one of the first things American GIs were given upon their arrival in Great Britain was a booklet that translated any number of words used by the English in one way and used by the GIs in another. For example, they were introduced to the word "fiddling." For American GIs fiddling typically meant playing a musical instrument. In Great Britain, during the war years, "fiddling" meant something quite different: It meant outwitting government regulations in minor ways—getting extra rationing coupons for food or gas, for example.

One important concept underlying the proposition that meaning is in people, not in words, is a process that communication scholars call "punctuation." Consider the following sentence:

Bert said Ernie give me that cookie.

With the simple manipulation of commas, quotation marks, and capitalization, you can create two very different sentences:

"Bert," said Ernie, "Give me that cookie."

Bert said, "Ernie, give me that cookie."

Note how these slight changes in punctuating the written message *entirely change* its meaning.

Interpersonal behaviors are subject to the same issues in interpretation. In interpersonal communication, punctuation refers to how people block off, or identify, the point when a sequence of words or behaviors starts and stops. Different people may perceive the same message or behavioral sequence as primarily an *effect* of previous behavior or a cause of further behavior, depending on where they believe the exchange began. They can, in effect, "punctuate" the behavior or message differently.

Courtesy of Garry Conner/PhotoEdit

Let's suppose Bert and Ernie are roommates, who are not getting along. Bert stays away from the apartment for long periods of time. When Bert comes home Ernie walks away from him; when Bert follows and attempts to start a conversation, Ernie gives him the cold shoulder, and Bert leaves. When Bert comes home again, he again tries to engage Ernie, who again cuts him off. At the urging of friends, Bert and Ernie sit down with a counselor and start discussing their problem. Bert says he stays away so much because Ernie treats him so badly. Ernie, on the other hand, says that he acts so unsociably because Bert is never around. What is happening here? The two room-mates are punctuating their interactions differently. Bert says Ernie caused the problem while Ernie believes that he is only responding to what Bert started. Punctuation problems lie at the heart of many interpersonal—and geopolitical—conflicts. Think of the longstanding "troubles" in Ireland and the Palestinian-Israeli conflict. Meanings do lie in people.

A second important concept is the tendency of people to label. For many people, certain specific words have intensely felt meanings. Using those words—or having those words used in their presence—elicits a wealth of personal emotions, ranging from highly positive to highly negative. For example, many people in relationships are hesitant to use the word "love." They hesitate, saying that they are "in like" or that they "really, really care" for one another. Why? Because "love" is a charged word when used in romantic relationships, and people know that using it may cause the relationship to change. Interestingly, the differences between behaviors that occur an hour before the word is first uttered and behaviors that occur an hour later may be very little. What actually changes are the emotional feelings and meanings that arise because the label is used. And what the label means is entirely in its symbolic value to you, your special other, and those around you. The meanings are in you, not the word.

5. Communication is irreversible.

"The Moving Finger writes; and, having writ, / Moves on," wrote the poet Omar Khayyam. "Nor all your Piety nor Wit / Shall lure it back to cancel half a Line, / Nor all your Tears wash out a Word of it." It is a simple, yet profound statement: Communication is irreversible. Once you say something, there is no way you can ever take it back.

Most of us learn this proposition the hard way. We say or do something that we later regret. To our chagrin, whatever we said or did cannot be erased. Arguments, especially, have a way of snowballing, and people sometimes reach a point where they say things they might not mean; or, upon reflection, would not want another to know or hear. Suppose you argue with a friend, and you say something that really upsets him—seriously bruising his self-esteem or his feelings about you or someone else important to him. Can you take back what you said? Not really. You can apologize, ask him to forget it, beg him to forgive you, plead that it was only the passions of the moment that made you say what you said, or insist that you did not really mean what you said. But even with all of these disclaimers, and even if he agrees to forgive and forget, he will carry some memory of what you said. And that exchange may affect, in innumerable ways, the future of your relationship.

> "It is far more accurate to think of communication as a tool that you can use to create problems as well as to solve them."

Long ago, the Greek poet Heraclitus wrote that you can never step in the same river twice. The first time you step in the river, that single step changes the river so profoundly that it is a different river by the time you take a second step. Similarly, with each communication with a person you permanently affect the relationship. Sometimes the effect is positive; other times it is negative. Sometimes the effect is miniscule, other times it is of such immensity as to totally alter the entire relationship.

6. Communication is a neutral tool.

Communication is neither good nor bad. Very often people attach a positive bias to the term communication—it solves problems, makes people happy, and generally is a useful, important, and good thing to do with others. But this belief in the inherent goodness of communication is inaccurate. For every instance in which communication can be shown to serve a good purpose, we can find another instance where it is used for ill. Remember the old adage "Sticks and stones can break my bones, but words can never hurt me?" Is it accurate? Of course not. We often find that words hurt us just as much as any stick or stone. Family spats that fester and grow to long-running disputes almost always have communication as a central component. And indeed, nearly every terrible event you can think of throughout human history has communication as a central aspect. Hitler rose to power, in part, because of his ability as a communicator. Wars of every sort begin with communication. In short, communication creates problems just as easily as it solves them. It would be a serious mistake to think of communication as a panacea for every, or even many, of your problems. It is far more accurate to think of communication as a tool that you can use to create problems as well as to solve them.

> **"Communication is not a natural ability, it is a learned skill."**

As you attempt to use interpersonal communication as a positive tool, remember that both quantity and quality are important factors in communicative success. People often seem to think that the quantity of communication is the only issue. Sometimes couples believe that if they simply spent more time communicating with one another, their disagreements would wither and their relationships would blossom. Young corporate executives think that if they only had increased "access" to their superiors, they would be more successful. Talkative individuals of all types assume that the more they talk, the more positively others will view them. In each of these cases people's communicative worlds are centered on quantity: Sheer frequency of communication is their central concern. Perhaps they are right; perhaps more talk might clear up the misunderstanding, cement the relationship, yield a promotion, or engender greater respect from others. But maybe they are wrong and talking more may well exacerbate the problem.

What these people may be forgetting is that quality of communication is as important as quantity. In many situations, people probably talk more than is necessary. A very small amount of high-quality talk can sometimes replace, and even improve on, large quantities of lower-quality talk. Rather than always maximizing the amount of communication, people might seek to achieve communication of greater depth. We make this observation not to say that only quality is important. Both quality and quantity are critical to effective interpersonal communication, alone and together.

7. Communication is a learned skill.

Communication is not a natural ability, it is a learned skill. This proposition is perhaps the most controversial of the propositions we have discussed here. When many people hear it for the first time, they reject it as untrue. Communication, they protest, is something that everyone does from birth. They offer as evidence the case of the crying infant who communicates to his mother, or they offer research in language development that suggests that some genetic structure for language is programmed into humankind. But careful analyses of both cases suggest that this position is ill considered. The child, at birth, does not communicate; it makes noises. Very soon, however, the child learns how to manipulate those noises to get desirable responses from others. At birth the child has no awareness that crying can, for example, elicit comforting responses from caretakers. Only after the caretaker demonstrates a consistent response does the child learn that crying may lead to comfort. The child, after learning that crying yields certain desirable outcomes, learns to use the wail as a signal and to communicate with the cry. In a simplistic sense, parents teach children to communicate via crying.

And what about language structure? Well, our proposition suggests that communication is learned, not that humans do not have a predisposition towards some language through which we communicate. Clearly we do have some cognitive structures built into us that help us understand and create language. But just because certain syntactic or grammatical structures are programmed into us, does not mean that at birth we know how to achieve our goals through language. Having an innate capacity to learn the structure of language says nothing about how well we will use the language when communicating.

Consider an analogy to this issue, the case of dating. Think back to the first date you ever had. How "well" did you do? Did everything go just perfectly? If you are like most people, your answer is a somewhat embarrassed "no." How about the dates that followed? If you think back you probably will come to conclude that you got "better" as your dating experience increased. People with many dating experiences develop dating skills that are better than those with more limited experiences. The same goes for communication. Those with more experiences and more practice are often far better communicators than those who lack the experience or practice. There are, in short, no natural-born daters, just as there are no natural-born communicators.

One reason why most people at first balk at this proposition is that they communicate constantly. Because they do it with such frequency, they come to assume that they are both competent performers and knowledgeable about what it is they do. But even if you see and do something every day, it does not necessarily mean that you truly understand it or can even remember basic aspects of it. Try this little exercise. Take out a pen, go to Exercise 1.1 and try to draw a penny. Right here. Right now.

Exercise 1.1. Draw a penny.

If you are like most people, you will find this exercise surprisingly difficult. Why? You have seen pennies nearly every day of your life as long as you can remember. And even if you are pretty sure you know, you may find that you drew an inaccurate picture. Just like your knowledge of that penny you see every day, your knowledge of communication may not be as good as you think it is. Communication is something we learn. As is true with just about everything we learn, there is always room for improvement.

Front of Penny	Back of Penny

---

8. Communication takes place in physical and psychological contexts.

Our final proposition is that communication always occurs in both physical and psychological contexts. This proposition ties together many of the other propositions we've discussed. Whenever we communicate we do so within a physical environment. Can that environment shape both what we say and how we say it? *Certainement!* After all, would you say the same thing in the same way in a small, intimate French restaurant as you would while standing in line for French fries at Six Flags over Texas? *Évidemment pas.* When making a presentation in a small room to three people, you are going to do very different things than if you are delivering the same presentation in an auditorium filled with 300 listeners.

Certain environments seem to enhance some kinds of conversations and reduce our willingness to engage in others. Environmental signals also provide a wealth of cues about what is appropriate to say, how words ought to be uttered, and how messages from others should be taken. In noisy environments we know to raise the volume of our voices and lower the intimacy of what we say. In social settings we know that our talk should be different than it is in work-oriented settings. Business meetings call for entirely different behavior than what is expected at company picnics. Smart communicators know how to interpret and structure the physical contexts in which they communicate. They work hard at creating environments conducive to what they want to communicate. Indeed, there is quite a large profession, variously called interior designers or environmental consultants, whose members create environments suitable to different sorts of communication.

Beyond the physical environment one also needs to consider the psychological context surrounding the message that is being sent and received. Because every interaction takes place within the very special perspectives of the people involved, a conversation can't be separated from the people holding it and what they bring with them to the exchange. When people participate in an interaction they come prepared to interpret what is said from their own points of view, based upon their highly individualistic experiences. An effective communicator recognizes that the psychological context shapes how every utterance is interpreted. Many times, less skilled communicators think that what they say will be taken in the same way, no matter the psychological context of the listener. This is an inappropriate judgment. Messages are understood by a listener only from his or her perspective.

Conclusion

This chapter has introduced you to the study of human communication. In this chapter, we have provided a definition of communication, a brief model of the communicative process, and eight propositions that introduce you to the fundamentals of interpersonal communication. By increasing your understanding of these basic concepts and by consciously working to improve your communication skills, you can increase your chances for a successful personal and professional life.

As we pointed out at the beginning of this chapter, the basic task in the workplace is communication. Any information that helps make you a more effective communicator will enhance your professional life.

Endnotes

1 For the first version of this model, see Shannon and Weaver's *Mathematical Theory of Communication* (Urbana: University of Illinois Press, 1949). The model was extended in 1954 by Wilbur Schramm, who gave more attention to the interpersonal processes of encoding and decoding. See his "How Communication Works" in Wilbur Schramm, ed., *The Process and Effects of Mass Communication* (Urbana: University of Illinois Press, 1954), pp. 3–26.

2 Paul Ekman and Wallace V. Friesen, "Nonverbal Leakage and Clues to Deception," *Psychiatry* 32:1 (1969), pp. 88–106.

3 Paul Watzlawick, Janet H. Beavin, and Don D. Jackson, *Pragmatics of Human Communication* (New York: W.W. Norton & Company, 1967).

4 David K. Berlo, *The Process of Communication* (New York: Holt, Rinehart and Winston, 1960).

Notes

CHAPTER 2

So What's Stopping You?

by John A. Daly

Objectives

After studying Chapter 2, you should be able to do the following:

- ☐ Distinguish between dispositional and situational anxiety.
- ☐ Know the major consequences of communication apprehension.
- ☐ Explain why people experience communication apprehension.
- ☐ List the major reasons why people experience stage fright.
- ☐ Use a variety of techniques to reduce your communication anxiety.

Key Terms

TERM	DEFINITION
cognitive restructuring	A therapeutic technique that helps people who are anxious reduce their fears by changing unrealistic beliefs to more realistic ones.
cognitive therapy	A type of therapy that helps alleviate people's fears through directed conversation.
communication apprehension	The general predisposition to avoid situations that require communication.
conspicuousness	Feeling that you are an unwelcome focus of attention.
dispositional communication anxiety	The anxiety you feel about communicating in most situations. Often called "trait-like anxiety."
labeling	The act of interpreting a situation and treating the interpretation as real.
learned helplessness	"Learning" through experience that you can't change a situation.
positive reinforcement	Reward for engaging in some activity. When an audience applauds you during a presentation, you're receiving positive reinforcement.
reframing	Recasting your interpretation of an event from a different perspective.
reticence	Shyness or communication apprehension.
rigid rules	Standards for behavior that people don't alter even when the situation warrants.
situational anxiety	The normal anxiety people experience when they find themselves in a stressful situation.
shyness	The tendency of a person to avoid social interaction.
stage fright	The anxiety a person experiences when speaking in public.
systematic desensitization	A therapeutic technique to help anxious people reduce their fears by associating communication with relaxation.
talkaholic	A person who is a compulsive communicator. He or she seemingly cannot "shut-up."
visualization	A therapeutic technique that helps anxious people reduce their fears by visualizing positive outcomes of future experiences.
writer's block	A sense of "stuckness" when trying to write.

Introduction

You know the feeling: You're about to give a presentation and you're feeling nervous. Your palms sweat; your hands shake; your mouth is dry. Your mind races frantically, thinking "Why am I here?" You start to speak and your mind goes blank. . . . Or how about this: You're about to interview for your dream job. Your prospective employer welcomes you, and your heart kicks out of control. You introduce yourself and stumble over your own name. And now you're blushing! Several eons later, when the interview is over, you can't remember the names of any of the people you just met. . . . Or this: It's the beginning of the semester and your stomach's killing you. You've got five new classrooms you've got to walk into, five new groups of strangers to avoid, five new professors to evade, five new opportunities for humiliation. . . .

Welcome to the worlds of stage fright and communication apprehension.

If you feel this way, you're not alone. In any number of surveys that ask people about their fears, speaking in public comes out near the top of the heap. A recent Gallup poll listed stage fright as Americans' second biggest fear—after snakes.[1] In the late 1970s, a famous (but unscientific) survey gained notoriety by claiming that people fear public speaking more than they fear death.[2] Experts in communication estimate that 10 to 15 percent of people are anxious even about talking in meetings and conversations.[3] Why the anxiety? And what can you do to control, if not eliminate, your fears about making a presentation, attending a meeting, or participating in an interview?

Almost everyone has butterflies when engaging in important communication activities. For instance, some degree of fear and anxiety is a normal reaction when preparing and delivering a presentation. It's also very normal to feel nervous before important interviews, meetings, or even some crucial conversations. Anxiety occurs when we feel we are being evaluated by others, and when we worry that we might not come across well. The issue to remember as you read this chapter is not *whether* you're apprehensive—we'll take that as given—but rather how you can control the degree to which you're apprehensive.

In this chapter, we'll begin by talking about how people differ in their general levels of communication anxiety. Then we'll move to the situation that makes most people particularly nervous—public speaking and the stage fright that often accompanies making a presentation. (The ideas that we offer about how to overcome stage fright in presentations apply equally to the anxiety you might experience in meetings or conversations.) Finally, we'll discuss strategies for dealing with extreme amounts of apprehension.

Understanding Communication Apprehension

The past 30 years have seen a plethora of academic research that studies how people systematically differ in their enjoyment, or avoidance, of communicating.[4] Under the rubric of communication apprehension, and sometimes shyness and reticence, scholars have found that some people love to talk; others are far more hesitant. Some find great personal rewards in speaking in conversations, at meetings, or in presentations. Others find those activities emotionally punishing. Some look forward to speaking in public; others will do almost anything to avoid it.

Figure 2.1 provides a typical instrument that measures general levels of anxiety.[5] The questionnaire is divided into four separate components—anxiety about group discussions, anxiety about speaking in meetings, anxiety about interpersonal interactions, and anxiety about making presentations. Take some time right now to fill out the questionnaire and total your score.

Media Box

Watch Professor James McCroskey talk about communication apprehension. His interviews are available in this chapter's folder in your Chapter Media Contents online.

Figure 2.1. Measuring your apprehension.

This instrument contains 24 statements that describe feelings about communicating with others.

Please indicate the degree to which each statement applies to you by marking whether you: Strongly Disagree = 1; Disagree = 2; Feel Neutral = 3; Agree = 4; Strongly Agree = 5

_2_ 1. I dislike participating in group discussions.

_1_ 2. Generally, I am comfortable while participating in group discussions.

_2_ 3. I am tense and nervous while participating in group discussions.

_1_ 4. I like to get involved in group discussions.

_4_ 5. Engaging in a group discussion with new people makes me tense and nervous.

_2_ 6. I am calm and relaxed while participating in group discussions.

_4_ 7. Generally, I am nervous when I have to participate in a meeting.

_____ 8. Usually, I am comfortable when I have to participate in a meeting.

_____ 9. I am very calm and relaxed when I am called upon to express an opinion at a meeting.

_____ 10. I am afraid to express myself at meetings.

_____ 11. Communicating at meetings usually makes me uncomfortable.

_____ 12. I am very relaxed when answering questions at a meeting.

_____ 13. While participating in a conversation with a new acquaintance, I feel very nervous.

_____ 14. I have no fear of speaking up in conversations.

_____ 15. Ordinarily I am very tense and nervous in conversations.

_____ 16. Ordinarily I am very calm and relaxed in conversations.

_____ 17. While conversing with a new acquaintance, I feel very relaxed.

_____ 18. I'm afraid to speak up in conversations.

_____ 19. I have no fear of giving a presentation.

_____ 20. Certain parts of my body feel very tense and rigid while I'm giving a presentation.

_____ 21. I feel relaxed while giving a presentation.

_____ 22. My thoughts become confused and jumbled when I am giving a presentation.

_____ 23. I face the prospect of giving a presentation with confidence.

_____ 24. While giving a presentation, I get so nervous I forget facts I really know.

SCORING:

Group discussion apprehension:

   18 − (scores for items 2, 4, & 6)   + (scores for items 1, 3, & 5)   = _____

Meetings apprehension:

   18 − (scores for items 8, 9, & 12)   + (scores for items 7, 10, & 11)   = _____

Interpersonal apprehension:

   18 − (scores for items 14, 16, & 17)   + (scores for items 13, 15, & 18)   = _____

Figure 2.1. Continued.

Public speaking apprehension:

18 – (scores for items 19, 21, & 23)   + (scores for items 20, 22, & 24)   = _____

TOTAL = _____

From J.C. McCrosky

Done? What was your total? If you scored above 80 you are probably generally nervous and uncomfortable when communicating. If you scored less than 51, you are likely the opposite—you enjoy, even seek out, opportunities to talk with others.

Scholars have identified two sorts of communication apprehension: situational anxiety and dispositional (also called "trait-like") anxiety. Everyone experiences situational anxiety, which occurs when we encounter specific high-stress situations. When we get embarrassed in an significant conversation, for example, many of us blush and get a tad tongue-tied. And when we have to make a very important speech, we all get a little nervous. In contrast, people who experience dispositional anxiety find that it affects them in *most* parts of their lives. People who are dispositionally shy, for example, experience shyness pervasively. It affects them everyday. The survey you just took measures dispositional apprehension, which is what we'll be talking about for the next few pages. (Later in the chapter we'll focus on stage fright, a common type of situational anxiety.)

Dispositional communication apprehension has consequences.

People who have dispositional anxiety about communication are profoundly affected by it. Anxiety permeates most parts of their lives—what they do, how they experience their relationships, and how others perceive them.[6] For example, highly anxious people don't do as well in classrooms as people who are less anxious. Why? Because in school you're often judged not only on what you know but also on how well you express it. Think about the number of classes you've taken that require—and grade on—"classroom participation." Teachers essentially punish students who are unwilling to verbally participate in their classes.

The problem starts early. Remember the reading groups in elementary school? How were you and your peers assigned to "high" or "low" groups? You probably were assigned a group based on your oral reading skills. As apprehensive people go through school, they miss many opportunities because of their fear of communicating. They don't get as much personal attention from teachers because asking for extra help—and even accepting help that's offered—requires communication. They don't volunteer to answer questions in classes, losing, as a consequence, numerous opportunities to impress teachers with their knowledge. They avoid highly interactive extracurricular activities that offer opportunities for leadership.

It's not surprising that in college, students with a good deal of communication apprehension do just as well as other students in large lecture classes, but they often receive lower grades in smaller courses. Why? It's because in small seminars, verbal participation is often a "must" for a good grade. To avoid this situation, many highly apprehensive students choose majors that they perceive won't require much social interaction. Once they graduate from college, communication apprehension continues to play a big role in their lives. Think about it: Most people get jobs through networking and oral interviews, both highly communicative activities. Further, but not surprisingly, researchers have discovered that people who are apprehensive receive job offers with lower starting salaries than other people who are less apprehensive about communication. Because apprehensive individuals choose occupations that require relatively little communication, they limit their own upward mobility. How? The higher people go in most occupations, the more important communication is to their success. (You'll seldom encounter a shy top executive.) And, in both school and work, shy people are evaluated less positively than their more outgoing colleagues.

> "People who are dispositionally shy, for example, experience that shyness pervasively . . . everyday."

Is the news completely bad for quiet people? No it isn't, for three reasons. First, it's just as possible for people to be too outgoing. Recent research on what scholars call "compulsive communicators" or talkaholics paints an equally negative portrait of people who never shut up.[7] Second, when apprehensive people are among people they know very well, many of the negative attributes associated with anxiety disappear. For example, shy people aren't very shy with their loved ones. Finally, reserved individuals can find perfect places for themselves in this world. Shy people do well, for example, as teachers of young children because kids are not evaluative.

Why are some people apprehensive about communicating?

Why do people differ, dispositionally, in their anxiety about communicating? While some evidence suggests a genetic component,[8] quite a bit of dispositional communication anxiety can be attributed to three environmental factors: inadequate positive reinforcement for communication, poor skill development, and a lack of good models of communicating.[9] If you experience dispositional communication apprehension, you may find in one or more of these explanations some understanding of *why*. And when you know why you experience what you do, you're well on your way to learning how to control it.

Courtesy of Tim Ridley/Dorling Kindersley Media Library

Inadequate positive reinforcement

Take the case of Tom. As a youngster he constantly heard his grandmother utter phases like "Children should be seen, not heard." His aunt, whose apartment he often visited, had cross-stitched a motto for her wall that read "A quiet child is God's child." At home, Tom's parents discouraged "yakking." When he would get home from school and try to engage his mother in conversation, she often responded with an exasperated comment such as, "Be quiet, Tom; I'm busy." At dinner, when he asked "too many" questions, his father would tell Tom to "shut up and eat." Tom learned, from an early age, that communicating was not a skill to be encouraged. In fact, he was rewarded for *not* talking. A bright student, he learned the lesson. Now that he's an adult, Tom simply avoids talking when he can. He stays silent in meetings, is reserved in conversations, and avoids making oral presentations.

Does this scenario sound familiar? Many people are raised to believe that speaking isn't good, and that staying quiet is the best approach. For them, quietness is reinforced; talking is discouraged. Take a moment to reflect on your own upbringing. What behavior received positive reinforcement in your family when it came to communication? Talking? Or staying quiet?

For some people, reinforcement-oriented apprehension about communication arises not from being punished for talking, but from receiving no response when they did try to communicate. Imagine that every time you said something, people ignored you. When you called to your siblings in the back yard, they "didn't hear" you. When you tried to talk at dinner, others talked right over you. When you suggested an activity, no one responded. Given enough experiences like these, what would you do? You might just give up using communication to accomplish your goals. People often withdraw when they constantly feel that their attempts to say something are futile. Over time, this sense of communicative impotence generates anxiety.

There's a third reinforcement explanation for communication apprehension, a state of being referred to as learned helplessness. People want and need consistency in their lives. We like to believe that particular actions lead to particular reactions. You turn the faucet on, you expect to get water. You flip the light switch on, you fully anticipate that light will appear. But what happens if sometimes you get the reaction you anticipate and other times you don't? What happens if one time when you flip the light switch the light comes on, another time nothing happens at all, and a third time you get a shock? And it keeps happening? At first, you'd try to figure it out. But if you continually receive random responses, you'd eventually just stop trying because it seems like nothing you would do could influence the outcome. The same can be applied to human communication. What if, as a child, one day you came home and your parents ignored what you had to say about school; another day, they were all ears? If on another day, you got yelled at for saying anything at all, and the next day, your parents accused you of "clamming up?" Soon, this kind of unpredictability would make you give up even trying to communicate. You'd withdraw, thinking "What's the use?" or "It's hopeless." At that point, you would have learned, through experience, to perceive yourself as helpless when it comes to communication.

Poor skill development

The idea behind the "poor skills" explanation for communication apprehension is that people who are currently anxious about communication either acquired fewer communication skills when they were young or gained those skills later than their peers. When you're not as skillful a communicator as others, you tend to avoid doing it. Over time, you get fearful and anxious about even attempting to communicate. And that nervousness is probably justified. It's like swimming: If you don't know how to do it, you'll be anxious about getting into water over your head. And if someone comes along and pushes you in, the fear you feel while trying to right yourself will confirm all the anxieties you had about drowning in the first place.

Consider the cases of Jose and Charlie. As Jose grew up, he was constantly given opportunities to develop his speaking skills. After attending a preschool that encouraged expression, Jose went to grade school, where he often volunteered for roles that required communication: He was the class weather boy in first grade, played the lead in the third-grade Thanksgiving skit, and won the job of captain of the safety patrol in fifth grade. By the time he got to high school, Jose was well-prepared for its debate team, and he was active on the team for all four years. Charlie, on the other hand, stayed home until he reached school age. In grade school he seldom got involved in social activities, preferring to read or watch TV. By the time he got to high school, Charlie had mastered the art of keeping a low profile. Now that they're both in college, which of these two people do you think might be more anxious about communicating? You're right if you say Charlie, who was exposed less often than Jose to vital communication opportunities while growing up.

When people first learn about the skills explanation for communication apprehension, they often respond, "Well then, why not just get up and get some experience now?" "Take a public speaking course," they say, "and you'll get over it." Unfortunately, that's much easier said than done. In fact, some researchers have found that when very apprehensive people enroll in a presentation skills class, they actually can become more anxious.[10] Why? Because logically, given their limited skills, they know that they're *likely* to do more poorly than others.

Take the case of Mary. For most of her life, she's felt uncomfortable making presentations. In fact, she finds every excuse to avoid making them and has consistently avoided opportunities to learn how to get better. The thought of making presentations scares her because she knows she's not a good public speaker. Now, upon the urging of her advisor, she's decided, with a great deal of trepidation, to enroll in a presentation skills class. During the first week of class, the teacher asks each student to stand up and make a brief introduction. One student—who turns out to have been an "all-star" debater in high school—volunteers to go first. She stands up and gives a great presentation. The instructor heaps praise on her. Then another—a theater major and gifted at delivery—leaps to his feet and offers a stunning speech laced with humor, insight, and iambic pentameter. The teacher says to the class, "Keep an eye on this guy; he's going to be great."

Now it's Mary's turn. How do you think she feels? She's thinking, "I don't want to do this. I'm not as good as those people." And she's right. Having never before given an impromptu speech, she walks to the front of the class, sees all the people staring at her, and feels faint. When she starts talking, she stumbles over words and loses track of what she wanted to say. When she finishes, she rushes to her seat and hides her face, burning with shame. What's the teacher to say? Given any level of sensitivity, it'll be something kind. But Mary—and everyone in the class—*knows* she did not do well. Mary is now even more convinced that public speaking is not for her. After her humiliating experience, she goes straight to the registrar to drop the class. Now, having "given it a fair try," she's more nervous than ever about speaking in public. Anxiety begets avoidance; avoidance limits skill development; poor skills lead to failure that, in turn, leads to greater anxiety.

Do you recognize yourself in Mary? If so, be proud of yourself that you've signed up for 306M and taken the first step. It's a hard one for you—much harder than for most people. But be aware that you can gain immensely from taking this class. It might even change your life! Just concentrate on doing what you can, and

remember to compare your new knowledge and skills only to your former abilities—not to the abilities of people who are already accomplished speakers.

Inadequate or poor models

People learn behaviors by watching others, and then imitating them. Most of us learned to dance by watching other people move; we learned how to socialize by mimicking others we thought socially talented. Luckily, most of us have managed to find good models for most of things we do—Stephen F. Austin, Mary Lou Retton, Mr. Rogers, the kid next door who helped you with math. But what happens if we have models that are barely adequate or even actively poor? We'll learn habits that will, in the end, hurt us.

> **". . . evaluation makes you experience anxiety."**

If, as we grow up, we consistently see people comfortably and competently communicate, we borrow many of their techniques, model their positive attitudes, and become comfortable and competent communicators ourselves. If, on the other hand, we have poor models, we won't be able to develop our skills as well. Consequently, when we do try to communicate, we may behave in ways that are less than effective. The negative response we get makes us want to avoid future speaking opportunities.

Take the case of Amy and Janine. Amy grew up in a household where both of her parents were adept communicators, and particularly adept public speakers. Her father is a trial attorney who has argued cases in front of the United States Supreme Court. Her mother is an English literature professor at a liberal arts college, teaching Shakespeare and Milton. Amy chose a small university and Communication Studies as a college major because she felt so comfortable and competent as a communicator. Janine, on the other hand, grew up in a household with parents who were not terribly social and who had absolutely no experience speaking in public—in fact, it scared them to death. Because of this, Janine always carried with her a fear of speaking in groups, in class and in social situations. She chose a large university where she could "disappear" and selected electrical engineering as a major, hoping she would not have to give presentations.

Understanding Stage Fright

Not everyone is disposed toward communication apprehension, and those who are vary in the degree to which they experience anxiety. Yet even people low in dispositional apprehension experience situational anxiety. One common form of situational anxiety is stage fright, which stops people from *desiring* to communicate in public. How come? Why does public speaking scare us so much? Learning why you fear speaking in public is the first step to coping with speech anxiety during presentations, meetings, and interviews, and other types of professional speaking.

So why *do* you experience stage fright?

Media Box
Read about feeling frozen at the podium in this chapter's folder in your Chapter Media Contents online.

You experience stage fright because you fear evaluation.

Few people enjoy being evaluated by others. But the bottom line is inescapable: When you give a presentation, you invite judgment. There you are, standing in front of an audience as its members think about what you're saying, how you're saying it, the way you dress, and even whether they like you. That's an awful lot of evaluation. And if you're like many people, fear of evaluation makes you experience anxiety.

How do you get over this fear? Winston Churchill is reported to have coped with his anxiety by imagining his audience naked. No doubt it worked: Imagining a bunch of overweight senior government officials in their birthday suits would reduce almost anyone's perception of them as powerful evaluators. To increase his confidence, Churchill redefined his audience from evaluative judges to globs of flesh. While you may not want to go that far—it's important that you retain respect for your audience—academic studies do support the value of reframing. People who ordinarily feel quite a bit of stage fright often don't feel scared at all when talking to young children or very old people. Why? It's probably because people don't perceive kids and our most senior of citizens as threats. Similarly, employees of all ranks are often more comfortable addressing subordinates than those they feel to be equals or superiors.

So, if you feel nervous when you speak because you feel as though you're being evaluated by people who have power over you, try to switch that feeling around and imagine yourself as confident. After all, you certainly know more than your audience about what you are talking about, you're obviously better looking than some of them—and you're the one who has the floor.

Another way of overcoming the fear of being evaluated is to understand that most audience members really want you to do well. Don't believe it? Next time *you're* in an audience, consider what you're thinking as the speakers are introduced. Are you hoping they'll fail? Or are you hoping that they'll be interesting and entertaining and worth listening to? If they falter, do you feel contempt or do you pull for them to pull it out? Bets are that you're as positive and supportive and empathic as you can be. And in that, you're no different from most audience members. Remember, your audience wants you to do well.

You increase your stage fright when you're unprepared.

When you're poorly prepared for a presentation, meeting, or interview, you know it. And that knowledge worries you—quite correctly. Confidence comes from preparation. If you want to reduce your evaluation-based stage fright in speaking, you'll need to be *very* prepared. (Luckily, the benefits of learning to engage in this level of preparation spill over into all other facets of your life, so it's well worth the effort.) Never underestimate how effective good preparation can be in reducing your anxiety. When you know what you want to accomplish, why you want to accomplish it, and what you are going to say, you'll be much less anxious. Most excellent speakers understand this fact. Indeed, a good friend of Winston Churchill once claimed that Churchill had spent the best years of his life writing "impromptu" speeches. Like Churchill, you too can be prepared.

> **"When you're poorly prepared . . . you know it . . . Confidence comes from preparation."**

Familiarity is your friend when it comes to speaking. New situations and new audiences often make us uncomfortable. An example: You agree to meet a friend at a party. You've never been to the apartment where the party's being held. As you walk in, looking for your friend, you find that you don't know anyone there. No one talks to you as you circulate . . . and your friend is nowhere to be found. How do you feel? Do you feel a little nervous, a little out of place? Contrast that feeling to another time when you arrived at a party held at one of your favorite places and attended by some of your favorite people. Didn't you feel more comfortable?

The same thing happens in communication. When you make a presentation to an audience you don't know, in an unfamiliar setting, you feel more anxiety than when you speak in a familiar situation to listeners you know well. Novelty begets anxiety.

So how do you cope with novelty? The answer is *not* to restrict yourself to making presentations only to people you know, in familiar settings. Instead, you should work hard, in advance, to acquaint yourself with both the unfamiliar audience and the unfamiliar setting. Discover everything you can about your audience before you make your presentation. Find out who they are. Talk to a few people who'll be there. Ask them who else will be attending and what sorts of things interest them. Look for ways that this audience is similar to other audiences you've known.

Just as important, get a feel for the setting. Get to the room early. Find out where you'll be standing to speak, talk out loud to gauge the acoustics, sit in a chair or two to see the room from the perspective of an audience member. Trial attorneys often use this strategy to help their witnesses focus. They walk the witnesses into the courtroom, sit them in the witness and jury boxes, have them speak into the microphone, and walk around the courtroom. Why do they do this? Because they know that people perform better when they're familiar with their surroundings. The less novel the setting, then the more comfortable the speaker will be.

The same techniques work for interviews and meetings. Suppose you really want a job with the Acme Company. The interviewer for Acme is coming to the College of Communication's Career Services office next month to recruit prospective employees. You know you'll be nervous because this is such an important interview. What should you do? First, use CCS resources to discover as much as you can about Acme. If you can, find out the interviewer who will be doing the interviewing. (Quite often the same interviewer comes each time.) Then, put yourself through practice interviews, signing up to interview with a few firms in advance so you can get accustomed to the questions that interviewers ask and become proficient in answering them. Preview the interview room if you can. Learn everything you can, so that the only novelty you face is your actual interaction with the interviewer.

In addition to making yourself familiar with your audience and setting, being prepared involves producing high-quality content to communicate. The more compelling your material, the more you *and your audience* focus on it, not you. Much of the remainder of this book discusses this subject, so we'll mention just a few key ideas here. First, choose a topic you know something about already, that you consider interesting and important, and that you're willing to explore in depth. Be an expert. If you know nothing about the weather, don't give a speech about the weather. Not only can audiences sense when you're bluffing, you'll put yourself through hell trying to "wing" it: What if you get questions you can't answer? What if you don't have enough to say? What if you're confused or wrong about something you say? What if you have to blather on and repeat yourself to fill time?

Second, prepare more material than you could ever use. Most of us are lousy at estimating how long it takes to talk about

something. So, if you're planning a 5-minute presentation, prepare enough material for 15 minutes, and then cut what you don't need as you practice. (Even if it turns out that you cut out a lot of information, just think how knowledgeable you'll sound during your Q&A.)

Third, do take the time to imagine the questions people might have about your topic. Come up with answers before you give your speech. Then incorporate the answers in your speech or hold them in readiness if that question is asked. Many well-known corporate leaders and public officials use this technique when planning to meet the press. A day or two before the press conference, staff members brief the leader on likely questions. The group hammers out appropriate answers. Then, when the speaker starts her speech, she feels comfortable knowing she already has answers to the bulk of questions likely to be raised.

You increase your stage fright when you feel conspicuous.

Even if you don't especially fear evaluation, and even if you're prepared to speak, you can experience the anxiety that brings stage fright just by thinking about being the focus of attention. Most of us don't like to feel conspicuous, and talking to a group of, say, 25 people means that you've got around 50 eyeballs staring at you. When you begin to think about all this attention, you can lose focus on your message and your audience and turn inward toward yourself. As you become more self-focused, the quality of your performance suffers and your anxiety increases.

Try this exercise. Say the phrase: "Four score and seven years ago," and think about what it means. Repeat it a few times, get used to the way it feels in your mouth. Now say it again, but this time, think about what your lips and tongue and jaws are doing. Finally, say it one last time, but this time place your hand gently on your throat and feel the vibrations as you speak. Did you notice that the more you thought about what you were *doing*, instead of what you were *meaning*, the more your speech slowed down? That's because the more you focus on yourself, the more you get distracted from your message. Being distracted hurts the quality of your delivery. That's why radio talk show hosts caution callers to turn down their radios before they get on the air; if they don't, they can become mesmerized by the sound of their own voices coming from their radios. And that's why TV broadcasters avoid looking at monitors while they're on camera. They know that if they start watching themselves they'll start thinking about the way they look and sound instead of the content of their communication.

> "As you become more self-focused, the quality of your performance suffers and your anxiety increases."

Some public speaking books suggest you should practice speeches in front of mirrors. What lousy advice! You're your own *worst* audience. Try it and you'll see why. As you talk to yourself, you'll start noticing your face, your hair, and your eyes. You'll notice your mouth moving and your tongue darting out from between your lips. Look at how pink it is! And your hands! What are you going to do with your hands? Just a few minutes of this and you'll be thinking very little about your message. Worse, because people become harsher in their self-judgments as they watch themselves, you'll be raising your anxiety level and increasing your stage fright. The tendency of people with a great deal of stage fright to become self-focused when speaking explains why research finds that they have difficulty remembering, after presentations, much at all about their audience, the room they were in, and what they said. They recall very well, however—and in exquisite detail—the many negative thoughts they had about themselves. People with less stage fright are far better at recalling audience members and their environment because they were focused on communicating their message, not themselves.[11]

So what should you do if you begin to feel self-conscious during a presentation? Years ago, speech coaches advised nervous people to find a point on the back wall of the room and talk to that point. The theory was that you could help yourself feel less overwhelmed by avoiding "live" interaction. Now we know that advice was wrong. Instead, focus every bit of your attention back onto your audience and the content of what you're saying. Talk to audience members as individuals. Pick out a friendly looking person and talk directly to him. Focus your attention on him. Decide that you're going to speak directly to him until he begins to smile. Then smile yourself (at an appropriate point) and you'll find that he smiles back. Then, move on to another audience member, in a different part of the room, and think, "I'm going to talk right at her until she nods her head." As you talk, nod your head (at an appropriate moment) and watch as she starts to reciprocate by nodding her head. What are you doing when you do this? You are redirecting your attention away from yourself and onto the audience, which allows your message to flow without anxiety.

Entertainers know this trick. If you've ever been to a comedy club, you know that there's one sacred rule: Don't sit in the front row unless you want to get picked on by the entertainer. When do entertainers start ribbing their audience? They do it when they want to take attention away from themselves. Any good comedian will tell you that sometimes nothing works: The audience is cold, even hostile. When that happens, the worst thing comedians can do is think about how they're bombing. Instead, they shift the audience's attention away from themselves. They get some breathing room by suddenly pointing out someone in the front row and making a "canned" joke about that person. The audience laughs and strains to see the person being mocked, while the comedian gets a little time to relax and recoup. Teachers do the same thing. When they forget what they want to say or get flustered, they'll often quickly ask for an informal classroom poll. "So how many of you have ever heard of. . . . "

The issue of conspicuousness is one reason you should never tell your audience that you're nervous. Sharing that information can only make your audience more aware of your nervousness—maybe they didn't even know you were nervous until you said it—and make you feel even more uncomfortable.

You increase your stage fright by holding yourself to rigid rules.

Years ago, a psychologist at UCLA, Mike Rose, started studying why people experience writer's block. What he discovered was fascinating.[12] After studying many writers, he found that those with writer's block had rigid rules about writing. These blocked writers believed, for example, that you need to have a perfect first sentence before you go on. So they slaved over that first sentence for hours, feeling that they would "never get it right," and quitting in despair. Writers who didn't suffer from writer's block knew that an opening sentence was important but decided not to worry about it if nothing immediately came to mind. They quickly moved into writing the body of their essay, knowing they could always go back to the introduction. The difference between "blocked" writers and those who comfortably wrote was that the former group let the rules run them while the latter group ran the rules.

The same is true with people suffering from stage fright. They often have very rigid rules about what, for example, a good presentation should look like. One mid-level executive at a computer company who often experienced stage fright said that he believed that "every good speech should start with a joke." Another very anxious scientist felt that "speeches should always have three main points." An engineer related that "every presentation must have visual aids with color graphics." All of these people dearly loved their rules about speaking. And all were haunted by them. If they didn't have a good joke, three (and only three) points, or color graphics, they got nervous. But, in reality, none of these are actually necessary rules for good speaking. Is it possible to give an excellent presentation without any jokes? Sure! Do all excellent presentations have three major points? Of course not! And many outstanding briefings have no graphics at all—color or otherwise. Please understand: There are no "must" rules of speaking (except, perhaps, the rule against talking while chewing gum). This book is, of course, filled with advice. But every piece of advice needs to be adapted to its situation. Is it sometimes all right to put your hands in your pocket while speaking? Yep! Is it acceptable, in some situations, to sit down rather than stand when speaking? Sure!

But some people don't know how flexible they can be when speaking. At some point in their lives they learned certain rules about speaking and now they believe they must follow those rules to the letter. The problem with rigidly following rules is twofold. First, sometimes the rules aren't appropriate. For instance, if you are talking to two of your best friends, it would be weird to stand behind a lectern. Second, when the rules you rigidly hold are not met or are violated, you'll get very uncomfortable. Imagine believing that only a presentation that begins with a barn-burner of a joke can be good. Further, imagine you dutifully start your presentation with a joke but no one gets it. Instead of the laughter you expected, there is absolute quiet. Now how do you feel? Awful, we suspect. Throughout the presentation, you'll be haunted by the fact that you failed to get it "right."

Here's something to think about: Most people are far more comfortable answering questions than they are giving formal presentations. At first glance, you'd think it would be the opposite because you can prepare for a presentation, but it's hard to prepare for every possible question that could be asked in the question-and-answer session that follows. You have to think "on your feet" when you answer questions, while you can do most of your thinking about a presentation beforehand. So it sounds like presentations should be far more nerve wracking. But that's not the case for most speakers. Why? Because both speakers and audiences have far fewer rigid rules about how a good Q&A session ought to go. Drop the rules for your presentation style and you'll feel much better speaking!

Related to rigid rules about speaking is the discovery that people often experience stage fright because they have unrealistic expectations about what's going to happen when they speak. They believe, for instance, that people in the audience will always pay rapt attention. Or they believe things will always go perfectly when they talk. As might be expected, most of these fond dreams are shattered very quickly. And when they are shattered, speakers get nervous.

Take the case of Vish, a 23-year-old college senior who was asked to give a speech at new student orientation. After carefully thinking about the occasion, Vish decides a serious talk on the perils of drinking will be both appropriate and useful, and he crafts a presentation about alcohol abuse that he knows will get the sober attention of listeners. As soon as he mentions the word "drinking," though, he loses the entire room as hundreds of 18-year-olds start giggling and whispering jokes to each other. Reflecting on the fact that the freshmen aren't where he is on the topic, Vish gets them back with wry humor and slowly brings them along to his serious topic. But what if Vish had clung rigidly to his early expectations that people would immediately take his message seriously?

> **"Most people are far more comfortable answering questions than they are giving formal presentations."**

This advice about easing your rigid expectations applies just as much to interviewing and meetings as it does to public presentations. Interviews have as many structures as people who give them. Some meetings follow an agenda; others are far more free-flowing. Life happens so relax those rules!

You increase your stage fright with negative self-talk.

Imagine that you're giving a presentation to an audience. At the end of the presentation, a communication researcher asks you how well you think you did and how nervous you appeared to your audience. The researcher also asks your audience members to rate you on the same questions. The point of the research is to see how closely your perceptions match those of your audience and how accurately you judged how your listeners saw you. When the ratings are collected and the researcher compares your judgments with the audience's ratings, what do you think you'll see?

In studies just like this, investigators find that people who suffer from high levels of speech anxiety think audience members see them as far more nervous and far less competent than the audience members actually report. The same is true for interviews.[13] These investigations confirm the existence of a common error speakers make: While you're the only credible judge of how you *feel* when you speak, you may not be a very good judge of how your performance comes across. Say that you make a presentation that didn't, in your mind, go very well; you couldn't help but feel nervous, uncomfortable, and uptight. But afterwards, as you brood, people come up and compliment you on it. You graciously thank your listeners for their kind words, but you say to yourself, "They're just being nice. What they really think is that I was lousy. They could see I was shaking and sweating all the way through that speech." But perhaps you're incorrect. Perhaps the audience really did see you as relaxed and comfortable. Maybe you really did give a fine presentation. Maybe you're not so good at gauging how nervous you actually appear.

And, for that matter, maybe you're not so good at gauging how you actually feel. Giving a presentation, conducting an important interview, or participating in a crucial meeting are physiologically arousing experiences. Your body gets "up" when you have to communicate in these sorts of settings: Your heart beats faster, your palms get sweaty, and your reflexes fire with scant provocation. When some people experience these feelings, they think, "I'm scared." When others experience *the same feelings*, they say "I'm excited." Physiologically, there's little difference between fear and excitement. What matters about a feeling is how you <u>label</u> it. Think of something adventurous you do by choice—riding a roller coaster, going scuba diving, eating five-alarm chili. What do you feel just before you start? Perhaps you feel a twinge of butterflies in the stomach, slightly sweaty palms, tight breathing? These physiological reactions are no different than the ones you have when you stand up to speak. The difference is that you call *some* of those activities fun—same physiology, different labels. The next time you are about to give a presentation, stop any negative self-talk and work to relabel the experience as positive. Rather than saying "I'm terrified," say "I'm psyched."

We can take the notion of labeling one step further. Communicatively anxious people often actually talk themselves into being more scared than they really are. Before they begin an interview or presentation they run an endless loop of negative conversation through their brains, saying things like: "This is going to be awful. . . . How did I get myself into this . . . ? I'm going to make a fool of myself. . . . People are going to laugh. . . . They'll hate me. . . . I'm going to look like an idiot. . . . " This kind of negative self-talk is particularly troublesome, because you can use it to talk yourself into believing the worst, *regardless of whether it's true.* Worse, you can use your negativity to make what you fear happen in fact. Why do this to yourself? Do what experienced speakers do: Set up a different kind of loop of self-talk: "I'm going to be great. . . . This is exciting. . . . What an opportunity. . . . This is going to work out fine. . . . I really know my stuff. . . . I'm so glad I'm here. . . . I'm really going to convince this audience."

One more thing about the arousal: Make use of the energy it offers. Before you give your presentation, walk around if you can, take some deep breaths, stretch. When you do start the presentation, move around the room and use gestures. Radiate the energy to your audience and relax!

Mark Leary, a psychologist who studies social anxieties, believes that stage fright is a function of two variables: How well you think you'll perform and how significant you believe the consequences of your performance will be.[14] Notice that both are perceptions. You can tell yourself that there's no way you'll perform well or you can persuade yourself that you'll be fine. Similarly, you can make yourself believe that an interview or presentation will be the single most consequential act you've ever done or you can understand that many, many things are more important in life than any one speech act. It's your choice. As Dr. Phil says, "There are no victims here, only volunteers."

Managing Your Fear of Communicating

When you understand stage fright and dispositional communication apprehension, you can begin to manage your fear of communicating. You can take a few simple steps to manage common stage fright. If you experience severe communication apprehension, you can achieve excellent results with professional help.

A few simple techniques to manage your stage fright.

People who suffer from stage fright can discover some very simple ways to better manage their anxiety. For lack of a better word these techniques fall under the rubric of "THINK!" Think before you make a presentation so you can control or avoid whatever makes you nervous:

- ❑ Suppose you discover that as you speak your hands shake. What to do? THINK! If there's a lectern, why not put your hands on it?
- ❑ Suppose your shaking hands make the notes you hold rattle? What to do? THINK! Why not put your note card on a clipboard? Clipboards don't shake very much. If you're so nervous that the clipboard shakes, lay it down on a table.
- ❑ Suppose you blush when nervous and that the blushing starts at chest level and slowly crawls up your neck. What to do? THINK! Why not wear a scarf or turtleneck instead of a shirt that reveals your nervousness?
- ❑ Or, suppose that you have a nervous habit of playing with change or the keys in your pocket when talking. What to do? You've got it: THINK! Why not get rid of the change or keys?

In meetings, we forget how helpful it is to project the agenda on a wall so that we can quickly glance to see our place in the schedule. In interviews, we forget to bring an extra copy of the resume, assuming that the interviewer has one. If you think in advance of the things that might make you nervous, you can do something about them.

How to treat severe communication apprehension.

If none of these ideas help you overcome your apprehension, you may want to try some more formal methods to reduce your anxiety, which include procedures used by professional clinicians and some highly trained teachers.[15] These therapies take work but with effort and good help, you can reduce your anxiety.

Systematic desensitization

Think about walking into a very attractive room and sitting down in a very comfortable chair. Peaceful music plays in the background. Greeting you at the door is Bill, a teacher trained in systematic desensitization. He briefly, but effectively, teaches you the basics of muscle relaxation. The setting and music add to your deep relaxation. As the music continues you find yourself getting more and more comfortable. At some point, Bill tells you he's going to ask you to think about situations that may or may not make you nervous. All have to do with communicating with others. Before he starts, Bill tells you that any time you feel even a little anxiety you should raise one finger. When you raise that finger, Bill will ask you to relax and then he'll start over describing the situations.

At this point, Bill starts by asking you to think of talking to a good friend about the weather. Next, he asks you to imagine chatting with a friendly store clerk about where to find a product. Then, he asks you to think of discussing a recent vacation at a family dinner. The process continues as he raises more situations that, based on pre-testing, are gradually more likely to make you nervous. What Bill is doing is going through a hierarchy of anxiety-producing situations. At the beginning, the situations he guides you to think about are mostly quite comfortable ones. As the process progresses, however, some are likely to make you nervous. For example, at one point, Bill asks you to think about making a brief presentation to some strangers. You feel a twinge of nervousness so you raise you finger. Bill then asks you to relax, the music plays on for a few minutes, and once you are relaxed Bill starts over again asking you to imagine again talking to a good friend about the weather. Over the two hours this therapy typically takes, you find yourself slowly beginning to associate communication events with relaxation rather than nervousness. The therapy is working.

This therapy is called systematic desensitization and it works amazingly well. The underlying notion is that stage fright arises when you mentally associate speaking with nervousness. After the treatment, you associate making a presentation with a sense of relaxation. Any number of studies confirms that the technique works. It is, by the way, a very common technique used to help people overcomes their phobias such as fear of snakes, elevators, or open spaces. It's also a technique used by nearly every professional sports team to aid players in coping with "clutch" moments, like when there's a tie game, a foul, and a single free throw standing between the team and victory. The player making the shot may "choke"—misjudge the shot and entirely miss the hoop. If she does, no win. Watch carefully how the player acts as she prepares to take the shot. Note how relaxed she is. Every muscle seems almost limp. What you are seeing is systematic desensitization at work. The player has learned that the more nerve-wracking the situation, the more relaxed she has to be.

Even if you don't seek professional help, understanding how systematic desensitization works can help you overcome your stage fright. You can teach yourself to relax, and if you do, you'll have less stage fright. Certainly this is easier said than done. But try deep breathing, peaceful mediation, stretches, and such when you feel yourself tense up. It will help.

Cognitive therapy

Systematic desensitization posits that if you are relaxed, stage fright won't be a problem. Cognitive therapies go a step further. When applied to stage fright, they're premised on the idea that you're afraid because you hold unrealistic beliefs about making presentations. You can challenge those beliefs, and make them fade in favor of beliefs that are more reasonable and useful to you. Consider the following transcript of a cognitive therapy session:

Teacher:	So you have stage fright.
Student:	Oh, yeah.
Teacher:	Why are you so scared to make a speech?
Student:	I don't know . . .
Teacher:	Really?
Student:	I guess because I'll look stupid.
Teacher:	What makes you think you'll look stupid?
Student:	I don't know . . . .
Teacher:	[silence].
Student:	OK, maybe because people will laugh at me if I make a mistake.
Teacher:	Now, let's think about that for a minute. Why do you think you'll make a mistake so bad that people will laugh at you?
Student:	I could.
Teacher:	Sure you could, and the Tower could fall over. Have you ever made a mistake while giving a speech that made people laugh at you?
Student:	No. . . . But it could it happen.
Teacher:	OK, let's assume it does happen, as rare as that is. What's so bad about making a mistake and having people laugh?
Student:	It would be embarrassing.
Teacher:	Yes, it would. So what? You'll live.
Student:	Yeah, but it would feel bad.
Teacher:	True, but you'd get over it, wouldn't you?
Student:	I guess so.
Teacher:	What do you mean you guess so? Do you think you wouldn't?
Student:	Well, sure I'd get over it, but still . . .
Teacher:	Still, what?

As you can see, this conversational process challenges and tries to change a person's unrealistic beliefs, in this case about the dangers of giving a speech. Most of the time, this student won't make a bad mistake. Most of the time people won't laugh, and even if they do laugh, it isn't the end of the world. Prior to the session all those unrealistic beliefs were making the student very nervous about speaking in public; during the session the student got the chance to examine the beliefs and decide if they're true. This therapy is called cognitive restructuring because it helps clients restructure their beliefs.

The take-home message with cognitive restructuring is that if you experience stage fright, you should try to challenge some of your fears. Get more realistic about what will happen when you give a speech. Really, it won't be *that* bad. Certainly, it won't be the end of the world. Challenge those negative beliefs that get in the way of speaking.

Another cognitive therapy is called visualization. Imagine, for a moment, that you're a professional golfer. You arrive at an important tournament two days early to get some practice on the course. To your chagrin, rain is pounding down in sheets, so heavy that going onto the greens would be foolhardy. So what to do? How do you get in the necessary practice? Many experienced golfers would tell you to find a good model of the golf course and study it carefully, in minute detail. Visualize each hole and how you would play it: Look at each green, imagine teeing off, feel the swing in your mind, watch the ball fly, feel the grass as you walk towards the hole. This sort of visualizing is as effective, some suggest, as physically practicing the round. As a speaker, you can do the same thing trying overcome your stage fright. Before your presentation, sit back and imagine making the speech. Think about how many smiles you'll receive as you start to talk, think about the nodding heads of agreement, think about the looks of interests you'll see in your audience, and think about how smooth your delivery will sound.

Conclusion

It's natural to experience some anxiety when you have to make an important presentation, complete a crucial interview, or speak at a meeting. The challenge is to overcome your nervousness and do a good job communicating. In this chapter we've discussed trait-like communication apprehension and situation-specific stage fright. We've discussed the causes of each and given practical advice for overcoming your fears, whatever their cause. Speaking is a human faculty; when you clear your mind of unrealistic fears, you'll find that it's also a human pleasure.

Endnotes

1   Summarized in *USA Today*, March 20, 2001.

2   David Wallechinsky, Irving Wallace, & Amy Wallace, *The Book of Lists* (New York: William Morrow and Company, 1977).

3   John A. Daly, James C. McCroskey, Joe Ayres, Tim Hopf, & Debbie M. Ayres, eds., *Avoiding Communication: Shyness, Reticence, and Communication Apprehension*, 3rd ed. (Cresskill, NJ: Hampton, 2004).

4   For an in-depth summary, see Daly, et al., *Avoiding Communication*.

5   James C. McCroskey, *An Introduction to Rhetorical Communication*, 4th ed. (Englewood Cliffs, NJ: Prentice-Hall, 1982).

6   To find out more about all these effects, see John A. Daly, John P. Caughlin, & Laura Stafford, "Correlates and Consequences of Social-Communicative Anxiety" in Daly et al., *Avoiding Communication*, 21–74.

7   Robert N. Bostrom & Nancy G. Harrington, "An Exploratory Investigation of Characteristics of Compulsive Talkers," *Communication Education* 48 (1999): 73–80; James C. McCroskey & Virginia P. Richmond, "Correlates of Compulsive Communication: Quantitative and Qualitative Characteristics," *Communication Quarterly* 43 (1995): 39–52.

8   Michael J. Beatty, Alan D. Heisel, Alice E. Hall, Timothy R. Levine, & Betty H. La France, "What Can We Learn From the Study of Twins About Genetic and Environmental Influences on Interpersonal Affiliation, Aggressiveness, and Social Anxiety: A Meta-Analytic Study," Communication Monographs 69 (2002): 1–18; Michael J. Beatty, James C. McCroskey, & Alan D. Heisel, "Communication Apprehension as Temperamental Expression: A Communibiological Paradigm," *Communication Monographs* 65 (1998): 197–219.

9   James A. Daly & Gustav Friedrich, "The Development of Communication Apprehension: A Retrospective Analysis of Contributory Correlates," *Communication Quarterly* 29 (1981): 243–55; Anne Van Kleeck & John A. Daly, "Instructional Communication Research and Theory: Communication Development and Instructional Communication—A Review," in Michael Burgoon, ed., *Communication Yearbook* 5 (New Brunswick, NJ: Transaction Books, 1982).

10 Daly & Friedrich, "The Development of Communication Apprehension."

11 John A. Daly, Anita L. Vangelisti, & Sam G. Lawrence, "Self-Focused Attention and Public Speaking Anxiety," *Personality and Individual Differences* 10 (1989): 903–13.

12 Michael Rose, *When a Writer Can't Write: Studies in Writer's Block and Other Composing Process Problems* (New York: Guilford, 1985).

13 Kenneth Savitsky & Thomas Gilovich, "The Illusion of Transparency and the Alleviation of Speech Anxiety," *Journal of Experimental Social Psychology* 39 (2003): 618–25.

14 Mark R. Leary, "The Social Psychology of Shyness: Testing a Self-Presentational Model" (doctoral dissertation, University of Florida, Gainesville, 1989); Mark R. Leary, "Social Anxiousness: The Construct and Its Measurement," *Journal of Personality Assessment* 47 (1983): 65–75; Mark R. Leary, Susan C. Atherton, Sara Hill, & Christine Hur, "Attributional Mediators of Social Inhibition and Avoidance," *Journal of Personality* 54 (1986), 704–16.

15 For reviews of different therapies, see Daly, et al., *Avoiding Communication*.

Notes

CHAPTER 3

Ethics and Professional Communication

by Celeste D.C. Simons

Objectives

After studying Chapter 3, you should be able to do the following:

- ☐ Describe the basic elements involved in a communication model in the context of ethical communication guidelines.
- ☐ Define academic integrity.
- ☐ What is scholastic dishonesty, its consequences and the rationale for its use.
- ☐ Know what blatant and unintentional plagiarism is, and be able to describe how students unintentionally plagiarize.
- ☐ Distinguish among common knowledge, proprietary knowledge, and accumulated knowledge.

Key Terms

TERM	DEFINITION
academic integrity	A commitment, even in the face of adversity, to honesty, trust, fairness, respect, and responsibility.
accumulated knowledge	Information that you acquire over time through instruction, research, and experimental learning.
blatant plagiarism	Purposefully stealing another person's work and representing it as your own original idea or expression.
cheating	Trying to get a better grade by trickery or deceit.
common knowledge	Information belonging to your culture as a whole, such as information obtained by your own senses, observation, logic, and reasoning.
credo	Statement of beliefs.
dilemma	A situation that demands that you make a choice among equally undesirable alternatives.
disclosure	The act of revealing previously unknown information.
ethics	The general study of the principle of right and wrong.
ethical action	The application of ethical principles in behavior.
expression	The actual words and symbols used in communication.
faulty paraphrasing	Plagiarism as a consequence of incorrectly rewording the meaning of another's work.
paraphrase	The act of putting someone else's idea into your own words.
plagiarism	Any submission of another's work as your own.

TERM	DEFINITION
proprietary knowledge	Information belonging to another person, including less well known facts, specific statistics, conceptual models, ideas, personal opinion, and critical analysis.
scholastic dishonesty	Any act designed to give unfair advantage to a student.
unintentional plagiarism	Plagiarizing without meaning to, usually because you don't understand the rules of scholarly documentation.

Introduction

In 2003, a year that saw corporate ethics scandals accelerate and "ethically challenged" business leaders doing "perp walks" in handcuffs and orange jumpsuits, the *New Yorker* published a cartoon with the caption "Moral Compass 2003." The drawing pictured a navigational compass lacking true north, its points reading "right (probably)," "it depends," "aesthetic decision," "completely personal choice," "wrong (for now)," "not sure," "it's a matter of cultural differences," and "who cares?"[1]

How you label the directional points on your own moral compass will dictate how you live your life—both personally and professionally. As college students, you currently face any number of situations that invite ethical decision-making. Some situations present genuine ethical dilemmas, which force you to agonize over competing principles of right and wrong. For example, your best friend is working two jobs to put herself through college, and she is struggling to get all of her homework done. Even though she is giving 150 percent effort, her work is starting to slip, and she is currently on academic probation. This semester, one more failing grade could cost her the education she is working so hard to obtain. Exhausted from another double shift, she suddenly remembers that she is due to give her presentation today in class. Out of desperation she asks you to help her write a presentation at the last minute, maybe like the one you wrote last week for this class. In such a case, it is not immediately clear what you should do. How do you help your friend? To what degree should you help her? Where do you cross the line between helping and cheating? Other situations simply call on you to take ethical action. In these cases, it may be fairly obvious what you should do— the only question is will you do it? Say, for example, that you discover that a group of your fellow students is blatantly plagiarizing and boasting about it. You know it is wrong. You know you should do something about it. Will you? Or will you "mind your own business?" Or will you decide to join in?

Exercise 3.1. An Ethical Violation You Have Encountered.

Please describe an ethical violation you have encountered on campus.

_____

_____

_____

_____

_____

_____

_____

_____

_____

_____

_____

_____

_____

_____

_____

_____

_____

_____

_____

_____

_____

_____

_____

Many students believe that the need to make ethical choices will fade away when you graduate into the adult world and finally get to associate with people who face life more thoughtfully. Have we got news for you! The ongoing revelations about the unethical behavior of Houston-based Enron executives Ken Lay, Jeffrey Skilling, and Andrew Fastow (to name just one case) should disabuse you immediately of any such notion.[2] People do not necessarily grow in moral stature as they grow in age, income, and responsibility. And ethical issues do not disappear when you have professional ambitions—in fact, they loom larger. As you face greater pressures in your career, not to mention the potential for greater rewards, the temptation to cheat will only intensify, particularly if you think that "everybody does it" and that you will be comparatively disadvantaged if you do not.[3] In fact, "How can I maintain my integrity while seeking success?" is perhaps the professional question in a public environment that often rewards dishonesty, writes former Harvard law professor Derrick Bell in his 2002 memoir *Ethical Ambition*.[4]

So get used to it. You will be called to make ethical choices at every stage of your professional life, and the same issues that make you uneasy now may metastasize into full-blown crises when the consequences of your decisions involve your career, your paycheck, your family, or your future. The time to form a well-thought-out ethical foundation for your career is now before the stakes loom so large that it is difficult to bring yourself to take risks.

Courtesy of AP/Wide World Photos

Media Box

All politicians lie, right?

Watch an interview with UT communications professor Mark Knapp as he talks about political deception. See this chapter's folder in your Chapter Media Contents online.

In this chapter, we will examine the meaning and importance of communication ethics and your professional responsibility to embrace academic integrity and avoid scholastic dishonesty. We will discuss what constitutes blatant and unintentional plagiarism and provide you with practical measures you can take to establish the habits of ethical professional communication.

Exercise 3.2. Personal Bill of Ethics.

As an ethical communicator in CMS 306M, I will

1. _____

   _____

   _____

   _____

2. _____

   _____

   _____

   _____

3. _____

   _____

   _____

   _____

4. _____

   _____

   _____

   _____

5. _____

   _____

   _____

   _____

Ethics and Communication

But what do ethics have to do with professional communication? According to communication scholar Richard Johannesen, ethics is "the general and systematic study of what ought to be the grounds and principles for right and wrong human behavior." Ethical issues apply to communication in the following instances:

❑ When the communication can be judged on a dimension of right and wrong,

❑ When the communication can involve possible significant influence on other humans;

❑ When communication reflects the communicator's conscious choice to seek specific goals; and

❑ When it represents the communicator's strategic decision to use communicative means to achieve those goals.[5]

Media Box
What is "ethics"? Watch UT communications professor Mark Knapp's interview, "Ethics of Deception" in this chapter's folder in your Chapter Media Contents online.

Your decisions about what to do in the "helping or cheating" and plagiarism scenarios above, for example, are profoundly ethical decisions in all four of the above situations. There is an additional dimension, however. Ethical decisions also include decisions about what you should say: Whatever decision you make will open your own communication to judgments of right and wrong, have a significant impact on others' lives (including your own), advance or retard your progress toward your own goals and represent your strategic use of communication to achieve those goals. As a student now, and in your future professional life, most of your communication decisions will be susceptible to ethical assessment. Professional communication, especially in its complex contexts of organizational cultures, pressures, interests, and constraints, is rife with ethical considerations.

It would be lovely to be able to say that being an ethical communicator means simply "always telling the truth," and then be done with it (a short chapter!). And, indeed, a source no less than Barbara Jordan, a former U.S. House of Representative from Texas, and the former Lyndon Baines Johnson School of Public Affairs professor, who achieved national prominence as the embodiment of moral conscience during the Watergate scandal, says ethical behavior, at root, means "being honest, telling the truth, and doing what you said you were going to do."[6]

To understand ethical communication, you must first understand that the sender of a message has an ethical filter, or a sense of what is right in a given situation. And, the receiver of a message also possesses an ethical filter. This means that the sender is not wholly responsible for ethical communication, but that all parties involved in a communicative exchange are responsible for the ethics of the situation. So, if you did relent and write that presentation for your friend because it was an "emergency," you are equally culpable of an ethical violation as the friend who asked for the favor.

Professional Communication Ethics

Communication ethics can be a complex topic in an interpersonal context. What about the professional context? The National Communication Association (NCA) is the professional face of many of your Communication Studies professors. In 1999, in recognition of the important link between professional ethics and professional communication, NCA's Ethics Commission created a credo for ethical communication among the organization's own members. Take some time to read this credo, reprinted in Figure 3.1.

Figure 3.1. National Communication Association (NCA) Credo for Ethical Communication.

Questions of right and wrong arise whenever people communicate. Ethical communication is fundamental to responsible thinking, decision making, and the development of relationships and communities within and across contexts, cultures, channels, and media. Moreover, ethical communication enhances human worth and dignity by fostering truthfulness, fairness, responsibility, personal integrity, and respect for self and others. We believe that unethical communication threatens the quality of all communication and consequently the well-being of individuals and the society in which we live. Therefore we, the members of the National Communication Association, endorse and are committed to practicing the following principles of ethical communication:

- We advocate truthfulness, accuracy, honesty, and reason as essential to the integrity of communication.
- We endorse freedom of expression, diversity of perspective, and tolerance of dissent to achieve the informed and responsible decision making fundamental to a civil society.
- We strive to understand and respect other communicators before evaluating and responding to their messages.
- We promote access to communication resources and opportunities as necessary to fulfill human potential and contribute to the well-being of families, communities, and society.
- We promote communication climates of caring and mutual understanding that respect the unique needs and characteristics of individual communicators.
- We condemn communication that degrades individuals and humanity through distortion, intimidation, coercion, and violence, and through the expression of intolerance and hatred.
- We are committed to the courageous expression of personal convictions in pursuit of fairness and justice.
- We advocate sharing information, opinions, and feelings when facing significant choices while also respecting privacy and confidentiality.
- We accept responsibility for the short- and long-term consequences for our own communication and expect the same of others.

—Credo, 1999, from the National Communication Association web site,
http://www.natcom.org/policies/External/EthicalComm.htm

> "... credos are ineffective ... unless people actually use the codes to govern their behavior."

Professional codes of ethics such as this one are useful in that they articulate values that may otherwise remain unsaid. These credos are ineffective, however, unless people actually use the codes to govern their behavior. The Enron Corporation, for example, published its own 64-page Code of Ethics in 2000. "We want to be proud of Enron and to know that it enjoys a reputation for fairness and honesty and that it is respected," wrote chairman and CEO Ken Lay in the book's foreword; "Enron's reputation finally depends on its people, on you and me. Let's keep that reputation high."[7] The ethics guide included a "Certificate of Compliance" that each employee was required to sign and return, promising to abide by the stringent ethical standards outlined in the book. As the Enron scandal broke in early 2002, employees auctioned off hundreds of copies of the Code of Ethics on eBay, joking bitterly that the books were in mint condition, never opened. "Did you expect 'em to be dog-eared and well-read?" asked *Business Week*, rhetorically.[8]

As Enron was a Texas-based company, its fate has been particularly significant to Texas educators. In early 2004, the University of Texas at Austin sponsored a conference on ethics, with an opening public lecture on "The Ethics of Enron: Lessons for the Future," given by William C. Powers, Jr., Dean of UT's School of Law.[9] Indeed, many schools, academic departments, and professors at the University are vitally interested in issues of ethics. Just go to the University of Texas home page and enter "ethics" in the search box and see how many items appear. In particular, the McCombs School of Business offers a Business Ethics Program for undergraduate and graduate students and the UT Bridging Disciplines Program offers an interdisciplinary program in Ethics and Leadership.[10]

The idea of ethics has to do with action. As Barbara Jordan might tell you, ethics is as ethics does. What, then, can you do to communicate ethically in your professional life? Communication scholar Robert Scott offers three simple guidelines: You can take responsibility for your own communication, you can treat others' communication with tolerance and respect, and you can muster the commitment and will to put your money where your mouth is.[11]

Take responsibility for your own communication.

Ethical communication requires that you acknowledge and take responsibility for your own communication, not hide it behind veils of secrecy, manipulation, and obfuscation. Many NASA engineers, when asked whether they gave permission to launch either Challenger or Columbia could be paraphrased as saying, "I said, at the time, that the conditions were such that I thought it would be okay to launch." No one took responsibility for the disasters by saying, "I said launch and that was a huge mistake." Disclosure (and lack thereof) is a perennial ethics issue in organizational communication, says UT professor Larry Browning, who states the basic principle as "whenever possible, put the light on something." If revealing the voice and strategy behind an instance of communication does not change the way you perceive your relationship to the communicator, the communication is likely to be ethical. This is because ethical decisions are "largely an issue of disclosure—when to disclose, how much to disclose."[12] However, as you approach the discussion, one thing is clear: Ethical communication is as much about effect as it is intent.

Treat others' communication with tolerance and respect.

Ethical communicators respect others' expressions and actions and tolerate the imperfect nature of their efforts, with the goal of attributing communication problems first to error and inevitably imperfect understanding, not to ill intention.[13] As the NCA credo says, "We strive to understand and respect other communicators before evaluating and responding to their messages. . . . We promote communication climates of caring and mutual understanding that respect the unique needs and characteristics of individual communicators."

There are a number of implications with this simple principle. More than simply black and white or good and bad, ethical situations involve complicated judgments about the locations of ethical fault lines, and it is relatively easy to suddenly find oneself on the wrong side of one. A single incident of ethical failure does not make a person inherently unethical, though. What matters is the person's response to crossing the line and the effect of that experience on the person's future behavior. Learning how to recover from ethical blunders is thus as important as our attempts to prevent them. The values of tolerance and respect are helpful in this regard.

Speak with commitment and will.

Ethical communicators will themselves to consciously participate in communicative behavior they consider right—not just easy or expedient.[14] "We condemn communication that degrades individuals and humanity through distortion, intimidation, coercion, and violence, and through the expression of intolerance and hatred," the NCA credo proclaims. "We are committed to the courageous expression of personal convictions in pursuit of fairness and justice."

Communication in organizational contexts is rife with ethical dilemmas that test individuals' commitment and will. Issues of power in organizations can create challenges, such as superior-subordinate relationships, which are fraught with ethical complications. If your boss asked you to withhold information from the company attorneys, for example, would you do it? What if you had to decide between your career and whistle-blowing?

The Harvard Business School case of Jonah Creighton illustrates the difficulties with such ethical communication decisions.[15] In this case, Jonah Creighton uncovered a case of racial discrimination in his organization, and chose to become a whistleblower. Although the organization was made accountable, the experience ultimately ruined Creighton's career. Ethical communication is difficult, but does not exist only in the workplace; it exists in the classroom as well.

Media Box

Do you know when someone is lying? Watch what the experts say.

Visit this chapter's folder in your Chapter Media Contents online and watch UT communications professor Mark Knapp discuss "Detecting Lies" and "Accuracy in Detecting Deception."

Exercise 3.3. Case Studies in Ethics.

Form groups of 5–6 students. Each group will be assigned one of the following ethical cases for discussion. Please be prepared to share your findings with the class.

CASE 1: WITHHOLDING INFORMATION

Researchers at the National Institutes of Health have discovered that a readily available, low-cost, over-the-counter drug can significantly reduce fatal heart attacks if taken every day. Generally the drug is safe even when taken in the large doses necessary to reduce heart attacks, although some patients will experience intestinal discomfort as a result of daily use of the drug. For about 1 in 300,000 patients, side effects could be serious. The beneficial effect of the drug is especially clear when used by individuals who are smokers or are overweight. However, even with this medication, these high-risk individuals are still more likely to die of heart attack than if they quit smoking or lose weight.

Several of the NIH researchers want to immediately launch a campaign to encourage the largest number of people to begin using the new treatment since thousands of lives could be saved each year. A few physicians suggest that the information about side effects be left out of the campaign materials since people who could benefit from the drug may incorrectly feel the risk of side effects is greater than the risk of heart attack. Others at NIH do not want to mention the benefits to smokers and overweight patients since these people may decide to take the drug without changing lifestyle in the belief the drug will protect them from the dangers of smoking or over-eating. Thus, the drug campaign could serve to give some people an excuse to continue dangerous habits. Still other researchers want to reveal all information about the drug, in the campaign, or in fine print on the bottle. What should NIH do?

CASE 2: PAID PUBLIC OPINION

William Armstrong, a radio commentator and talk show host who owns and operates a small public relations firm, accepted a $25,000 contract for PR from the U.S. Department of Education to build public support for the "No Child Left Behind" (NCLB) program. Initially, Armstrong's firm organized conferences and "media opportunities" for NCLB advocates, publicizing their position. A week ago, Armstrong was informed by Bush administration officials that when he was hired, they expected him to personally advocate the program on his talk show and in other media appearances on a regular basis as a part of the contract.

Both before accepting the contract and since, Armstrong has advocated the NCLB program because he personally believes the program is a good one. Recently, a new staffer at the agency suggested there is a conflict of interest with Armstrong's personal, on-air advocacy of NCLB once he began taking money from the

Department of Education, especially because he has not made public the PR contract he accepted. Armstrong replies that all he is doing is repeating a long-held opinion that has not changed since accepting the contract and that the PR firm's activities are independent of his media activities. The staffer believes Armstrong should give back the money or quit advocating for NCLB as a commentator. It remains uncertain how the radio network that carries Armstrong's show or the hosts of TV programs that he appears on would react if they knew he had accepted money to support NCLB. What should Armstrong do? Was it ethical for the administration to use public funds to pay an apparently independent commentator to argue for a specific political program?

CASE 3: PRIVACY OF FAMILIES

A well publicized kidnap/murder case serves as the basis for a "new journalism" docu-novel. The actual case involved a group of escaped convicts who kidnapped a young couple and their two children, held them captive for three days in a deserted factory, and eventually tortured and killed all of the family members. Later the criminals killed themselves in a shootout with police. The docu-novel written by a famous author is completely accurate with respect to all known facts in the case. However, little is known about exactly what went on (and was said) during the period of captivity and torture of the family (except what the medical records show). The author has "invented" dialogue between family members and criminals to illustrate the terror the family must have felt. The author feels this dialogue, while literally fictional, is appropriate and necessary to the story so that readers will understand the kind of men who committed the crime. He notes that the convicts' fictional acts are developed from profiles provided by a police psychologist.

Relatives of the victims have read a manuscript of the docu-novel and have asked that it not be published (at least in its present form). They object to dialogue which shows the victims begging for their lives and not always standing up for each other. The relatives say this fiction demeans the young family unnecessarily, and perhaps falsely. The author says the dialogue is consistent with what normal people do in such a situation. Relatives also object to the inclusion in the book of facts about the couple's sexual problems calling such material an invasion of privacy and unfair since the couple (and the relatives) are victims and did nothing to put themselves in the public eye. The author counters with the observation that this crime is a public matter and that people need to understand how such terrible events can happen and how they can be prevented. He argues that his book will serve a good purpose in revealing the causes of such crimes. What should be done about the book?

CASE 4: ACADEMIC FREEDOM

A tenured professor at St. John's College, a Roman Catholic liberal arts college, has determined after long study that (in his view) a proper understanding of the *Bible* and other Christian traditions does not indicate that abortion is morally wrong. This, of course, puts him in opposition to official church doctrine; therefore, church authorities and school officials have pressured him to cease teaching ideas which are contrary to church doctrine. [Church authorities feel that as a religion professor at a Catholic school he "represents" the Church.] The professor is unwilling to change his views of teaching, arguing that the tradition of academic freedom gives him the right to teach the truth as he sees it as long as he functions as a serious professional within his area of scholarly expertise. College officials must consider several courses of action. They could continue to let him teach religion (even if it isn't orthodox Catholicism) in defiance of Church doctrine. They could attempt to fire him for insubordination (defying the meaning of "tenure"). Or they could move him into a non-teaching job at the college (where he would not be able to teach his views). What should the administrative officials at the college do?

Exercise 3.3. Continued.

CASE 5: NEGATIVE CAMPAIGNING

Mary Mikesell, a candidate for the state legislature, turns on the TV to discover that her opponent is running ads which attack her voting record during a previous term of office. She recognizes that the facts in these ads are technically correct, but they are used in a way that misrepresents their meaning. For example, one ad cites what appears to be a large number of absences during votes; however, the fact is that these votes were nearly all on minor procedural matters and occurred when Mary was in legislative committee meetings. (Her opponent's ad suggests that, "She just didn't show up for work.")

Several of Mary's advisors press her to respond immediately to these ads. (Research shows quick responses are often effective counters). Some think she should deny wrongdoing and simply interpret the record correctly. Others want her to attack her opponent and they have some specific "negatives" (all true and documented) that can be used. (Research also suggests this can be effective). Mary doesn't like the idea of dignifying the attacks on her with a reply and she wants to avoid becoming negative herself. However, she doesn't want to lose the election because of false and unfair campaign tactics and she doesn't want to look weak in the face of an attack. What should be done?

Academic Integrity

Up to this point in this chapter, we have been talking rather abstractly about ethical and professional communication. Now let's get practical. At the same time as you are studying to enter a future profession, you are already filling a professional role, which has its own concrete ethical responsibilities and challenges—the role of student.

The work you do is scholarship. If, before you arrived at UT, you felt that homework was just busy work and thus unrelated to your "real life," and if you have carried that attitude over into college, you may be missing the boat. College is not the place to kill time while waiting for your adult life to begin. Your adult life is already in progress. What you do at college stays with you the rest of your days—especially at a school like UT, where any professional or personal relationship you begin may last a lifetime. Think of the maps you see at the heads of trails in state parks. Paths radiate in all directions. An arrow marks your current location. "You are here," the arrow says. As you consider each course of action, you decide which trails you will follow and which trails will open up the terrain in front of you. The professional habits you develop now and the work standards you set for yourself, will determine what opportunities rise to meet your steps and how you will meet the challenges facing you. If you treat your work in college as tedious and irrelevant, and you choose to take the path of least resistance in meeting your professional responsibilities, then that may well be the adult life that will rise before you. On the other hand, if you make the decision to view your coursework as your own work, the work takes on a new significance as you realize that you do it not for your professors' sake, or for your parents' sake, but for your own sake. And if you begin to see the importance of taking the right steps because they are right, you will also begin to understand the ways in which the work you do now can contribute to your future professional growth.

> "The professional habits you develop now . . . will determine . . . how you will meet the challenges facing you."

As a student doing the work of scholarship, your major ethical responsibility is to avoid scholastic dishonesty, generally defined by the University of Texas as "any act designed to give unfair academic advantage to the student."[16] (For the specific definition, see Figure 3.2.) In a 2002 story about the prevalence of scholastic dishonesty in America's high schools, CNN quotes a student's matter-of-fact assessment of the practice of "cutting corners" by some students:

> What's important is getting ahead. . . . The better grades you have, the better school you get into, the better you're going to do in life. And if you learn to cut corners to do that, you're going to be saving yourself time and energy. In the real world, that's what's going to be going on. The better you do, that's what shows. It's not how moral you were in getting there. . . . Cheating is a shortcut and it's a pretty efficient one in a lot of cases.[17]

Imagine this student's future and the "better" life she thinks she is creating for herself. If high school is too stressful for her, how is she going to cope with college and her responsibilities in the professional world?

Figure 3.2. Definition of Scholastic Dishonesty at the University of Texas at Austin.

"Scholastic dishonesty" includes, but is not limited to, cheating, plagiarism, collusion, falsifying academic records, misrepresenting facts, and any act designed to give unfair academic advantage to the student (such as, but not limited to, submission of essentially the same written assignment for two courses without the prior permission of the instructor) or the attempt to commit such an act.

—from Section 11.802, "Scholastic Dishonesty,"
in Appendix C, "Institutional Rules on Student Services and Activities,"
of the UT catalog *General Information, 2003–2004*,
http://www.utexas.edu/student/registrar/catalogs/gi03-04/app/appc11.html.

It is not lost on your instructors that this justification for cheating accompanies many students into college. In a 1999 survey of students on 21 U.S. campuses, Donald L. McCabe of Rutgers University found that over 75 percent of students admitted to "some" cheating, with one-third admitting to "serious" cheating on exams and half admitting to "serious" cheating on papers.[18] Indeed, few aspiring professors make it through their first semesters as teaching assistants and instructors without confronting academic dishonesty.

Are so many of your fellow students really so ethically challenged? The story is mixed at UT, according to a 2001 survey on academic integrity conducted by the Student Affairs Research team. Nearly 87 percent of UT student respondents disagreed with the following statement: "There is really nothing wrong with cheating, other than the risk and consequences of being caught." Still, nearly 64 percent of these same students also disagreed with the statement, "Most students who cheat are unethical people."[19]

How can this discrepancy be reconciled? Miriam Schulman of the Markkula Center for Applied Ethics cites the work of sociologists Gresham Sykes and David Matza, who analyzed the thought processes that allow people to feel ethical while behaving unethically: "Yes, this behavior is wrong, and society is justified in making rules to disallow it," goes the thinking. "But special circumstances make it OK for me to ignore this rule."[20] These thought processes take four general forms:

❑ Denying an injury or victim. "No harm, no foul." Since no one is damaged by your cheating, you have done nothing wrong.

❑ Appealing to higher loyalties. Sure, it's wrong to cheat, but you are not doing it for yourself, you are doing it for your parents: It would hurt them if you let them down by getting a bad grade.

❑ Denying personal responsibility. You did not want to do it but circumstances forced you to do so. If only that book you needed had been at the library. Besides, you didn't know it was wrong to copy from the Internet. . . .

❑ Condemning the condemner. You would not have had to cheat if the University had not made you take this class; if your professor had been more competent, more helpful, or kinder; if your TA had kept more office hours. . . .

> ## ". . . people do not spend time and energy rationalizing behavior they are happy to acknowledge publicly."

Recognize these thought processes? Each is a type of rationalization that allows you to preserve your good opinion of yourself at the same time you give yourself permission to do something you know is wrong.

However, people do not spend time and energy rationalizing behavior they are happy to acknowledge publicly. Some thought will explode each of these justifications for bad behavior: First, there is harm done. You do not honor your parents by cheating. Your choices are your responsibility. Other people's bad behavior does not excuse your own. Not true? Then imagine calling someone you admire, and saying: "Hey! Guess what! You know how much I want you to respect me, so I'm calling to tell you that I cheated on my midterm today. Yep! The instructor isn't very understanding; and, I heard that other people were going to cheat, so I just thought, "What the heck, I'll do it too." Yeah, we'll probably all get an A—and blow the curve for the other idiots! Aren't you proud of me?" If this does not sound like something you would care to say or admit, it is time to get your actions in line with your beliefs. Moreover, you really do yourself a disservice by using rationalizations such as these as crutches. Do you really think you will have less pressure in your career than you have in college? You would do far better to start good professional habits here and now.

So far, we have been talking about the negative but private consequences of cheating—the effects that occur even if no one else ever finds out you cheated. Often, though, other people do find out, and then the consequences can wreck havoc on your professional standing, now and in the future.

Scholastic dishonesty risks academic consequences.

When professors become aware that a student is cheating and begin the process of inquiry and punishment with Student Judicial Services, students are often aghast at the severity of the punishment and the weight of the system that comes crashing down on them. Depending upon the student's college at UT, the professor in charge of the particular course, and the extent of the dishonesty (as determined by the professor, who represents the victim and is the initial judge), punishment may range anywhere from failure on the single assignment to dismissal from the University (see Figure 3.3). If the student has already graduated when the dishonesty is discovered, the University can revoke the degree. Seriously (see Figure 3.3).

Figure 3.3. Penalties for Scholastic Dishonesty at the University of Texas at Austin.

A faculty member . . . or the dean of students or hearing officer may impose one or more of the following penalties for scholastic dishonesty:

1. Written warning that further scholastic violations may result in a more severe penalty;
2. No credit or reduced credit for the paper, assignment, or test in question;
3. Retaking of examination or resubmission of assignment;
4. Failing grade or reduced final grade for the course.

The dean . . . or the hearing officer . . . may impose one or more of the following penalties for violation of a regents' rule, University regulation, or administrative rule:

1. Admonition;
2. Warning probation;
3. Disciplinary probation;

4. Withholding of grades, official transcript, and/or degree;

5. Bar against readmission, and/or drop from current enrollment, or drop from enrollment in one or more courses;

6. Restitution;

7. Suspension of rights and privileges, including, but not limited to, participation in athletic or extracurricular activities and residing in or entering University housing;

8. Failing grade for an examination or assignment or for a course and/or cancellation of all or any portion of prior course credit, or other academic penalty;

9. Denial of degree;

10. Deferred suspension;

11. Suspension from the University for a specified period of time;

12. Expulsion (permanent separation from the University);

13. Revocation of degree or withdrawal of diploma;

14. Other penalty as deemed appropriate under the circumstances.

—from Sections 11.503, "Authorized Academic Penalties," and 11.501, "Authorized Disciplinary Penalties," in Appendix C, "Institutional Rules on Student Services and Activities," of the UT catalog *General Information*, 2003–2004, http://www.utexas.edu/student/registrar/catalogs/gi03-04/app/appc11.html#11-501.

Why such radical punishment for what may seem to you to be a minor infraction? Because responsible and honest scholarship is the very foundation of academic life; when you attack that foundation, you strike at the very heart of academic integrity. The Center for Academic Integrity at Duke University's Kenan Institute for Ethics defines academic integrity as "a commitment, even in the face of adversity, to five fundamental values: honesty, trust, fairness, respect, and responsibility."[21] In its own statement on academic integrity, The University of Texas at Austin notes that UT was founded by mandate of the 1876 state constitution,

> . . . which called for the establishment of "a university of the first class." This ideal has shaped the University's mission since its founding and continues to guide the policies of the University today. As a university of the first class, The University of Texas also participates in a larger mission: the advancement of knowledge. The sharing of knowledge forms the heart of university life. Scholars, teachers, and students all participate in a community of learning, where the ideas and information that have been developed over centuries are disseminated, elaborated upon, and added to in a continual process of intellectual advancement. . . . Without academic integrity, neither the genuine innovations of the individual nor the progress of a given field of study can adequately be assessed, and the very foundation of scholarship itself is undermined. Academic integrity, for all these reasons, is an essential link in the process of intellectual advancement.[22]

And, speaking practically,

> In the marketplace where graduates compete for jobs, the value of a University of Texas degree is largely related to the reputation of the University. Incidents of scholastic dishonesty reflect poorly on the institution's integrity and lessen the worth of the education attained by all University students.[23]

This is what cheating means to the University. But what does cheating mean to you? Say that you cheat, you are found out, and your professor fails you on just the one assignment (not the whole course) and chooses not to involve the dean's office. On subsequent assignments with that professor, you can bet that you will be seriously scrutinized, and you may have a much harder time making good grades. Furthermore, the professor may share information about you informally with your adviser and other members of the faculty and staff, who will also inspect your work with critical care. And from that point on, you will never know if your professors see your name on their class rosters at the beginning of a semester and think, "oh, the cheater." If your professor decides to fail you for the entire class, you will have to take the course over if it is a required course, perhaps with the same professor. That will be a long semester—as well as perhaps delaying your graduation, embarrassing you in front of your friends and family, and costing you time and money. If your professor decides to escalate the case to the dean's office, you may eventually find yourself dismissed from the University. In that case, you may find it difficult to continue your degree at another institution, even if you are able to transfer most of your credits. Do you think your professors are going to write you letters of recommendation? Or if they do, what do you think the letters will say? And how are you going to explain your dismissal from this University to another school or to an employer? If you tell the truth, you run the risk of rejection. If you lie or withhold the truth, you have created another ethical problem for yourself, one that will potentially be even greater if you are discovered.

Scholastic dishonesty risks professional consequences.

Careers rise and fall largely on the basis of reputation of work you've performed. When you exit the university and begin your job hunt, your reputation and character will be as important to your success as your resume. From here on out, each time you are considered for promotion, for salary increases, for bonuses, and each time you are considered for hire at a new job or in a new department within the same company, your personal credibility will factor heavily into the equation. People want to work with someone they can trust. Organizations want to hire people in whom they can be confident, and there is no shortage of eligible persons who would like to fill the positions. You are one among many, and your personal credibility and integrity is something that will either set you apart from the crowd or cause you to be lost therein.

"People want to work with someone they can trust."

Recommendations are one key to your success. As many of you are already learning, finding professors to write recommendations for you can be a difficult task. Getting those professors to write positive recommendations can mean the difference between getting into the graduate or professional school or getting the job you want . . . or not. Some professors will not write a letter of recommendation for you unless you waive your right to see it, and many professors consider it their professional responsibility to write the truth about you as they see it. You should concentrate on making sure that "the truth" is something you would want a future employer to see. The world is not as tolerant of duplicitous behavior as it once was, and taking the easy way out now may cost you far more than you can imagine in the future.

Scholastic dishonesty risks life-long consequences.

Surveys show that many college students believe that the risk of getting caught is slight. So what about that? What if you plagiarize your work and avoid getting caught? What if you make it all the way through your academic career and come out the other side with a diploma and a career? You are home free, right? Perhaps this was true in the past, but no more. Every plagiarized assignment you hand in is a potential career-ender. In recent years, blatant plagiarism has skyrocketed because of the ease of cut-and-paste copying from the Internet. To fight back, professors have begun using the Internet and other software-based methods to detect plagiarism. Many professors now require that you hand in your work as an electronic file. If your professor passes the file along to a "plagiarism-prevention" service like Turnitin.com, your paper will be compared to billions of pages of content on the Internet, millions of scholarly works (including journal articles), and millions of student papers turned in from colleges throughout the country—a database that grows every day.[24] Perhaps you plagiarize from a book that has not yet been digitized. If, in the future, your paper matches new content added to the database, your professor will be notified—even years after you graduate.

In addition, once your college work makes it into databases, it will be potentially available for anyone to read at any time. Think of the 2004 presidential race and the scrutiny the candidates faced for their behavior while in college in their early 20s, decades ago. And think how little information was available on those candidates as compared to the information that will always be available about you. Numerous political and professional people have been forced to resign or removed from their positions for "minor" offenses as far back as their undergraduate degrees. Think of former Railroad Commissioner Lena Guerrero, a Texas Democrat who falsely claimed to have graduated from UT, and whose Cinderella political career ended at age 34 (when Republican political operative Karl Rove tipped the *Dallas Morning News* to the fact that she had lied on her resume). For ethical and practical reasons, it's best to avoid scholastic dishonesty.

Avoiding Scholastic Dishonesty

Let's assume that you want to avoid scholastic dishonesty. The two most prevalent kinds of scholastic dishonesty are cheating and plagiarism. It's pretty easy to avoid cheating, since cheating is nearly always intentional. Plagiarism is a different, more complex matter. In addition to committing plagiarism blatantly, people can plagiarize without intending to do it, or sometimes without even being aware that they are doing it. In a worst-case scenario, you could be expelled from the University for doing something wrong that you did not know that you were doing.

> "... people can plagiarize without intending to do it, or sometimes without even being aware that they are doing it."

How can this be?

Plagiarism is not defined by intent, it is defined by effect. Think of many store policies about breakage: "You break it, you buy it." It is immaterial whether you intended to break that vase; the vase is broken and you are the one who broke it. In the same way, unintentional plagiarism (also called "accidental plagiarism, inadvertent plagiarism, or negligent plagiarism") is still plagiarism. Saying "I didn't know!" will not help: Because you are a professional student, and because scholarship is the professional work you do, it is your professional responsibility to know what plagiarism is and how to avoid it. Would Greg Maddux say that he did not know he was not allowed to intentionally throw a baseball at a player?

What is cheating?

The University has a long, specific definition of cheating that you will see in Figure 3.4. Avoid doing anything covered in that list and you probably will be okay. There are other things you need to think about besides cheating, however, when communicating ethically in this course. Some of these are outlined for you here:

- ❑ **Group assignment.** Pull your own weight! Make sure you are doing your part of the assignment, and give it your best effort! Failing to show up for meetings, not answering emails or returning phone calls, or even coming to meetings late, showing up unprepared, or turning in shoddy work are all forms of unethical communication. You are telling your group that you just do not care and you are dragging their grade down with your own. Do not be a dead weight to your team, be the support they need to put together an excellent presentation!

- ❑ **Informative and persuasive assignments.** Do not "share" a presentation outline with your roommate, so that both of you give the same presentation in two different 306M sections. Your instructors talk. Do not try to "adapt" a research paper you wrote for another class into your informative or persuasive presentation in this one. Each class requires that you prepare original work, unless you have worked something out in advance with your instructor.

- ❑ **Impromptu assignment.** This is perhaps the easiest assignment in which you can avoid plagiarism. You will not have time to collect mounds of research. However, those facts and figures you do choose to use in your presentation should be cited.

- ❑ **Tests.** Do work with friends and study groups to prepare well for the test. Do not cheat, make up excuses to take the test at a later date, or try to get test questions from friends in earlier sections. If you are offered what someone presents as a copy of the test for sale, do not buy it. Show some dignity and self-respect, and plan ahead to prepare well. If you are having trouble, communicate with your professor to find out about study sessions ahead of the test date.

Figure 3.4. Definition of Cheating at the University of Texas at Austin.

"Cheating" includes, but is not limited to,

1. Copying from another student's test paper;
2. Using during a test materials not authorized by the person giving the test;
3. Failing to comply with instructions given by the person administering the test;
4. Possession during a test of materials which are not authorized by the person giving the test, such as class notes or specifically designed "crib notes." The presence of textbooks constitutes a violation only if they have been specifically prohibited by the person administering the test;
5. Using, buying, stealing, transporting, or soliciting in whole or part the contents of an unadministered test, test key, homework solution, or computer program;
6. Collaborating with or seeking aid or receiving assistance from another student or individual during a test or in conjunction with other assignment without authority;
7. Discussing the contents of an examination with another student who will take the examination;
8. Divulging the contents of an examination, for the purpose of preserving questions for use by another, when the instructor has designated that the examination is not to be removed from the examination room or not to be returned to or kept by the student;
9. Substituting for another person, or permitting another person to substitute for oneself to take a course, a test, or any course-related assignment;
10. Paying or offering money or other valuable thing to, or coercing another person to obtain an unadministered test, test key, homework solution, or computer program, or information about an unadministered test, test key, homework solution, or computer program;
11. Falsifying research data, laboratory reports, and/or other academic work offered for credit; and
12. Taking, keeping, misplacing, or damaging the property of the University, or of another, if the student knows or reasonably should know that an unfair academic advantage would be gained by such conduct.

—from Section 11.802, "Scholastic Dishonesty," from Appendix C, "Institutional Rules on Student Services and Activities," of the UT catalog *General Information, 2003–2004*, http://www.utexas.edu/student/registrar/catalogs/gi03-04/app/appc11.html.

What is blatant plagiarism?

The University defines plagiarism generally as "any use of another's work and submitting that work as one's own."[25] Plagiarism "includes, but is not limited to, the appropriation of, buying, receiving as a gift, or obtaining by any means material that is attributable in whole or in part to another source."[26] That pretty much covers "intentional," or blatant plagiarism. For any course at this University, including this one, you cannot honestly buy work off the Internet (or copy and paste it either) and claim it as your own. You cannot accept it as a gift from your graduating roommate or lift it from your sorority or fraternity's files. You cannot copy it from a friend at another school.

And it is not just whole works that you cannot appropriate, buy, receive, or obtain by any means. UT regulations specify that you also cannot take any part of someone else's "words, ideas, illustrations, structure, computer code, other expression, and media."[27] That means that you will not protect yourself from charges of plagiarism by taking one main point each from two or three different sources and cobbling them together. If your professor interprets the rules strictly, theft of a single sentence from a single source can send you packing. And if you found a beautifully worded sentence on the Internet that you could not resist grabbing, your instructor can read it, appreciate it, suspect it and Google it—in 0.17 seconds. When you get caught with blatant plagiarism, it is hard for you to make any claim whatsoever in your defense: What you did was clearly intentional and clearly wrong.

In our experience, many CMS 306M students are in particular danger of committing blatant plagiarism, because they think the standards for academic integrity do not count for oral presentations. This dangerous attitude, for example, ended Delaware Democratic Senator Joe Biden's Presidential candidacy in 1987. In a heartfelt passage in a stump speech, Biden had said,

> I was thinking as I was coming over here, why is it that Joe Biden is the first in his family ever to go to a university? Why is it that my wife, who is sitting out there in the audience, is the first in her family to ever go to college? Is it because our fathers and mothers were not bright? Is it because I'm the first Biden in a thousand generations to get a college and a graduate degree that I was smarter than the rest? . . . Those same people who read poetry and wrote poetry and taught me to sing verse? Is it that they didn't work very hard, my ancestors who worked in the coal mines of Northeast Pennsylvania and would come up after 12 hours and play football for four hours? Is it because our fathers and mothers were not bright? . . . No, it's not because they weren't as smart. It's not because they didn't work as hard. It's because they didn't have a platform upon which to stand.[28]

A powerful sentiment—but one that quickly turned into buffoonery when the Dukakis campaign compiled a video tape comparing Biden's speech with a speech by British Labor leader Neil Kinnock, who had recently said this passage (and several others in the speech) in a campaign speech of his own:

> Why am I the first Kinnock in a thousand generations to be able to get to university? Why is Glenys the first woman in her family in a thousand generations to be able to get to university? Was it because all our predecessors were thick? Did they lack talent, those people who could sing and play and write and recite poetry? Those people who could make wonderful beautiful things with their hands? Those people who could dream dreams, see visions? Why didn't they get it? Was it because they were weak? Those people who could work eight hours under ground and then come up and play football? Weak? Those women who could survive eleven child-bearings? Were they weak? Does anybody really think that they didn't get what we had because they didn't have the talent or the strength or the endurance or the commitment? Of course not. It was because there was no platform upon which they could stand.[29]

When reporters started looking, they found that Biden had plagiarized speeches by other public figures, too; when they started digging, they found that he had been disciplined for serious written plagiarism decades earlier while in law school at Yale.[30] As you can see from your own response to the passages above, discovery of oral plagiarism is even more shocking than discovery of written plagiarism because words that you write have a separate existence, while words that you say are part of you. And as Joe Biden found out, oral speech can be just as permanent as written speech, if it is recorded . . . like your presentations in this class. In either oral or written plagiarism, the culpability is the same—theft of intellectual property is theft.

Blatant plagiarism can be an issue in any CMS 306M assignment. To avoid blatantly plagiarizing in this course, follow these guidelines:

- ❏ **Group assignment.** Do not forget to cite those slides! PowerPoint, or whatever visual medium you use to get your point across, requires citations. Be sure to cite your visual evidence, your photographs, and other information. Failing to do so is plagiarism! While we see less of this on the group project because there are more eyes on the ball, so to speak, it still happens more often than we would like. Cite orally, cite in the outlines, cite in the visual aids.

- ❏ **Informative, persuasive, and impromptu presentations.** Do not purchase or copy presentations from the Internet. Do not use or "adapt" presentations from friends who have taken the class before you, or ask a friend to write the presentation for you because you do not know what to say. Avoid appropriating interesting ideas you see or hear. Cite them. It is one thing to take a great line and think about how you could follow in the footsteps of an accomplished speaker with your own sayings or phrases; it is quite another thing to simply claim to have made the footprints yourself. Do not steal images and use them without attribution in your visual aids.

You can avoid blatant, intentional plagiarism the same way you avoid cheating: Just don't do it.

What you can do to avoid unintentional plagiarism.

Remember, plagiarism is the act of taking someone else's work and claiming it as your own. Most unintentional plagiarism results from students' technical problems with the technique of paraphrasing. Paraphrasing is the act of borrowing (not stealing) someone else's idea and putting it into your own words. (Remember: To fairly borrow an idea, you must credit it to its source.) Paraphrasing is an essential tool of both speech and scholarship, so it is to your benefit to learn how to do it properly.

All paraphrases retain a source's original idea. When students paraphrase incorrectly, they generally make one or more of three mistakes: (1) They remove the quotation marks around a direct quotation; (2) They alter a passage's wording, but retain its original structure; or (3) They do not cite their source. Students sometimes believe that paraphrasing an idea in one of these three ways makes the idea their own. But faulty paraphrasing is plagiarism. Let's look at each of these three kinds of faulty paraphrasing.

Removing quotation marks from a direct quote

The first way to plagiarize by faulty paraphrasing is to remove the quotation marks from a direct quotation, perhaps altering the words slightly, but leaving the quotation substantially intact. Compare the following final sentence of Joe Biden's anecdote to the final sentence of Neil Kinnock's original story. It is almost identical in its words, and it is completely identical in its structure. In fact, it appears an (almost) direct quotation masquerading as a paraphrase:

> Kinnock: It was because there was no platform upon which they could stand.
>
> Biden: It's because they didn't have a platform upon which to stand.

With this type of faulty paraphrase, Biden stole (rather than borrowed) Kinnock's direct words as his own. Because he took Kinnock's words and idea, Biden committed plagiarism.

Disguising your copying

The second way to plagiarize by faulty paraphrasing is to retain an author's idea and structure, but "revise" the text by systematically altering the actual words. Compare Biden's speech to Kinnock's original sentence. It is identical in idea and structure, but substitutes "fathers and mothers" for "predecessors," "bright" for "thick," and so on. This process is called "disguised copying,"[31] and it is plagiarism:

> Original: Was it because all our predecessors were thick? . . . Was it because they were weak? Those people who could work eight hours under ground and then come up and play football?
>
> Biden: Is it because our fathers and mothers were not bright? . . . Is it that they didn't work very hard, my ancestors who worked in the coal mines of Northeast Pennsylvania and would come up after 12 hours and play football for four hours?

With this type of faulty paraphrasing, Biden kept everything of value from the original except its actual words. Because he took the original author's idea and structure, it is plagiarism.

Hiding the sources

The third way to plagiarize by incorrectly paraphrasing is to omit or hide its source, providing the reader with no clue that the idea is not original. This entire excerpt from Biden's speech constitutes this kind of plagiarism: "I was thinking as I was coming over here . . . ," Biden said, claiming that the anecdote to follow was not only original, but fresh. "Filing the serial marks" off prose—taking another person's idea, words, or structure without attribution—is plagiarism.

How to use other people's words and ideas properly.

Remember, plagiarism is the act of taking someone else's work and claiming it as your own. When you give proper attribution to someone else's work, you automatically avoid even unintentional plagiarism. You can use other people's words and ideas correctly in two ways: (1) You can directly quote their words, and cite your source; and (2) You can paraphrase the relevant idea, and cite your source.

Direct quotations

At times, you may want to borrow another person's actual words—say, when they are particularly meaningful, beautiful, precise, or concise. In that case, you would use direct quotations. When you quote someone, by citing your source, you are telling your audience that the words you are quoting are material penned by another person, and that you are ethically and legally borrowing them. Imagine if Senator Biden had simply quoted Kinnock and acknowledged his source:

> Yesterday, while I was watching C-SPAN, I saw part of a speech by Neil Kinnock, who's running for Labor party leader in England. "Why am I the first Kinnock in a thousand generations to be able to get to university?" he said. "Why is Glenys the first woman in her family in a thousand generations to be able to get to university? . . . Was it because our predecessors were thick? . . . Of course not. It was because there was no platform upon which they could stand."

> Ladies and gentlemen, those questions hit home. And I ask you today, why is it that Joe Biden is the first in his family ever to go to a university? Why is it that my wife, who is sitting out there in the audience, is the first in her family to ever go to college?

Had Senator Biden simply acknowledged his source, and quoted the relevant words, he would not have put himself in hot water.

Correct paraphrasing

Sometimes you do not need the other person's actual words; you just want to borrow an idea. Directly quoting another person can be time-consuming, and it can take attention away from your own point. In that case, just put the idea in your own words and credit the source:

> In his campaign for British Labor leader, Neil Kinnock has been asking audiences why it is that society seems to leave whole groups of disadvantaged people behind. Is it that these people are stupid, or weak, or lazy? . . . No, he says, it's that they lack a "platform" from which they can launch their efforts. I'm committed to making sure that we continue to build that kind of platform to support all Americans.

This kind of correct paraphrase extracts the "gist" of Kinnock's idea, compresses it, completely rewrites its structure and words (other than the directly quoted "platform"), and takes care to attribute the idea to its author.

How do I know what ideas need to be cited?

In the extended example we have been using of Joe Biden's use of Neil Kinnock's words, it is quite clear that Biden improperly "filed the serial marks" off Kinnock's idea. But things are not always so clear. How do you know when an idea needs to be cited? Think of a continuum with two clear ends and a muddled middle. Some information belongs to you as part of your cultural birthright; it is called common knowledge and you may incorporate it in your own work without attribution. Well-known facts are common knowledge. The idea that the earth is round, for example, is a common part of our culture's knowledge, and you can use it as your own.

Other information is clearly of specific origin—information such as less well-known facts, specific statistics, conceptual models, ideas, personal opinions, and critical analysis. This kind of information is called proprietary knowledge and you must cite it if you use it. Your responsibility to these two very different types of information is perfectly clear. For example, although you do not need to credit the fact that the world is round, you do need to cite a particular individual's unique experience of that fact:

> We all know that the earth is round—or at least we think we do. But a very few people know the earth is round from their own personal experience. Gemini 11 astronaut Pete Conrad is one of them. "Eureka, Houston," he said on September 14, 1965, when he and he and his fellow astronauts became the first humans to see the whole earth from space, "The earth is really round."[32]

Between the two poles of common knowledge and proprietary knowledge lies a whole (round) world of facts, ideas, and images, which comprise what we might call accumulated knowledge. How do you know what among the knowledge you have accumulated over your lifetime you can use as your own and what you ought to document? How do you know if information is proprietary knowledge or common knowledge? The answer is that it is a matter of judgment, based on your own sense of integrity and whether your use of the material is fair. How do you judge whether a use is fair? *The Chicago Manual of Style* (which is the major authority in professional publishing), suggests the following test: Is the information yours to use, or are you "taking a free ride" on another author's labor?[33]

The safest answer is this: When in doubt, cite your source.

What if I do not know where I got an idea?

Think about that idea that has been hanging around in your head for a week or so that you plan to use in your presentation. Take a moment to ponder your intellectual habits. Is it as if you've come up with this particular kind of phrase or image out of nothing? Does it sound like something you would say? Or could it possibly bear some resemblance to song lyrics you've heard on the radio, or some forwarded e-mail message that you found particularly amusing, or the article you read last night for class? If you conclude that the idea did not spontaneously occur to you, and you want to use it, you should find your source. (What you must not do is invoke that most lame of source credits: "As an anonymous person once said. . . ." Either own the idea yourself or credit the source that does own it.)

Think it is hard to track down the source of an idea or phrase? It isn't any longer—just Google it.

Being an Ethical Audience Member

Finally, if someone else is speaking, remember that you are equally responsible for making the situation ethical. In other words, it is critical to be an ethical audience member. If it is a presentation day, even if it is not your own day to speak, show up. Simply being there demonstrates a level of respect for the speaker's time and effort and the class as a community. Pay attention. You are responsible for providing constructive and useful feedback to presenters, a task that becomes impossible if your mind is wandering throughout the talk. Do not walk out. Yes, it is possible to wait through the entire presentation before excusing yourself to the restroom. Certainly, if the speaker is saying things that are offensive or inappropriate, respectfully question the speaker about the statements at the end of his or her presentation. Give verbal and nonverbal feedback. Of course, you are required to provide written feedback for some speakers, and that feedback should be specific, constructive and honest. However, your nonverbal feedback is equally telling—if you are reading the *Daily Texan* in the middle of someone's presentation, you are being not only disrespectful to the speaker, but downright rude. Central to being an ethical audience member is treating presenters as you wish to be treated when it is your turn to present.

> "... remember that you are equally responsible for making the situation ethical."

Conclusion

You may be thinking at this point that this is a lot of heavy information to throw at you. You are right. It is essential information, though, as essential as the knowledge you will have to master to thrive in whatever profession you enter. Hopefully, we have given you a beginning—a roadmap, if you will—to take with you on your journey to becoming an ethical communicator. We began by discovering the link between ethics and communication, and exploring the ways in which the great communicators of our time, including your professors, have utilized ethical communication to flesh out and understand the dimensions of ethical communication. Although we only began to touch on the complexity of the concept of ethical communication, we did find ways to bring the concept home, and discussed just how ethics applies in our everyday lives as students, and how important it is to this very course. This chapter is not intended to be read and then forgotten, but to be used again and again as a reference—a guide for you to turn to when you need to touch back and look for some understanding, or a place to go for more resources when you are not sure how to approach a dilemma of ethical communication.

Ethical communication is a complex subject that cannot be mastered in one chapter in one textbook. Still, we have made a start. We hope you use this discussion to help you reflect on your own communication and begin applying some of these principles so that they will become habits by the time you graduate.

One final word of advice, which may become one of the best pieces of advice in this chapter: If you are not sure whether you are crossing a line of ethical or legal communication—ask, and ask before you hand something in for a grade. Your professors are marvelous resources and they are here for your education. Never hesitate to go to a professor's office, make an appointment, or ask for a few minutes after class to work through an ethical dilemma or get clarification on a proper citation format. It is much better to ask than to make assumptions and discover too late that you were wrong. Your grade, your academic career, any professional reputation are far too important to let slide because you did not take time to ask your professor for help. We wish you the best of luck on your ethical journey.

Media Box

Watch the sample student speech, "Informative Speech: HIV/AIDs Home Testing."

You will find the speech in this chapter's folder in your Chapter Media Contents online.

As you watch the speech, consider whether or not you think the speaker is ethical. Why or why not?

Endnotes

1   Roz Chast, "Moral Compass 2003" (cartoon), *New Yorker*, September 1, 2003.

2   See Peter Behr and April Witt, "The Fall of Enron," a *Washington Post* investigative report, published July 28–August 1, 2002, http://www.washingtonpost.com/wp-dyn/articles/A9783-2002Jul27.html.

3   See "Everybody Does It," chapter 1 of David Callahan's *The Cheating Culture* (New York: Harcourt, 2003).

4   Derrick Bell, *Ethical Ambition: Leading a Life of Meaning and Worth* (New York: Bloomsbury, 2002), 1.

5   Richard L. Johannesen, *Ethics in Human Communication*, 5th ed. (Prospect Heights, NJ: Waveland, 2001), 1–2.

6   Barbara Jordan, quoted in "Ethics and The University of Texas System: A Brief Practical Guide," http://www.utsystem.edu/ogc/Ethics/Ethguide.htm. For more information about Jordan, see http://txtell.lib.utexas.edu/stories/j0001-full.html.

7   *Enron Code of Ethics* (July 2000), 2; document scanned and made available by The Smoking Gun, http://www.thesmokinggun.com/enron/enronethics1.html.

8   "Enron Collectibles on eBay," *BusinessWeek*, February 4, 2002, http://www.businessweek.com/magazine/content/02_05/c3768019.htm.

9   For information on the UT ethics conference, see http://www.engr.utexas.edu/cofe/ethics2004/.

10 For information about the McCombs Business Ethics program, see http://www.mccombs.utexas.edu/dept/msis/ethics/About_Program.htm. For information about the UT Bridging Disciplines Program on Ethics and Leadership, see http://www.utexas.edu/student/connexus/bdp/ethics.html.

11 Robert L. Scott, "On Viewing Rhetoric as Epistemic," *Central States Speech Journal* 18 (1967): 16–17.

12 Larry Browning, in conversation with the author, October, 2003.

13 Scott, "On Viewing Rhetoric as Epistemic," 16–17.

14 Scott, "On Viewing Rhetoric as Epistemic," 16–17.

15 For information about the Creighton case, see http://doi.contentdirections.com/mr/hbsp.jsp?doi=10.1225/490090.

16 University of Texas at Austin Student Judicial Services (SJS), "Academic Integrity," http://deanofstudents.utexas.edu/sjs/academicintegrity2.html.

17 "Survey: Many Students Say Cheating's OK," CNN, April 5, 2002, http://www.cnn.com/2002/fyi/teachers.ednews/04/05/highschool.cheating/.

18 Statistics from the web site of The Center for Academic Integrity (CAI), Kenan Institute for Ethics, Duke University, http://www.academicintegrity.org/cai_research.asp.

19 UT Student Affairs Research Team, "Academic Integrity Survey, Spring 2001 Survey Results," http://www.utexas.edu/student/research/surveys/results/spring2001/dssrv004/results/index.html.

20 Miriam Schulman, "Cheating Themselves," *Issues in Ethics* 9 (Winter 2003), http://www.scu.edu/ethics/publications/iie/v9n1/cheating.html, summarizing and adapting the work of Gresham M. Sykes and David Matza, "Techniques of Neutralization: A Theory of Delinquency," *American Sociological Review* 22 (1957): 664–70.

21 The Center for Academic Integrity (CAI), Kenan Institute for Ethics, Duke University, "The Fundamental Values of Academic Integrity," http://www.academicintegrity.org/pdf/FVProject.pdf.

22 UT SJS, "Academic Integrity," http://deanofstudents.utexas.edu/sjs/academicintegrity2.html.

23 UT SJS, "Academic Integrity," http://deanofstudents.utexas.edu/sjs/academicintegrity2.html.

24 Information from Turnitin.com, http://www.turnitin.com/static/products_services/plagiarism_prevention.html.

25 UT SJS, "Academic Integrity," http://deanofstudents.utexas.edu/sjs/academicintegrity2.html.

26 Section 11.802, "Scholastic Dishonesty," from Appendix C, "Institutional Rules on Student Services and Activities," of the UT catalog *General Information, 2003–2004*, http://www.utexas.edu/student/registrar/catalogs/gi03-04/app/appc11.html.

27 Section 11.802, "Scholastic Dishonesty," from Appendix C, "Institutional Rules on Student Services and Activities," of the UT catalog *General Information, 2003–2004*, http://www.utexas.edu/student/registrar/catalogs/gi03-04/app/appc11.html.

28 Maureen Dowd, "Biden Is Facing Growing Debate on His Speeches," *New York Times*, September 16, 1987.

29 Neil Kinnock, 1987 speech excerpt transcribed by Michael Pearce from 1987 Labour Party Broadcasts archived at the Election Broadcast Archive, University of Leeds, http://www.psr.keele.ac.uk/area/uk/pebs/lab87.htm.

30 Larry J. Sabato, "Joseph Biden's Plagiarism; Michael Dukakis's 'Attack Video'—1988," part of "Media Frenzies in Our Time," a Washintonpost.com special report, March 27, 1998, http://www.washingtonpost.com/wp-srv/politics/special/clinton/frenzy/biden.htm.

31 University of Chicago Press, *Chicago Manual of Style*, 15th ed., University of Chicago Press, Chicago, 2003, p. 136.

32 "Pete Conrad Remembers," streaming video of Pete Conrad speaking of viewing the whole earth, *Air and Space Magazine*, http://www.airspacemag.com/asm/web/site/QT/FlatEarth.html.

33 University of Chicago Press, *Chicago Manual of Style*, 15th ed., University of Chicago Press, Chicago, 2003.

Notes

CHAPTER 4

Listening

Objectives

After studying Chapter 4, you should be able to do the following:

☐ Understand what listening entails.
☐ Define the various types of listening.
☐ Identify who the listener is and what his or her needs are.
☐ Figure out contextual barriers to good listening skills.
☐ Learn how to become a better listener.

Key Terms

TERM	DEFINITION
backchanneling cues	Cues to let the speaker know you're listening.
discriminate	To mark or perceive the distinguishing or peculiar features of; to distinguish by discerning or exposing differences.
evaluate	To determine or fix the value of; to determine the significance, worth, or condition of, usually by careful appraisal and study.
hear	To gain knowledge of by hearing. To listen to with attention.
interpret	To explain or tell the meaning of; to conceive in the light of individual belief, judgment, or circumstance.
listen	To pay attention to sound. To hear something with thoughtful attention: give consideration.
receive	The first stage of hearing is when you receive the message (or listen to it).
remember	To bring to mind or think of again; to keep in mind for attention or consideration.
respond	To say something in return: make an answer; to react in response.
subjective listening	Listening that is peculiar to a certain individual; the listening skills are modified or affected by personal views, experience, or background, i.e., a subjective account of the incident.
understand	To grasp the meaning of; to accept as a fact or truth or regard as plausible without utter certainty.

Introduction

All of our lives, people say to us, "Are you listening? Did you hear me?" It's a rhetorical question that doesn't really merit a response, but we always say, "Of course, I'm listening," whether or not we are. The truth is, of course, that we probably aren't listening—at least not intently or purposefully. We may hear part of what has been said, but each of us has natural filters that affect the way we listen, so we hear only what we want to hear.

An example comes to mind. A psychology professor had dedicated his life to teaching and worked hard to prepare interesting lectures, yet he found his students sitting through his talks with glassy-eyed expressions. To learn what was wrong, and also find out what was on his students' minds on the off chance that they were not focusing on psychology, he would, without warning, fire a blank from a gun and then ask his students to record their thoughts at the instant they heard the shot. Here is what he found:

- ❑ Twenty (20) percent were pursuing erotic thoughts or sexual fantasies.
- ❑ Twenty (20) percent were reminiscing about something (they weren't sure what they were thinking about).
- ❑ Twenty (20) percent were worrying about something or thinking about lunch.
- ❑ Eight (8) percent were pursuing religious thoughts.
- ❑ Twenty (20) percent were reportedly listening.
- ❑ Twelve (12) percent were able to recall what the professor was talking about when the gun fired.

Media Box
Listen as Professor Melissa Beall discusses the difference between *listening* and *hearing*.
Visit this chapter's folder in your Chapter Media Contents online.

What would you have been thinking about if this demonstration happened to you?

Actually, the category you fell into would probably change from moment to moment, depending on the circumstances at that time. If you were hungry, you'd be thinking of lunch. If you were bored, you might be thinking of something erotic. If you were fascinated by the speaker, then you might be paying attention, at least for part of the time.

Many different circumstances affect our ability to listen, including our state of mind, our physical state, our beliefs, our intentions, our interest in the subject, our own history and predilections, our ability to stay focused, the speaker's presentation, etc. As a listener, you hear more than one billion words a year. How much of that information do you retain and how much goes past you and into the stratosphere, never to be retrieved again? As a presenter, how can you possibly get and keep the attention of a roomful of listeners—at least long enough to impart valuable information to them?

In this chapter, we will define the act of listening, present various listening methods, and identify barriers to listening. We'll focus on how to improve your critical listening skills, show what makes a good listener, and learn how as a presenter you can "read" your audience and catch its attention.

What Is Listening?

To listen is to pay attention to sound or to hear something with thoughtful attention. There is a difference between hearing and listening. Hearing is the physical process of sound waves bouncing off an eardrum. Listening is active and involves a series of five steps: receiving, understanding, remembering, evaluating, and responding. The process is represented in Figure 4.1.

Figure 4.1. This five-step model defining the process of listening draws on a variety of models that listening researchers have developed (Courtesy of Alessandra, 1986; Barker, 1990: Brownell, 1987; Steil, Barker & Watson, 1983).

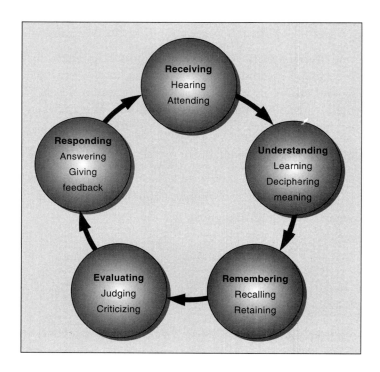

Receiving.

Unlike listening, hearing begins and ends with the first stage, which is <u>receiving</u>. Hearing is what happens when you get within earshot of some auditory stimulus. Listening is quite different; it begins (but does not end) with receiving a speaker's messages. (Note that we're using the term "speaker" to relate to anyone who is speaking, not just someone on a podium giving a speech.) The messages a listener receives are both verbal and nonverbal; they consist of words, as well as gestures, facial expressions, variations in volume and rate, and lots more.

At this stage of listening, you recognize not only what is said, but also what is not said. For example, if you are listening critically, you will hear the message delivered—for example, your professor says that this will be a hard class with lots of work, versus the undelivered but implied or understood message—you're going to be spending a lot of time in the library if you want to earn a good grade!

Receiving messages is a highly selective process. You don't listen to all the available auditory stimuli. Rather, you selectively tune in to certain messages and tune out others. Generally, you listen most carefully to messages that you feel will prove of value to you or that you find will be particularly interesting. At the same time, you give less attention to messages that have less value or interest. Thus, you may listen carefully when your instructor tells you what will appear on an exam, but listen less carefully to an extended story or routine announcements that he delivers.

Tips for being a better critical listener:

- ❑ Look at the speaker; make your mind follow your body and focus attention on the person speaking.
- ❑ Focus your attention on the speaker's verbal and nonverbal messages, on what is said and on what isn't said.

❑ Avoid attending to distractions in the environment, such as what is going on outside or that flickering light.

❑ Focus your attention on what the speaker is saying, rather than on any questions or objections you may have to what the speaker is saying.

Rushing to judgment.

Most people have biases that come out when they listen to a speech about something they disagree with, whether it is politics, religion, or the best way to cook salmon. Instead of listening to the theory and the supporting arguments, they tick off in their heads all the things that are wrong with what the speaker is saying. Not only does this do the speaker an injustice, but it also hurts the listener. First, the listener misses salient points of the presentation because he is pursuing only the thoughts in his head that negate what the speaker is saying. Second, the listener is interpreting the speaker's comments without necessarily hearing them or the gist of what is being said. So, the next time you are listening to a speech where you have preconceived notions about the speaker, try the opposite—try listening without judgment first and see if you learn something new.

Understanding.

Understanding a speaker means grasping not only the thoughts that are expressed, but also the emotional tone that accompanies these thoughts; for example, the urgency or the joy or sorrow expressed in the message. To enhance understanding, try the following practices:

❑ Relate the new information the speaker is giving to what you already know.

❑ See the speaker's messages from the speaker's point of view; avoid judging the message until you fully understand it as the speaker intended it.

❑ Rephrase (paraphrase) the speaker's ideas into your own words as you continue to listen.

Interpreting

The essence of understanding lies in interpretation and how you figure out what the words mean not only to you and your sensibilities, but to the world. If the sender sends out a message that you interpret incorrectly, then the message gets lost. People interpret messages based on their own background: What they've read, how they were raised, what similar messages have meant to them, and how they think. Take a look at the following note to see how differently one situation can be interpreted, based on the sender and receiver's information and communication pathways.

Levels of interpretation

Message from Bob: "We need to talk."

Level 1 Interpretation—Bob wants me to shut the door and discuss something. I decide to listen. Bob asks about my family and tells about his. I continue to listen.

Level 2 Interpretation—Bob wants to talk privately. He will bring up his topic after a few conversational exchanges. I'm supportive and curious, and decide to listen. Bob tells me that he is concerned about losing his job. I continue to listen.

Level 3 Interpretation—Bob is worried, feels vulnerable, and is concerned about others learning of his predicament. I feel honored that he trusts me enough to discuss it with me. I will listen as long as he needs to talk. Bob tells me has seen a reorganization chart and doesn't see his job title on it. He is worried about maintaining his health insurance.

Level 4 Interpretation—Bob does not have evidence that he will lose his job. He may even be up for another position and promotion, so far as the chart is concerned. I wonder why he brought up health insurance in particular. I will continue to listen to discriminate between what Bob knows and what he is guessing. I will listen for messages that explain his focus on health insurance.

Discriminating

Discriminating listeners choose to listen carefully and <u>discriminate</u> between information and propaganda, between facts and personal experience, between official business and small talk, and between research that keeps them abreast and information on which they must take action. Discriminating skills must be used at every level of listening. In other words, the discriminating listener hears, processes, and evaluates the information, figuring out what is important to keep and what can be left behind as inconsequential. Discriminating listeners do not prejudge a situation before they actually hear and listen to it.

Remembering.

Some messages we remember, most we forget. What is the difference between those that stick with us and those that are literally in one ear and out the other? What you <u>remember</u> is not actually what was said, but what you think (or remember) was said. Memory for speech is not reproductive; you do not simply reproduce in your memory what the speaker said. Rather, memory is reconstructive; you actually reconstruct the messages you hear into a system that seems to make sense to you. Only if you reconstruct a message into something that makes sense to you and is therefore salient to you will you remember it.

If you are trying to remember salient points of something, use the following tips to enhance your memory:

- ❑ Identify the thesis or control idea and the main points.
- ❑ Summarize the message in a more easily retained form, being careful not to ignore crucial details or important qualifications.
- ❑ Repeat names and key concepts to yourself.
- ❑ Identify the organizational pattern and use it (visualize it) to organize what the speaker is saying.

Evaluating.

When you <u>evaluate</u>, you judge the message and the speaker's credibility, truthfulness, or usefulness in some way. At this stage, your own biases and prejudices become especially influential. These will affect what you single out for evaluation and what you'll just let pass. They will influence what you judge to be good information and what you judge to be bad information. In some situations, evaluation is more in the nature of critical analysis.

> "... empathic listeners identify with the speaker, try to see the situation from that person's point of view, and seek to understand how it makes the person feel."

When evaluating what you've heard or listened to, use the following criteria:

- ❑ Resist evaluation until you feel you understand (at least reasonably well) the speaker's point of view.
- ❑ Distinguish facts from inferences, opinions, and personal interpretations that you're making, as well as those made by the speaker.
- ❑ Identify any biases, self-interests, or prejudices that may lead the speaker to slant unfairly what he or she is presenting.
- ❑ Identify any biases that may lead you to remember what supports your attitudes and beliefs and to forget what contradicts them.

Evaluative listening is particularly important when listening to persuasive speakers. In this case, you should measure the value of the topic, the soundness of the reasoning, and the quality of the support for the argument. We take on roles, or rather identities, in the listening process. A person's listening identity changes in response to his or her evaluative listening. A listener may choose to take on an objective, detached identity or a subjective, empathetic role. Objective, detached listeners distance themselves from issues to collect facts without personal bias. Detachment requires distancing oneself from "whatever threatens to distort the understanding of what is there." Subjective, empathic listeners identify with the speaker, try to see the situation from that person's point of view, and seek to understand how it makes the person feel. This does not mean empathetic listeners always agree with the speaker or the message, but they try to see another person's perspective without judging too carelessly or quickly. We could all be better empathetic listeners!

> **"We could all be better empathetic listeners!"**

Responding.

Responding occurs in two phases: (1) nonverbal (and occasionally verbal) responses you make while the speaker is talking; and (2) responses you make after the speaker has stopped talking. Responses made while the speaker is talking should support the speaker and show that you are listening. These include what nonverbal researchers call backchanneling cues or gestures that let the speaker know that you're listening, such as nodding your head, smiling, and leaning forward—anything to encourage the speaker. Remember that anyone who is speaking to you expects you to listen and respond.

> **"Remember that anyone who is speaking to you expects you to listen and respond."**

Responses made after the speaker has stopped talking are generally more elaborate and might include questions of clarification, expressions of agreement, and expressions of disagreement. All of these would be appropriate responses.

Potential responses, both verbal and nonverbal, to the speaker include the following:

❑ Use a variety of backchanneling cues to support the speaker, because using only one cue, like nodding constantly, will make it appear that you are not listening but are on automatic pilot. Or you could be interpreted as being rude.

❑ Support the speaker in your final responses by saying something positive and encouraging about the speech or presentation.

❑ Own your own responses. State your thoughts and feelings as your own, and use I-messages. For example, say "I think the new proposal will entail greater expense than you outlined," rather than "Everyone will object to the plan because it will cost too much."

Who Is the Listener?

Like speakers, listeners have purposes in mind; they are partners in speech transactions. The way they think about what is said is affected by their purposes, knowledge of and interest in the subject, level of listening skills, and attitudes toward self, speaker, and the ideas presented.

The listeners' purposes.

Listeners always have one or more purposes when they come to a speech. No less than speakers, they are looking for something, be it information, confirmation of prior judgments about ideas or people, or simply entertainment. Good speakers will take into account their listeners' purposes or risk rejection by the audience.

The listeners' knowledge and interest levels.

In speaking situations, listeners' knowledge of and interest in the subject will significantly affect how they respond to the message. It is the speaker's job to figure out how much the listeners know in advance about the topic and whether or not they have a personal stake in it. Beyond assessing knowledge and interest, it is incumbent upon the speaker to analyze cultural differences, if any, and how they will affect the presentation.

The listeners' command of listening skills.

Listeners vary in their abilities to process oral messages. Cultural differences may place greater responsibility on the speaker to ensure that the ideas are clear; otherwise, the audience will tune out. Furthermore, even though college audiences have been listening to instructors for several years, they still want to know why they should listen to you. Motivating audiences to use the skills they have is as important as recognizing when they are not comprehending your message because of inadequate skills.

The listeners' attitudes.

As the model in Figure 4.2 suggests, listeners' attitudes toward themselves, the speaker, and the subject affect how they interpret and respond to speeches. Listeners with low self-esteem, for example, tend to be swayed more easily than those with stronger self-images. Listeners who feel their opinions are confirmed by the speaker also are more easily influenced than those holding contrary ideas. Moreover, as a rule, people seek out speakers whose positions they already agree with and retain longer and more vividly those ideas of which they strongly approve.

Audience analysis is one of the keys to speaking success, because you need to know about people's attitudes before you can reach them.

*Figure 4.2. A model of the speechmaking process. (Courtesy of **Principles and Types of Public Speaking**, 15th Ed.)*

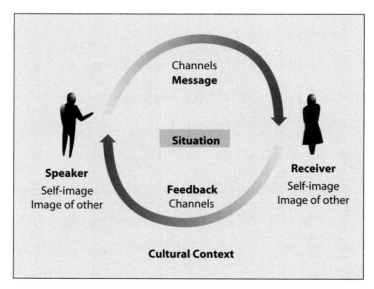

Feedback.

Often, we interpret public speaking as communication flowing in one direction—from speaker to listener. Information, feelings, and ideas, however, flow the other way as well. Feedback is information that listeners return to you about the clarity and acceptability of your ideas (see Figure 4.3)

Listeners may provide immediate feedback in the form of verbal or nonverbal responses during an interaction. Some immediate feedback is direct, such as when the audience asks questions, whereas some is indirect, such

Figure 4.3. Various types of feedback given from the audience (listeners) to the speaker. (Courtesy of Principles and Types of Public Speaking, 15th Ed.)

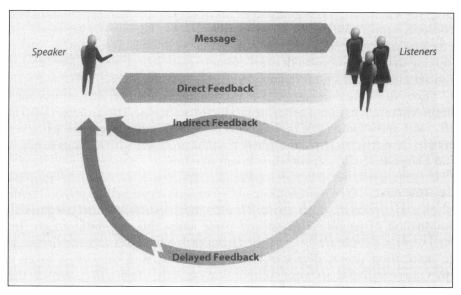

as when speakers look for frowns, smiles, and other nonverbal cues to audience reaction. Being able to read feedback for signs of comprehension and acceptability is important, as this skill allows the speaker to make midcourse adjustments in his speech, as necessary.

However, in some cultures, it is considered to be impolite to show disapproval through feedback. Instead, people smile cordially, as if all is well, when in reality they might not understand anything you say or be angry you said it. Knowing in advance how different cultural values govern responsiveness will help you develop a sound perception of how effectively you have communicated your ideas. In some cases, you may not be certain until you have received additional concrete evidence through delayed feedback, which takes the form of oral, auditory, or visual signals received after the message has been transmitted.

Contextual Barriers to Good Listening Skills

All communication occurs in a context, and each context has communication noise—that is, something that interferes with communication. Three contexts in particular shape listening experiences—location, culture, and gender.

Location matters.

Interference in environment weakens listening capabilities. Physical noise is specific to the immediate environment, or location, of the communication. Interviewers, for instance, like to control the location so that the interviewee will not be distracted.

Location helps frame the communication. For example, chastising a coach in a locker room in front of his team is very different from chastising him in a private office. Also, critical comments have added impact when the location is such that someone is humiliated or embarrassed because of where you chose to criticize.

Cultural differences.

Cultural presumptions shade meanings, especially in regard to how directly a message is stated, the appropriateness of interactions (who may speak to whom, when, where, and about what), and whether groups or individuals are more highly valued.

Cultural vocabulary mismatches often cause communication errors. For example, communicators may use different languages that have similar words, but with different meanings, so their audience becomes confused by a misplaced word. Or the audience may not understand the use of technical, professional, or other jargon used by the communicator. Always be aware of your audience and ask if you think they are confused by a concept or terminology.

Media Box

Does culture impact listening strategies?

Professor Melissa Beall discusses basic tips for listening in intercultural contexts.

Visit this chapter's folder in your Chapter Media Contents online.

Gender styles cause confusion.

Men and women also listen differently. Women are more likely to use listening to build relationships, and men are more likely to listen to get information. Deborah Tannen says women and men listen so differently that it is as if they were speaking different languages. If the communicators are either two men or two women, they are more likely to anticipate how the other will interpret the message.

> "... women use listening to further their primary goals of building rapport and establishing closer relationships."

However, when men communicate with women, the women are more likely to position themselves as the listeners, and the men are more likely to be lecturers and take on the roles of expert and authority. Women do more nodding and "uh-huhs" to indicate they are listening than do men. Men are more likely to interrupt for dominance, but women are more apt to interrupt to "join" the speaker. Typically, women use listening to further their primary goals of building rapport and establishing closer relationships. Men value listening because they get information that helps them solve problems. No one style is necessarily better than another, but in our culture, we value the person speaking—that person is perceived to have control. This is a tendency we must fight constantly in order to be better listeners.

Becoming a Better Listener

The good news is that listening skills can be improved, but it will take some effort on the part of the listener. First, you will have to identify what type of listener you are. Second, you will need to focus on the areas where you need to improve. Following are some tips to help you further your listening skills.

Adapt to the speaker's delivery.

Good listeners focus on a speaker's message, not on his or her delivery style. To be a good listener, you must adapt to the particular idiosyncrasies that some speakers have. For example, you may have to overlook or ignore a speaker's tendency to mumble, speak in a monotone voice, or fail to make eye contact. Or even more difficult, you may have to forgive a speaker's lack of clarity or coherence in the delivery.

Even if the speaker is well-polished, he or she may not have much of a message to deliver. Beware of the smooth-talking salesperson that convinces you to buy something without your carefully considering the content of his or her message. As a good listener, always concentrate on the message, not the messenger.

Listen with your eyes as well as your ears.

Although body language can be distracting and lead the message astray, that doesn't mean that you should ignore it. Nonverbal clues play a major role in communicating a message. Some experts even suggest that most communication is nonverbal. So much for valuing the person speaking! Even though this statistic does not apply in every situation, emotion is primarily communicated by unspoken messages. For example, facial expressions help identify the emotions being communicated, and a speaker's posture and gestures can reinforce the intensity of emotion. The idea is to pay attention to nonverbal cues, but not watch speakers judgmentally.

Monitor your emotional reaction to a message.

Heightened emotions can affect your ability to understand a message. If you become angry at a word or phrase a speaker uses, then your listening comprehension decreases. Depending on cultural backgrounds, religious convictions, or political views, listeners can become emotionally aroused by certain words, particularly words that connote a negative opinion about their beliefs.

How can you keep your emotions in check when you hear something that sets you off? First, recognize when your emotional state is affecting your rational thoughts. Second, use the skill of self-talk to calm yourself down. Focus on your breathing to instill a sense of calm. Finally, tell yourself that you are not going to let anger get in the way of your listening and understanding the speaker.

> **"Heightened emotions can affect your ability to understand a message."**

Avoid jumping to conclusions.

Don't jump to conclusions prematurely about a speaker's content. Give that person time to develop and support his or her main point before you decide whether you agree or disagree or whether the message has any value. If you mentally criticize a speaker's style or message, your listening efficiency will decline. So, even if the guest lecturer walks into class wearing a tee-shirt that says, "Gig 'Em Aggies!", your job is to avoid concluding she is therefore incompetent or irritating—listen for the content and try not to judge the package.

Be a selfish listener.

Being a selfish listener can help you maintain your powers of concentration. If you find your attention waning, ask yourself questions such as, "What's in it for me?" and "How can I use the information from this talk?" Naturally, you will find more useful information in some presentations than others, but be alert to the possibility of good information in all speeches. Find ways to benefit from the information you are listening to, and try to connect it with your own experiences and needs.

Listen for major ideas.

Good listeners listen for major ideas, concepts, and principles, rather than just the facts. Facts are useful only when you can connect them to a principle or a concept. In speeches, facts as well as examples are used primarily to support major ideas. Try to mentally summarize the major idea that the specific facts support.

In 1933, Franklin Delano Roosevelt delivered his first inaugural address, with the key idea in the fourth sentence of the speech: "This great Nation will endure as it has endured, will revive and will prosper. So, first of all, let me assert my firm belief that the only thing we have to fear is fear itself." A good listener would immediately identify this last statement as the core of the speech.

Identifying the major ideas in a speech is not as difficult as you might imagine. A competent speaker will offer a preview of major ideas early in the speech. If no preview is provided, listen for the speaker to enumerate major points, such as "My first point is . . ." Transitional phrases and a speaker's internal summaries are other clues that can help you identify major points. If your speaker provides few overt indicators, you may have to discover them on your own. In that event, mentally summarize the ideas that are most useful to you.

> **"Good listeners listen for major ideas, concepts, and principles, rather than just the facts."**

Identify your listening goal.

A typical student will spend over 80 percent of his day involved in communication-related activities, of which 9 percent is spent writing, 16 percent reading, 30 percent speaking, and 45 percent listening (see Figure 4.4).

There are at least four different listening goals: listening for pleasure, to empathize, to evaluate, and to gain information. Being conscious of your listening goal will allow you to listen more effectively. For example, if you are listening for pleasure, you need not listen at the same intensity as you would if you were trying to remember something for a test later.

Listening to empathize usually means that you are attempting to feel what the speaker is feeling. Usually, empathetic listening occurs in one-on-one listening situations with a good friend. On the job, it might involve a customer, a client, or a co-worker. Listening to empathize requires these essential steps:

1. *Stop.* Stop what you are doing and give complete attention to the speaker.
2. *Look.* Make eye contact and pay attention to nonverbal cues that reveal emotions.
3. *Listen.* Pay attention to both the details of the message and the major ideas.
4. *Imagine.* Visualize how you would feel if you had experienced what the speaker had experienced.
5. *Check.* Check your understanding of the message by asking questions to clarify what you heard and by summarizing what you think you heard.

Figure 4.4. How we spend our time communicating in any given day.

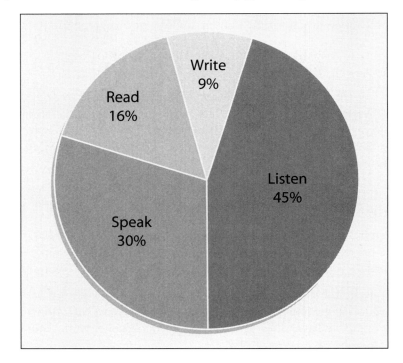

When you evaluate a message, you are making a judgment about its content. You are interested in whether the information is reliable, true, or useful. When evaluating what you hear, the challenge is to not become so critical of the message that you miss a key point the speaker is making. Rather, you must juggle two very difficult tasks. You must make judgments, as well as understand and recall the information you are hearing.

When you are listening to a message and also evaluating it, you have to work harder than at other times to understand the speaker's message. Your biases and judgments act as noise, often causing you to misunderstand the intended meaning of the message.

Since elementary school, you have been in listening situations in which someone wanted you to learn something. Keys to listening for information are listening for the details of a message and making certain you link the details to major ideas. Poor listeners either listen only for facts and pieces of a message or are interested only in the "bottom line." By concentrating on both facts and major ideas, while also mentally summarizing the information you hear, you can dramatically increase your ability to remember messages. Also, remember to compare unfamiliar information to ideas and concepts with which you are familiar.

Knowing your listening goal can help you develop an appropriate listening strategy. Be conscious of what you are seeking from the message.

As a speaker, it is also important for you to know your audience's objectives. If you planned to deliver an educational lecture, but it turns out your listeners are there only for pleasure, then you will have to make some quick adjustments to meet your audience's needs. Audience-centered speakers consider the listening goals of their audiences.

Practice listening.

Because you spend 45 percent of your day listening, you need to practice listening skills. Listening skills do not develop automatically. Researchers believe that poor listeners avoid challenge. For example, they listen to and watch TV situation comedies rather than documentaries or other informative programs. Skill develops as you practice listening to speeches, music, and programs with demanding content.

Taking notes.

Good listeners are usually good notetakers. Always take notes on a speech, if at all possible, because taking notes reinforces good listening skills. It forces you to identify key points of the speech and also highlight important substantiating information. You can also write down questions that you'd like to query the speaker about later.

Of course, in a one-on-one situation, it would be rude to take notes, but you can still take notes in your head. Listen and clarify what is important about what the other person is saying. Then check back with that person to make sure you heard what they wanted to say correctly.

Become an active listener.

An active listener is one who remains alert and mentally re-sorts, rephrases, and repeats key information when listening to a speech. You can listen to words much faster than a speaker can speak them. Therefore, it's natural that your mind may wander. But you can use the extra time instead to focus on interpreting what the speaker says.

- ❑ First, use your listening time to re-sort disorganized or disjointed ideas. If the speaker is rambling and throwing out unorganized ideas, seek ways to rearrange them into a new, more logical pattern.
- ❑ You can also rephrase or summarize what the speaker is saying. This mental activity will help you stay alert so that you can follow the speaker's flow of ideas. Listen for main ideas, and then put them into your own words. You are more likely to remember your mental paraphrase than the speaker's exact words.
- ❑ Do more than just rephrase the information as you listen to it. Periodically, repeat key points you want to remember. Go back to essential ideas and restate them to yourself.

  If you follow these steps for active listening, you will find yourself feeling stimulated and engaged instead of tired and bored as you listen to even the dullest of speakers.
- ❑ An additional active listening strategy is to look for "information handlers" provided by the speaker. In the opening few minutes of the speech, an effective speaker should give an overview of the message; listen for this preview. During the speech, listen for the speaker to identify major ideas by using transition phrases or signposts; signposts occur when the speaker says something like "My first point. . . ." Concentrate on the conclusion of the speech. Does the speaker clearly summarize the major ideas? Listening for the overall structure of the message as evidenced through an overview, transitions, signposts, and summary statements can help you remain actively involved as a listener.

Conclusion

Fostering good listening skills early in life will stand you in good stead for the rest of your natural life. Every aspect of life requires listening in some form or other. If you can learn to listen and process information correctly, then you will have more successful relationships, career paths, and life experiences. If you do not have good listening skills, it is not too late to develop them. Rather, it is imperative that you practice listening and note taking in order to lean how to get the important information in any given situation.

Endnote

1 This chapter is largely based on Raymie E. McKerrow, et al., *Principles and Types of Speech Communication,* 14th ed., Pearson Education, 2000; and Joseph A. DeVito, *The Elements of Public Speaking,* 2nd ed., Pearson Education, 2006.

Exercise 4.1. Say What?! A Lesson in Active Listening.

Visit this chapter's folder in your Chapter Media Contents online and listen as communication scholar Melissa Beall discusses guidelines and suggestions for improving your listening skills.

Then, listen to the inauguration of Barack Obama as the 44th President of the United States. On Tuesday, January 20, 2009, Supreme Court Chief Justice John G. Roberts administered the oath to Obama . . . incorrectly! President Obama had to be sworn in a second time.

Where else have you seen the benefits of *active listening*?

_____

_____

_____

_____

_____

_____

_____

_____

_____

_____

_____

_____

_____

_____

_____

_____

_____

_____

Notes

CHAPTER 5

Audience Analysis

by Melody Chatelle, Ph.D.

Objectives

After studying Chapter 5, you should be able to do the following:

- ☐ Define audience analysis and its key components.
- ☐ Explain the importance of audience analysis for effective presentations.
- ☐ Articulate presenter and audience benefits of audience analysis.
- ☐ Identify various methods of audience analysis.
- ☐ Define specific methods for conducting audience analysis.
- ☐ Understand the importance of certain specific details on your audience.

Key Terms

TERM	DEFINITION
attitudes	Audience members' likes and dislikes.
audience	Those upon whom the ideas, feelings, information, e.g. the message, are presented.
audience adaptation	Modifying or changing the structure, design and/or delivery of your speech to your listeners to enhance message clarity, as well as making your examples and illustrations specifically applicable to your audience to help achieve and maintain audience interest.
audience analysis	Proactively and systematically gathering and reviewing information about those to whom you will be presenting your message in an effort to increase presentation effectiveness.
audience-centered presenter	One who is ever-mindful of the audience in making his/her presentation, and who adapts to the changing nature of message delivery given the human facets of audience members.
beliefs	What audience members hold to be true or false.
demographics	Statistical data about an audience.
demographic profile	A way of better understanding your audience by compiling statistical data relative to audience members' backgrounds.
message	Ideas, feelings, information, and the like presented to an audience through a variety of methods as selected by the presenter, and preferably developed at all times with the audience in mind.
psychographic profile	A way of better understanding your audience by compiling attitudinal information relative to values, beliefs, and ideology of your audience.
values	What audience members judge to be right or wrong.

Introduction

Imagine this: You have tickets to see the Rolling Stones in New York's Madison Square Garden. You grew up listening to the Stones with your parents and have been a lifelong fan of the band. And now, here you are in New York waiting to hear what promises to be the concert of your life! As the band takes the stage, Mick Jagger swaggers to the microphone in typical cocky form. He looks out into the audience and shouts above the almost deafening roar of the crowd: "Hello, Los Angeles!"

Is it a bad dream, or just a bad example? No doubt one does not become a musical legend over decades and knighted by the British Royals as Mick Jagger has by making a huge *faux pas* like welcoming adoring concert goers in New York by saying "Hello, Los Angeles." Yet this simple example argues a monumental point: Knowing your audience is critical to effective presentations, whether it's in a business setting, academic classroom, fraternity house, or on the musical stage.

An anonymous, smart person once said, "A poor presenter quits talking when he or she is tired." A good presenter quits *before* the audience is tired. Here are some key foundational concepts for making effective presentations: (1) knowing your audience *before* you make your presentation is the fundamental key to effective presentations; (2) developing audience-centered messages must be at the core of every single presentation, regardless of how small or large your audience (including the beginning of a concert at Madison Square Garden before thousands); (3) knowing your audience matters whether or not you are speaking, singing, or shouting your <u>message</u>; and (4) audience-centered messages must be at the root of every presentation whether you are speaking impromptu to your sorority sisters or delivering the State of the Union from the nation's capital. Having your audience foremost in your mind is critical—whether you are speaking to inform or to persuade.

In sum, regardless of the particulars, audience matters.

Defining Audience Analysis

Audience analysis involves creating a profile of the individuals gathered for a presentation. All presenters benefit from knowing their audience's basic <u>demographics</u>: age, sex, race, religious background, education level and so on. This information helps speakers when creating a presentation in everything from selecting a topic to choosing supporting evidence to verbal and nonverbal delivery. How? Let's look at an example. If you are presenting to your campus environmental group, you would want to pick a topic related to environmental issues such as drilling in the Arctic National Wildlife Refuge rather than a topic like "how to pick the right jeans for your body type." In addition, knowing your audience cares about and is involved in environmental defense, you would know they would believe scientific data from the Sierra Club over

> "... Knowing your audience is critical to effective presentations ..."

Courtesy of AP/Wide World Photos

> "... the more specific information you can learn about your audience, the better able you are to tailor your presentation to their particular needs."

Courtesy of Teri Leigh Stratford/Pearson Education

opinion cited by oil company lobbyists. You would also understand that your audience is already aware of much of the basic terminology surrounding environmentalism, and would not spend 45 minutes defining jargon. In all, just knowing a few facts about your audience can help make your presentation a successful one. In turn, the more specific information you can learn about your audience, the better able you are to tailor your presentation to their particular needs.

So how does an effective presenter consider the audience? Now that the definitional groundwork has been set, various themes, strategies and ideas for considering the audience will be presented in the following sections, beginning with the benefits to both presenter and audience members when an audience analysis is conducted.

Benefits of Audience Analysis

The benefits of audience analysis are many and varied. A few of the benefits are presented here to give you every advantage when making your presentation.

The advantages of audience analysis for the presenter.

Can you imagine going to a job interview without knowing the name of the person with whom you are meeting? Can you imagine presenting yourself as a viable candidate for a particular job without knowing the details of the job, the people who make up the company, or the mission of the organization? What if Martin Luther King Jr. had not conducted an audience analysis prior to his *I Have a Dream* speech, and thereby left his audience wondering about the details of that dream? How much less effective would King's historical speech have been if he had *not* known about his audience, and the passion they shared with him in ending racial discrimination?

The presenter benefits the most from conducting an audience analysis. At the end of any presentation, the presenter obviously hopes to have accomplished his or her objectives, whether those objectives are to persuade or inform. Like audiences themselves, a presenter's objectives can be large—mobilizing masses of people to participate in a march on Capitol Hill; or they can be small—simply asking your fraternity brother or sorority sister a question. Presenter objectives can involve large audiences, like asking masses of people to advocate for certain causes at capitol buildings, or they can be between only two people, such as when you are applying for a job and must present yourself to the personnel manager of a company. Regardless of the size of the audience or the nature of the situation, the presenter has a much better chance of accomplishing the desired goal if she conducts an audience analysis before the presentation.

The next time you make a presentation of any kind, even something as simple as asking a fellow student to take notes for you in a class you are going to miss, consider the following benefits to thinking ahead about the person or persons to whom you will be making the presentation:

❑ An increased chance of reaching your presentation goals;

❑ A reduced chance of poor presentation performance;

❑ The increased likelihood of audience connection and responsiveness;

❑ A reduced chance of embarrassment because you do not understand your audience;

❑ Increased sensitivity to and recognition of diversity within audiences;

❑ An increased confidence level and self-assuredness on the part of the presenter;

❑ Reduced chance of *out of body* experiences on the presenter's part due to nervousness or acute anxiety;

❑ Increased chance of repeat requests for similar presentations;

❑ And a reduced chance of being rejected.

What additional benefits come to your mind?

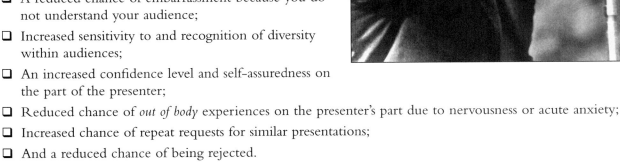

Courtesy of Tophamthe Image Works

What are audience benefits of audience analysis?

The audience also benefits from audience analysis when a presenter does his homework before making a presentation. How many boring presentations have you sat through—or slept through—simply because the presenter had not done any homework, and therefore did not know the audience? How many meetings have you attended in which a presentation was made that bombed because the perspectives or backgrounds of the audience members themselves were not considered by the presenter? How many presentations have you seen that started with an apology from the presenter because she did not have enough handouts for every single person in attendance? How many sales presentations have been stopped short because frustrated audience members do not care to be distracted by someone who fails to say their names correctly?

> **"When a presenter conducts an audience analysis, audience members are more likely to listen to the presentation itself."**

When a presenter conducts an audience analysis, audience members are more likely to listen to the presentation itself. In sum, audience members must be engaged in the process of communication or they will not give you their time or attention, thereby diminishing presenter effectiveness. And the way you engage an audience is to make the effort to thoroughly understand their <u>beliefs</u>, <u>attitudes</u>, and needs.

Audiences gain three major benefits from effective analyses:

❑ Greater understanding of the topic;

❑ Increased interest in the subject;

❑ And, the ability to act based on an informed opinion.

First, if an audience analysis is conducted prior to a presentation, the audience is more likely to be addressed "on their level," or at the level of understanding common to the members of that audience. In other words, the presentation is not too simplistic, nor too technical—information presented at the right level means a greater likelihood your audience walks away really understanding the topic you presented. Second, with understanding comes interest. It is unsurprising that audiences who really "get" a subject find themselves more interested in it—wine connoisseurs are more interested in wine simply because they *know* something about it; food enthusiasts are the same way with gourmet cuisine, motorcyclists with the benefits of owning a Harley Davidson. So, not only does a quality audience analysis mean a greater chance for learning, but it also equates to an increased appreciation for the subject. Finally, because audiences feel knowledgeable and intrigued, they are far more capable of acting based on informed opinion rather than naivety or misunderstanding. And, ultimately, that makes audiences more responsible "consumers" of information.

Getting Started with Audience Analysis

Now that we have discussed the conceptual foundations of doing your homework as a presenter, including focusing on benefits to both the presenter and the audience, as a result of audience consideration and analysis, the question becomes "how does a presenter get started in doing an audience analysis?" Because audiences are made up of human beings who are complicated, complex, mobile, and always changing, there is no simple formula for studying audiences. There is also no right or wrong way to conduct an audience analysis. In fact, a student conducting an Internet search on the term audience analysis might find more than 170,000 hits on that term alone, suggesting not only that the issue is an extremely important one within the context of effective presentations, but also that multiple perspectives exist for conducting audience analyses.

One such perspective comes from a public speaking author, Lenny Laskowski, who offers an acronym on the word AUDIENCE as a reminder of the steps in conducting an audience analysis. These steps are presented in Table 5.1.

Table 5.1. An Acronym for AUDIENCE.		
A	Analysis	Who is your audience? How many will be in attendance?
U	Understanding	What is your audience's knowledge of the subject?
D	Demographics	What are the majors, hometown and year in school of your audience members?
I	Interest	Why is your audience in attendance? Who asked your audience to attend?
E	Environment	Where will you stand before your audience to give your presentation? Can all the members of your audience see and hear you? What visual aids will you be using in conveying your message, and how will they be received within your setting?
N	Needs	What are the needs of your audience? What are your needs as the presenter?
C	Customized	What specific needs should you address with your audience?
E	Expectations	What does your audience expect to learn or hear from you?

Do your homework by analyzing your audience.

Core to any audience analysis are three broad concerns about which you should think: (1) the *needs* of your audience; (2) the *types of people* who comprise your audience; and (3) the *logistics and details* of your presentation, specifically as they relate to your audience.

Answering the three statements above is an excellent way to begin your homework when conducting an effective audience analysis. Also, the notion of conducting an audience analysis as a homework project is an important one given that any effective audience analysis must take place long before you actually begin the presentation to your audience. If you find yourself thinking about your audience for the first time as you walk up to the podium (whether your audience is comprised of 10 people or 100), you should know that you have immediately placed yourself in a compromising situation as a presenter—you have failed to do your homework long before you begin to speak.

So that we do not make the same mistake in not fully considering the components of audience analysis, let us begin our homework for analyzing an audience by examining these three concepts in depth.

Think about the needs of your audience

Collectively and individually, every single member of your audience has needs. Some people need to be told what to do. Some people need to show off in front of others; and, others need to be left alone. Some people need to hear only the bottom line. Some people need to have you stop talking as quickly as possible so that they can move on to the next thing on their "to-do" list. The list of needs can and does go on and on.

Your job as an audience-centered presenter is to recognize, anticipate, and respond to those needs as best as humanly possible, understanding that no one individual can be all things to all people. Yet if you want to be a truly effective presenter who gets across the intended message to an audience, you should strive diligently to address the needs of the individuals in your audience.

One way to address the needs of your audience is to *understand* those needs. Psychologist Abraham H. Maslow is widely known for outlining a theoretical framework by which people are motivated to move from one need to the next. As you begin to develop your presentation, think about Maslow's hierarchy of needs in terms of your audience. What are the needs of your audience? Where is your audience heading in terms of reaching their needs? What do Maslow's needs mean for the particular individuals before whom you are conveying your message? How can you apply Maslow's need theory to your audience?

Exercise 5.1. A.U.D.I.E.N.C.E. Analysis.

Using the AUDIENCE acronym, conduct your own analysis of your class members or another group in front of whom you are presenting in the near future:

Analysis:

Understanding:

Demographics:

Interest:

Environment:

Needs:

Customized:

Expectations:

Outlined below in Table 5.2 is a general framework of Maslow's Hierarchy of Needs.

Professional speaking coach Stephen C. Rafe suggests that most of the audiences he has observed over 25 years of giving professional presentations function within the level of "Social Needs." Nonetheless, an effective presenter should develop a general understanding of *all* of the needs, and tailor her remarks to recognize that audience members do not always snugly fit into any one particular need group. Audience members will not all fit into one particular level—for things are not that simple or easy. In fact, presenters who have done their homework should assume in advance that members of the audience have all of the needs outlined above at different times of their lives. Thus to be truly effective, presenters should make every attempt to appeal to a wide variety of needs in an effort to motivate the entire audience: presenters should focus on audience adaptation.

Because audiences are made up of people who are at various stages of their lives on any given day, who are thinking and worrying about a million different issues, and who collectively present a daunting challenge to presenters, Maslow's theory represents a good way to begin to do your homework prior to making a presentation.

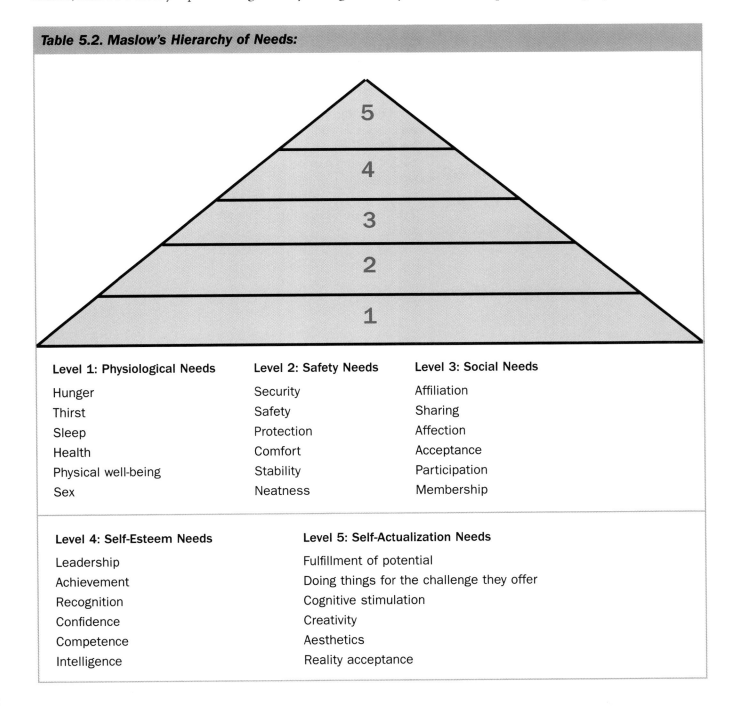

Table 5.2. Maslow's Hierarchy of Needs:

Level 1: Physiological Needs

Hunger
Thirst
Sleep
Health
Physical well-being
Sex

Level 2: Safety Needs

Security
Safety
Protection
Comfort
Stability
Neatness

Level 3: Social Needs

Affiliation
Sharing
Affection
Acceptance
Participation
Membership

Level 4: Self-Esteem Needs

Leadership
Achievement
Recognition
Confidence
Competence
Intelligence

Level 5: Self-Actualization Needs

Fulfillment of potential
Doing things for the challenge they offer
Cognitive stimulation
Creativity
Aesthetics
Reality acceptance

Maslow's hierarchy builds from level to level, assuming that people will be motivated to ultimately search for self-actualization. An effective presenter is challenged to anticipate where audience members may fall on the hierarchy, and then develop remarks in concert with those needs. For example, if you are making a presentation before a group of highly paid corporate Chief Executive Officers (CEOs), you might assume that the CEOs would fall along Maslow's level four, "Esteem," in which there is a strong need for recognition, achievement, competence, intelligence, and the like. However, if some of those same CEOs had just been informed of drastically falling stock values on Wall Street or corporate mergers that might result in job terminations, they might quickly be moving from the Esteem level back to level two, "Safety," or possibly even level one, "Physiological" needs, depending on the severity of the situation. The reference to Maslow's need theory is a recognition that audience members have all kinds of needs, and effective presenters must be mindful of those needs in an effort to motivate people to listen.

Think about the types of people who comprise your audience

One basic way of beginning an audience analysis is to ask: What types of people will be in my audience? Another way of thinking about this question is to ask: Whom am I trying to reach, and why should they listen to me?

> "... demographic profile of an audience is a way of enhancing your understanding of your audience by developing statistical data relative to your audience ..."

Two ways of answering these questions are to draw a demographic and psychographic profile of your audience.

Demographic Profile: Demographics relate to statistical data about an audience. A demographic profile of an audience is a way of enhancing your understanding of your audience by developing statistical data relative to your audience members' backgrounds. Conducting a demographic profile should be a key component of any audience analysis. Listed below in Table 5.3 are tips and strategies for developing a demographic profile:

Table 5.3. Demographic Profile.

Questions to Ask	Strategies to Implement
Who will your audience members be?	Conduct a survey of your audience members before your presentation to gather demographic data.
Where do they live? What do they do for a living?	Interview specific leaders and members who will be in the audience.
What is the age range of your audience?	Interview previous presenters who have appeared before the same audience.
What is the gender makeup of your audience?	Gather data on your audience from demographic sources such as the U.S. Census Bureau based on items such as zip codes, metropolitan areas etc.
What is the religious background of your audience?	

Questions to Ask	Strategies to Implement
What is the socio-economic status of your audience? What is the educational level of your audience? What is the sexual orientation of your audience? What is the general family background of your audience?	Conduct a thorough analysis of the professional affiliation of your audience, e.g. review the demographic data relative to teachers and parents if you are speaking before a group like the National Parents Teachers Association (PTA). Review performance reviews of previous presenters who have appeared before your audience. Review attendance rosters of your audience before you present.

Psychographic Profile: Moving beyond statistical data, the second key component is developing a psychographic profile: identifying and reflecting on attitudes, ideology, values, and beliefs. Table 5.4 outlines some questions and strategies for developing a psychographic profile.

Table 5.4. Considerations for Developing a Psychographic Profile.

Questions to Ask	Strategies to Implement
What are the values of this audience? What are the ideals of this audience? What are the beliefs of this audience? What does this audience like? What does this audience dislike? What does this audience's organization stand for? What are its guiding principles? How does this audience define right? How does this audience define wrong? What does this audience hold as true? What does this audience hold as false?	Conduct an attitudinal-specific survey of your audience members before your presentation. Conduct an opinion survey of specific leaders and members who will be in the audience. Ask previous presenters who have appeared before the same audience for their general viewpoints on the attitudes and beliefs of the audience. Search for psychological profiles of professions that will be represented in your audience, e.g. teachers, doctors, construction workers, healthcare providers, accounting clerks, and others. Thoroughly review the vision, mission, strategies, objectives, guiding principles, and other such data relative to your audience's organization. Review existing stands on legislative or policy issues of importance to your audience.

Audience Types: In addition to gathering demographic and psychographic data, there are many other tools to use in thinking about your audience prior to your presentation. Whatever system or combination of systems you devise that works for you is what you should use. The primary message is one that is worthy of restating: thinking about your audience ahead of time is a critical ingredient, if not *the* critical ingredient, to being an effective presenter.

For example, some presenters think about their <u>audience</u> in terms of the types of people before whom they are presenting. A presenter's life would be simple if audiences could be easily tagged using certain categories or types, but such is not the case. Within every audience exists a multitude of personality types. Let's take a look at some of the generally agreed upon types of personalities who may comprise your audience as presented in Table 5.5. In thinking about this information, the important point to remember is that you need to do everything you can to reach all of the different personality types in your audience as you are able to identify them in your audience analysis homework. Such lists are based on loose generalizations, as offered by numerous communication practitioners in a variety of forms—they are by no means exhaustive. Not all people fit neatly into one or more of the personality types as presented in the table. The categorization of personality types is, however, a viable tool for thinking ahead about your audience.

Table 5.5. Personality Types.

Model presented by Barbara Miller, internationally known instructor of a *"Thinking on Your Feet"* seminar.

Personality Types	Characteristics	Possible Professional Representatives	Most Interested in Hearing/ Seeing/Knowing	Presentation Tips and Strategies
Intuitors (Conceptual)	"Big-picture" people Future-oriented Conceptually creative	Some CEOs Strategic planners Some architects City Planners Artists	Where the organization or talk is going How things will be better in the years ahead	Paint a picture of where you are headed with your presentation Tell stories Use analogies Use photographs and images to tell your story
Thinkers (Analytical)	Statistical people Analytical people Logically-driven, think in linear fashion Consistent, stable	Accountants Systems analysts Attorneys 60% Some architects Stock market analysts Quality control or assurance personnel Bankers	Charts, graphs How you came to your conclusions Statistical data Background reading materials Matrix, flow-chart documents	Prepare and distribute background handouts Walk thinkers through the processes you used to obtain your information Present statistics and quantifiable data
Feelers (Relational)	Emotional thinkers Appreciate testimonials Likes "touchy-feely" information, warmth and human interest stories	Healthcare givers Sales & Marketing Actors Wedding planners Personnel managers Teachers Daycare providers Ministers	What others think about the information you are presenting How people are affected by your data The human aspects of your information "Hallmark" images and stories	Tell stories about people by name Personalize your data Create visuals involving people and real-life situations Tell the "before" and "after" of peoples' stories

Personality Types	Characteristics	Possible Professional Representatives	Most Interested in Hearing/ Seeing/Knowing	Presentation Tips and Strategies
Sensors (Practical)	Bottom-line oriented Most everything is urgent Move fast Appreciate brevity	Some CEOs Multi-tasking individuals with little time Military personnel, e.g. master drill sergeants Consultants paid by the hour Some stock brokers	What you are actually wanting your audience to do Bottom-line results Last-action steps Call-to-action information Benefit analysis	Give sensors your bottom-line message first, and then work backwards quickly Offer a one-page "bottom-line" sheet with hard and fast evidence Issue a call to action page Provide information on where to go if you need help, and then leave people alone Reduce amount of handouts and discussion about processes

As stated earlier, presenters must be cautious in trying to neatly categorize audience members into those categories presented above and other similar personality types. Nonetheless, thinking about personality types is an effective tool for audience analysis. In fact, Miller suggests that in any given audience, a possible general breakdown based on the above-stated personality types might look like the following in Figure 5.1:

> "... thinking about personality types is an effective tool for audience analysis."

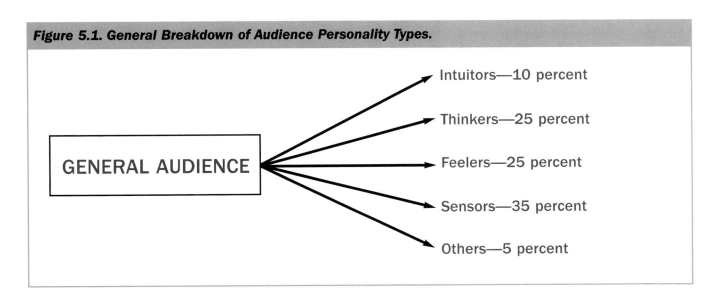

Figure 5.1. General Breakdown of Audience Personality Types.

GENERAL AUDIENCE

- Intuitors—10 percent
- Thinkers—25 percent
- Feelers—25 percent
- Sensors—35 percent
- Others—5 percent

Think about the logistics and details of your audience and its setting

How many times have you heard presenters begin their presentations with jokes that are inappropriate to their audiences? How many times have you tuned out to a presentation because the presenter showed his ignorance by incorrectly referring to an acronym involved in the organization's mission? What do you think of presenters who show overheads written in miniscule type, despite the fact that they are presenting before audiences of several hundred people? What is your immediate impression of presenters who incorrectly pronounce the names of high-ranking individuals before whom they are presenting? What is your expectation of the quality of presentations you will hear from presenters who arrive late to give their presentations and blame traffic for their tardiness? If for some reason you find that you cannot or do not conduct a full-scale audience analysis as outlined in this chapter (an unwise decision under *any* circumstance), at a minimum you *must* make certain that you are well-informed as to the logistics and details of your audience and the audience setting prior to giving your presentation.

From a bottom-line perspective, before you ever begin a presentation to an audience, you must gather general data to complement your needs assessment, demographic and psychographic profiles, and consideration of personality types. The minute you find yourself making a presentation, regardless of whether that presentation involves a job interview, a conversation with a professor about a grade, a talk before the leaders of your rugby team, or a commencement address in front of 300, you *must* do your homework in gathering some basic information that will help you conduct an audience analysis.

There are many questions that must be asked ahead of time in conducting an in-depth audience analysis with respect to logistics and details. One general way of thinking about logistics and details relates to answering the journalistic questions of *Who, What, When, Where, Why* and *How?*

Table 5.6 offers a template for gathering basic audience logistics and informational details. Presenters should complete this type of questionnaire before every single presentation, to the degree most appropriate.

Table 5.6. A Template for Audience Logistics, Analysis and Details.

Presentation/audience specifics	
Name of group/acronym	
Time Frame for Presentation (outline breaks)	
Date	
Location (specific site, address, city—request map to presentation location)	
Web site address	
Contact person(s)	
Title of Contact Person(s)	
Contact person(s): address Office phone Cell phone Home phone Pager	
Appropriate dress of presenter	
Audience attire	
Audience analysis	
Audience's purpose(s) in convening?	
Expected number in the audience	
Audience needs, e. g. basic; safety/security; belonging; esteem; self-actualization	
General demographic data of audience, e.g. age, occupation, income, genders	

Table 5.6. A Template for Audience Logistics, Analysis and Details (continued).

Audience analysis	
General psychographic data of audience, e.g. attitudes, ideals, values, beliefs, mission statement	
General personality types, e.g. sensors, feelers, thinkers, intuitors, etc.	
Presentation topic(s)	
Sensitive areas?	
Other speakers on the program (including phone numbers)	
Prior speakers from years past on your topic (including phone numbers)	
Knowledge levels of audience members to topic(s) you are presenting	
Additional presentation logistics and details	
Room arrangement, e.g. podium, head table, round tables, conference style, visual aids, equipment	
Key members of audience/organization from whom to gather more detailed information (include names and telephone numbers)	
General Notes	
Follow-up items	
Post-speech evaluation notes/follow-up information	

Conclusion

Once you have conducted your in-depth audience analysis as you prepare to give a talk or carry on a persuasive conversation, you can use the information you've gathered on your audience when practicing your message delivery. Scholars in academia, movie actors on Hollywood sets, comedians in nightclubs, and consultants who travel the country earning their living making public speeches all point to the value of knowing your audience in delivering effective messages.

Courtesy of Laima Druskis/Pearson Education

Understanding the members of your audience will help you connect with audience members both individually and collectively. You will be more comfortable in how you physically present yourself on the day of your talk, how you project your message with voice clarity and tone and inflexion, and in terms of what words you use, stories you tell, and statistics you offer in order to reach a majority of audience members, each with their own individual personality types.

Another benefit to conducting an in-depth audience analysis is to use the information to determine which audience you are actually speaking to—the one *inside* the room and/or the much bigger one *beyond* the walls of the room in which you are speaking, also known as the expanded target market (Wilson-Smith, 2005). Scholars suggest that when we give a public presentation, in most all cases we are trying to reach two audiences: those persons inside the room and the larger constituencies they represent. In other words, although you are presenting to 25 people ages 18–22, they represent all college-age people outside the classroom. Thus understanding the membership of those in the room can give you important information about the larger target market you may be trying to reach in order to maximize your effectiveness in message delivery.

Another next-step benefit from audience analysis relates to audience environment. Conducting a thorough audience analysis can expose possibly unanticipated pitfalls in effective message delivery, such as the presence of an audience member who will be publicly negative or even the presence of an entirely hostile audience. Professional speaker Larry Tracy (2005) suggests there are always those in an audience who would rather jeer than cheer. Thus, effective communicators must do their audience-analysis homework in advance in order to expose the possibility of hostile situations that reduce communication effectiveness.

Famed speaker and author Leo Buscaglia once said "there is no secret to being a successful communicator–just prepare, know your subject and care." Your homework is complete. You now *know your subject* by knowing your audience. Audience analysis will help you succeed in being an effective presenter and meeting your objectives, whether you are trying to talk your way out of a parking ticket, discuss a grade with a professor, persuade the college band to take a trip to a certain location, get that important job you want, deliver a commencement address, or even start a musical concert once you become famous like Mick Jagger. Presentations are a daily part of our lives, and thinking ahead about your audience is the key to success.

This chapter has suggested the following: (1) doing your homework via audience analysis is the critical component to the preparation and delivery of effective presentations; (2) audience analysis is a complex yet imperative process to effective communications; (3) audience analysis should take place long before a presenter comes before his or her audience; (4) audience analysis should take place regardless of the size of the audience; and (5) there are many different ways to conduct audience analyses, including thorough needs assessments, demographic and psychographic profiles, and personality assessments.

Former National Football League tackle, sports broadcaster and actor Merlin Olsen once said: "One of life's most painful moments comes when we must admit that we didn't do our homework, that we are not prepared." Audience analysis is about doing your homework so that you will succeed as a presenter. From hence forward, think and do your homework before you speak.

Courtesy of Dorling Kindersley Media Library

References

1 Beebe, S.A., Beebe, S.J., Ivy, D.K., Schmidt, W.V., Conaway, R.N., Richmond, V.P., & McCroskey, J.C. (2001). *Professional Communication Skills*. Boston, MA: Allyn & Bacon.

2 "Catapult yourself to the top—become an electrifying public speaker!" (2002, June) *Executive Focus, 19*.

3 Hartley, D. (2003). "Impressive communication makes a difference." *Nation's Cities Weekly, 26*, 8–9.

4 Laskowski, L. (2002). *A.U.D.I.E.N.C.E. Analysis—it's your key to success*. Power Pointers. Retrieved from http://powerpointers.com/showarticle.asp.

5 Miller, B.B. (1991, March). *Thinking on your feet*. Executive coaching seminar conducted at a management meeting of Living Centers of America, Inc. in Austin, Texas.

6 Rafe, S.C. (1990). *Think on your feet and make the best presentations of your life*. New York: Harper Business, A Division of Harper & Row Publishers.

7 Smith, T.E. & Frymier, A.B. (2006). "Get real: Does practicing speeches before an audience improve performance?" *Communication Quarterly, 54*, 111–125.

8 Tracy, L. (2005). "Taming hostile audiences." *Vital Speeches of the Day, 71*, 306–312.

9 Verderber, R.F. (2000). *The challenge of effective speaking*. Belmont, CA: Wadsworth/ Thompson Learning.

10 Walters, L. (1993). *Secrets of successful speakers—how you can motivate, captivate, and persuade*. New York: McGraw-Hill, Inc.

Notes

PART 2

Interpersonal and Group Communication

CHAPTER 6

Interviewing for Information Gathering

by Amy Schmisseur

Objectives

After studying Chapter 6, you should be able to do the following:

☐ Explain the three factors that distinguish an interview from other interactions.
☐ Prepare a schedule of questions for a moderately structured interview.
☐ Use a variety of techniques to polish your schedule of questions.
☐ Prepare an effective interview opening and closing.

Key Terms

TERM	DEFINITION
brainstorming	The creative process of generating uninterrupted, unevaluated ideas.
closed question	A question that invites a limited, shortened response.
clustering	The process of grouping similar ideas together to identify particular themes or topic areas.
dialogic interview	An interview in which all parties both ask and answer questions.
directive interview	An interview in which all questions are asked by the interviewer and answered by the interviewee.
double-barreled question	A question that simultaneously asks two questions.
formal interview	A premeditated interview that consists of a planned schedule of topics.
guessing question	A question that guesses at its own answer without waiting for input from the respondent.
impromptu interview	An interview that arises spontaneously in the course of conversation.
interaction	A dynamic, communicative exchange that occurs between two or more parties.
interpersonal communication	Human communication that occurs when people interact simultaneously with each other and attempt to mutually influence each other.
interview	The purposeful asking and answering of questions between two parties.
interview structure	The design of a schedule of questions for the interview.
interviewing	An interactive process between two parties where at least one of those parties has a predetermined and serious purpose and where the interaction involves the asking and answering of questions in achieving that purpose.
leading question	A question that attempts to steer the interviewee toward a particular response.
neutral question	A question that leaves the interviewee free to respond in a genuine, unbiased way.
open question	A question that invites an elaborated, detailed response.
panel interview	An interview that can consist of multiple interviewers and/or multiple interviewees.
primary question	A question that introduces a new topic or a new idea within a topic.
purpose	Your goal for the interview.
rapport	A sense of relationship, "we-ness."

TERM	DEFINITION
secondary question	A specific question that is derived from a primary question and probes for additional information.
speedy question	A question that follows another without giving the respondent a chance to respond.
spontaneous secondary question	A secondary question that arises out of information provided during an interview.
starter	The words you use to begin a question.

Introduction

Helping you develop sound professional communication skills is our goal in CMS 306M. Much of the process of learning professional communication skills is learning to recognize the ways your communication changes as a result of your audience—whether it is one, a few, or many individuals. Beginning with this chapter, the second part of the book is devoted to communication strategies appropriate for one-on-one and group communication in a professional setting.

Professional communication serves an essentially *strategic* function—that is, when at least one of the parties involved has a specific goal in mind other than just "chatting" with someone. This chapter focuses on common, strategic interpersonal interactions that typically take place between two people in a professional setting when one person is trying to gain information from another.

When you think of the word "interview," you may see yourself (neatly attired and tense) sitting across a desk from a potential employer, answering formal questions about yourself and your abilities. But you engage in less formal interviews nearly every day: When you meet with a professor to discuss an assignment or even when you network with co-workers at a work-sponsored happy hour, you are—whether you know it or not, and whether you are doing it *well*, or not—interviewing. This chapter focuses on the formal processes of interviewing, but you will find you can apply these skills in countless informal situations.

What is an Informational Interview?

What distinguishes an informational interview from other forms of interpersonal interaction, such as routine interactions with strangers, hanging out with friends, or telephone calls home? An interview is the kind of interaction that might occur when you make an appointment with your adviser to discuss your major, meet with a prospective landlord about an apartment, participate in research projects for departmental faculty, or gather information from individuals as part of a class project. Each of these scenarios clearly displays three characteristics that experts Charles Stewart and William Cash outline as essential to the idea of interviewing: (1) an interactive process between two parties, (2) during which at least one party has a strategic purpose or goal in mind, (3) which is to be accomplished through the asking and answering of questions.[1]

> **"... interviewing involves the exchange of communication through an ongoing, dynamic process of interaction."**

Let's explore each of these characteristics.

Interviews involve an exchange between two parties.

As with any type of interpersonal communication, interviewing involves the exchange of communication through an ongoing, dynamic process of interaction. We say that the interview exchange takes place between two "parties" rather than between two "individuals" because interviews often involve more than two individuals, while still representing two (and only two) distinct interests. For example, large corporations often meet potential entry-level employees in an interview format called a panel interview, in which multiple interviewee(s) represent one party while those conducting the interview represent the second party. (When communicative exchanges occur among *more* than two parties, we speak of small-group interactions, rather than interviews.)

Interviews involve a strategic purpose or goal.

For a communicative exchange to qualify as an interview, at least one of the two parties must have a strategic purpose or goal in mind. This stipulation is the first consideration that distinguishes an interview from other forms of interpersonal interactions. If neither party to the interaction is strategically pursuing a goal, then the conversation is just that, a conversation.

In informal situations, conversations can turn instantly into interviews—and interviews back into conversations—as the interaction flows and individual purposes form and fall apart. Say you are chatting on the 40 Acres bus with a stranger who sees your textbook and mentions a communication course that she is taking. And it is one for which you are thinking about registering! And your date with the registrar is tomorrow! Suddenly you form a purpose and start conducting an impromptu interview.

> You: Is it good? Is it hard? Is it worth taking? How's the professor?
>
> Stranger: Well . . . Actually, I'm taking it at Baylor. I'm just in town visiting my brother.

Just as suddenly your purpose dissolves and you are back in conversation. Now your would-be respondent forms a purpose of her own: She is thinking of transferring and now she wants to interview *you*, to find out what you know about the Communication Studies department, how you like UT, and what it is like to live in Austin. In the space of a few sentences, each of you has been an aimless conversationalist, an informal interviewer, and an informal interviewee.

> "... formal interviews ... are distinguished by planning, preparation, structure, and design, in service of a predetermined goal."

More formal interviews are usually premeditated, and are distinguished by planning, preparation, structure, and design, all in service of a stable and predetermined goal. That goal can include gathering important information for your own purposes, exploring your respondent's values and beliefs, establishing rapport, making a positive impression, or exchanging perspectives and viewpoints on different issues. As with any strategic interaction, the goals of the various parties may coincide or collide. "Newsmaker" interviews between journalists and public figures, for example, often show the alignment of compatible purposes, as in the *Meet the Press* interview between NBC host Tim Russert and President George W. Bush during the 2004 Primary season, when both the interviewer and interviewee had an interest in putting the president in front of the nation.

Interviews involve the asking and answering of questions.

The final and perhaps most recognizable feature of an interview is the asking and answering of focused, specific questions. While conversations often contain questions and answers, interviews feature questions and answers as their primary content, especially questions that are planned in advance to elicit specific information.

Some interviews, known as directive interviews, consist primarily of an interviewer who asks all the questions and an interviewee who does all of the answering. These types of interviews typically are done as survey research. If you have ever picked up your phone to find yourself participating in a market research study or political poll, you may recall that you were given few opportunities to ask your own questions. Other types of interviews, less directive in nature, take the form of a dialogue in which both parties feel free to initiate topics. While the interviewer still asks a larger percentage of the questions in such a dialogic interview, the interviewee participates more actively in creating the interview's content than in the directive approach. Many employment interviews are structured as dialogues. Although the potential employer continues to ask most of the questions, the interviewee is encouraged to ask questions throughout the interview (or at certain points during the interview), creating a more interactive interview for both parties. Both directive and nondirective approaches have their place in gathering useful information and in meeting specific communication objectives.

> "... interviews feature questions and answers as their primary content ... to elicit specific information."

The purposeful asking and answering of questions is much of what differentiates an interview from a conversation. Paradoxically, a good interview feels very much like a conversation as it unfolds. Think about conversations you have on a daily basis. In many instances, those conversations are easy and comfortable, and the interaction is fairly smooth and seamless. A good interview should feel much the same way—interesting and engaging, not stilted and mechanical. Although preparing for an important formal interview requires research, planning, and practice (as does preparing for a musical recital, for example), the resulting performance should *flow*. And that outcome is likely only when you are prepared enough to genuinely participate in the real-time exchange actually taking place.

> "... a *good* interview feels very much like a conversation as it unfolds."

How *do* you prepare for an interview? The perspective of this chapter is that of the interviewer, who has the responsibility of directing the interview. (Keep in mind that interviewees should prepare for formal interviews as well, especially when the interview will have an impact on the interviewee's own life.)

Preparing for an Interview

While an impromptu interview consists of spontaneous questions generated in the inspiration of the moment, a formal interview—especially an important formal interview—should be carefully thought out in advance. The purpose of the interview, the structure you select, the topics you generate, and the types of questions you ask in your interview greatly determine the quality of the answers from your respondent.

Courtesy of Pearson Education

Decide on a purpose for your interview.

Before you engage in any interview, you should define its <u>purpose</u>. Having a clearly defined purpose will help you construct a meaningful, cohesive schedule of questions, which will guide your prompts and direct your interviewee's answers. As you define your purpose for any interview, think about what you hope to get from the interview in its content and relationship dimensions. Perhaps you are seeking certain information, but you are looking to develop your professional network as well. Also give some thought as to why your interviewee is participating. Why has this person agreed to the interview? What does this person want to accomplish through the interaction?

Exercise 6.1. Your 5-Point Agenda.

To stay focused during an information-gathering interview, it is helpful to have a clear idea of what you want to learn from the interaction. To keep from rambling, you might use a 5-point agenda to stress the most important pieces of information you want to gather from your expert interviewee.

To put together your 5-point agenda, consider the following questions:

What are the 5 most important things about this topic I need to ask?

What 5 things about this topic are unclear which require clarification?

What 5 things might you be able to ask only an expert about this topic?

1. _____

   _____

   _____

2. _____

   _____

   _____

3. _____

   _____

   _____

4. _____

   _____

   _____

5. _____

   _____

   _____

Choose an interview structure.

Once you have defined your purpose for conducting the interview, you should consider the interview's structure. Your choice of structure is determined by its purpose. The structure you choose, in turn, determines the degree of preparation you will need for the interview and the flexibility of questions you can ask. If, for example, you intend to interview a number of people and you want to make sure that you ask each interviewee the same questions, you should create a standardized schedule of questions. Similarly, if you want to be sure to ask your respondent very specific questions, you will want to prepare those questions in depth and in advance. In contrast, if you want to let your interviewees' individual responses impact the questions you ask, or your questions are more general and unordered, then you will want to create a much broader, less defined schedule of questions. Generally speaking, an interview structure can be highly scheduled, nonscheduled, or moderately scheduled.[2]

Highly scheduled interviews

As you might expect from its name, a highly scheduled interview structure is a detailed flowchart that contains all questions the interviewer is to ask. It allows no deviation in either the order or the wording of questions, thus requiring the interviewer to ask the same questions of each respondent in the same way.[3] (See Figure 6.1 for examples of questions from a highly scheduled interview.) You may want to use a highly scheduled interview structure when you want to replicate the interview and compare responses, such as when you are surveying a large population of people. Faculty in the Department of Communication Studies often use highly scheduled interviews when collecting survey data so that they can analyze and compare responses across hundreds of participants. Human resources representatives for large corporations often use this approach for employment interviews to ensure that all applicants receive the same interview protocol.

The major advantage of the highly scheduled approach is that it allows those gathering information to maintain consistency and comparability across responses. The highly scheduled interview has two major disadvantages: First, it ties the hands of interviewers and dictates exactly what can and cannot be said. Second, it leaves little room for interviewees to expand their responses or volunteer unexpected but potentially valuable information.

Nonscheduled interviews

As an interviewer, you may encounter situations in which you have little time to prepare for an interview or your purpose for conducting the interview is so broad that you want to let the conversation itself direct the structure of the interview. It is in these instances that you may want to conduct a nonscheduled interview, which consists of questions that introduce general topic areas and ideas, not specific issues.[4] (See Figure 6.2 for an example of questions from a nonscheduled interview.)

The advantage of the nonscheduled approach is that it allows you to go into an interview without preconceived ideas or expectations. In addition, with this approach and the amount of latitude it provides, you *may* be able to get your interviewee to expound on topics in unusual depth. However, given its loosely constructed nature, the nonscheduled approach has significant disadvantages: You run the risk of losing control over both time and content, especially with interviewees who tend to veer off course with their responses. When you conduct a nonscheduled interview, you need to monitor your time carefully and be able to redirect your respondent to the original line of questioning, if necessary.

Figure 6.1. Questions from a Highly Scheduled Interview.

I. What three courses have you taken at UT that helped you most in your career?

[Name of first course] _____

[Name of second course] _____

[Name of third course] _____

> **Figure 6.1. Continued.**
>
> A. Let me ask you a few questions about [name first course].
> 1. Why did you take [name first course]?
> 2. How has [name first course] proved valuable to you?
> 3. What grade did you get in [name first course]?
>
> B. Now, let me ask you a few questions about [name second course].
> 1. Why did you take [name second course]?
> 2. How has [name second course] proved valuable to you?
> 3. What grade did you get in [name second course]?
>
> C. Finally, let me ask you a few questions about [name third course].
> 1. Why did you take [name third course]?
> 2. How has [name third course] proved valuable to you?
> 3. What grade did you get in [name third course]?

> **Figure 6.2. Topics for a Nonscheduled Interview.**
>
> Some topics to bring up include the following:
>
> - The experiences that have been most valuable to the interviewee while at UT.
> - The classes that the interviewee is glad he/she took.
> - The lessons the interviewee wishes he/she had learned at UT, but didn't.

Moderately scheduled interviews

The moderately scheduled interview structure divides the interview into specific, major questions with possible probing questions under each.[5] (See Figure 6.3 for an example of questions from a moderately scheduled interview.) Because this type of interview structure leaves room for follow-up questions and probes beyond those on the original schedule, it gives you freedom to adapt the interview to the actual flow of conversation. You may want to use a moderately scheduled structure when you want to explore your respondent's thoughts and opinions in depth, or you need flexibility to ensure that the respondent's answers are accurate and complete. The advantage of this structure is that it preserves your ability to direct the interview while allowing for the exchange of rich, insightful information. The major disadvantage is that you give up some control over the interview's direction and leave some issues to chance.

> **Figure 6.3. Question from a Moderately Scheduled Interview.**
>
> 1. What classes did you take at UT that you've found particularly valuable in your job?
> a. Why did you take them?
> b. What did you learn?
> c. How aware were you at the time that the classes would be valuable to you?
> d. How have you used what you learned in your job?

Generate topics for your interview.

Once you have decided your interview's purpose and the type of schedule that you should use, your next task is to begin generating the topics you want to cover. While this task may seem straightforward, it is our experience that most students struggle when coming up with meaningful topics to both themselves and their subjects. Indeed, "What should I ask?" is one of the most frequent questions we get from students working on their first schedule of questions.

One way to begin this task of generating topics is to borrow techniques from the literature on <u>brainstorming</u>. The term "brainstorming" was coined more than 50 years ago by advertising executive Alex Osborn, who taught a set of creative techniques to help, as he said, the brain *storm* a creative problem "in commando fashion." To brainstorm a problem, you generate a great many ideas without pausing to censor or criticize those ideas. The wilder and more exaggerated the idea, the better. This is especially true at this early stage of the creative process because it is easier to rein in an idea later than it is to come up with original ideas in the first place.[6] An elementary technique for associating those ideas is <u>clustering</u>, so called because it involves the nonlinear grouping together of related concepts to establish topics or themes.

Begin the process of generating topics by jotting down—in no particular order—everything you can think of that you might want to ask your respondent. At this point, you are brainstorming, so don't worry about how the question is phrased, worded, or even spelled. Simply write down as many questions as you can think of without limiting your ideas and thoughts. Write fast, and write for no more than, say, 10 minutes. Figure 6.4 shows a brainstorming list created by a UT student about to interview a CMS graduate about her job and career opportunities in her field. (Notice the bad handwriting, spelling, and grammar.)

Figure 6.4. A Brainstorming List for an Interview about Career Opportunities.

Job—what like about it, don't like?

How'd you <u>know</u> that your field was what you'd be interested in?

Obstacles on job?

How get started in field?

What classes did you take in college to help you prepare for this job? Useful?

College—where?

Why choose your major?

Where headed in future?

How can your field improve?

What *do* you do in your job?

What would you change about your job?

Once you have brainstormed a substantial list of possible questions, look for similarities, or themes—that is, look for the way that some of the questions you want to ask seem to "hang together," or *cluster* into themes. The list in Figure 6.4 seems to cluster around the interviewee's present job duties, past experiences, and future expectations. (Depending on your purpose for an interview, of course, the themes you will find will differ.) Notice how the questions in each cluster begin to *look* like they belong together. Figure 6.5 shows how a student has taken a list of brainstormed questions about wellness and clustered them into potential themes or topics.

As shown in Figure 6.6, once you have identified several clusters of questions, determined and labeled the identifying theme or topic that holds each cluster together, you can continue to add more questions as they relate to each topic and begin to "clean up" your questions so that they are clear, concise, and properly phrased (we will address this more specifically later). As you continue to brainstorm questions for each potential theme or topic, you will notice that your themes may change slightly. The student in this example went from one set of themes and then modified those themes as he or she added more questions. Thus, as your questions become crystallized, so do your topics.

Figure 6.5. Clusters of Brainstormed Questions about Challenges to Wellness.

Cluster 1—Wellness related questions

What defines wellness?

Challenges to wellness?

How do I achieve wellness?

What should I change about my lifestyle to achieve wellness?

Cluster 2—Western v. Eastern Philosophies

How did you get interested in Western philosophies of wellness?

How did you get interested in Eastern philosophies of wellness?

What training exists?

Cluster 3—Wellness-related careers

What courses did you take in college to help you prepare for this job?

College—where?

Why choose your major?

Figure 6.6. Clusters of Additional Brainstormed Questions about Wellness.

Wellness-related Career Questions

How did you get started in the field?

Where did you go to college?

How did you know you'd be interested in this field?

Describe courses in college that helped you prepare for this job.

Why did you choose the major that you did?

Questions about Symptoms

What symptoms signal a lack of wellness?

What are some of the obstacles to achieving wellness?

What do you do personally to maintain wellness?

What would you change about your lifestyle?

Questions related to effects of lack of wellness

What effects does being "unwell" have in a person's life?

What are the physical manifestations?

How can I learn more about treatment?

What treatments are available?

Describe different challenges to treatment.

At the end of the brainstorming and clustering exercises, you will not need to ask yourself, "What will I talk about?" You will have generated a number of solid topics and the beginnings of your questions, as shown in Figure 6.7.

Figure 6.7. List of Topics Generated through Brainstorming and Clustering.

Topics for interview:

Preparing for a career in wellness

Managing the career

Understanding the field

Understanding symptoms of wellness

Responses to poor wellness

Construct your schedule of questions.

Let's pause for a brief recap: You have determined your purpose. (Check!). You've chosen an interview structure. (Check!). And, you have used brainstorming and mind-mapping techniques to generate your topics. (Check!). Excellent. Now it is time to construct your actual schedule of questions. A moderately scheduled interview should contain roughly one major question for each two minutes of the planned interview. For example, a 30-minute interview should have about 15 questions.

So why can't you just take your rough list of topics and questions and call it a day? Because creating interview questions is something of an *art*.[7] Do you think that Barbara Walters or Ted Koppel just "wing it?" Do you think that Jon Stewart's own brand of short "newsmaker interviews" just happens to be thought provoking *and* funny? How well you plan your questions determines the quality of the responses you receive.[8] In a brief interview, you may lack the time to let a conversation meander and find its own shape. Think how disappointed you would be to end an interview without anything really being said, and without getting the quality and quantity of information you were seeking.

> "... creating interview questions is something of an *art* ... How well you plan your questions determines the quality of the responses you receive."

Design your interview questions to invite the quality and quantity of information you want.[9] As you craft each question, keep two technical issues in mind: First, make sure you create both primary and secondary questions. Second, make strategic decisions about when to ask open and closed questions.

Primary and secondary questions

Within the topics you choose for your interview schedule, some of the questions you write will be primary questions and some will be secondary questions. Primary questions are designed to open up new topics or areas within a topic and can be clearly understood independent of the sequence in which they are asked. In other words, primary questions make sense standing alone, without other questions to give them context. Here are a few examples of primary questions:

What three courses at UT have helped you most in your career?

How did you get your current job?

What challenges do you face on your job?

In contrast, secondary questions (also called *probing questions*) are designed to delve deeper into a topic that you have already opened with a primary question. You use probing questions to engage your interviewee and gather additional meaningful and relevant information. Here are some examples of secondary questions that would fit under the primary question above:

> Why did you take that particular course?
>
> How has it helped you?
>
> Did you do well in it?

For a moderately scheduled interview you should plan several secondary questions under each primary question in your schedule. Depending on the interaction that emerges between you and your interviewee, you will find that some of your planned questions will become irrelevant as new information becomes available—and other, unplanned questions will arise. This situation is perfectly normal. Indeed, a proficient interviewer often "probes off the schedule"—that is, asks <u>spontaneous secondary questions</u> based on the verbal and nonverbal cues of the interviewee. Spontaneous secondary questions cannot be planned in advance because they simply occur "in real-time." You use them to gather more information on a single idea or issue as well as to offer varying degrees of topic control for the interviewer.[10] Here are some examples of more spontaneous secondary questions:

> Really? Were you surprised that it worked out that way?
>
> It sounds like that was a real learning experience for you. . . .
>
> And so what helped you feel comfortable working with people you didn't know?

In addition to the content-specific secondary questions that you plan or spontaneously generate, you can use four *strategic* types of secondary questions to invite specific kinds of answers from your respondent: nudging probes, restatement probes, summary probes, and closing probes. Each of these types of probe has its own distinct purpose; it is likely that you will use all four of them during the course of your interview.

Nudging probes. You can use verbal or nonverbal nudging probes (also called *encouragement probes*) to encourage a respondent who has stopped short of providing sufficient information or hesitates about revealing more information.[11] Verbal nudges include statements as simple as the following:

> Go on.
>
> Really?
>
> Uh-huh.
>
> And . . .?

Nonverbal nudges can include encouraging hand gestures, interested facial expressions, and affirmative nods of the head—anything that implies that you are engaged and want to hear more.

Restatement probes. You can use restatement probes to ask a question in a different way. Restatement probes are useful to steer a respondent back onto topic, reintroduce an aspect of a question that hasn't been answered, reframe a question that was not understood, or exert subtle pressure in the face of a reluctance to answer:

> We were talking about classes you took at UT. What was another class you took?
>
> You talk about how hard it was. What did you do to *overcome* these challenges?
>
> What I *meant* to ask you just now was . . .
>
> If you don't want to talk about it, I understand, but it would help me see . . .

Using restatement probes allows you to control and direct the flow of conversation.

Summary probes. You can use summary probes to recap or paraphrase the ideas and thoughts of your respondent and reflect them back for comment. Summary probes are especially useful when your respondent's answers are vague or unclear and you want to make sure that you understand your respondent's intentions, or you want to confirm that your respondent is prepared to "own" a statement:

> So what you mean is that . . .
>
> So what I hear you saying is that . . .
>
> If I understand you correctly, you believe . . .
>
> Am I correct in saying that . . .

Using summarizing statements helps you make sure that you are interpreting your respondent's words in a responsible way, so that you can report the interview fairly. Summarizing statements help you become both a credible and trustworthy interviewer.

Closing probes. You can use closing probes to "close the door" on a particular question or larger topic area as you prepare to move on to another secondary or primary question. With a closing probe, you can take one last opportunity to gather information you may have missed and invite your respondent to conclude the topic with a final response. Your closing probe also signals to the interviewee that you are seeking to move onto the next topic or idea within a topic. Closing probes include the following examples:

> I'd like to move to my next question now.
>
> Before we move on, I'd just like to ask you one more thing.
>
> Is there anything else you'd like to add before we move on?
>
> I think I understand now; thanks for covering that issue in such depth.

Using closing probes allows you to shape the interview and keep your respondent aware of the interview's structure (and that it *has* a structure).

Closed and open questions

The second issue to keep in mind when writing your schedule of questions is the difference between <u>closed questions</u> and <u>open questions</u>. Closed questions tend to restrict an interviewee's response to just a few options—and in many cases, to only two: "yes" or "no." As shown in the following example:

> You: Did you like your first job?
>
> Her: Yes.

In contrast, open questions give interviewees more freedom in determining the degree to which they will respond.

> You: Tell me about your first job.
>
> Her: Well, at first I was a little intimidated because I'd never been in that kind of situation before. After a while, though, when I got more comfortable . . .

Notice how you are much more likely to receive interesting and rich information when you ask a question that is open rather than closed. An open question invites an interviewee to provide information filtered through personal insight, at whatever length seems appropriate.

This observation does not mean that you *never* want to use closed questions; in fact, they are especially efficient when you want "just the facts, ma'am." In the following example, the first two sets of closed questions and answers set the stage for the final open question and its open answer:

You:	When did you graduate?
Her:	Nineteen ninety-six.
You:	When was the last time you were back?
Her:	Oh, probably 2000.
You:	Have things changed much?
Her:	Are you kidding? I remember when I first came to UT, you could . . .

Interviewers generally structure *most* of their primary and secondary questions as open questions, letting any necessary closed questions "just happen" as spontaneous secondary questions. For the interview schedule you write as part of your interviewing assignment in this course, do not include *any* closed prompts at all. Why not? Just imagine conducting an interview like this:

You:	Did you like UT?
Her:	Sure.
You:	Did you like it a lot?
Her:	Yeah, I liked it a lot.
You:	Was Austin different when you were here?
Her:	Yeah, really different.
You:	Could you elaborate?
Her:	Nah.

For a five-minute interview like this, you would need about a hundred questions!

(Remember Chris Farley's excruciating interview with Paul McCartney on *Saturday Night Live*? Farley: "You remember when you were with The Beatles?" McCartney: "Yeah, sure." Farley: "That was awesome!" McCartney: "Yeah, it was.")[12]

One trick when crafting open questions versus closed questions is to pay attention to the words you use to begin the question, the starter. Examples of starters such as *do, will, can, is* and their variations (*did, would, could, was,* etc.) often lead to closed questions:

Do you intend to stay with your current employer?

Would you recommend starting with a large or small company?

Can you tell me how I can get into this line of work?

Is your job interesting?

In contrast, starters such as *tell me about, what, describe,* and *explain* help you develop open questions:

Tell me about the pros and cons of staying with your current employer.

What do you recommend for people looking at both large and small companies?

Describe what I should do to get into this line of work.

Explain what makes your job interesting.

Notice that you can arrange any content into either closed or open prompts:

Closed: *Do* you intend to stay with your current employer?

Open: *Tell me about* the benefits of staying with your current employer.

Two powerful starters are the words *what* and *how*, which can begin either closed or open questions, depending on the subsequent words. For example, a question such as "What courses did you take in college?" may feel like a closed question to respondents, who may then simply list the different classes they took rather than tell you something meaningful about them. On the other hand, a question such as, "What did you study in college?" may feel much more open. Similarly, "How important is *x* to your work?" may elicit the one word answer "very;" whereas "What is the relevance of *x* to your work?" may yield a more interesting and in-depth response.

Examine your questions for language problems.

So far you have determined your purpose, chosen an interview schedule type, generated topics, written primary and secondary questions, and crafted those questions to emphasize openness. You have finished now, right? Not quite. Now it is time to polish your interview schedule by examining it for evidence of ambiguous or complex phrasing, irrelevant or offensive content, leading questions, and speedy or guessing questions.

Ambiguous and complex phrasing

How you phrase your questions often determines the type of response you receive. Ambiguous and overly complex phrasing creates questions that introduce misunderstandings between interviewer and respondent. No matter how good the content of your questions, poor phrasing will diminish your rapport with your respondent and compromise the value of the information you receive.

Try not to use ambiguous phrasing. Use language that is simple, specific, concrete, and clear.[13] You do not want your respondent to spend valuable time during the interview deciphering your meaning. Even an apparently simple question such as, "Did you go to a large high school?" can get you in trouble. (Another reason why you should not ask closed questions!) What you mean by "large" and what your respondent may mean can be vastly different—you may come from a west Texas town where 300 students would be very large indeed; your respondent may come from Dallas, where 2,000 students is not remarkable. You ask the question; your respondent answers; and you have started your exchange based on different understandings about your topics. (This is yet another reason to use restatement and summary probes.) As part of the polishing process, read your schedule of questions to see if any of them can be easily misunderstood—then fix them.

Exercise 6.2. Open and Closed Interview Questions.

Part of the research you might gather for your presentations might come from interviews conducted with experts on a topic. For this reason, it is critical you understand how to organize and facilitate a great interview. Often, we do not realize how many closed-ended questions we ask in everyday conversation. In an interview, it is important to avoid closed-ended questions as much as possible. This activity can be used to help you practice this skill.

Activity:

Find a partner. You will ask your partner questions about him/herself for 3 minutes. Then, your partner will ask you questions about yourself for 3 minutes. If your partner asks you a closed-ended question, please only give a one-word answer and stop talking.

When you ask a closed-ended question and receive only a one-word answer, try to rephrase the question such that it is open-ended and elicits a richer response from your interviewing partner.

Example:

Closed-Ended: Do you think this activity is a good one?

_____

_____

_____

_____

_____

_____

Now Open-Ended: What is challenging about this activity for you?

_____

_____

_____

_____

_____

_____

A second phrasing issue is what Stewart and Cash refer to as *complexity*.[14] Avoid asking complicated, wordy, and detailed questions that leave respondents wondering what exactly you want to know. Most complexity issues occur because the interviewer is trying to get a question to accomplish too much at once. For example, the double-barreled question (also called a "two-in-one") literally asks two questions in one:

> Why did you choose this particular career and how do you feel about your decision after so many years?

Notice the connecting conjunction. Using *and*, *but*, and *or* is a clue that you are heading toward a double-barreled question. When you ask a two-in-one question, you make your respondent expend unnecessary effort deciding which part of the question to answer first. Furthermore, in trying to answer both questions, the respondent may not answer either one very well.[15]

Questions also can be complex by being too broad. For example, "Tell me about yourself" a question frequently asked in interviews, is so broad and reveals so little about the interviewer's purpose, that interviewees are often unsure how to answer. Not knowing the direction in which you (as the interviewer) would like the interview to go, your respondent may choose a response at random, which is unlikely to further your goals. As part of the polishing process, read your schedule of questions to see if any of them are overly complex, then revise your questions, keeping them short and focused.

Irrelevant and offensive content

Another issue to consider as you polish your schedule of questions is what they communicate about your intentions—or lack thereof.[16] The two major problems with content are irrelevance and potential offensiveness. Irrelevant questions betray a lack of focus on your part, undercut your credibility, and derail the interview into a rambling conversation. While irrelevant questions can provoke interesting answers, they distract your respondent from providing the information you want to receive. Study your schedule of questions and ask yourself whether each question you have written advances your purpose. If it does not, take it out.

During the interview itself, avoid opportunities to spontaneously follow (or take) your respondent down a rabbit hole. Another exchange from the immortal *Chris Farley Show*:

McCartney: . . . No, no, no, Chris. I get asked that all the time in interviews. Maria Shriver asked the same question last week.

Farley: Really? Did you know that she's married to Arnold Schwartzenegger?

McCartney: Yeah. I've heard that.

Farley: Did you see *Terminator?*

McCartney: No, I missed that one.

Farley: That was a pretty awesome flick. OK . . . Remember . . . you remember when you were with The Beatles. . . .[17]

If irrelevant questions make you seem less credible, offensive questions make you seem unfriendly—not generally a recipe for a productive interview (unless, of course, you work for Chris Matthews or Bill O'Reilly). Questions that may seem relevant and innocuous to you, such as "How old are you, anyway?" "How much money do you make?" may offend your respondent. Review your schedule of questions for those questions that are potentially offensive. Rewrite them or remove them entirely, if you can. If they are absolutely essential to the interview, word them as delicately as possible and move them to a position that is toward the end of interview, after you have established trust and rapport. By that time, your respondent may feel more comfortable and respond even if offended—or may decline to respond without taking offense.

Leading questions

A third problem with many interview schedules is the presence of leading questions, which indicate to the respondent that you prefer one type of response over another.[18]

Can you believe that he's skipping the meeting? You aren't, right?

Is this is a great class, or what?

You won't mind taking notes for me, will you?

While these examples demonstrate a blatant desire for a particular answer ("yes," "yes," and "no"), leading questions can be much less obvious, expressing bias subtly through verbal innuendo or nonverbal gestures and facial expressions, such as the following:

Would you say that you are in favor of the proposed tuition increase?

Like all good Texans, do you enjoy barbecue?

It's sad when people like us have to do this work alone. Can I sign you up?

The above examples suggest which response is desired by assuming one answer as the norm. Rarely do interviewees want to contradict normative attitudes and beliefs; to the extent that questioners assert that one view is better than the other, interviewees may feel more compelled to answer "yes," even if they really mean "no."

Sometimes interviewers ask unintentionally leading questions. In other cases, interviewers plot leading questions to force or trap respondents into providing answers that they would not ordinarily give. Intentional or not, the outcome is still the same—the interviewee isn't given the opportunity to respond in a way that is open, honest, and freely chosen. Read your schedule of questions to make sure that you transform either type of leading question into a <u>neutral question</u>.

You can neutralize unintentional leading questions by making them open (rather than closed) and by ensuring that starters come at the beginning of the questions (rather than at the end). You can neutralize intentional leading questions by removing your point of view. Each example in Figure 6.8 shows the effects of all three types of neutralization.

Figure 6.8. Neutralizing leading questions.

Leading question	Neutral question
You are going to the game, aren't you?	Are you going to the game?
Don't you just hate that new tax plan?	What do you think about the new tax plan?
Wasn't the original movie better than that awful remake?	How do you think the remake compares to the original?

Speedy and guessing questions

Finally, purge your interview of questions that actually prevent the respondent from responding. Two types of questions that cause this problem are the speedy question and the <u>guessing question</u>—both are more likely to appear in the interview you conduct than the schedule of questions you write.

<u>Speedy questions</u> occur when you ask two or more questions back to back, without giving the interviewee time to answer one before you ask another. Interviewers often ask speedy questions because the interviewer is anxious to get a number of questions in, and thus runs ahead of the interviewee. Examples of speedy questions include

Why did you come to UT? Was it because of the sports?

Are you going to the concert? What other plans do you have?

Taking time to listen to your respondent's answers is the solution to this problem. You also may fall into the habit of asking speedy questions if your respondent pauses to think before answering the question. Uncomfortable with the silence, you may begin to rephrase the question before the interviewee has had a chance to answer it. Remember that silence is sometimes necessary as the interviewee thinks about how to properly respond to your question. Try not to cut off this process. Give the interviewee ample time to respond and pay attention to nonverbal clues before jumping in with another question.

The other type of question that prevents the respondent from responding is the guessing question,[19] in which you jump ahead of the interviewee to answer your own question, rather than waiting for the interviewee's thoughts and opinions. Whatever answers the respondent ends up giving will be altered by responding to your characterizations. Some examples of guessing questions include

Guessing: Did you approach her about the problem because you were angry?

Correct: Why did you approach her about the problem?

Guessing: Do you go to UT because of the strong athletic program?

Correct: Why do you attend UT?

Interviewing Principles in Practice

As you watch the sample interview in class, write down examples of the following types of questions. In what ways was the outcome of the interview affected by the kinds of questions asked? If some of these questions had been asked differently, would the interview have been more or less effective? Were any obvious or important questions omitted? Share your thoughts with your instructor and classmates.

Was this interview directive or dialogic?

List two examples of the interviewer's <u>primary</u> questions:

1.

2.

Please list a <u>spontaneous secondary</u> question:

Please provide examples of a(n):

○ Open question:

○ Closed questions:

○ Leading question:

○ Nudging probe:

○ Restatement probe:

○ Summary probe:

○ Closing probe:

○ Guessing question:

Were the interviewer's questions:

Ambiguous or unambiguous?
Examples:

Irrelevant or relevant?
Examples:

Offensive? Why or why not?
Examples:

Speedy?

Special thanks to Becky LaVally, The University of Texas at Austin

Putting It All Together

Now that you have prepared the body of your interview, you need to prepare a memorable, if much less formal, opening and closing to the interview to capitalize on the power of first and last impressions. Although you will not write a script, or memorize what you will say, it is good to invest some time in planning.

Prepare a confidence-building opening.

Good openings are necessary for putting your respondent at ease, building rapport, and establishing a clear agenda or procedure for the interview. You have a very brief window of opportunity to make a good first impression, so giving some attention to the initial few seconds of interaction will serve you well in the long run. Don't forget about the value of what you *do* as well as what you say.

In advance of the interview, clearly explain why you have chosen your respondent and what you hope to accomplish in the interview. This will help your respondent feel confident about participating and getting into the proper frame of mind. Make sure to dress appropriately for the interview. Do not overdress *or* under dress. (When in doubt, err toward professional rather than casual dress.)

The opening of the interview itself should consist of an introduction, a rapport-builder, and an orientation. (See the sample interview outline at the end of this chapter.)

- ❏ **Introduction.** Meet your respondent with a clear, confident introduction, good eye contact, and a firm handshake to convey sincerity. Avoid a handshake that is too strong (i.e., "the death grip") or one that is too soft and mild (i.e., "the limp rag"). State your name and the purpose of your interview.

- ❏ **Rapport-builder.** Spend the first few moments initiating rapport-building exchanges. Make each exchange count with situation-specific small talk. Avoid generic cocktail party ice-breakers such as "How are you?" and "Great weather, huh?" Instead, speak to the specific situation. You can convey greetings from a mutual acquaintance, such as "My uncle asked me to tell you hello," or observe items and artifacts unique to the interviewee and ask about them.[20] If, for example, you notice a UT diploma hanging on someone's wall, you can raise a question about their years at UT, beginning an informal conversation that builds a sense of commonality.

- ❏ **Orientation.** Before turning to your schedule of questions, discuss procedures involved with the interview. Give your interviewee a sense of the topics you plan to cover. Be particularly specific about how long the interview will take. People are much more likely to enjoy the interview process and be willing to engage in it again if they understand what to expect and if the interviewer respects their time. Make sure to ask interviewees if they have any questions before you begin. This courtesy allows them to resolve any concerns or questions they may have and will help them feel more comfortable in providing thoughtful responses to your questions.

Prepare a satisfying closing.

Imagine how disappointing it would be to sit through a stimulating interview but have it end on a sour note. Just like first impressions, final impressions are crucial in developing new relationships. Often, the interview closing is what the interviewee will remember most. However, as even experienced interviewers know, breaking away from the flow of conversation and concluding the interview can be a tricky and rather awkward process.[21]

Just before the allotted time comes to an end, offer to close the interview—whether you have finished or not. If you have finished, signal the close of the interview and forewarn the interviewee that the interview is ending by using such phrases as "Well, it's nearly time for us to conclude," or "I want to thank you for your time today." If you have not finished, mention that the time is nearly up and suggest arranging another meeting time to conclude the interview. By giving your respondent the choice of continuing the interview past its allotted time now or continuing it another day, you signal a clear respect for the interviewee's time—something that will go a long way in developing and maintaining long-term relationships. At this point, the interviewee can either agree to continue or accept your invitation to close.[22]

After your "bid" for a close has been accepted, the closing of the interview itself should consist of a brief summary, a desire for future contact, and the expression of appreciation. (Again, see the sample interview outline at the end of this chapter.)

- ❑ **Summary.** Provide your respondent with a brief summary of what you learned in the interview and how it will be particularly helpful to you. Doing so makes interviewees feel as though agreeing to the interview was a worthwhile investment of their time.

- ❑ **Future contact.** Make sure to establish an expectation of some degree of future contact with your interviewee. Remember that interviews create relationships that do not necessarily end with the interview. Finding a way to make future contact with your interviewee helps to build relationships and future contacts. Ask the interviewee if you can call with additional questions. Offer a business card and suggest that you would appreciate talking with them again in the future.

- ❑ **Appreciation.** Continue building rapport with the interviewee by thanking your respondent. After you leave, follow up by writing a brief thank-you note, which can be handwritten, typed, or sent as an email, depending on the overall context, purpose, and general tone of the interview.

Conclusion

This chapter has provided practical, step-by-step instructions for creating and conducting a successful interview. We have distinguished an interview from other types of interactions as an interpersonal interaction that generally requires motive and planning. Additionally, we discussed ways to plan for and construct a schedule of questions. Finally, we articulated strategies for asking questions, probing for greater depth in an interview, and making the most of any length of interview time with which you may have to work. With this chapter as a guide, we hope you feel greater confidence conducting and participating in interviews. Our next chapter explores another element of interpersonal behavior, and that is small group communication.

Endnotes

1 Charles J. Stewart & William B. Cash, *Interviewing: Principles and Practices*, 11th ed. (New York: McGraw Hill, 2006), 4.

2 Raymond L. Gorden, *Interviewing: Strategies, Techniques, and Tactics*, Revised ed. (Homewood, IL: Dorsey, 1975), 62–65.

3 Gorden, *Interviewing*, 64–65.

4 Gorden, *Interviewing*, 63–64.

5 Stewart & Cash, *Interviewing*, 78.

6 Alex F. Osborn, *Applied Imagination: Principles and Procedures of Creative Problem-Solving* (New York: Charles Scribner's Sons, 1953).

7 Stanley L. Payne, *The Art of Asking Questions* (Princeton, NJ: Princeton University Press, 1979).

8 Robert L. Kahn & Charles F. Cannell, *The Dynamics of Interviewing* (New York: John Wiley & Sons, 1957), 107.

9 Gorden, *Interviewing*, 424–425.

10 Gorden, *Interviewing*, 426; Stewart & Cash, *Interviewing*, 52.

11 *Saturday Night Live: The Best of Chris Farley* (DVD), Vidmark/Trimark, October 10, 2000.

12 Kahn & Cannell, *The Dynamics of Interviewing*, 108; Ken Metzler, *Creative Interviewing: The Interviewer's Guide to Gathering Information by Asking Questions*, 3rd ed. (Needham Heights, MA: Allyn & Bacon, 1997), 35.

13 Stewart & Cash, *Interviewing*, 129.

14 Payne, *The Art of Asking Questions*, 102; Stewart & Cash, *Interviewing*, 61.

15 Kahn & Cannell, *The Dynamics of Interviewing*, 121.

16 *Saturday Night Live: The Best of Chris Farley*.

17 Kahn & Cannell, *The Dynamics of Interviewing*, 127.

18 Stewart & Cash, *Interviewing*, 62.

19 Stewart & Cash, *Interviewing*, 69–70.

20 Metzler, *Creative Interviewing*, 19.

21 Metzler, *Creative Interviewing*, 22.

22 Stewart & Cash, *Interviewing*, 84–85.

Notes

CHAPTER 7

Working with Teams

by John A. Daly

Objectives

After studying Chapter 7, you should be able to do the following:

- ☐ Learn the benefits and challenges of working in teams.
- ☐ Define roles within teams and their functions.
- ☐ How to lead a team.
- ☐ Recognize various leadership styles.
- ☐ Building consensus within a team framework.
- ☐ Take advantage of working in meetings.

Key Terms

TERM	DEFINITION
affective or interpersonal stage	This stage of meetings is typified by disagreements among members of the team.
assigned leader	A leader who is "officially" chosen.
brainstorming	A team technique for generating ideas.
collective sampling bias	A tendency to focus on shared information.
conflict stage	A stage of a meeting that occurs after the project or problem is defined. It is the time in which team members work through problems.
consensus	Informed and deliberate agreement.
content	Substantive material that can be processed.
democratic leader	This type of leader wants to reflect the team's wishes.
emergent leader	An informal leader in the team whose ranking could compete with the assigned leader's role.
evaluation apprehension	Fear of being judged or assessed, hence a team member will not present his or her idea.
groupthink	Doing what is easiest or what the majority wants without regard to new or different ideas.
laissez-faire leaders	This type of leader demonstrates no leadership skills.
orientation stage	The first stage of meeting, which is characterized by defining the problem or project.
participative leaders	This type of leader will consider input from the team before making decisions.
procedural conflict	A sub-stage of the conflict stage of meetings, which is characterized by disagreement surrounding the process.
process	The running or operations of a meeting.
production blocking	An obstacle that prevents a team from operating optimally (e.g., only one person at a time can present an idea).
reinforcement stage	The final stage of meetings, after agreement has been reached, where the team comes together again for congratulations.
resolution stage	This stage of meetings is where teams reach agreement about what to do.
social leaders	A person in this role primarily maintains social harmony.

TERM	DEFINITION
social loafing	The tendency of team members to not give "100%" when other resources are allocated to the team.
substantive conflict	A sub-stage of the conflict stage, which is characterized by disagreements over issues.
task leader	A person whose role within a team is to ensure that tasks are accomplished.
team	A small number of people, with complementary skills, who are committed to a common purpose or goal.

Introduction

In today's world, a great deal of work gets accomplished in teams. Why? Because most challenges that we face in the professional world require talents that no one individual possesses.

The basic presumption of teamwork is that together people get more things done, and more effectively than they would individually. Research consistently has shown that teams often do better than individuals on many tasks. Teams can be amazingly smart. For instance, back in the early 1900s, a statistician asked a large group of people to estimate the weight of a bull. When the group's estimates were averaged, the statistician found the average was almost exactly what the bull weighed. On the television show *Who Wants to be a Millionaire*, contestants are allowed to seek help from two sources when they are stymied—a person who they believe is an expert and the audience. When studying which is a better choice for the contestant, they find that the audience—composed of a wide variety of people—are more accurate than the purported expert.

> ". . . together people get more things done, and more effectively than they would individually."

Not surprisingly, we all spend a good amount of our time on teams, whether they are sports teams, study groups, committees, or even collections of friends or family members. Teams offer any number of benefits. When solving problems you get more resources (physical or mental), you see different approaches to problems, and you often make more accurate decisions because others may correct mistakes you have made. You also get psychological advantages: People are more likely to buy into decisions when they have been involved in making them as well as the sense of inclusion that comes from being part of a team. Teams, however, also create problems—not only does teamwork take a lot of time but people working on teams will often go along with decisions they don't really agree with, as well as let others do their work. Conflicts often arise in teams that can, if poorly handled, scar relationships.

Should You Use a Team?

Before we go any further, let's be clear. Teams are sometimes unnecessary. For instance, when a task only requires one person to accomplish it, why use a team? Only one person can type a letter on a keyboard at a time. Sometimes, teams are unnecessary when you have a very talented individual. For example, if only one person on a team knows how to code software, what advantage is there to have the other team members involved in trying to write code when they don't have the necessary skills? Teams also take time so sometimes wise people make decisions and complete tasks by themselves—they simply don't have the time to work with others to get something done. Many students actually prefer to work on a term paper by themselves because, in the past, they have found that they can get a paper done more efficiently alone than with others.

Exercise 7.1. Why work in teams?

First, answer the questions by yourself without consulting your laptop or anyone around you. Second, get together with your presentation team and see how many questions you can answer. The answers are at the back of the chapter.

1. Name the four men who made up the world famous band, *The Beatles*.

2. Name the 13 provinces and territories of Canada.

3. In Harper Lee's novel, *To Kill a Mockingbird*, what is the name of the neighbor who never comes out of his house?

4. What are the names of the seven dwarfs from Snow White?

5. What are the four states that border Texas?

6. Name the fifth through tenth U.S. President.

7. What are the first names of the five members of the Simpsons family?

8. What is the tallest mountain in the world?

9. What is the largest desert?

10. What is the largest animal?

11. What is the fastest animal?

Teams are also unnecessary when decision makers don't value the opinions of teams. In many companies, executives will put together a team to study some issue and make recommendations. However, if decision makers already know what they are going to do, regardless of what the team recommends, why waste team members' time and energy? A final case where teams may not be the best choice is when the performance of the weakest person on the team determines the success of all. For example, suppose you are a wonderfully gifted swimmer or runner. You regularly win individual events. One day your coach, a generous fellow, tells you that you will be competing in relay races this week. You will run or swim with three other people. The problem is that the three are the weakest competitors on the team. No matter how hard you run or swim, there is no way you are going to win.

There are also people who simply prefer not to work on teams. These individualistic people really have a hard time putting up with everything that teams require. If you had to identify people who work well in teams they probably value teamwork, are willing to rely on others to do their parts, care about both team members and achieving a good outcome for the team, are willing to put up with all the common challenges teams experience, and are willing to abide by team decisions. Some people simply cannot or will not conform to these ideas. The problem for these people is that they are sorely limited in what they will be able to accomplish in life. Very few professions don't require substantial teamwork.

What is a Team?

Jon Katzenbach, who studied successful teams in organizations, suggested that a good definition of a team is "a small number of people with complementary skills who are committed to a common purpose, performance goals, and approach for which they hold themselves mutually accountable." Let's unpack this definition: First, teams are composed of a small number of people. How many people should be on a team? There is no hard and fast rule, although some people suggest the best number is between 4 and 6 people. Jeff Bezos, the founder of Amazon, once said that a good team was composed of the number of people it took to eat two large pizzas.

> "Team members bring with them skills that complement one another."

Team members bring with them skills that complement one another. Why would you want people with exactly the same skills on a team? Even though they have complementary skills, team members all agree on the purpose and goals of the team along with how they are going to address the issue on which they are working. In a team, you don't want different people having different goals. That would lead to confusion. And, very importantly, team members understand that they are mutually accountable—no one succeeds unless every one succeeds. One of the worst things that can happen to a team is when one or more members believes that he can get more accomplished by working around the team than working with the team. You can see all of these characteristics on a successful sports team. Each member brings a different skill but all agree on how the team will approach the game, which roles they will play, and the overall goal of winning. Most importantly, no one tries to take all the credit.

When Katzenbach examined successful teams he noticed there were some common indications that the team was doing well. These indicators include the following:

❑ **Themes and identity.** On effective teams, members identify with their team: You become the team. Symbolically, it can be as simple as sport teams wearing shirts with their team logos etched across them.

❑ **Enthusiasm and energy.** When working on many team projects, people start off with great enthusiasm. "This will be a great project . . . it will be fun to do!" But as time goes on, their enthusiasm fades. The thought of going to another team meeting is painful. On successful teams, however, enthusiasm stays the same and may even get stronger. You look forward to meetings.

❑ **Event-driven history.** Successful teams have a history—that is, team members think in terms of the events their team has experienced. If you have ever gotten together with friends who you played with on a sports

Courtesy of Craig Cozart/the Stock Connection

team years ago, you understand this idea. You may not remember the team's record or even where each game was played but you do recollect some special moments—the time the team left someone behind, the day a few team members got sick and threw up on everyone else, the silly play that actually worked. Smart team leaders know that when building a strong team, the team has to experience early on some "events" together.

❑ **Personal commitment.** A sure sign of an effective team is that team members feel a strong personal commitment to the team. Even when they don't feel like it, they go to meetings. Even when pressured to do other tasks, team members don't want to let down their team by not accomplishing their assignments.

❑ **Optimism.** Effective teams know they will succeed. There is no doubt that they will accomplish their ultimate goal. Of course, the optimism needs to be realistic. No professional baseball manager believes that his team will win 162 games in a season. But he does believe that they will win each game.

❑ **Performance results.** An effective team gets things done. They accomplish their goals in measurable ways. Ineffective teams, on the other hand, wallow—never seeming to get past the talking phase about what they plan to do. Smart teams know the wisdom of getting something done every meeting.

Those are some of the signs of a successful team. However, anyone reading this chapter most likely will have worked on a team that didn't work out the way they should have: A group project that should have been easy but instead became a soap opera; a sports team with great talent who never won anything. Why do teams fail? Academic studies suggest there are many reasons, including the following:

❑ Unclear goals.
❑ Changing objectives that were poorly communicated.
❑ Poor leadership.
❑ Lack of mutual accountability.
❑ Having the wrong people on the team.

❑ Not prioritizing the team.

❑ Misunderstanding of roles.

❑ Too much unhealthy conflict.

❑ Bad process management (how the team is organized and run).

❑ No rewards for teamwork.

Courtesy of Russell Sadur/Dorling Kindersley Media Library

Exercise 7.2. Team Bill of Rights.

Create a working document for your presentation team that dictates how you will work together to get your presentation finished. For example, your rules can be ones of personal/team rights (e.g., each member has the right to disagree respectfully with another); or regulations (e.g., team members must contribute one slide to the PowerPoint presentation).

1. _____

_____

_____

_____

2. _____

_____

_____

_____

3. _____

_____

_____

_____

4. _____

_____

_____

_____

5. _____

_____

_____

_____

Goals matter in teamwork.

Effective teams begin with goals. These goals shape everything that happens on the team—who is on the team, what gets done, and how issues that arise are prioritized. When you are placed on a team, one of the first tasks you and your teammates need to clarify is exactly what the team is to accomplish—that is, what is the team's mission? Good goals have some common characteristics. They are specific (e.g., "We need to complete a class presentation on water issues the state is facing in the next 10 years."), time-limitation (e.g., "The presentation will be in two weeks."), measurable (e.g., "We need to have at least 10 slides, we need each team member to talk for at least three minutes, and we need to get an A"), and the goals must be acceptable to all team members (e.g., "We all agree that we will do this assignment.").

> "Probably the single most important issue revolving around goals is that everyone on a team agrees with the goals."

It is good when goals are challenging (e.g., "This will be tough but we can do it!") and interesting to team members (e.g., "Water will be one of the major issues the state will face and I plan to live in this state for years to come."). Probably the single most important issue revolving around goals is that everyone on a team agrees with the goals. Disputes over goals wreck havoc on teams.

Roles matter as well.

One of the challenges of a successful team is that it requires each person to make an individual contribution to the team. Each person plays some important role in the group. There are many different types of roles in a team. An obvious one is the leadership role (and we will discuss this role later). There is also the recorder role, the person(s) who keeps minutes; the organizer role—the person(s) who gets things organized for each meeting; the researcher role—the person(s) who studies the issues the team is addressing; the tension-relieving role—the person(s) who cracks jokes at just the right time, and a host of other roles. Two problems emerge for some teams when it comes to roles: First, no one is willing to take on some important role. No one wants to do the organizing, or the research. Without people assuming these vital roles, teams often falter. Second, sometimes there is role conflict—too many people want the same role. When team members fight about who is willing to do what, they waste valuable energy and time. And, if the conflict persists, the team's deliverables are often poor.

> "One of the challenges of successful team is that it requires each person to make an individual contribution to the team."

Generating Creative Ideas

One of the biggest challenges any team faces is coming up with creative ideas—new solutions that will solve the challenges they face. Not surprisingly, there has been a good amount of research done which examines how successful teams generate creative ideas. One of the major strands of this research focuses on something called "brainstorming." Brainstorming was the brainchild of an advertising executive, Alex Osborne, who was concerned that people in his firm were not being creative enough. To this day, many companies celebrate brainstorming as a way to come up with innovative notions.

> "... brainstorming has been seen as a great way to come up with new ideas."

Brainstorming has a few ground rules. First, the goal of brainstorming is to generate as many ideas as you can as a team. Quantity matters. Second, wild ideas are encouraged. Even if crazy ideas might not make a lot of sense, say them anyway. Why? Because of a third rule: Try to "piggyback" on the ideas of others. One person may throw out some idea. Another person may use that notion as a prompt for another, even more creative idea. Fourth, only one person should talk at a time. Finally, don't evaluate others' ideas. Don't say an idea will never work or is bound to fail. Instead, just keep generating more ideas.

For the past 50 years, brainstorming has been seen as a great way to come up with new ideas. It seems to work. Many companies use it to this day. But when scholars started investigating the effectiveness of brainstorming, they made a surprising discovery: Brainstorming is not as good as people think it is for generating ideas. In studying any communication activity, it is important to have what researchers call a "control"—that is, something you can use to determine whether that activity actually gets you where you presume it will. The obvious control group for brainstorming is to take some people and have them generate ideas individually and compare how many ideas they come up with the number of ideas a similar collection of people produce when brainstorming together. Surprisingly, the group of individuals working independently of one another, called a "nominal group," will come up with more ideas. When you think about it this makes sense: Only one person at a time can talk when brainstorming in groups. This production blocking means that when people are alone they can continually come up with ideas, while people working in groups must often sit quietly when others are talking.

Another reason why brainstorming may not be as effective as people presume may be because of evaluation apprehension. Some people don't like to talk in front of other people. They are shy. Even extroverts might fear that people around them may consider some of their ideas odd. So they don't volunteer those ideas. One way to overcome evaluation apprehension in brainstorming is to have people anonymously brainstorm via a networked computer. Put a group of people in a room. At every desk is a computer. Ask each person to start typing ideas into the computer. In the front of the room there is a screen displaying what each person writes. As they contribute their own ideas, they can see the ideas of others. This technique, called "electronic brainstorming," eliminates both production blocking (each person can type simultaneously) as well as evaluation apprehension (the contributions are anonymous).

Leading Teams

Crucial to any effective team is good leadership. Scholars have discovered that there are three different dimensions of team leadership. They are as follows: (a) assigned versus emergent leadership, (b) task versus social leadership, (c) autocratic-participative-democratic, and laissez-faire leadership.

Courtesy of Rick Gomez/Corbis Images

Assigned vs. emergent leadership.

In many teams someone is assigned to be the official leader. It may be a boss or someone appointed by the boss. The teacher might say to one student "You are in charge of this project." This person is called the assigned leader. He or she is officially "in charge." Often, though, as a team progresses through its tasks, one or more members of the team slowly emerge as informal leaders. People on the team start listening more to the informal leader than the assigned leader. What should the assigned leader do? Beat up the emergent leader? No, of course not. What the assigned leader should do is to celebrate the emergent leader or leaders. The assigned leader should let them take some responsibility and not be threatened by them. The emergent leader clearly has some sway over the group, so fighting him or her will only make the assigned leader look bad. This notion even can be applied to families. One parent may be the assigned leader. At times, though, the other parent, or even a child, may become the emergent leader. Mom may be the official leader but one of the kids actually may play more of a leadership role on some issues than Mom.

Task vs. social leadership.

In any group some people just want to get the work done. They feel pressured by perhaps time and other tasks to move quickly through a project. They are task focused. They don't want to waste time. They just want the project done. These are your task leaders. Other people are just the opposite. They will walk into a meeting carrying drinks and a DVD they want to watch. They will switch on their computer and show you some videos they just downloaded. They will tell a joke and add some delicious gossip. These people are often called "social leaders." Task leaders and social leaders drive each other crazy. The social leader might say, "All work and no play, what a stupid life . . . no one on his death-bed ever said I wish I had put more time into the job." On the other hand, the task leader might respond, "If you don't do the task, you won't have the job!" For a team, both people are essential. The task leader ensures tasks get done and the social leader maintains some degree of harmony in the group. Again, think of family life. In many families, Mom is the task leader and Dad is the social leader. Mom calls "Time for dinner right now!!!" and Dad says, with a smile and wink, "Relax, let's finish the game and then we'll go in." While Mom and Dad probably didn't always like their roles, the different approaches probably made family life better for the kids.

Other leadership styles.

Leaders also vary in how they handle the input of team members. At one extreme are autocratic leaders. These individuals are effectively dictators. "Do it my way!" is their mantra. Then there are participative leaders, who consider the input of team members but still make their own decisions. The next type is the democratic leader. These people, who do not necessarily vote-count, try to reflect the team's wishes. Finally, there are leaders who are best called "laissez-faire leaders" (a term translated loosely from French meaning "free for all" or "leave it alone"). These people demonstrate no leadership whatsoever. Which is the best form of leadership? The answer is "it depends." Clearly there are appropriate situations for each style. For instance, in an emergency, the last thing you want is someone who wants too much input. If there is a fire in the building, you don't want the team leader to say, "Let's discuss how we might leave the building." Instead, you want an autocrat, "We are leaving out this door right now and meeting up outside!" On the other hand, when you are brainstorming an idea, you might want a laissez-faire leader. When planning a party, you might prefer a democratic or participative leader.

> "The more versatile your leadership skills, the more effective you will be."

In reading this section, consider the following: First, most of us are not at any one extreme. We may be more social than task-oriented, but if need be we can be highly task focused. We have pointed out the extremes, understanding that most people fall closer to the middle of each range. Second, you may notice you have a preference for one or two different approaches. You might be thinking that you are mostly a task-oriented person who, if given a choice, might be a tad autocratic. No problem. That works in some contexts and on certain tasks. However, it would be wise for you to consider practicing a different approach. Next time you are in a meeting, relax. Let someone else take charge. On the other hand, if you are mostly a social leader with a tendency to be laissez-faire, you might try taking a more assertive role when working on your next team project. The more versatile your leadership skills, the more effective you will be.

How to Build Consensus on a Team

Everyone knows that effective teams share consensus about the important issues they have to address. Sports teams, to be successful, must work together seamlessly. Similarly, teams with a laser-like focus on getting a project accomplished must find ways to build cohesion. Luckily, we know a great deal about how cohesion is created in teams. Cohesion is enhanced when team members meet the following criteria:

- ❑ **Share similar goals.** Few things destroy a team quicker than people who do not agree on why they are together. When people are aligned around the same goals, cohesion is enhanced. When teams start to wallow, smart team members often review the goals of the team.

- ❑ **Have a common enemy.** Having an "evil empire" builds cohesion. School spirit is built by having a competing school that brings students in the school together. Why else does A&M exist?

- ❑ **Spend time together on both task and non-task activities.** The more time you spend with people, the more you get to know them. You come to understand why they do what they do and hopefully appreciate everything they bring to the team. It is easier to work with someone you know than a stranger.

- ❑ **Work at respecting and trusting one another.** A team isn't your family. You don't have to love your fellow team members but you do need to respect and trust them. Disrespect and lack of trust wear out teams quickly. One note here: When internal politics become highly charged, teamwork disappears. When a person believes she or he can get more credit, or more accomplished, by working around the team than through the team, teamwork falters.

- ❑ **Have a series of successful experiences together.** Successful teams punctuate their history by a series of small accomplishments. These "milestones" give every team member the sense that the team is going somewhere together.

When Consensus Fails You

As a general rule, smart teams seek consensus. There are times, however, when consensus may actually hurt teamwork. Two particular cases are (1) social loafing, and (2) groupthink.

Social loafing challenges teamwork.

Imagine a tug of war with one person at each end of the rope. Each person can pull 50 pounds. Now imagine we add another person to each side of the rope. Each of these individuals also can tug 50 pounds. Logically, each side should now be able to pull 100 pounds. But do they? Not often. They will, instead, pull perhaps only 90 pounds. Now we add another person to each side and again each has the ability to pull 50 pounds. We would anticipate that each side would now be able to pull 150 pounds. But, in fact, they will pull something like 125 pounds. What is happening? Every time we add another person to the team, the overall team performance goes down. Researchers call this tendency "social loafing"—we let others do our work. We've all experienced this on group projects. It seems we end up doing the work of everyone, as our team members just sit around and watch. Don't feel too bad, though. Haven't we all loafed ourselves? Think about a time when you helped someone move. Everyone hefts a couch and with noisy grunts carries it up some stairs. You are part of the team carrying the couch and you are moaning like everyone else. Truthfully, though, you are barely touching the couch.

What can teams do to reduce social loafing by their members? Here are three suggestions:

- ❑ **Make the work more interesting.** People contribute more when they are highly involved in what is happening, when they feel some responsibility for the process or project; when they feel they are doing something important. When people get excluded, they don't feel ownership, or they feel that what they are doing doesn't really matter. Why should they work hard on a project? Make sure your team members are working on tasks they feel are interesting and important. Remember, different people may feel different tasks are vital. Someone might think research is crucial; another might value most creating the slides for a team presentation.

- ❑ **Make work identifiable.** Years ago a young woman was attacked and killed in New York City. While she was being attacked any number of people heard her screams. Yet no one called the police. Why? Perhaps because New Yorkers are cold and uncaring? Of course not! Instead, every witness presumed that someone else would call law enforcement. This phenomenon of assuming that someone else will do something is

Courtesy of John Serafin/Silver Burdett Ginn

called the "diffusion of responsibility." When others are working on something, why should we get involved? The way to overcome this diffusion of responsibility is to make people individually identifiable. Suppose you walk out of class one day and your teacher falls to the floor unconscious. Obviously, something is very wrong. Don't shout to the crowd "Someone call EMS! Someone call the police!" Instead, point to one individual and say "You! Call EMS!" And look at someone else and tell them specifically to call the police. Team members are less likely to loaf when they have individual and public responsibilities. Therefore, it is not surprising that social loafing occurs more often on large rather than small teams. You can easily get lost on a large team. Smart team leaders know the value of making specific assignments.

❑ **Manage the team process.** Social loafing occurs more when people are tired. When people are fresh they are more willing to make substantial contributions. Though when team meetings last too long, when they are scheduled at the wrong time of day, people's attention and involvement start fading. Similarly, when there are too many distractions people often lose interest in a team project. If your team is meeting at someone's apartment and a highly touted football game is on a big screen television, what would you expect most people to do?

Groupthink challenges teamwork.

Many years ago, Irving Janis, a famous psychologist with a deep interest in history, made a perplexing observation: Often, groups of very smart and successful people sit down together as teams and make atrocious decisions. Think back to some historical cases: Pearl Harbor where the military lined up planes in straight rows making it easy for attacking planes to destroy them *en masse*; the Watergate affair where senior-level White House executives made really stupid decisions that, in the end, toppled a Presidency; the Enron Corporation, filled with brilliant people, who came to believe they were invincible; NASA, literally stocked with rocket scientists who, together, made terribly consequential decisions when it came to the shuttles *Challenger* and *Columbia*. The list could go on forever—smart, talented people working together to craft terrible decisions. Why does this happen?

> **"Often, groups of very smart and successful people sit down together as teams and make atrocious decisions."**

Janis felt these teams were suffering from what he labeled <u>groupthink</u>. When you put a team together composed of people who share many common beliefs (same political party, same organization, and so on), and then place them under stress (time pressure, political challenges, war, public approval, legal issues), they can end up becoming both highly cohesive and, simultaneously, very concerned about maintaining harmony. Their cohesiveness results in suffering from illusions that they are invulnerable (e.g., "We're the United States . . . no one can attack us!"), that they are morally superior to other organizations and teams (e.g., "God is certainly on our side"), and a tendency to stereotype outsiders ("We know better than others—they are just dumb"). If we are invulnerable and so much better than everyone else, we don't need to think through our decisions. Cohesive teams under stress often emphasize harmony over anything else—we need to get along and not "rock the boat." So team members are often (1) close-minded about ideas that might challenge what the team "knows;" (2) pressure is put on team members who dissent too often from what the team "knows;" (3) self-censored because they are fearful that others might not like them if they were to dissent; and (4) they are seduced by an illusion of unanimity—that is, if people don't disagree aloud then they must agree.

> **"Cohesive teams under stress often emphasize harmony over anything else—we need to get along and not 'rock the boat.'"**

The consequences of groupthink can be profound. Teams don't explore important alternatives when making decisions, they isolate people who could bring in new valuable information, and they don't consider how their decisions could go awry. In class projects, groupthink often results in mediocre projects that, oddly enough, team members felt were quite good when they were submitted.

How do teams make sure that they don't fall in the trap of groupthink? Four moves may help:

❑ **Reduce mindless conformity.** Smart leaders should never announce what they are thinking until every team member has enunciated his or her position. If a leader were to say, "I think we should do X" there may be team members who nod in agreement even through they are thinking to themselves "X is a really stupid move. But I can't buck the boss?" An important way of reducing mindless conformity is have team members vote on issues anonymously. Public voting often encourages people to go along with decisions even if they disagree. This is especially so when they feel their opinion may be in the minority. Good leaders also know the value of asking one person at each meeting to serve as a "devil's advocate." In this role, the person challenges the decisions of the team. Of course, it is important to rotate that responsibility among team members. If any one person is regularly cast in this role, she or he will begin to be ignored by others.

❑ **Build in checks and balances.** Effective teams find ways to check their decisions. Rather than a pall-mall race to make a decision, smart teams take time effectively to ensure that their decisions are optimal. When facing a problem, one very useful technique is to break the team into sub-teams. Ask each sub-team to independently arrive at a decision. Then, see if each sub-team reaches the same decision. If one sub-team thinks their team should approach a project using Method A, and another sub-team thinks they should use a different method, then perhaps more discussion is warranted. On the other hand, if both teams independently adopt Method A, you have some assurance that the decision is reasonable. Some very smart teams also know the wisdom of inviting valued outsiders to their meetings occasionally to critique assumptions and what is being done. A fresh perspective can do wonders by challenging assumptions. More broadly, smart teams scout for new information as they make decisions and complete projects. They know and appreciate the fact that they don't know everything.

❑ **Modify how decisions are made.** An important move you can make in reducing groupthink is to hold "second-chance meetings." We have all experienced the momentum of team decision-making. After we have reached a decision, we want to move on quickly. Sometimes, though, the best thing is to sleep on a decision and then discuss it one last time. We all have woken up in the morning and thought that something we agreed to the previous day wasn't the wisest. Another useful tactic to reduce the threat of groupthink is to spend some time discussing how your group's decision will be implemented. Ideas are easy—implementing them is hard. So spend some time laying out step-by-step what it would take to get the idea accomplished

❑ **Reduce stress.** Groupthink emerges when teams feel highly stressed. Think about what happens when you feel overly stressed: You focus narrowly on exactly what you need to do, ignoring lots of others things—relevant or not to the decision you need to make. You make simple decisions emphasizing quantity rather than the quality. You feel a strong need for closure: "Let's just stop talking and get this thing done!" If you can somehow reduce the amount of stress your team feels, groupthink is less likely to occur. If you wait until the evening before your project is due to start working on it, you'll be overly stressed. Obviously, you don't want to eliminate every iota of stress—a modest level of stress actually can help performance.

Handling Value Decisions

Most teams work on projects where the deliverables are seemingly straight-forward—that is, a paper needs to be completed, a project needs to be outlined and finished, or someone has to be selected for some task. While in the beginning, team tasks appear easy, experienced team members know that often there are unexpected disagreements. Suppose your team must nominate someone for a scholarship award. You have five viable candidates. Who do you choose? Team members may disagree because they think one or the other candidate is more deserving. What drive these disagreements are team members' differing values. Effective teams use a four-step process when making "value" decisions:

❑ **Brainstorm criteria.** In this stage, team members brainstorm every possible criterion that might affect the decision they have to make. For example, facing the challenge of selecting the scholarship recipient criteria might include academic performance, extra-curricula participation, family needs, diversity, potential, interests, and so on. At this stage, no team member disagrees with any other team member.

❑ **Rank order criteria.** After every potential criterion has been listed, the team discusses which ones are more important. Their goal is to generate a rank-ordering of all the criteria. Is academic performance more important than need? Does diversity trump potential, and so on? This is where the major debate happens.

❑ **Match choices to ranks.** The team now takes each alternative decision and matches it to the ranked criteria.

❑ **Check the results.** Obviously, when the final decision is made team members may look askance and ask "How did we end up with that decision?" The team may decide to renegotiate their choices.

Working in Meetings

Meetings are the bane of many people's existence. In many meetings it seems that not much is accomplished, even though many people have put in a good amount of time. Many very productive people claim that meetings are their biggest wastes of time. Yet meetings are essential to many tasks. You need the input of others to make a decision or create some sort of product. In this section we look at what you can do to make team meetings more effective and efficient.

There are two crucial components to any meeting: (1) the <u>content</u> of the meeting and (2) the <u>process</u> of the meeting. Even the best content can be destroyed by poor process, and the best process won't make up for bad content. In this section we will focus mostly on process issues. It is up to you to make sure that meetings are substantive.

All of us have attended awful meetings. What annoys you most in those meetings? Some of the biggest complaints people have about meetings include the following:

❑ Getting off track

❑ Having no goals or an agenda

❑ Lasting too long

❑ People coming poorly prepared to the meeting

❑ No decisions are made at the meeting—nothing gets done

❑ Some people do not take any responsibility

- ❑ No leadership
- ❑ Lots of wasted time at the meeting
- ❑ The meeting started late
- ❑ Too many interruptions and distractions
- ❑ Someone dominates
- ❑ Meetings are regularly cancelled or postponed

> **"In many meetings it seems that not much is accomplished, even though many people have put in a good amount of time."**

To make sure that these problems don't happen to you, there are a number of things that can be done to enhance the quality of your team meetings. Before the meeting begins there are three things you might want to consider:

❑ **Establish objectives for each meeting.** People get more done when they have goals. Each meeting should be framed by some specific objectives—that is, what exactly do we want to accomplish at the meeting? By the end of the meeting, we will have accomplished what? The best objectives are ones that are important to team members. They also need objectives that can be realistically accomplished during a meeting. You may need to break down objectives into smaller units so that team members can get them accomplished at the meeting. Ask yourself questions like: "What is the purpose of this meeting? What will the team do? What should be done by the end of the meeting?

❑ These objectives can be translated into an agenda. A good agenda is one that is simple; it clearly communicates the purpose and goals of meeting; it is distributed before the meeting; it describes when, where, who, how, and how long; it assigns roles for people when appropriate (who will do what); and it may even include time points (e.g., we will spend 20 minutes on item A).

❑ In many meetings, the best agenda items are not topical but are instead decision-based. Rather than list an item like "Research" you might want to list "How should we approach Topic X." Notice that it is impossible for people to really prepare for the topical item. How do you spend any time getting ready for "Research?" But you could think ahead of time what you know about "Topic X."

❑ **Create the right environment for the meeting.** A smart team member makes sure the setting is appropriate for the meeting. The room should not be filled with distractions. Too often, students hold meetings in their apartments or rooms. Think about the distractions. There is the TV, video games, the kitchen filled with food and drinks, a couch that is perfect for lounging. No wonder so little gets done. You want a meeting place where there isn't much to do or see other than what is relevant to the meeting. You want to make sure that all the equipment is ready to go before the meeting starts. If you are going to use a computer, make sure it is on and plugged in prior to the meeting; if you are going to use pens and paper, make sure they are available. Some people actually suggest that the best meetings are held while standing up. They are often quicker for sure. Where a meeting should happen is not a trivial question. You might decide to meet in a room at the library or Union rather than at someone's apartment. You might decide to avoid places like Starbucks, given its many distractions.

> ## "Crucial to an effective meeting is well-prepared participants."

❑ **People should come prepared.** Crucial to an effective meeting is well-prepared participants. Too often, team members walk into a meeting not having done any prior work—that is, they haven't reviewed what has been accomplished in prior meetings; they don't bring items (computers, research, etc.) that are vital to what will be discussed; and they haven't done the work they committed to do before the meeting. So the meeting is filled with exasperation and excuses. Smart teams make sure every participant comes well-prepared.

Once the meeting begins there are five major considerations to remember, if you want the meeting to be effective.

1. **Keep the meeting structured.** A good meeting is one where things get done. Smart team leaders only hold meetings when there is a need to meet. Nothing annoys people more than to attend an unnecessary meeting. To get things done, effective team members stick to the agenda. They continually remind their colleagues about the goal of the meeting. At points during the meeting, they summarize what has been accomplished so far. They manage time by moving on if a decision obviously cannot be made. If people get off-topic, the team leader may suggest that the off-topic item be placed in "a parking lot," which includes ideas that were interesting but not particularly relevant. The team will consider them after all the topic-relevant issues have been covered.

   Crucial to effective teamwork is making sure that people participate and make important contributions. The reasons we include people on a team is because each person can contribute something that no one else can contribute. Yet, when academic studies examine what actually happens at meetings, the finding is that people talk mostly about ideas and information they have in common. Suppose I ask a team of five people to solve a knotty problem. Every team member shares some clues to the problem in common. And, each person has at least one clue that no one else has. What does the team spend most of its time discussing? The items they all have in common. But, obviously, the most important information is probably what the team members don't share in common. This tendency to focus on shared information is called the <u>collective sampling bias</u>. What can you do to overcome this tendency of people to ignore non-common information?

   - Early on recognize what unique information or skills each person brings to the team.
   - Have the leader repeat (and even write on a poster) unshared information that people contribute.
   - Ask, over and over again, "Does anyone else have anything to contribute?"
   - Have people distribute their ideas and information before the meeting through emails or handouts.
   - Have the meeting go longer—lengthier meetings lead people to volunteer new ideas.
   - Encourage people to be "critical"—in a positive way, create some disagreements that prompt people to add new information.

2. **Build consensus.** When people complete a good meeting they feel like things have been accomplished and that there is some <u>consensus</u> among team members about what was decided. Effective team leaders can build consensus by doing the following:

- Not always arguing for only their ideas, but rather soliciting and using ideas volunteered by other team members.
- Focusing on the team's goals, not their own.
- Avoiding easy conflict-reducing techniques early (e.g., a quick vote) in favor of longer discussions.
- Continually summarizing areas of agreement.
- Regularly listening and checking understandings.
- Using group pronouns (us, we, our) rather than self-oriented ones (I, me, my).

3. **Understand the stages of meetings.** Most decision-making meetings go through four stages. The first is called the <u>orientation stage</u>. This is where people get acquainted and start talking about the issue or problem they need to resolve. They try to define the project or problem. This stage is followed by the <u>conflict stage</u>. Here team members work through problems—"I think we should approach the issue this way." "No," replies another member, "we should do it my way." This stage is an often difficult stage because conflict usually arises and most people don't like conflict. It is important to note that there are three sorts of conflicts many teams experience during this stage:

- <u>Substantive conflict</u>: Disagreements over issues. "I think the largest lake in the world is in the U.S." "No," says someone else, "the largest lake is in Russia." Substantive conflict is, up to a point, a good thing for teams. It generates better and more accurate ideas.
- <u>Procedural conflict</u>: Disagreement surrounding the process. "What we need to do first is look at what is on the Web." "No," says someone else, "we should first outline the questions we have." Like substantive conflict, procedural conflict, up to a point, is not bad for teams.
- <u>Affective or interpersonal conflict</u>: Disagreements about each other. "You are so lazy! You must not care a bit about this project!" "Hey," says someone else, "I don't like the tone of your voice. And, I am really tried of your complaining." Interpersonal conflict is almost always dysfunctional. It creates all sorts of problems—grudges, anger, and absence to name but three. A smart team always works hard to avoid affective conflicts.

    The third stage of meetings is the <u>resolution stage</u>. This is where teams reach agreement about what to do. The final stage is the <u>reinforcement stage</u>. After agreement has been reached, team members spend time congratulating one another about their work together. Team members might relax over drinks talking about what a good project they have completed.

4. **Follow-through on commitments.** One of the biggest problems for many teams is that some members never keep their commitments between meetings. At a meeting they promise to accomplish tasks and at the next meeting nothing has been completed. Smart teams know how important it is to follow through on commitments. To encourage people to follow-though you might do the following:

- Be very specific about what each person should do by laying out (1) what they are to do, (2) when it should be done, and (3) how it needs to be done. The more specific the assignment, the more likely it will be completed.
- Follow-up before the next meeting. Have people email their work to everyone before the meeting.
- Do it right away. Procrastination is often the real reason people don't get their work done. They commit but then other things come up. Get everyone to commit to doing their assignments the next day.

5. **Being a good team member.** While team leading by arranging the process, structuring the meeting, and understanding the stages of meetings, building consensus, and following through on commitments are crucial to effective meetings, there are many things every team member needs to do to make sure that their meetings go well. Here is a checklist to assess your team behavior:

- Get to your meeting on time.
- Come prepared.
- Participate.
- Listen.
- Deal with issues at the meeting, not afterwards.
- Don't monopolize the discussion.
- Stick to the agenda.
- Support others; build on other's ideas.
- Be optimistic.
- Respect others; criticize ideas, not people.
- Perform follow-up actions as promised.

Conclusion

Teams are a part of our everyday reality, for good or ill, as students and as professionals. A team is a small number of people with complementary skills who share a common goal and are ultimately accountable for the performance of the team. Team members take on different types of roles and leadership responsibilities to get projects accomplished. Great teams work by arriving at consensus through creative means such as brainstorming and nominal group techniques, and they avoid traps like groupthink and social loafing. Even more importantly, great teams know the value of effective and efficient meetings and work to create rules and environments that produce the best results. We hope that this chapter enables you to work more productively on teams—to be a better teammate and to have a clearer sense of some strategies that will improve your team overall. After all, being on a team can be an incredibly rewarding experience as long as each member contributes to the fullest.

Answers to: Why Work in Teams?

1. John Lennon, Paul McCartney, George Harrison, Ringo Starr
2. British Columbia, Alberta, Saskatchewan, Manitoba, Ontario, Quebec, Prince Edward Island, Nunavut, Newfoundland, Nova Scotia, Yukon Territories, Northwest Territories, New Brunswick
3. Boo Radley
4. Dopey, Sleepy, Grumpy, Doc, Bashful, Happy, Sneezy
5. Louisiana, Arkansas, Oklahoma, New Mexico
6. Monroe, Adams, Jackson, Van Buren, Harrison, Tyler
7. Homer, Marge, Bart, Lisa, Maggie
8. Everest
9. Sahara
10. Blue whale
11. Cheetah

Media Box

Watch the sample group presentation in this chapter's folder in your Chapter Media Contents online.

What communicative strategies do the presenters use to strengthen their delivery?

Facilitating a Group Problem-Solving Meeting

According to Sue DeWine, prominent organizational communication scholar and consultant, most managers spend 2–3 days a week in unproductive meetings. Each year, as many as 30 working days and up to $71 million are wasted on meetings that accomplish nothing. Many business professionals complain that meetings are ineffective for the following reasons: lack of preparation, no goals or agenda, disorganization, ineffective leadership and control, and getting off the subject.

Goal: Your goal of this assignment is to help you overcome these obstacles and develop skills necessary to design and conduct an effective and productive problem-solving meeting. To reach this goal, you and your group members will facilitate a problem-solving meeting with the class based on a case study. As meeting facilitators, you will set the meeting's agenda, guide the class through this agenda, and work with the class to develop and select the best solution to your case's problem.

- ❑ Introduce the problem (Step 1)
- ❑ Define and analyze the problem (Step 2)
- ❑ Establish criteria (Step 3)
- ❑ Generate possible solutions (Step 4)
- ❑ Evaluate possible solutions (Step 5)

Your Group's Responsibilities

1. First, your group will need to choose a case study. This step involves locating and researching a current problem existing within the university community or in the Austin community. This problem will be addressed in the meeting presentation. Your group must provide a written description of your case prior to your scheduled presentation date (See your instructor for specific dates). The description of your case should be based on information obtained from at least two current sources. **Your case must be approved by your instructor prior to your scheduled presentation date.**

2. You and your group will have until your class presentation time to meet, discuss the case, create an agenda, and prepare to lead the class through the Reflective Thinking Procedure. How you and your group members define and analyze the problem will determine your agenda for the meeting. Prior to your presentation day, your group must define and analyze the problem (Step 2). On your presentation day, you must begin the meeting by introducing the problem (Step 1) and presenting a summary of how your group defined and analyzed the problem. Then, you must establish criteria for possible solutions (Step 3), generating possible solutions (Step 4), evaluating solution alternatives (Step 5), and finally selecting the best alternative and making plans to implement the chosen solution. You must involve the class (at *minimum*) in steps 4 and 5. Please refer to your in-class instruction for specific information about how to accomplish this.

3. Remember that you are running a meeting in which everyone in the class is a participating member of your organization. Your challenge is to ask questions of class members, encourage discussion, and carefully process and consider their feedback to arrive at a decision. Most importantly, your focus should be on helping members solve the problem at hand by taking them through the steps of the *Reflective Thinking* process—not on solving the problem for them. You are to act as "expert meeting facilitators" and your audience will become members of the organization in your case.

4. Your group will have 18 to 22 minutes in which to run this meeting. If your group facilitates for less than 18 minutes, or more than 22, your group grade will be penalized. For example, if a meeting is less than 18 minutes, one point will be deducted for each 15-second interval. For example, a meeting that is 1–14 seconds short, would lose 1 point; a meeting that is 15–29 seconds short, would lose two points, etc. **Please, time your meeting when you practice.**

5. Limit your notes to **your instructor's requirements**. Include only KEY WORDS to prompt your thinking on notes. Do not write out whole sections (or the entire presentation) on your notes. If you choose to ignore this advice, expect to be penalized 5 points.

6. You must incorporate at least **four** computer-generated visual aids that enhance your meeting by adding to the audience's understanding of the meeting process/progress.

7. Each group member must participate in conducting the meeting. All members of your group will receive the same grade on this assignment.

8. Your delivery should include professional language and all team members should strive to generally engage the audience. Plan carefully for what each member will accomplish during each step. Also, make sure your dress is appropriate for the type of organization and context of your meeting.

9. Submit the following items (one folder per group) to your instructor on the day of your presentation:

   ☐ A copy of your group's agenda

   ☐ Instructor's Evaluation for Problem-Solving Meeting

   ☐ Presentation notes (place these in the folder following your presentation)

   ☐ Printouts of visual aids (these may be full slides or "handouts")

   ☐ A bibliography containing at least two sources used for your presentation. Put them in APA, MLA or another appropriate academic style. If listing a web source, be sure to name the entity that maintains the website so we know it is a credible source.

Points Possible	Meeting Facilitation	30
	Individual Evaluation	5
Total Points Possible		35

10. Following your meeting, each group member will write his or her own evaluation of your group's process. For instructions on completing this assignment, see "Evaluating Your Group's Problem-Solving Meeting."

Evaluating Your Group's Problem-Solving Meeting

The purpose of this evaluation is to reflect on the importance of group work and to apply it to your personal experience with this assignment. **You must view the videotape of your presentation before writing this essay.** You are to write a 3–5 page evaluation essay that assesses your group participation and communication. This essay should be typed and double-spaced, using a standard 12 point font (with 1" margins). Please **do not** exceed the 5 page maximum. This assessment is due ONE WEEK after your meeting facilitation.

The essay should include an introduction, body, and conclusion and must include specific examples to support each argument. Divide the body into the following sections:

1. Describe the performance of your team members during the preparation for your meeting facilitation. Describe each person's behavior (task, "social," and/or nonfunctional) during the course of the project. Provide specific examples to support each assertion and be sure to describe the roles/functions that each member performed. Consult the chapters in your textbook, as well as information provided in class about group communication, in making this analysis. Don't forget to describe *your* behavior as a team member. Explain your behaviors and discuss what you did well and what you'd like to improve in future group experiences. Again, focus on specific examples and use your text and lecture to support your analysis.

2. Describe the performance of your team during the actual meeting facilitation. Did everything go as planned? Did your group perform as expected? You should address each of the following questions:

   ☑ Were the problem and its consequences explained well? Explain.

   ☐ Were the criteria clear and explained well? Explain.

   ☑ Did the class have ample opportunity to express opinions/offer suggestions? Explain.

   ☐ Did your team effectively use the class' opinions and suggestions? Explain.

   ☑ Was your team organized? Did you work well together? Explain.

   ☑ Did your delivery allow you to engage the audience? Explain.

3. Evaluate your experience with this team as a whole. In doing this, select any two group communication concepts and discuss how well your group met your objectives in relation to these concepts. For example, you might choose to focus on groupthink, group stages, emergent leadership (or any other communication concept in your text or discussed in class) and comment on your group's ability to employ these skills in your preparation meetings and/or in the meeting facilitation itself. In other words, choose two of the concepts that you learned about group communication and demonstrate how you saw them at work in your own group.

This evaluation MUST be in ESSAY form. Again, in the body of the essay, you should address each of the three content areas above, providing examples for each. This means you cannot simply create a numbered list. You will be graded on your content and how well you evaluate your group. Remember to check spelling, punctuation, and grammar. Be sure to utilize your textbook to support your claims (i.e., by quoting or paraphrasing relevant material).

Because this essay does not affect the group grade (which is based upon the presentation), please do not feel that you must try to convince your instructor that your group was effective or not. Rather, your goal is to analyze the events and behaviors that took place during the preparation and performance of the meeting assignment (positive and negative), explain what they were, why they occurred, and the outcomes of these events and behaviors.

Peer Evaluation: Group Presentation

Group Members' Names:_____

Please complete evaluations for the presentation you have been assigned to evaluate. Turn evaluations into your instructor at the end of class.

Rate when prompted (1=poor; 7=excellent) & please make comments for each.

Is the group's objective made clear?

1   2   3   4   5   6   7

Explain score.

Are team members organized/work well as a team? (Consider individual and group presentation styles, ordering)

1   2   3   4   5   6   7

Explain score.

Consider realism, research, rationale

Is the presentation **plausible**? (Consider realism, research, rationale)

1   2   3   4   5   6   7

Explain score.

Is the presentation **original**? (Consider product creation, presentation, creativity)

1   2   3   4   5   6   7

Explain score.

How professional was the presentation?

(Consider verbal/nonverbal skills, delivery, dress, visual aid, Q&A)

1   2   3   4   5   6   7

Explain score.

The strongest feature of this presentation was:

My suggestion to improve this presentation is:

Feedback Initials:

Peer Evaluation: Group Presentation

Group Members' Names:_____

Please complete evaluations for the presentation you have been assigned to evaluate. Turn evaluations into your instructor at the end of class.

Rate when prompted (1=poor; 7=excellent) & please make comments for each.

Is the group's objective made clear?

1   2   3   4   5   6   7

Explain score.

Are team members organized/work well as a team? (Consider individual and group presentation styles, ordering)

1   2   3   4   5   6   7

Explain score.

Consider realism, research, rationale

Is the presentation **plausible**? (Consider realism, research, rationale)

1   2   3   4   5   6   7

Explain score.

Is the presentation **original**? (Consider product creation, presentation, creativity)

1   2   3   4   5   6   7

Explain score.

How professional was the presentation?

(Consider verbal/nonverbal skills, delivery, dress, visual aid, Q&A)

1   2   3   4   5   6   7

Explain score.

The strongest feature of this presentation was:

My suggestion to improve this presentation is:

Feedback Initials:

Peer Evaluation: Group Presentation

Group Members' Names:_____

Please complete evaluations for the presentation you have been assigned to evaluate. Turn evaluations into your instructor at the end of class.

<u>Rate when prompted (1=poor; 7=excellent) & please make comments for each.</u>

Is the group's objective made clear?

1   2   3   4   5   6   7

Explain score.

Are team members organized/work well as a team? (Consider individual and group presentation styles, ordering)

1   2   3   4   5   6   7

Explain score.

Consider realism, research, rationale

Is the presentation **plausible**? (Consider realism, research, rationale)

1   2   3   4   5   6   7

Explain score.

Is the presentation **original**? (Consider product creation, presentation, creativity)

1   2   3   4   5   6   7

Explain score.

How professional was the presentation?

(Consider verbal/nonverbal skills, delivery, dress, visual aid, Q&A)

1   2   3   4   5   6   7

Explain score.

The <u>strongest feature</u> of this presentation was:

My <u>suggestion to improve</u> this presentation is:

Feedback Initials:

Peer Evaluation: Group Presentation

Group Members' Names:_____

Please complete evaluations for the presentation you have been assigned to evaluate. Turn evaluations into your instructor at the end of class.

Rate when prompted (1=poor; 7=excellent) & please make comments for each.

Is the group's objective made clear?

1   2   3   4   5   6   7

Explain score.

Are team members organized/work well as a team? (Consider individual and group presentation styles, ordering)

1   2   3   4   5   6   7

Explain score.

Consider realism, research, rationale

Is the presentation **plausible**? (Consider realism, research, rationale)

1   2   3   4   5   6   7

Explain score.

Is the presentation **original**? (Consider product creation, presentation, creativity)

1   2   3   4   5   6   7

Explain score.

How professional was the presentation?

(Consider verbal/nonverbal skills, delivery, dress, visual aid, Q&A)

1   2   3   4   5   6   7

Explain score.

The strongest feature of this presentation was:

My suggestion to improve this presentation is:

Feedback Initials:

Peer Evaluation: Group Presentation

Group Members' Names:_____

Please complete evaluations for the presentation you have been assigned to evaluate. Turn evaluations into your instructor at the end of class.

Rate when prompted (1=poor; 7=excellent) & please make comments for each.

Is the group's objective made clear?

1   2   3   4   5   6   7

Explain score.

Are team members organized/work well as a team? (Consider individual and group presentation styles, ordering)

1   2   3   4   5   6   7

Explain score.

Consider realism, research, rationale

Is the presentation **plausible?** (Consider realism, research, rationale)

1   2   3   4   5   6   7

Explain score.

Is the presentation **original?** (Consider product creation, presentation, creativity)

1   2   3   4   5   6   7

Explain score.

How professional was the presentation?

(Consider verbal/nonverbal skills, delivery, dress, visual aid, Q&A)

1   2   3   4   5   6   7

Explain score.

The strongest feature of this presentation was:

My suggestion to improve this presentation is:

Feedback Initials:

Peer Evaluation: Group Presentation

Group Members' Names:_____

Please complete evaluations for the presentation you have been assigned to evaluate. Turn evaluations into your instructor at the end of class.

<u>Rate when prompted (1=poor; 7=excellent) & please make comments for each.</u>

Is the group's objective made clear?
1   2   3   4   5   6   7
Explain score.

Are team members organized/work well as a team? (Consider individual and group presentation styles, ordering)
1   2   3   4   5   6   7
Explain score.

Consider realism, research, rationale

Is the presentation **plausible**? (Consider realism, research, rationale)
1   2   3   4   5   6   7
Explain score.

Is the presentation **original**? (Consider product creation, presentation, creativity)
1   2   3   4   5   6   7
Explain score.

How professional was the presentation?
(Consider verbal/nonverbal skills, delivery, dress, visual aid, Q&A)
1   2   3   4   5   6   7
Explain score.

The <u>strongest feature</u> of this presentation was:

My <u>suggestion to improve</u> this presentation is:

Feedback Initials:

Notes

CHAPTER 8

Leadership and Decision Making in Groups

by Geoffrey R. Tumlin

Objectives

After studying Chapter 8, you should be able to do the following:

- ☐ Understand critical elements that are inherent in the study of leadership.
- ☐ Conceptualize a method for critically analyzing leadership that includes a focus on the leader, the followers, and the situation.
- ☐ Know the limitations of a trait-approach to leadership.
- ☐ Be able to compare and contrast different leadership styles and theories and understand how those styles and theories influence leader decision making.
- ☐ Understand some of the leadership challenges that you are likely to face in your professional future.
- ☐ Assess obstacles that you are likely to face while leading a change initiative.
- ☐ Understand practical suggestions for improving leadership effectiveness.

Key Terms

TERM	DEFINITION
authoritarian	Leaders who seek minimal input from their followers.
authority-compliance management	Leaders who have a low concern for people, but a high concern for production.
contingency theories	Leadership theories that postulate that a leader's effectiveness depends primarily on the situation.
country club management	Leaders who have a high concern for others, but a low concern for production.
democratic	Leaders who allow their followers to have significant influence over their decisions and, consequently, a significant impact on their exercise of leadership.
egalitarian	The idea that everyone should be treated equally.
Fiedler's Contingency Theory	The most well-known contingency theory which states that the right type of leader should be selected for a particular situation, or the situation should be modified to best fit the particular leader.
high LPC	A leader who is primarily relationship-oriented, as measured by the LPC scale.
impoverished management	Leaders who have a low concern for people, and a low concern for production.
interactional framework	A framework conceptualizing leadership as occurring at the intersection of three elements: the leader, the follower, and the situation.
least-preferred coworker (LPC) scale	A survey instrument that determines a leader's predilections towards task- or people-orientation based on a description of the person that the leader works with least well.
leadership	A dynamic, interactive process whereby one person (or group) influences another person (or persons) to move toward a particular goal or objective.
Blake and McCanse's leadership grid®	A taxonomy of leadership styles that categorize leaders across two dimensions: concern for people and concern for production.
low LPC	A leader who is primarily task-oriented, as measured by the LPC scale.
middle-of-the-road management	Leaders who have a moderate amount of concern for others, and a moderate amount of concern for production.
Situational Leadership Theory®	A leadership theory that matches appropriate leader behaviors based on the readiness level of followers.

TERM	DEFINITION
team management	Leaders who have a high amount of concern for others, and a high amount of concern for production.
trait approach	A theoretical leadership approach that maintains that there are certain characteristics that people possess making them more or less likely to be effective leaders.
transactional leader	A leadership exchange relationship where the leader trades rewards and/or punishments in return for followers' efforts.
transformational leader	A leadership relationship where the leader gains influence from followers through a process that appeals to followers' values and belief in a higher purpose to spur change in the status quo.

Introduction

Chapter 7 introduced you to the concept of groups, group dynamics, and collaboration in the workplace. This chapter builds on the ideas presented in chapter 7 by exploring the concept of leadership and considering different ways that leaders make consequential decisions for groups and teams. Specifically, this chapter will answer the following questions about leadership and a leader's decision making in groups:

- ❑ What, exactly, is leadership?
- ❑ What do effective leaders look like?
- ❑ Are there certain traits that can predict leadership effectiveness?
- ❑ What are some different leadership styles and theories and what are their influence on leader decision making?
- ❑ What is the role of followers in the leadership process?
- ❑ What are some common challenges that leaders face?
- ❑ What is some practical advice for effectively leading others?

By the end of this chapter, you will have a better understanding about the answers to these questions, along with practical suggestions about your role as leader and follower in different groups that you will likely encounter throughout your professional career. With these questions as our guide, let's begin our look at leadership.

What, Exactly, Is Leadership?

It would be nice if we could take a pass on this tricky question by simply defining leadership as "the things that leaders do to get the job done," and then move on with the rest of the chapter. In fact, it would be easy to borrow one of a multitude of available leadership definitions. Distinguished leadership scholar Bernard Bass notes that "there are almost as many different definitions of leadership as there are persons who have attempted to define the concept."[1] Many leadership sources begin by acknowledging this challenge inherent in pinning down a definition of leadership and echo the well-cited phrase by Pulitzer Prize winner James MacGregor Burns: "Leadership is one of the most observed and least understood phenomena on earth."[2]

It is important for our purposes to select from a multitude of leadership definitions one that will provide a clear definition of leadership and simultaneously clarify and delimit what we are talking about when we say leadership.[3] After reviewing many sources on leadership and scrutinizing leadership definitions, we propose the following definition of leadership for our use in this chapter:

> Leadership is a dynamic, interactive process whereby one person (or group) influences another person (or persons) to move toward a particular goal or objective.[4] From this operational definition, we see that leadership: (1) is a process; (2) is dynamic and interactive; (3) involves influence; and (4) is purposeful.

Let's briefly unpack each of these critical elements of our definition.

Leadership is a process.

Leadership is a process and not a discrete action or even a series of discrete actions. Rather, leadership is more accurately conceptualized as progressive, ongoing actions, events, and behaviors that may or may not lead to a culminating event. For example, let's say that you are the president of a student organization that is trying to lobby the university administration to have a fall break (similar to a spring break). As president of this organization, let's call it Students for Fall Break (SFB for short), your leadership responsibilities might likely include chairing formal meetings of your organization, meeting with leaders of other student organizations to find common support for your initiative, communicating with university administrators, and making the SFB's views known in local media outlets.[5]

Your leadership is not best illustrated by looking at each individual activity or event in which you participate, but rather your leadership is a gradual and an all-encompassing accumulation of everything that you do as president of Students for Fall Break. Although you will be granted some positional authority as president of SFB, your leadership is more like a gestalt of everything you do as a leader. So, leadership is not accurately conceptualized as a one-shot phenomenon but rather as a macro perspective embodying all of your behaviors, actions, and activities.

> "Leadership is a process and not a discrete action or even a series of discrete actions."

Leadership is dynamic and interactive.

As president of Students for Fall Break, you will undoubtedly exert some influence over your members. However those members also will exert an influence over you! Few leaders can charge forward blindly without taking the views of their followers into account, thus revealing a critical principle of leadership: Leadership involves a give and take between the leaders and the led. As we will discuss later, leaders can vary according to how much influence their followers have over them. Some leaders tend to be more authoritarian in nature, meaning that they seek and follow little input from their followers. Other leaders tend to be more democratic in nature, allowing their followers to have a great influence over their decisions and, consequently, a significant impact on their exercise of leadership.

> "Leadership involves a give and take between the leaders and the led."

As you probably can gather by this point in our discussion, leadership is not a static concept! Leadership is, at its core, a dynamic, interactive, and evolving process that is ever changing. Since we have already touched upon the idea of influence in leadership, let's look at that particular tenet of our leadership definition.

Leadership involves influence.

Fundamentally, leadership involves the practice of influence. In leadership's simplest form, a leader attempts to influence followers to achieve some goal. Regardless of the particular manner in which a leader goes about achieving these goals, influence is a precious commodity of leadership. You might think of influence as the fuel of leadership.

We already mentioned that followers can influence a leader. As president of Students for Fall Break, you will likely find yourself influenced by things other than just your followers. You might be influenced by the university administrators, professors, your friends and family, and even the very media outlets that you are using you get your message across. Leadership authors Richard Hughes, Robert Ginnett, and Gordon Curphy point out that leadership occurs at the intersection of three elements: the leader, the follower, and the situation[6]. They call this approach—that which considers the leader, the followers, and the situation—the interactional framework and we will use this helpful framework throughout this chapter as we consider the nature of leadership.[7]

> "Leadership is, at its core, a dynamic, interactive, and evolving process . . ."

Using the interactional framework, we can see that the act of leadership itself is influenced not only by the leader, but also by the followers and by the situation with which the leaders and the led find themselves dealing. We have already discussed how the leader and the followers can exert influence in our example as the president of Students for Fall Break. Now, let's consider the situation.

The situation also can exert a significant influence on the process of leadership. For example, it would likely be much easier to get support for a fall break if some recent high-profile studies found that having a fall break dramatically increased student and faculty productivity. Let's speculate that these studies were well-regarded and became the lead story on the local news, which then led to a surge in grassroots support for a fall break. These events might make your job much easier as president of Students for Fall Break.

> "... leadership involves the practice of influence."

Suppose, on the other hand, that the same highly regarded studies found that having a fall break had a negative influence on student productivity and the potential cost of a fall break was exorbitant to the university, leading to a groundswell of opposition to the idea. In this case, the situation would likely exert a significant negative influence on your efforts as president of the SFB. Both cases illustrate how the situation would influence the process of leadership.

Leadership is purposeful.

Finally, leadership is purposeful. Leaders are fundamentally *trying to get something done*. Quite often, leaders are viewed as change agents within organizations and within society. As noted leadership and change scholar John Kotter points out, "leadership ... is about coping with change."[8] (We will talk more about the challenges of leading change later.)

Our focus on leadership as purposeful is directly related to the overall premise of this book about strategic communication. Like communication, leadership is also strategic and purposeful. And, the vehicle of leadership is communication, which is why a chapter on leadership appears within this book on strategic communication.

> "... often, leaders are viewed as change agents within organizations and within society."

People have long recognized that leadership and communication are solidly intertwined. John Gardner notes that "Communication is, of course, the prime instrument of the leader/motivator."[9] Communication studies researcher J. Kevin Barge also recognizes these interconnections and states that "leadership is best understood from a communication standpoint."[10] And Michael Hackman and Craig Johnson, echoing this opinion state: "We believe that leadership is best understood from a communication perspective."[11] Communication is the vehicle of leadership, enabling leaders to direct influence through purposeful, strategic communication.

So, we have determined from our definition that leadership is (1) a process, (2) dynamic and interactive, (3) involves influence, and (4) purposeful. Now that we have a good definition of leadership, let's take a look at what effective leadership looks like.

What Do Effective Leaders Look Like?

Are good leaders tall or short? Are they good speakers? Do they have above average IQs? Do effective leaders have more physical stamina and endurance than the general population? These are questions that have been asked and answered, to varying degrees in a multitude of empirical studies since the early 1900s.[12] This search for innate leadership qualities is called the trait approach to leadership. The trait approach holds that there are certain characteristics that people possess that make them more or less likely to be effective leaders.

Are there certain traits that can predict leadership effectiveness?

The trait approach to leadership has a certain intuitive appeal. It seems reasonable to think that certain attributes, like intelligence and sociability, might predict leadership effectiveness. However, one large drawback to the trait approach to leadership is that it has been hard to nail down a definitive set of traits that accurately predict leadership effectiveness. Moreover, studies have shown that a wide array of traits can predict successful leadership, resulting in a massive number of variables that could possibly influence leader effectiveness.[13]

You can probably see these problems with the trait approach simply by thinking about some good leaders from your life. Some of those leaders might have been good speakers, and some might have been shy or felt a bit awkward addressing others. Some leaders that you know might be short and some others tall. Some outspoken and others more reserved. In short (pardon the pun), there is no definitive set of traits that guarantees leadership effectiveness. While you might benefit as a leader from having a good speaking ability or a keen intellect, those traits by themselves do not guarantee effectiveness, nor do those traits consistently predict leadership effectiveness. I am sure we can all think of smart, articulate people who are not the best leaders (and who, in fact, might be some of the worst leaders that we know!). Arguably what is most important to take from studies of the trait approach is what *was not* found—namely, that no discernable trait or set of traits consistently predicts leadership effectiveness.

> **". . . leaders are made, not born."**

So, we can answer the two questions posed above in the following manner, taking the second one first: Are there certain traits that predict leadership effectiveness? No. What do effective leaders look like? Leaders come in all shapes and sizes, all creeds and colors. They have all levels of education from the most advanced degrees possible to having almost no formal education at all. In short, leaders do not have a particular *look* at all!

Are leaders born or are leaders made?

Based on our discussion of the trait approach, we have come a long way toward answering the question of whether leaders are born or made. Given the difficulties of trait researchers to determine a set of traits that accurately and reliably predicts leadership effectiveness, we can say that leaders are made, not born. Adding another voice to our proclamation that leaders are made, leadership author John Gardner states:

> "Many dismiss the subject [of leadership development] with the confident assertion that 'leaders are born not made.' Nonsense! Most of what leaders have that enables them to lead is learned. Leadership is not a mysterious activity. It is possible to describe the tasks that leaders perform. And the capacity to perform those tasks is widely distributed in the population."[14]

Gardner echoes a notion that many educators have known for years: Leadership can be taught and people can be progressively developed to be effective leaders. In fact, many business, governmental, and non-profit organizations devote significant time and resources to developing leaders. So, we have established that leadership can be taught. Now, for the next question . . .

Is leadership an art or a science?

The answer to this question depends largely on who you ask. Many people believe that leadership is an art, implying that people lead by trusting a certain sense of intuition and gut feeling to guide their decisions and actions.[15] Other people (as well as some leadership theorists who we will discuss later) believe that leadership is more of a science than an art. People holding this view believe that people can lead effectively by using systematic methods of analyzing and determining leadership decisions based on available information or by simply plugging the right kind of leader into the applicable leadership situation.[16]

For our purposes, let's consider leadership as both an art and a science, although we will focus more on the science piece in the pages to come. We do this for a reason: If we can cover some basics about the science of leadership, meaning that we can equip you with some systematic understanding of leadership and effective leader decision making, you will be free to focus individually on the art of leadership as you begin to accumulate leadership experiences. And, over time you will feel more secure experimenting with different actions in different leadership situations and hone your craft of leadership into something both authentic and unique.

Leadership Styles and Theories and Their Influence on Leader Decision Making

There are countless theories of leadership and limitless descriptions of different leadership styles (see Figure 8.1 for a listing of some of these styles). We will focus on a few of these leadership theories and styles so that we can provide an appropriate scheme for understanding how different types of leaders make decisions. A good place to begin our discussion of leadership styles and their influence on decision making is Blake and McCanse's Leadership Grid.®[17]

Blake and McCanse's Leadership Grid.®

Blake and McCanse's Leadership Grid® provides a taxonomy of leadership styles by categorizing leaders across two dimensions: *concern for people* and *concern for production*. As such, the Leadership Grid® offers a way of classifying leaders based on their focus on relational (people-oriented) versus task-oriented behaviors. Leaders can be characterized as being either high or low across these dimensions, resulting in five different leadership style possibilities.[18]

Leaders who have a low concern for people and a low concern for production are characterized as impoverished management. These leaders often do the bare minimum to get by, generally operating as withdrawn and distant from their subordinates. This type of leader often presents a twin threat to organizations: They are unconcerned both about getting the job done and the well being of their followers. These leaders do not make decisions based on what is good for their followers or what is best for the organization, but rather based on other criteria, such as what is easy or expedient.

Figure 8.1. A Listing of Selected Leadership Theories and Typologies.

Trait leadership

Situational leadership theory

Contingency theory

Path-goal theory

Leader-member exchange

Normative decision theory

Transactional and transformational leadership

Team leadership

Charismatic and visionary leadership

Ethical leadership

Servant leadership

Principle-centered leadership

Autocratic, democratic, and laissez-faire leadership

Directive, negotiatative, consultative, participative, and delegative leadership

Authoritarian and egalitarian leadership

Leaders who have a low concern for people but a high concern for production are characterized as <u>authority-compliance management</u>. These leaders believe that accomplishing the mission is more important than the well-being of their followers. Authority-compliance leaders see their subordinates as vehicles for task accomplishment and little else, often communicating with them only to the extent necessary to impart instructions. Authority-compliance leaders primarily make decisions based on what will get results.

The third type of leadership style delineated by the Leadership Grid® is <u>country club management</u>. These leaders are high in their concern for others and low in their concern for production. As the name implies, leaders with these predilections are more concerned with interpersonal harmony than they are with task accomplishment. Country club leaders tend to avoid confrontations and be uncontroversial, favoring harmony and protecting an agreeable status quo. Country club leaders make decisions based on what is best for their followers and what will best maintain social harmony in the group or organization.

Leaders who are high in their concern for others and high in their concern for production are classified as <u>team management</u> in Blake and McCanse's Leadership Grid.® These leaders place dual priority on getting the job done and on the welfare of their subordinates. They believe that task and social requirements can be mutually supportive in that a job well done will often facilitate team development and foster harmonious working relationships. Team management leaders make decisions based on the dual considerations of their desire for results and their concern for their subordinates.

A final leadership style described by the Leadership Grid® is <u>middle-of-the-road management</u>. These leaders have a moderate amount of concern for others and a moderate amount of concern for production. Perhaps best thought of as compromisers or balancers, these leaders seek acceptable, judicious levels of task accomplishment and place a moderate amount of concern on the interests of their followers. Middle-of-the-road managers make decisions based on their balancing of subordinate's welfare with task accomplishment.

Blake and McCanse's Leadership Grid® is a good starting point for our discussion of leadership styles and decision making because it allows us to look at leaders as they differ on the dimensions of task-oriented behaviors (concern for production) and social behaviors (concern for people). We will come back to this task, social balance, throughout this chapter as it is one of the most common ways of classifying leaders. The five resulting leadership styles that form the Leadership Grid® help illustrate how leader orientation on these two dimensions can result in very different decision-making processes. Next, let's look at a comparison between two other leadership types that are very well known in the leadership literature and are often compared to each other: transactional and transformational leadership.

Transactional and transformational leadership.

The first widespread conceptualizations of transactional and transformational leadership came from James MacGregor Burns' landmark book *Leadership*.[19] Burns maintained that leaders could be classified as either transactional or transformational in nature. A <u>transactional leader</u> uses a system of rewards and punishments to exert influence over followers. In a way, transactional leadership can be considered as an exchange relationship where the leader trades rewards and/or punishments in return for followers' efforts. A common transactional leadership exchange might be a leader that trades money (a reward) for work from the subordinate. Or, a transactional leader could withhold a promotion (a punishment) in an attempt to coerce a follower to work harder or longer. Some other examples of transactional leaders are politicians who trade favors for constituents for their votes or salespeople who wheel and deal to make a sale to a client.

"A transactional leader uses a system of rewards and punishments to exert influence over followers."

One critical tenet to transactional leadership is that once the leader is out of rewards or punishments, the leader's influence dissipates. Leaders and followers only remain connected as long as a mutually beneficial exchange relationship exists between the two parties. For this reason, transactional leaders tend to make decisions based on two factors: (1) what the leader desires to accomplish; and (2) the leader's ability to offer a salient reward or punishment to secure compliance. Once a transactional leader determines his goal, he must then determine if he has sufficient ability to secure compliance through a transactional exchange with his followers.

A <u>transformational leader</u>, by contrast, gains influence from followers through a process that appeals to followers' values and belief in a higher purpose to spur change in the status quo.[20] Transformational leaders are generally excellent communicators who inspire their followers with a vision of the change event, and they have the charismatic ability to elevate their followers' thinking. In many cases, transformational leaders are able to see and articulate a better plan for the future than their followers would otherwise envision. A transformational political leader, for example, might convince his or her constituents that sweeping changes to the tax code were necessary to prevent the transference of large amounts of debt to future generations.

Transformational leaders make decisions by first determining the vision and direction of the group and organization, and then by galvanizing and inspiring their followers through their charismatic articulation of the vision. Transformational leaders are often considered to be change agents who can implement bold innovations in organizations and engender fierce loyalty.

> **"Transformational leaders . . . are often considered to be change agents who can implement bold innovations in organizations and engender fierce loyalty."**

Now that we know a little about transactional and transformational leadership, it is important to understand some ideas about how the two theories work. First, remember our definition of leadership where we said that leadership was a dynamic and interactive process? The implications of this dynamism are that leaders can demonstrate both transformational and transactional leadership styles at different times, in different situations. While many leaders invariably have a preference towards the type of style that they favor, we will often find ourselves in leadership situations where a transactional style is more appropriate at some points, and a transformational style is more effective at others.

Second, it is important to understand that one style is not necessarily better than the other. Although transformational leaders tend to attract more attention due to their charisma and inspirational ability, transactional leaders can also be extremely effective. Here is where the situational nature of leadership plays a key part in determining leadership effectiveness: One style might be more appropriate and effective than another, depending on the leadership context. Recall also our earlier discussion of the interactive model of leadership from Hughes, Ginnett, and Curphy, which says that leadership occurs at the intersection of the leader, the followers, and the situation?[21] "Good, were flattered that you remember." Let's finish our discussion of leadership styles and their impact on leaders' decision making by looking at two theories that analyze multiple components from the interactive model of leadership. First, consider situational leadership theory, which looks at the matching of particular leader behaviors with particular followers. Then, we will turn to contingency theory, which explores the combination of the leader and the situation.

Situational leadership theory.

<u>Situational leadership theory</u> was developed by Paul Hersey and Kenneth Blanchard as a way of matching appropriate leader behaviors based on the readiness level of followers.[22] According to the theory, followers' readiness level can be characterized by two variables: (1) ability and (2) willingness. Ability refers to the followers having the competence and the skills to complete the requisite tasks assigned to them. Willingness describes the followers' motivation and interest in performing the required tasks as well as their confidence in their potential for successful task completion.

Once a leader has determined the followers' readiness level, the leader selects the leadership style that best fits with the readiness level. The possible leader styles are broken down into two types of leadership behaviors: (1) directive and (2) supportive. These leader behaviors refer to the ways that a leader communicates, assigns, and supervises the tasks that they have given to their subordinates. As the names imply, *directive leaders* take a more direct role in task communication, explicitly describing the task to subordinates in what is usually one-way communication.[23] *Supportive leaders*, on the other hand, facilitate teamwork and follower efforts through a two-way communication process that includes such behaviors as active listening and collaborative problem solving. The way that situational leadership theory divides leadership behaviors into directive and supportive is similar to the way that Blake and McCanse's Leadership Grid® classified leaders based on their concern for people or their concern for production. Both of these classification schemes highlight the recurring distinction among leaders: the split between task and relational leadership behaviors and activities.

According to situational leadership theory, once the leader is aware of the followers' readiness level, the leader matches that readiness level (R1 – R4) with the appropriate leader style (S1 – S4), such that the leadership style match for R1 is S1, for R2 is S2 and so on. Followers with low readiness are best led with a directing telling style; low to moderate readiness with an explaining/selling style, and so on. See Figure 8.2 for the matches between follower readiness levels and appropriate leadership styles according to Hersey and Blanchard's Situational Leadership Theory.

Figure 8.2. Leadership Styles Appropriate for Various Readiness Levels.

READINESS LEVEL	APPROPRIATE STYLE
R1, Low Readiness Unable and unwilling or insecure	S1, Telling High task-low relationship
R2, Low to Moderate Readiness Unable but willing or confident	S2, Selling High task-high relationship
R3, Moderate to High Readiness Able but unwilling or insecure	S3, Participating High relationship-low task
R4, High Readiness Able and willing or confident	S4, Delegating Low relationship-low task

Situational Leadership theory states that leaders should make decisions based primarily on the readiness status of their followers: "in Situational Leadership, it is the follower who determines the appropriate leader behavior."[24] Situational leadership theory indicates that the very manner in which a leader interacts with subordinates should be based on what the follower needs. In this way, situational leadership theory places a primacy on the followers; you can say that situational leadership theory is follower-centric. It should be duly noted that this theory assumes that leaders can modify their behavior with a certain degree of ease in response to followers' readiness levels. While this is consistent with our definition of leadership and we certainly believe that leaders are capable of modifying their behavior and style as required, it should be noted that some people are more likely than others to be able to transition from one style to another. These are idiosyncratic differences that add variety to the practice of leadership.

Contingency theory.

Although a number of theories could be described as contingency theories, the best such known theory is Fiedler's contingency theory.[25] Fiedler's contingency theory differs from situational leadership theory in one critical way: In situational leadership theory, leaders are instructed to change their leadership behaviors based on their followers' readiness level; however, in Fiedler's contingency theory, leaders are presumed to be much more fixed in their leadership styles and less able to change their leadership behaviors. Therefore, the heart of Fiedler's contingency theory is the idea that the right type of leader should be selected for a particular situation, or the situation should be modified to best fit the particular leader.[26]

Contingency theory begins by classifying leaders in a manner in which we are becoming familiar, by determining if the leader is task-oriented or people-oriented. Fiedler does this using the <u>least-preferred coworker (LPC) scale</u>, which is a survey instrument that determines a leader's predilections toward task- or people-orientation based on a description of the person that the leader works with least well. Once the leader has been given a LPC score as either <u>high LPC</u> (relationship-orientation) or <u>low LPC</u> (task-orientation), it is possible to make some predictions about which types of situations that leader might be most effective. Again, remember that contingency theory assumes that it is easier to fit a specific type of leader to a particular situation than it is for a leader to change his or her style or orientation.

> "... the heart of Fiedler's contingency theory is the idea that the right type of leader should be selected for a particular situation ..."

Contingency theory next seeks to classify the leadership situation based on overall favorability. To determine overall situational favorability, three subconstructs are used: (1) leader-member relations, (2) task structure, and (3) leader position power.[27] Leader-member relations refer to the general affinity, confidence, and loyalty that the followers have for their leader. Task structure refers to the extent to which the nature of the followers' work tasks are clearly delineated and explicitly stated. Leader position power refers to the amount of legitimate authority and positional power that a leader has. Figure 8.3 shows how the different combinations of the three situational variables come together to predict which type of leader orientation will be most effective in dealing with a particular situation.

In a nutshell, contingency theory predicts that task-oriented leaders are best suited to either highly favorable or highly unfavorable situations and that relationship-oriented leaders work best in situations that are in between—neither highly favorable nor highly unfavorable.[28]

The Role of Followers in the Leadership Process

Throughout the course of this chapter, we have addressed followers as one of the three main components in the process of leadership (along with the leader and the situation). It is important to highlight them again because they are the one element in the leadership process most likely to be de-emphasized when you are thinking about leadership. Part of this is probably due to our natural attraction to leaders as opposed to followers. After all, we can probably list many movies and television shows that we have watched in the past year that have focused on a particular leader, but how many movies or television shows do we watch that are focused on followers? There is a similar correlation in the books we read and the movies we watch, as well as many leadership textbooks and academic articles.[29]

> "In spite of this, followers will always be a critical variable in the process of leadership."

In spite of this, followers will always be a critical variable in the process of leadership. Practically, you are encouraged to get to know your followers to the best of your ability and factor this knowledge into your decision making. And, as a follower, you should understand that you really do play a critical role in your organization, group, or team; and, therefore, plan accordingly to be an effective follower, just as you will plan to be an effective leader.

What are some common challenges that leaders face?

As a leader, you will invariably face a number of different challenges throughout your professional career. Let's take a look at three challenges that you are almost certain to face as a leader.

Figure 8.3.

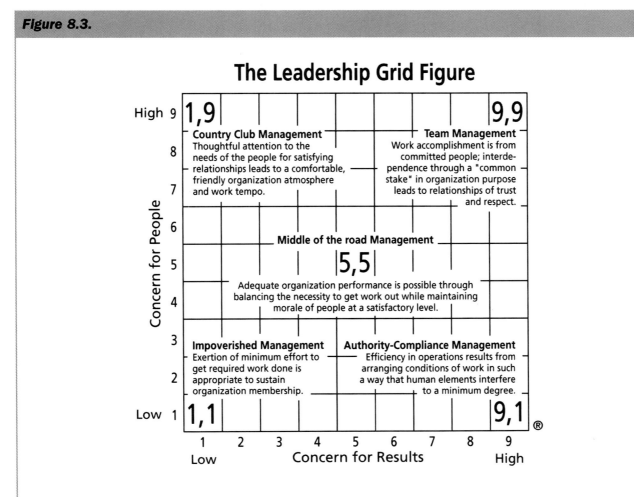

The Leadership Grid Figure

Source: The Leadership Grid® figure, Paternalism Figure and Opportunism from *Leadership Dilemmas—Grid Solutions*, by Robert R. Blake and Anne Adams McCanse (Formerly the *Managerial Grid* by Robert R. Blake and Jane S. Mouton). Houston: Gulf Publishing Company, (Grid Figure: p. 29). Copyright 1991 by Blake and Mouton, and Scientific Methods, Inc. Reproduced by permission of the owners.

Leading a change effort

As we discussed when we talked about transformational leadership, some conceptualizations of leadership assume that leaders are primarily change agents. There are many books written on leading change, and the primary thesis seems to boil down to the fact that the leader has to overcome significant resistance in almost any change effort.[30] It is important to highlight the critical role of communication in a leader's successful facilitation of a change effort. As you can see from Figure 8.4, communicating—specifically communicating a vision—is critical to the successful implementation of a change effort. While there are multitudes of ways to conceptualize change, all of us can think of a leader who faced change on either a small or a large level. Throughout your leadership career, you are likely to routinely implement change efforts on a small level, perhaps even weekly or monthly. On a larger level, you might only be leading a large change effort a few times over the course of your entire career. Regardless of the scope and the magnitude of the change effort, the centrality of communication remains.

One reason you only may encounter large-scale change is that change brings great stress and uncertainty to an organization so effective communication is imperative. And, in conditions of stress and uncertainty, organizational members and stakeholders have a desperate craving for information. Failure to provide timely, accurate information results in the rumor mill and the grapevine taking over, and it will result in misinformation about the change effort.

> ### Figure 8.4. Eight Reasons Why Change Efforts Fail.
>
> 1. Leaders allow for too much complacency
>
> 2. A sufficiently powerful guiding coalition is not created
>
> 3. Leaders underestimate the power of a vision
>
> 4. The vision is under communicated by a factor of 10 (or 100 or even 1000)
>
> 5. Obstacles are permitted to block the new vision
>
> 6. Leaders fail to create short-term wins
>
> 7. Victory is declared too soon
>
> 8. Changes are not anchored firmly in the corporate culture
>
> Adapted from John Kotter, *Leading Change* (Boston: Harvard Business School Press, 1996, pp. 4–14).

Preventing groupthink and facilitating open communication

As discussed in Chapter 7, groupthink is a challenge that leaders must actively guard against. As leaders build up influence and authority over time, the possibility exists that followers might become less and less likely to challenge the leader and to provide the kind of good, sound advice that all leaders need. Groupthink is prevented by a number of countermeasures. First, to the extent to which you, as a leader, actively consider your followers and involve them in appropriate ways in the decision making process will automatically hedge against groupthink. Second, establishing open lines of communication prevents groupthink. Third, fostering a culture where candor is encouraged and rewarded will go a long way in the fight against groupthink. Finally, appointing someone to be a devil's advocate in meetings and at other (or at *all*) critical junctures can help prevent against groupthink.

> "... groupthink is a challenge that leaders must actively guard against."

Ethics and Leadership

Invariably, at some point in your professional career, you are going to face an ethical challenge. While it might be something as transparent as a bribe or a pay-off, it is more likely to be opaque, such as having to determine if you should fire a veteran of your company who has not been able to "right the ship" after a series of personal tragedies. There are scores of books written that deal with the ethical component of leadership. Our purpose here is to provide some practical advice when you are faced with ethical leadership challenges.

First, we highly recommend that you think through challenging situations before they occur. You should try to find your own ethical compass when the seas are smooth as opposed to in the middle of the storm. In the middle of an ethical crisis is hardly the time to contemplate your ethical bearings for the first time.

Second, do not discount your intuition when making ethical decisions. As the writer Robert Louis Stevenson once said: "If your morals make you dreary, depend on it, they are wrong."[31] Many times, we know the answer to the ethical challenge but we are simply in the middle of the crisis and we cannot take the time to adequately listen to our intuition. So, make the time to listen, and listen closely, to what your gut is telling you.

Third, understand that sometimes you will have to lead by exception. While <u>egalitarian</u> principles may seem conceptually appealling, in practice, leaders must often treat people differently.[32] And, at some point in your leadership career, you are likely to make a "rule," only to turn around and break it when you see that an exception needs to be made. Do not be dismayed by this. There are not any hard and fast rules for leaders, rather principles and ideas to use as guides. Sometimes, leadership by exception is the most appropriate leadership strategy.

Conclusion

In conclusion, we wish you the best of luck as you continue to experiment and refine your leadership style. We encourage you to be gentle on yourself and remember that leadership is a lifelong process that involves a great deal of trial and error. Remember, leaders are made and not born, and the "making" of a leader takes a lifetime to perfect! But, the good news is that it's not all an uphill struggle. Some of your best moments are likely to happen when you are leading a group of people towards a worthwhile and challenging end. Those bonds are authentic and some may last a lifetime. So, be kind to yourself and enjoy the journey. Be courageous and, when appropriate, be bold in your leadership. Your followers are depending on you. Good luck!

Review Questions

1. How do you personally define leadership? Is there anything that you would add or remove from the chapter's definition?

2. Do you agree with the chapter's statement that leaders are made and not born? Why or why not?

3. Please explain, in your own words, the relationship between leadership and communication.

4. How effective do you think the interactive model of communication (leader, follower, and situation) is in helping to explain leadership? How might you modify the theory to make it more effective?

5. Explain the difference between task (concern for production) and social (concern for people) leaders.

6. Give an example of a leader behavior that is transactional in nature. How do you think this behavior leads to influence?

7. Give an example of a leader behavior that is transformational in nature. How do you think this behavior leads to influence?

8. Argue either for or against Fiedler's proposition that leaders are relatively fixed in their leadership style.

9. What is the role of followers in the leadership process? Frame your answer using at least two of the ideas or theories presented in the chapter.

10. Which of the leadership theories presented in the chapter makes the most sense to you? Why?

11. What are some common challenges that leaders face?

12. Describe some obstacles frequently encountered when leading a change effort.

13. Explain ways to guard against groupthink.

14. Describe in your own words the relationship between leadership and ethics.

15. Offer your own suggestions for effective leadership.

Endnotes

1 Bass, B. M. (1990). *Bass and Stogdill's handbook of leadership* (Third ed.). New York: Free Press, p. 11.

2 Burns, J. M. (1978). *Leadership*. New York: Harper and Row, p. 2.

3 See Rost, J. C. (1993). *Leadership for the twenty-first century*. Westport, CN: Praeger, pp. 37–95 for a rigorous chronology of leadership definitions.

4 Although this definition of leadership is our own, it bears the influence of Richard Hughes, Robert Ginnett, & Gordon Curphy from their textbook *Leadership: Enhancing the lessons of experience* 3rd ed. (Boston: Irwin/McGraw-Hill, 1999) and from their interactive model of leadership, which is discussed later in the chapter. Hughes, Ginnett, & Curphy use the following definition of leadership which is from C.F. Roach & Orlando Behling, "Functionalism: Basis for an Alternate Approach to the Study of Leadership." In *Leaders and Managers: International Perspectives on Managerial Behavior and Leadership.* ed. By J.G. Hunt, D.M. Hosking, C.A. Schriesheim, and R. Stewar (Elmsford, NY: Paragon, 1984).

5 Thanks to John Daly for supplying this example.

6 Hughes, R. L., Ginnett, R. C., & Curphy, G. J. (1999). *Leadership: Enhancing the lessons of experience* (Third ed.). Boston: Irwin/McGraw-Hill, p. 26.

7 Although Hughes, Ginnett, & Curphy developed the interactive model of leadership, looking at (a) leaders, (b) followers, and (c) the situation as essential leadership variables was documented earlier in Fred Fiedler, *A Theory of Leadership Effectiveness* (New York: McGraw-Hill, 1967) and in Edwin Hollander, *Leadership Dynamics: A Practical Guide to Effective Relationships* (New York: Free Press, 1978).

8 Kotter, J. P. (1998). What Leaders Really Do. In *Harvard Business Review on Leadership* (pp. 37–60). Boston: Harvard Business Review Paperback, p. 40.

9 Gardner, J. W. (1993). *On Leadership*. New York: Free Press, p. 51.

10 Barge, J. K. (1994). *Leadership: Communication Skills for Organizations and Groups*. New York: St. Martin's, p. vi.

11 Hackman, M. Z., & Johnson, C. E. (1996). *Leadership: A communication perspective*. Prospect Heights, IL: Waveland Press, p. 4.

12 For a good review of trait research in leadership, see chapters 4 and 5 in Bass, B. M. (1990). *Bass and Stogdill's handbook of leadership* (Third ed.). New York: Free Press.

13 Northouse, P. G. (2004). *Leadership: Theory and Practice* (Third ed.). Thousand Oaks, CA: Sage, p. 23.

14 Gardner, J. W. (1993). *On Leadership*. New York: Free Press, p. xix.

15 For example, see Max DePree, *Leadership is an Art* (New York: Dell, 1998).

16 A good example of using a scientific model to make a leadership decision (specifically whether or not to involve subordinates in the decision making process) is the normative model of decision making from Victor H. Vroom, A Normative Model of Participation in Decision Making in *Handbook of Industrial and Organizational Psychology*, ed. M.D. Dunnette (Chicago: Rand McNally, 1976). A good example of a theory that advocates putting the right kind of leader in specific situations is Fielder's contingency theory: Fred E. Fielder, A contingency model of leadership effectiveness. In L. Berkowitz (ed.) *Advances in experimental social psychology* (Vol 1, pp. 149–190, New York: Academic Press, 1978).

17 Blake and Mouton's first conceptualization of the leadership grid (then called the management grid) appeared in Robert R. Blake and Jane S. Mouton, *The Managerial Grid* (Houston, TX: Gulf Publishing, 1964). They subsequently updated their thoughts in 1978 and 1985.

18 The good visual depiction of the leadership grid is found in Robert R. Blake and Anne A. McCanse, *Leadership Dilemmas—Grid Solutions* (Houston, TX: Gulf Publishing, 1991, p. 29).

19 James MacGregor Burns, *Leadership* (New York: Harper and Row, 1978). The term transactional leadership was first used by James V. Downton in *Rebel Leadership: Commitment and Charisma in a Revolutionary Process* (New York: Free Press, 1973).

20 Hughes, R. L., Ginnett, R. C., & Curphy, G. J. (1999). *Leadership: Enhancing the lessons of experience* (Third ed.). Boston: Irwin/McGraw-Hill, p. 291.

21 Hughes, Ginnett, and Curphy, *Leadership*, p. 26.

22 The tenets of situational leadership theory were first articulated in Paul Hersey & Kenneth Blanchard, Life Cycle Theory of Leadership. *Training and Development Journal* 23 (1969), pp. 26–34. They have refined and republished their theory multiple times since then. A recent description of their situational leadership theory can be found in Paul Hersey, Kenneth Blanchard & Dewey Johnson, *Management of Organizational Behavior: Leading Human Resources*, 8th Ed. (Upper Saddle River, NJ: Prentice Hall, 2001).

23 Northouse, *Leadership*, p. 89.

24 Paul Hersey. Kenneth Blanchard & Dewey Johnson, Management of Organizational Behaviour: Leading Human Resources, 8th Ed. (Upper Saddle River, NJ: Prentice Hall, 2001), p. 188.

25 Fred Fiedler originally postulated his contingency theory in Fred Fiedler, A Contingency Model of Leadership Effectiveness in L. Berkowitz (ed.), *Advances in Experimental Social Psychology,* Volume 1, pp. 149–190 (New York: Academic Press, 1964). It was refined in Fiedler, *A Theory of Leadership Effectiveness* (New York: McGraw-Hill, 1967).

26 Hughes, Ginnett, and Curphy, *Leadership*, p. 63.

27 Northouse, *Leadership*, pp. 110–111.

28 Northouse, *Leadership*, p. 111.

29 Robert Kelley's work on followers is an exception to the tendency to focus on followers: Robert Kelley, *The Power of Followership* (New York: Currency Doubleday, 1992) and Robert Kelley, In Praise of Followers in *Harvard Business Review* 66, no. 6 (1988, pp. 142–148).

30 Two good books on change leadership are John Kotter, *Leading Change* (Boston: Harvard Business School Press, 1996) and James O'Toole, *Leading Change: Overcoming the Ideology of Comfort and the Tyranny of Custom* (San Francisco: Jossey-Bass, 1995). A good book on communicating change is T.J. Larkin & Sandar Larkin, *Communicating Change: Winning Employee Support for New Business Goals* (New York: McGraw-Hill, 1994).

31 Quote retrieved from http://www.worldofquotes.com/author/Robert-Louis-Stevenson/1/.

32 This is the central premise of a good book by Marcus Buckingham and Curt Coffman called *First, Break all the Rules: What the World's Greatest Managers do Differently* (New York: Simon and Schuster, 1999).

33 Although *Rules and Tools for Leaders* by Perry M. Smith (New York: Avery, 1998) is pretty good at laying out some general rules and guidelines.

Notes

CHAPTER 9

A Primer in Intercultural Communication

Objectives

After studying Chapter 9, you should be able to do the following:

☐ Understand the communication process and characteristics of competence.

☐ Recognize the need to self-monitor communication competence especially in intercultural situations.

☐ Develop skills in selecting and using a variety of communication strategies and responses based on situational contexts, goals, and needs.

☐ Have a greater understanding of cultural and ethnic diversity.

☐ Increase your communication competence by increasing your communication complexity, nuance, and sophistication.

☐ Develop an appreciation for intercultural communication.

Key Terms

TERM	DEFINITION
collectivism	The broad value tendencies of a culture in emphasizing the importance of the "we" identity over the "I" identity, group rights over individual rights, and in-group needs over individual wants and desires.
culture	A learned system of meanings which helps us make sense of and explain what is going on in our everyday surroundings.
face	Our public selves that make up who we want to be seen as.
flexible intercultural communication	Being adaptive, creative, and experimental in your communication style.
globalization	The changes in culture, the industrialization of work, the shift from villages to towns and cities, the rise of individualism, decline of community, and the technological advances that account for our present social situation.
high-context culture	A culture in which the emphasis is on how intention or meaning can best be conveyed through the context and nonverbal channels.
individualism	Cultures like the US, Canada, and Western Europe who value individual identity over group identity, individual rights over group rights, and individual needs over group needs.
intercultural communication	The symbolic exchange process whereby individuals from two or more different cultural communities negotiate shared meanings in an interactive situation.
large-power distance	Hierarchical cultures where there is a clear chain of command and communication interactions are dependent on where one's position falls on the hierarchy.
low-context culture	A culture in which meaning is expressed through explicit verbal messages.
mindful communication	Being consciously aware of, and paying attention to our communication behavior.
small power distance	Cultures that work together to achieve a democratic and egalitarian decision-making process and power structures.
strong uncertainty avoidance	Cultures that view conflict as a threat and to be avoided.
weak uncertainty avoidance	Cultures that view conflict as natural and potentially positive.

This chapter aims to increase your professional communication competence by increasing your knowledge and skills about intercultural communication. With increased globalization, or the changes in culture, the industrialization of work, the shift from villages to towns and cities, the rise of individualism, decline of community, and the technological advances that account for our present social situation, and demographic changes in the U. S., it is inevitable that you will be communicating with people who do not look like you, think like you, and communicate like you.

When we use the word culture, we refer to a learned system of meanings which helps us make sense of and explain what is going on in our everyday surroundings.[1] This meaning system consists of patterns, traditions, beliefs, values, norms, meanings, and symbols that are passed on from one generation to the next and are shared to varying degrees by interacting members of a community.

Culture influences all that we do—from our recreational activities to what we eat, to how we celebrate, to how we worship, to how we deliver public presentations. But culture is not always simple. Culture is a slippery, elastic concept that takes on multiple shades of meaning. On one level, culture can refer to the trivial—like when we cut down a tree, move it inside, and decorate it once a year. Culture can also refer to the momentous, as in what people will die for.

What Is Culture?

Start with a cage containing five monkeys. Inside the cage, hang some bananas on a rope and place a ladder under the bananas. Before long, a monkey will go to the ladder and will climb towards the bananas. As soon as he touches the ladder, spray all of the other monkeys with cold water. After a while, another monkey makes an attempt with the same result—all the other monkeys are sprayed with cold water. Pretty soon, when another monkey tries to climb the ladder, the other monkeys will try to prevent it. Now, put away the cold water. Remove one monkey from the cage and replace it with a new one. The new monkey sees the bananas and wants to climb the ladder. To his surprise and horror, all of the other monkeys attack him. After another attempt and attack, he knows that if he tries to climb the ladder, he will be assaulted. Next, remove another of the original monkeys and replace it with a new one. The newcomer goes towards the ladder and he is attacked. The previous newcomer takes part in the punishment with enthusiasm! Likewise, replace a third original monkey with a new one, then a fourth, then a fifth. Every time the newest monkey takes to the ladders, he is attacked. Most of the monkeys that are beating him have no idea why they were not permitted to climb the ladder or why they are participating in the beating of the newest monkey. After replacing all the original monkeys, none of the remaining monkeys have ever been sprayed with cold water. Nevertheless, no monkey ever again approaches the ladder to try for the bananas.[2]

Why Study Intercultural Communication?

Although intercultural communication, or the symbolic exchange process whereby individuals from two or more different cultural communities negotiate shared meanings in an interactive situation, is not a new area of study, its importance has grown in recent years for an obvious reason: our world is changing. Many years ago, a white American businessman could predict the race, gender, average age, and even religion of most audience members—they would look like him, speak like him, and share many of the same attitudes, beliefs, and values.[3]

Today, such audiences are rare.

Now, direct contact with cultural different people in our neighborhoods, community, schools, and workplaces in an inescapable part of life.[4] Therefore, knowing how to deliver public presentations to those of a different cultural background will be extremely useful to both future business persons and sojourners who plan on traveling the world, and those who plan on staying in the increasingly diverse United States.

A Homogenous Audience:

Courtesy of Photofest.

A Diverse Audience:

Courtesy of Savage Productions, Inc.

Cultural Value Dimensions

Culture is an elastic term, making the relationship between culture and communication complex and messy. This presents a problem for us when we attempt to offer broad generalizations about how to deliver presentations to people of different cultures. Many years ago, people who studied intercultural communication compared different countries. For example, they would look at how France was different from the U.S., or how Nigeria was different from China. This approach had two problems. First, currently there are an estimated 195 countries in the world. Comparing them to one another would be a daunting task! Second, often there is more variability *within* a nation than there is *between* nations. There are perhaps more differences between a person raised in the Valley in Texas and someone from the Bronx than there are between someone from Monterrey, Mexico and someone from the Valley. Thus, scholars sought to find a few underlying dimensions of cultures that nations and people could be placed on. Since that intellectual move was made, we've organized many cultural differences into five main cultural value dimensions: low and high context, individualism and collectivism, small and large power distance, weak and strong uncertainty avoidance, and feminine-masculine roles.

Exercise 9.1. How to be both appropriate and effective in your communication style.[5]

Brian Holtz is a U.S. businessperson assigned by his company to manage its office in Thailand. Mr. Thani, a valued assistant manager in the Bangkok office, has recently been arriving late for work. Holtz has to decide what to do about this problem.

After carefully thinking about his options, he decides there are four possible strategies:

1. Go privately to Mr. Thani, ask him why he has been arriving late, and tell him that he needs to come to work on time.

2. Ignore the problem.

3. Publically reprimand Mr. Thani the next time he is late.

4. In a private discussion, suggest that he is seeking Mr. Thani's assistance in dealing with employees in the company who regularly arrive late for work, and solicit his suggestion about what should be done.

What would your choice be? Why?

_____

_____

_____

_____

_____

_____

_____

_____

_____

_____

_____

_____

_____

_____

_____

_____

_____

Holtz's first strategy would be effective, as it would accomplish his objective of getting Mr. Thani to arrive more promptly, but given the expectations of the Thai culture, which are that one person never directly criticizes another, such behavior would be very inappropriate. Conversely, Holtz's second strategy would be appropriate but not effective, as there would probably be no change in Mr. Thani's behavior. The third option would be neither appropriate nor effective because public humiliation might force Mr. Thani, a valuable employee, to resign. The fourth option, which is the best choice is both appropriate and effective because using indirect means to communicate his concerns, Mr. Thani is able to save <u>face</u> while Holtz's accomplishes his strategic goals.

Low and high context.

Edward T. Hall, a prominent intercultural scholar, coined the terms low-context and high-context to account for the differences in the degree to which the amount of information implied by the context rather than just the specific words that are spoken affects what we understand when people are speaking.[6]

In a _low-context_ culture, meaning is expressed through explicit verbal messages. The U. S., for example, is a relatively low-context culture where people are expected to say what they mean and mean what they say. Speakers are expected to present facts in a clear, direct, and explicit style. Jerry Jones, billionaire owner of the NFL's Dallas Cowboys, offers a great example of low-context public speaking. On giving advice on how to ask an audience for their money, he said there are five important points to remember: "Number one," Jones said, "is ask for the money. And I forgot the other four." Jones' no-nonsense approach might work for a U. S. or Western Europe audience, but let's compare that direct, low-context approach to how that message could be interpreted in a high-context culture.

In _high-context_ cultures, emphasis is on how intention or meaning can best be conveyed through the context and nonverbal channels. In other words, high-context cultures require much more reading between the lines because communicators must consider the background and history of the speaker-audience relationship. In a high-context culture, Jones' direct appeal for the audience's money would be met with disdain and rejection. The audience would feel insulted because Jones not only failed to take the time to develop a relationship with the audience members, but failed to petition them in a nuanced manner.

Here is another good example of the differences between low and high-context: Imagine two neighbors talking over their shared fence and one says to the other, "I hear your daughter practicing the violin constantly. You must be so proud of her diligence and discipline. She works so hard, even in the early mornings and late at night. She is no doubt going to grow up and become a star." How might this message be interpreted? If this were a low-context culture, the neighbor would say thank you and accept their neighbor's surface level compliment. But in a high-context culture, the neighbor might respond with regret and apologize, for the subtle, deeper meaning is that the daughter's violin playing is annoying their neighbor.

Exercise 9.2. The following situations can help you sort out whether you prefer high or low-context communication.

1. When you enter a room full of people, if your typical reaction would be to seek out a stranger and introduce yourself that would be more low-context. If your typical reaction is to blend in and not be noticed, you would be more high-context.

2. Suppose you had two job offers to choose between. If you choose the position that will result in greatest job satisfaction that would be more low-context. If your choice would be based on location of the job in relation to your close friends and family that would be more high-context.

3. Imagine that you and your co-worker are up for the same company promotion. You just heard that you got it, but your co-worker did not. What will you say when your co-worker asks if you have heard any news? If you tell your co-worker you got the promotion that would be more low-context. If you would tell your co-worker you have not heard anything yet that would be more high-context.

4. A controversy has developed in your workplace, and you need to take a position. Which is your most likely course of action? If you analyze the controversy on your own and voice your position that would be more low-context. If you discuss the controversy with your friends and take their views into account that would be more high-context.

5. New Year's is right around the corner and you've already planned a long weekend off, with early notification. Your manager asks you to work the New Year's Eve weekend at the last minute because everyone else wants the day off. If you say "No thanks..." directly with no reason given that would be more low-context. If you say, "No thanks..." in a tactful way—and offer a reason and apologize that would be more high-context.

6. Your parents do not approve of your romantic partner. What do you do? If you tell your family to respect your partner and treat him or her properly that would be more low-context. If you tell your partner that he or she must make a great effort to "fit in" with the family that would be more high-context.

7. Throughout the semester, your professor constantly mispronounces your name. What do you do? If you correct your professor—you do not want the error to continue—that would be more low-context. If you say nothing and let it go that would be more high-context.

8. Your neighbor has been loudly playing music for the past 3 nights past 1 a.m. If you approach your neighbor assertively that would be more low-context. If you grin and bear it—and hope the music will stop eventually that would be more high-context.

Individualism and collectivism.

Suppose you graduate from UT and are presented with a choice of jobs. In one, no one is singled out for personal honor but everyone works together. In another, personal autonomy is encouraged and individual initiatives are achieved. If you are from an individualistic culture like the U. S., or Sweden, there is more than a 90% chance you would choose the second job. But if you were from a collectivistic culture like Japan or Singapore, there is less than a 50% chance of you choosing the second.

Individualism. Individualistic cultures value individual identity over group identity, individual rights over group rights, and individual needs over group needs. Individualism promotes self-efficiency, individual responsibility, and personal autonomy, and emphasizes personal achievement and standing out from the group.[7]

Collectivism. The values expressed in U. S. Western culture, however, reflects only 25% of the world's population. Most of the world's population, including cultures found in many Asian, African, Latin, & Arab countries, tend to be team players, concerned with harmony, and group cohesion more than individuals' personal feelings. Collectivism refers to the broad value tendencies of a culture in emphasizing the importance of the "we" identity over the "I" identity, group rights over individual rights, and in-group needs over individual wants and desires. Collectivistic cultures promote relationship interdependence, ingroup harmony, and ingroup collaborative spirit more so than individualistic cultures. It is revealing that the word for "I" in Chinese, a very collectivistic culture, looks very much like the word *selfish* and the word *"different"* is the same as the word for *wrong*.[8]

Collectivistic Sayings

- ❑ "One finger cannot lift a pebble."

- ❑ "The nail that sticks up will be hammered down."

- ❑ "When spider's webs united, they can tie up a lion."

- ❑ "No need to know the person, only the family"

- ❑ "It takes a whole village to raise a child."

Small and large power distance.

The third cultural value dimension refers to how important power and status are to communication interactions.

Large power distance. Large power distance cultures are hierarchical, much like the military where there is a clear chain of command and communication interactions are dependent on where one's position falls on the hierarchy. Cultures with large power distance like Japan and China tend to accept unequal power distributions based on age, seniority, and rank. If you were in a meeting with members of a large power distance culture, you would need to be very careful about overtly criticizing anyone above you in the power hierarchy. Comments that did not fit within the chain of command would not be welcomed. In a speaking situation, you would address the majority of your presentation to the top people in the room, and perhaps pay less attention to everyone else.

Small power distance. Small power distance cultures value equal power distributions, equal rights and relations, equitable rewards and punishment based on performance. In these cultures, there is less of a power hierarchy and more equality. Because these cultures tend to be more egalitarian, it would be acceptable, within reason, to voice your criticism of both subordinates and superiors in public situations. In presentations, you would speak to the entire room and consider everyone's feedback as equally important.

Weak and strong uncertainty avoidance.

The fourth cultural value dimensions refers to the extent to which members of a culture do not mind conflict or uncertain situations and the extent to which they try to avoid those uncertain situations.

Weak Uncertainly Avoidance. In weak uncertainty avoidance cultures conflict is perceived as natural and potentially positive. Cultures found in Singapore, Denmark, and the U. S. encourage risk taking and conflict-approaching modes. They don't mind change.

Strong Uncertainty Avoidance. Alternatively, in strong uncertainty avoidance cultures, conflict is perceived as a threat and to be avoided. Cultures found in countries like Greece, El Salvador, and Japan tend to avoid conflict, prefer clear procedures and conflict-avoidance behaviors.[9]

The difference between weak and strong uncertainty avoidance cultures becomes apparent during the Question-and-Answer session after the presentation. Audience members from weak uncertainty avoidance cultures would not have a problem telling you they disagree with you or that you are simply wrong. They might even interrupt you during your presentation to voice these qualms and they would expect a cogent defense from you. An audience member from a strong uncertainty avoidance culture, in contrast, would rarely interrupt, saving his or her qualms for a later, perhaps more private, time.

Feminine-masculine sex roles.

The final cultural value dimension refers to how much gender roles are clearly complimentary and distinct or are fluid and overlapping.[10] Geert Hofstede, a prominent intercultural researcher, makes a distinction here between masculine cultures with clear and rigid sex roles and feminine cultures with overlapping sex roles and more gender equality.

In masculine cultures, "men are men" and "women are women" and there is little ambiguity. Think about the stereotypical masculine image and stereotypical feminine image here and you'll have an idea of what the ideal image males and females are supposed to fit in to in these cultures. In cultures with high masculinity scores like Japan, Italy, and Mexico, men are supposed to be task-oriented, tough, assertive, and value material success, while women are supposed to be more modest, feminine, tender, and concerned with the quality of life.

High femininity cultures like Sweden, the Netherlands, and Costa Rica, have sex roles that are more fluid, overlapping, and less rigid. For example, there is less of a distinctive and idealized masculine or feminine image in these countries. Both men and women can be modest, observant, and tender. In this dimension, the U. S. is moderate, displaying neither very high masculinity scores or very high femininity scores.

Where a culture falls on the masculine/feminine sex role continuum has a profound impact on how you should approach your public presentation. In both content and delivery, masculine cultures would expect you to strictly adhere to traditional gender norms as you speak, while feminine cultures would not have those same expectations. This should inform everything from your dress, gestures, and posture, to the types of stories you tell and the way you structure your arguments.

Exercise 9.3. The Rosemary Parable[11]

ROSEMARY is a young woman about 21 years old. For a long time she has been engaged to a young man named HERNANDO and she is coming from a great distance to meet him for their scheduled wedding. The problem she faces is that between her and her betrothed there lives a river. No ordinary river, mind you, but a deep, wide river infested with hungry crocodiles.

ROSEMARY ponders how she can cross the river. She thinks of a man who has a boat, whose name is SVEN. She approaches SVEN and asks him to take her across the river. SVEN replies, "Yes, I'll take you across the river if you'll spend the night with me."

Shocked at this offer, she turns to another acquaintance, LEE PAI, and tells him her story. LEE PAI responds by saying, "Poor ROSEMARY, I understand your problem, but I don't see how I can help. It's really your problem, not mine."

ROSEMARY, in desperation, decides to return to SVEN and hooks up with him. In the morning SVEN takes her across the river. She completes her journey and arrives in time.

Her reunion with HERNANDO is warm, but on the evening before they are to be married, ROSEMARY feels compelled to tell HERNANDO how she succeeded in getting across the river. HERNANDO responds by saying, "I can't believe you would do such a thing. I wouldn't marry you if you were the last woman on earth." And he banished her as a soiled woman.

Finally, at her wit's end, ROSEMARY turns to our last character, SEIICHI. He listens to her story and says, "What a terrible thing to happen. ROSEMARY, I don't love you, but I will marry you." And that's all we know of the story.

Write down, in rank order, the character you MOST APPROVE to LEAST APPROVE, plus a brief sentence explaining your first choice, second choice, and so on.

In groups of four to six, take turns sharing your first choice, second choice, third choice, and so on. Probe each other for the reasoning behind the rank-order decision-making process.

Discuss and arrive at a **group consensus** of the rank-order choices. One member of the group should be responsible to record group choices and report back to the entire class.

Individual Rank-Order Choices

1. Most approve:
2. Least approve:

Reflection Analysis

1. On an individual level, who was your top-ranked choice? What values were you defending? Who was your bottom-ranked choice? What values were you rejecting?
2. Where did you learn your cultural/personal values? Identify your influential sources.
3. Did you change your rankings to the group consensus rankings wholeheartedly? Explain your decision or dilemma.
4. Recommend 2–3 constructive ways to understand your own values and other people's values mindfully.

Intercultural Communication Guidelines
General communication guidelines.

Gestures. Be aware of how cultural differences influence how we interpret gestures. For example, sitting at a table during a meeting, crossing your legs, and showing the soles of your feet to the audience is normal in most U. S. settings, but it could be viewed as an impolite and insulting action in many others.[12] Pointing to an audience member and using the "A-OK" gesture is all right with U. S. audiences, but the gesture can be insulting in some cultures.[13] For instance, in France and Belgium, it means your worth is zero. In Greece and Turkey, it is a vulgar sexual invitation, usually meant as an insult. Even the traditional "hook 'em horns" symbol—a closed fist with the index and pinkie fingers raised—can be offensive in some countries. For you, it probably means that you are a proud member of the Longhorns. But in some Mediterranean countries, this same gesture implies that a man's wife has been unfaithful. In American Sign Language, the gesture translates into "bullshit." And of course, for heavy metal fans, the sign is a compliment.[14]

Courtesy of AP Wide World Photos.

Self-disclosure. Be aware of how cultural differences influence when and how much you self-disclose. The U. S. is a high self-disclosure culture. In the U.S., it is appropriate to talk about one's family. In several other cultures, people would look askance if a speaker disclosed information about his or her family.

Formality. Cultures vary in the degree to which a speaker needs to appear formal when presenting. In the U.S. culture, informal presentations are almost always the norm. A speaker will sit on a desk as they talk, wander about the room, and speak "off the cuff." In other cultures, a speaker is supposed to be more formal. In your classes at U.T., you seldom see a professor standing behind a podium, reading a prepared text as a lecture. Study abroad in some nations and the professor, always dressed in a suit, makes no eye contact because he or she is reading word-for-word to his or her audience.

Eye contact. Be aware of how cultural differences influence how much and when you should engage another in eye contact. In the U. S. and Western European cultures, people expect those with whom they are communicating to look them in the eye as eye contact is read as a sign of respect and attentiveness. But direct eye contact is not read to be universally appropriate. In fact, in some cultures direct eye contact is considered rude. For example, in Japan people direct their gaze to a position around the Adam's apple and avoid direct eye contact. Chinese, Indonesians, and rural Mexicans lower their eyes as a sign of deference—to them, too much eye contact is a sign of bad manners. Arabs, in contrast, tend to look intently into the eye of the person with whom they are talking— to them direct eye contact demonstrates keen interest.[15]

Public speaking guidelines.

Speak slowly and clearly. Unless audience members are fluent in English, they must translate your words into their own language. This takes time and cognitive effort, so speak slowly and clearly. In addition, pause more often so they can catch up with you and enjoy a brief mental break. Do not over-do this, however, so that you come across as patronizing or condescending. Use the audience's non-verbal feedback to find the right balance.

Use multiple modes of presentation. Once again, if your audience is not fluent in English, it is wise to use visual aids. Visual restatements, such as pictures, graphs, gestures, or written summaries can help reinforce your points and keep your audience tracking with your verbal message. Be more thorough with non-native English speakers, as well. Use full sentences and complete statements rather than just prompts and key words on your PowerPoint slides and handouts as most non-native English speakers are better readers than listeners. Also be careful of assuming someone who can speak English can also read English. This is not always the case.

Elevate your level of formality. In general, use a more formal style when speaking to international audiences. Keep in mind what you learned about power distance and employ those principles here. Use proper names and titles unless directed not to. Elevate your dress, as well. Finally, adjust your speaking style to match the formality expected by your audience. Leave phrases such as "like," "totally," "dude," and "OMG" for the Gossip Girl viewing parties.

Avoid humor. Humor rarely translates well. This goes for international audiences, as well as domestically diverse audiences. Comedian Jerry Seinfeld succeeded in the U. S. He flopped in Asia. When giving public presentations, failed humor can kill your credibility. Verbal word plays like puns and funny sayings are often too idiosyncratic to one's own culture. Additionally, certain topics are taboo in some cultures that would be perfectly acceptable in the U. S. A joke about a senator's affairs could entertain a U. S. audience while the same joke about a member of the royal family in Sweden would be met with distain.[16] This also means avoiding U. S. clichés. Every language and culture has unique clichés or sayings that do not translate well. "That's the way the ball bounces," "It's six one way, half a dozen the other," "Better safe than sorry" may make sense to a U. S. audience while those sayings may leave others scratching their heads.

Understand local politics. You can be linguistically fluent in another culture but still act like a cultural fool if you do not master the appropriate norms of speaking in a particular cultural context.[17] The more you understand context, the more you can adjust your message to fit your audience's desires. Speeches on topics like the death penalty, welfare, or police brutality may be interpreted in very different ways depending on whether you are speaking in Westlake or east Austin. So will jokes or anecdotes about Paris Hilton's under garments, Michael Jackson's misgivings, or Bernie Madoff's financial prowess. Understanding context can be aided by understanding local politics. It is helpful to pay attention to the local news before addressing a diverse audience so you can understand what they might be experiencing at that given moment. But remember, as a guest in the culture, you want to appreciate, not evaluate, their news. This can help with your topic content and a potentially hostile question-and-answer period.

Courtesy of Landov Media.

Conclusion

<u>Mindful communication</u> means we are consciously aware of, and pay attention to our communication behavior. <u>Flexible intercultural communication</u> means we are adaptive and creative. It means we make detours and have the courage to try again. It means we are other-centered. It is our hope that this chapter has helped you to do just that.

Culture Quiz[18]

A fundamental component of intercultural communication competence is an appropriate level of knowledge about the culture in which you are communicating. Use these questions as a litmus test of how much you know about other cultures. Hopefully, this will encourage you to be mindful of the connection between intercultural knowledge and intercultural competence.

True or False:

1. A "thumbs up" in some Islamic countries is a rude sexual sign—true or false?
2. Forming an "O" with the thumb and the forefinger in Japan means that we can now discuss money—true or false?
3. Scandinavians are more tolerant to silent breaks in conversations—true or false?
4. Laughter in Japan can be a sign of confusion, insecurity or embarrassment—true or false?
5. In the UK, to compromise is seen as a positive sign of both parties winning—true or false?
6. Wearing gloves in Russia when shaking hands is considered polite—true or false?
7. Leaving right after dinner in Central America is considered well-mannered as it means you've been well fed—true or false?
8. In Sub-Saharan Africa it is normal to arrive half an hour late for dinner—true or false?
9. If you tell your female friend from Africa that she's put on weight during her holiday, it means she's had a good holiday and is physically healthier than when she left—true or false?
10. In Brazil, flicking your fingers under your chin is a sign of disgust—true or false?
11. If you want to show your respect for an elder in Africa, do not look them directly in the eye—true or false?
12. Keeping your hands in your pockets while negotiating in Russia is rude—true or false?
13. It is seen as polite to not accept an offer of food or drink in Persia immediately on being offered it, instead you should refuse a few times before accepting the gift—true or false?
14. In France, dinner is commonly served at 5 p.m.—true or false?
15. In Brazil, purple flowers are a symbol of friendship—true or false?
16. In Mediterranean cultures, being boisterous in the streets and public places is widely accepted—true or false?
17. In Australia, a single male passenger should sit in the back seat—true or false?

Fill in the blank:

18. What is the capital of Nigeria?

   _____

19. What is the largest city in Italy?

   _____

20. What is the longest river in Russia?

   _____

21. What is the biggest state in the U.S.?

   _____

22. What is the national language of India?

   _____

Answers to Culture Quiz:

1–5: True

6: False—you need to remove your gloves when shaking hands in Russia.

7–9: True

10: False—this means you don't know the answer to a question in Brazil

11–13: True

14: False—in France, it is common to eat dinner at 7 p.m. or later and it tends to be a light dinner.

15: False—Purple flowers in Brazil are often seen at funerals. Avoid giving a host purple flowers.

16: True

17: False—A single male passenger should sit in the front seat in Australia.

18. Abuja

19. Rome

20. Volga

21. Alaska

22. Hindi

Endnotes

1 Ting-Toomey, S., & Chung, L.C. (2005). *Understanding intercultural communication.* Los Angeles: Roxbury Publishing Company.

2 Activity available through: http://www.businessballs.com/stories.htm#monkey.

3 Daly, J., & Engleberg, I. (2005). *Presentations in everyday life: Strategies for effective speaking.* Boston: Houghton Mifflin Company.

4 Ting-Toomey, S. (1999). *Communicating across cultures.* New York: The Guilford Press.

5 Lustig, M., & Koester, J. (1996). *Intercultural competence: Interpersonal communication across cultures.* New York: HarperCollins.

6 Hall, E. (1976). *Beyond culture.* New York: Doubleday.

7 Ting-Toomey, S., & Chung, L.C. (2005). *Understanding intercultural communication.* Los Angeles: Roxbury Publishing Company.

8 Samovar, L. A., & Porter, R. E. (2001). *Communication between cultures.* Belmont, CA: Wadsworth.

9 Ting-Toomey, S., & Chung, L.C. (2005). *Understanding intercultural communication.* Los Angeles: Roxbury Publishing Company.

10 Hofstede, G. (1991). *Cultures and organizations: Software of the mind.* London: McGraw-Hill.

11 Adapted from Weeks, W., Pedersen, P. & Brislin, R. (1979). A manual of structured experiences for cultural learning. LaGrange Park, IL: Intercultural Network.

12 Raymie E., McKerrow, B. E., Gronbeck, D. E., & Monroe, A.H. (2003). *Principles and types of public speaking* (15th Ed). Boston: Pearson Education.

13 Urech, E. (1998). *Speaking globally: Effective presentations across international and cultural boundaries.* Dover, NH: Kegan Page.

14 Donahue, K. (2005, January 22). What "hook 'em, horns" symbol means elsewhere. Fanblogs.com. Message posted to http://www.fanblogs.com/big12/003614.php.

15 Samovar, L. A., & Porter, R. E. (2001). *Communication between cultures.* Belmont, CA: Wadsworth.

16 Raymie E., McKerrow, B. E., Gronbeck, D. E., & Monroe, A.H. (2003). *Principles and types of public speaking* (15th Ed). Boston: Pearson Education.

17 Ting-Toomey, S., & Chung, L.C. (2005). *Understanding intercultural communication.* Los Angeles: Roxbury Publishing Company.

18 Culture Quiz. Portions taken from http://skill-assessment.suite101.com/article.cfm/quiz_on_intercultural_competence.

Notes

PART 3

Preparing Public Presentations

CHAPTER 10

Sources for Your Presentation: Effective Research and Citation in the Context of Professional Communication

by Joshua Hanan and Meredith Bagley

Objectives

After studying chapter 10, you should be able to:

☐ Understand critical elements to gathering and preparing research for presentations.
☐ Navigate the major research databases.
☐ Critically evaluate the integrity of online sources.
☐ Assess how to properly cite various types of research into your preparation outline.
☐ Understand practical suggestions for integrating research into the delivery of your presentation.

Key Terms

TERM	DEFINITION
abstracts	Short summaries of an entire article that help the reader grasp the main points of the study.
academic journals	Periodical publications produced by scholarly presses; usually dedicated to one area or sub-area of research; usually searchable online.
Academic Search Complete	A major research database of scholarly sources available through the UT library homepage. Also known as EBSCO.
APA style	A particular method for organizing research into an outline and bibliography. Very popular in the social sciences and stands for the American Psychological Association.
bibliographic citations	A comprehensive approach toward referencing sources in the end of your outline.
Boolean Operators	Special language codes that facilitate database searches by combining terms in particular ways and by specifying the way information is retrieved.
citation style	A method of organization that allows you to integrate research into your outline and bibliography in a particular standardized fashion.
closed domains	Website address types that are available only to certain sources that have been verified and authenticated; educational (.edu) and government (.gov, .mil) sites are closed.
databases & indexes to articles	A link found on the UT library homepage that allows users to search a wide variety of online data bases of scholarly resources.
direct quoting	The process of stating verbatim, in a presentation, information derived from an author other than oneself.
domain	The final letters in a website address indicating, in general, the nature of that site in terms of content and credibility
edited books	A type of book that does not consist of one comprehensive study but instead a number of studies written by various authors.
Editorial columns (opinion pieces)	A type of newspaper article, written either by editors of the newspaper or approved guest writers, that expresses an opinion rather than delivering neutral reports on the news.
ethos	The Greek word meaning "credibility."
fields	Areas of the citation—like author, title, journal title, abstract or full text—that are found in various journals.
jargon	Specialized and complicated terminology used by a particular discipline
Lexis Nexis Academic	A subscription-only database that gives users access to nearly every newspaper printed around the world.
logos	From the Greek for "the word;" it is translated as logic.

TERM	DEFINITION
ombudsmen	An individual responsible for fielding complaints directed to an organization and providing explanations to these inquiries.
open stacks	A way organizing a library system that allows users to retrieve their own books as opposed to having a librarian find such books for the users.
oral citations	The organization style used for referencing citations in your actual presentation.
paraphrasing	The process where you rearticulate, in your own words, what you learned from consulting the research of an original author.
parenthetical citations	A method that allows a public speaker to integrate research into the body of their text.
peer reviewed	Designation of an academic journal that indicates that its articles have been approved by experts in the field
periodical	A source published on a regular but not daily basis that can encompass a wide array of publication styles.
Perry-Castaneda Library	UT's largest library, named after Ervin S. Perry—the first African American to be appointed to the academic rank of professor—and Professor Carlos E. Castañeda—a central advocate and developer of the Benson Latin American Collection.
qualifier	A statement used in your presentation that demonstrates why the source you are referring to is credible.
sponsor	The individuals and groups responsible for a website's existence and content.
subjective bias	Describes the particular partisan stance a source may have on the contents it is reporting.
UT library catalogue	The electronic listing of all UT's library holdings.

Introduction

One of these skills you need when preparing professional presentations is an ability to gather and collect research in an invigorating and professional manner. Without adequate research skills, even the most competent presenter will be rendered ineffective. Why is this, you ask? There are three primary reasons why gathering research for presentations is necessary (all of which, you may note, tie back to previous chapters that you have read).

First, conducting adequate research is necessary for appearing credible. As Aristotle pointed out in his book *The Rhetoric*, credibility, or ethos, is a central dimension of good public speaking. Unless you can convey a sense of credibility in your presentation, your words can be great, and you're appeals alluring, but listeners may approach your research with uncertainty and skepticism. While certain people exude ethos strictly because of their name or occupation, most professional communicators must develop ethos as they talk. Although you may be disappointed, then, to learn that you are not innately credible, the good news is that by simply taking time to conduct quality research you can create the perception of credibility in the eyes of your audience.

The second reason is that consulting ample research helps you support the various claims you make whenever you communicate professionally. Supporting one's claims falls in the realm of logic, or logos, which is the principal means through which people reason with one another. Exhibiting logos requires having good research and data to back up the claims that you make. Think back to your own experiences. Do you feel more motivated to listen to someone when they have an abundance of research to back up their claims or when they have very little? If you're like most people, you prefer the latter. Ample research is indeed one of the most preferred qualities of a good public presentation.

The final reason gathering thorough research is necessary is that it is the ethical thing to do! As noted in chapter 3, as a professional communicator you have an ethical imperative to present information in an honest and open way. To illustrate the importance of being ethical, just think about the following hypothetical scenario. If you were being sold a new health product on the market that was extremely expensive but claimed to work wonders, you would expect this presentation to be based on careful and scrupulous research. If you later found out the claims your salesperson made were biased, or even worse fabricated, you would almost certainly be irritated.

For these reasons, and many more, learning how to gather research and use it in presentations should be a central part of your 306M education. Not only will learning research skills help you in this class but it will help you in every future class you take. In this chapter we will cover the central aspects of preparing for public speaking presentations such as locating, evaluating, and referencing sources in your outline, bibliography, and presentation. We begin the chapter by discussing the physical and virtual aspects of UT's library system. Then, we turn our attention to the variety of sources that you may come across in the process of gathering research for a 306M presentation. Finally, we focus on referencing sources in your presentation both during the speech and in the bibliography that you give to your instructor. By the time you finish reading this chapter you should be in the position to become a better overall professional speaker and researcher and hopefully have a better understanding of how conducting thorough research aids in the overall process of communication.

Doing Research in College: In the Library and Beyond

Like many college students today, there is a good chance you have never set foot in a University of Texas library. While this may make your 306M instructor cringe, the reality is that this scenario is not uncommon. With the advent of the Internet, the necessity of visiting university libraries for research has decreased significantly. Moreover, as has always been the case, the library is not considered by most undergraduate students to be the most exciting place around. Many students would rather spend their time with friends and family.

That said, in this section our goal is to convince you that exploring the libraries at UT should be a top priority! Not only do UT libraries offer an environment that is conducive to learning, they also provide a variety of tools that allow you to conduct more thorough and accurate research.

Why visit the library at UT Austin?

The University of Texas at Austin has one of the best library systems of any public university in the United States. With many different libraries on campus, as well as four major research and archive centers that contain over eight million volumes it's no wonder the library system of UT Austin is ranked 6th in the nation.[1] Theoretically speaking, there are enough books at UT for each undergraduate to check out 200 at time!

Most likely, out of all the various libraries at UT, you will use the Perry-Castaneda Library, UT's largest and most expansive library collection.[2] The PCL is located just east of the UTC classroom building, just west of Jester Dorm, and diagonal from the Gregory Gym—you can't miss it! Named after two prominent faculty at UT, Professor Ervin S. Perry—the first African American to be appointed to the academic rank of professor—and Professor Carlos E. Castañeda—a central advocate and developer of the Benson Latin American Collection—PCL is one of the most happening places to be on the entire UT campus. The four levels of stacks at PCL contain 70 miles of books—about how far it is from Austin to San Antonio—and 2.5 million volumes. Not convinced yet? Here are three other major reasons to visit the PCL in person.

First, there are computer terminals in the PCL, enabling you to research and prepare your presentation at the same time. These computers are located on the first floor and sign-up is facilitated through an automated system. Documents can also be printed at the PCL and simply require a basic copy card on which you can load dollar amounts at any time. In addition, the library staff often holds classes on using the library computer system and other web-based research tools inside the Periodical room on the ground floor of PCL. You can learn browsing techniques from the pros and then put them to work for yourself.

The second reason to visit the PCL is to take advantage of the open stacks. Some libraries have closed stacks, when a staff member must retrieve any book you request. While that sounds pretty luxurious, open stack libraries allow you to find your own books. This gives you the important advantage of browsing the shelf on either side of your item. More often than not, other books that may be helpful will be located just next to the one you found on the shelf. In many cases you can get enough research for your entire presentation just by doing one initial search of the open stacks.

Finally, the third reason to visit the library may seem obvious: the librarians! You may have an image in your head of a librarian as some stern elderly lady, wearing glasses, who shushes people and never leaves her desk. This, however, could not be farther from the truth. Librarians at prestigious academic libraries like UT's are some of the smartest and most resourceful people on campus. While they can't do your research for you, they can make the experience less time consuming, more productive, and even more fun and enjoyable. The main information desk at the PCL is located about 50 feet inside the front doors, on the right, just across from the Circulation desk. It is open from 8 a.m. to 8:45 p.m. Monday through Friday, and noon to 8:45 p.m. on weekends.

In sum, visiting the PCL should be part of every college student's experience. The PCL provides UT students with an irreplaceable resource that cannot be mimicked in any virtual environment. So next time you're scanning the web and cannot find any research go check out the PCL *before* you tell your 306M instructor that you cannot find any research!

Using the library catalog

For those homebodies out there, don't get too freaked out, you can still conduct excellent research via the UT libraries from your bed, desk, cafeteria, or nearby grassy knoll (provided you get wireless coverage). The way you'll do this is through the UT Library Catalog (http://catalog.lib.utexas.edu), the electronic listing of all UT's library holdings. The Catalog is found on the homepage of the UT libraries, most easily accessed from the left-hand menu of the main UT homepage under "Libraries & Museums, University Libraries." Once you're on the library homepage, the menu of Research Tools will drop down automatically and the catalog is your first option on this menu. It is also first on the list of "QuickLinks" on the left-hand menu. We are going to discuss three online library resources in this section: the Catalog and two search tools under the Databases & Indexes options on this menu. As you gain confidence with the library page and databases, we encourage you to explore the catalog more fully.

The UT catalog: The Library Catalog allows you to search all UT library holdings and most research and archive collections. You can build your search in a number of ways:

- ❏ *Keywords*—this is the default setting when you enter the catalog, and allows you to type a string of words related to your topic (no punctuation needed). For example, if you're speaking on greenhouse gas emissions, you might type "global warming greenhouse" and hit Go. As of the publication of this chapter, that string of words resulted in 301 entries.

- ❏ *Advanced Search*—this is helpful when your topic is really broad, or when you're just starting your research. You still enter a string of key words, but then you can limit the search by library location (since you now know where the PCL is, maybe limit it to there?), language, and publishing year. This last one is especially helpful if your 306M instructor has rules about how old a source can be in your presentation.

- ❏ *Author and Title*—this option is helpful if you know part of a citation, maybe you heard it on the radio or in conversation, or if your author's name or book title is one you remember.

Research Databases: Sometimes you want to find something other than a book or bound volume. You might want recent newspaper or magazine articles about your topic (we'll get into the reasons why you want different types of sources in the next section). While the library catalog can tell you if the library carries *Time*, *The Houston Chronicle*, or *Popular Mechanics*, it can't tell you what articles are in each of these magazines. To do that, you have to use the <u>Databases & Indexes to Articles</u> link from the Research Tools menu. Clicking on this link gives you a ton of options. Luckily, the website suggests some of the major databases that will be most useful for you. We will discuss two: Lexis-Nexis Academic and Academic Search Complete (also called EBSCO Premier).

First, <u>Lexis-Nexis Academic</u> gives you access to nearly every newspaper printed around the world. It is a subscription-only database which means that ordinary people at home don't get to use this amazing tool; it also means that part of your tuition and fees go towards keeping UT's subscription working, so why not get your money's worth! (You'll notice that when you log onto Lexis-Nexis from a non-UT network you have to enter your EID.) It also allows you to access major papers like the New York Times without creating an account on each paper's website and risk receiving solicitations, web cookies or any other unwanted attention from commercial sites. At Lexis-Nexis, you literally have the world at your fingertips.

Searching strategically is especially important in a database this size. There are three major search areas you can control from the "Easy Search" page when you enter Lexis-Nexis. First, you can use <u>Boolean Operators</u>, or those funny abbreviations that allow you to manage your search term (e.g., punctuation marks, "and," "or").

The second factor you can control is what type of newspapers to search. The default setting on Easy Search is "Major World Publications"—this is a huge list and perhaps beyond the scope of your 306M presentation. A drop down box allows you to Select Sources, under which you can specify United States papers, types of publications (legal, magazines) or even major titles like the *New York Times* and *Washington Post*. This is a head start towards finding those credible sources your 306M instructor will demand.

Finally, and most easily, you can control the date range in which you search. A simple drop down box gives you options here, and you can run your same search terms several times to find the proper range of entries—for some topics it may take searching a two year range to find enough credible, substantive articles, while for some others it may only take searching the scope of one month.

The second database you'll want to use is <u>Academic Search Complete</u>, or <u>EBSCO</u>. Instead of finding newspaper and magazine articles, this database allows you to find research articles in academic journals. Again, we'll discuss the characteristics of each source in the next section, but for now think of these sources as the studies you hear cited on the evening news, or the studies your professors work hard to complete and get published. It's also like going right to the horse's mouth, as the research found at EBSCO tends to be original and non-partisan. Such high quality research, however, doesn't have to be hard to track down as using the EBSCO database is very much like using the Library Catalog or Lexis-Nexis. To this end, there are three important steps that you should know when searching EBSCO:

Getting there: After clicking the Databases & Indexes to Articles option on the Research Tools menu of the library homepage, look just above the Lexis-Nexis option for Academic Search Complete. This link takes you to the EBSCO host main page. The default page is the Advanced Search, which is perfect because this is where you want to start.

Select a Field: In a way similar to doing keyword or title searches in the library, EBSCO lets you select a field in which to search for your terms. Fields mean areas of the citation like author, title, journal title, abstract or full text. We will discuss just these main fields, but you can explore all of them.

- ❏ *Author*: Use this if you already know of an author who wrote a particular study or paper that you're trying to find. For example, if Dr. Stepjan was interviewed on CNN about his research related to what you are interested in, then enter his name.

- ❏ *Title*: This is like your keyword search in the library. Enter your main topic terms here and select Title to find any articles with these words in their title. You can also use your same Boolean Operators (e.g. AND, OR) in the three boxes provided to you if you need to narrow your search.

- ❏ *Journal Title*: You can be specific or general in this field depending on how much information you have. For example, if you know you're looking for something that appeared in the *Communication Monographs* you can write out the name of the journal word for word.

- ❏ *Abstract*: This will locate terms in the brief paragraph each author provides to summarize their article. Searching here is fine if you have a big topic or a common term. If you don't, use Full Text.

- ❏ *Full Text*: This will search entire articles for your search terms. If you enter a commonly used term here, beware that you may get thousands of results.

Finally, you can combine search terms and fields to really narrow your search. For instance, I might build a search that looks for an author named Jones in a journal that has Health in the title and discusses HPV in the full text.

- ❏ *Peer-Reviewed*: **This is a crucial step**. In the larger box just below the searching box, there is a small square to check next to the words "Scholarly (Peer Reviewed) Article". Be sure you check this box before doing your search! This will ensure you get the original source, the most credible research out there, and meet your instructor's requirement for an academic journal source.

Safety in Numbers: Using Sources in Your Presentation

Why do teachers make such a big deal about sources? Believe it or not, your 306M instructor has strict source requirements for reasons much beyond torturing you the night before your presentation. As noted at the start of this chapter, having a variety of good sources in your presentation is a guaranteed way to make your presentation stronger.

In gathering a variety of sources for your presentation, it is important to know the types of material that you want in advance. In this section, we will discuss familiar types of sources in terms of how they are produced. In doing so, we hope to help you better understand the benefits and limitations of each type of source.

Academic Journals

When professors and other researchers at places like the National Institute of Health complete a study, they publish their results in academic journals. These are special periodicals that are printed anywhere from one to twelve times a year, are read by other professionals in a given field, and are considered to be the most credible source for expert research on any topic for two main reasons. Reason one is the credentials of the authors: professors, doctors, scientists, award winning specialists, etc. Reason two is that most academic journals are peer-reviewed, meaning that each study published by one of these experts has been read, edited and approved by other experts in the field. This is an incredibly strict standard for publishing articles and signifies why it is so important to check the "Peer Reviewed" box in your database searches. Each type of source has different standards to meet before publication, but only articles in academic journals have been vetted by other equally trained experts before reaching your eyes.

Peer review and quality of authorship are two of the major benefits derived from using academic journals, but there are others as well. For example, with academic journals you are seeing raw data and original research, and you'll often see graphs or tables that can be used as visual aids in your presentation (see chapter 3 on how to cite a table or graph). Journal articles often have lengthy bibliographies from which you can find more sources for your presentation.

While academic journals are excellent sources, there are downsides. One major drawback is that since this is the highest level of expert research you may encounter a high level of jargon, or specialized and complicated terminology. These studies can also be quite long and often assume a high level of prior knowledge about the subject. Articles contain abstracts, or short summaries of the entire article that will help you grasp the main points of the study. Finally, in many fields it takes quite a long time for studies to appear in journals, so you may not find data on current events in an academic journal.

Books

You may be more familiar with finding and reading books, and certainly many experts write books too. Once again, understanding the production process of books helps us understand their advantages and disadvantages. Books begin as manuscripts, submitted by the writer, that then are reviewed extensively by editorial staffs who often employ fact-checkers to verify the facts and figures in the book. Revisions and further editing will occur, adding the time it takes to write and publish a book. For this reason books sometimes take even longer to come out than peer reviewed articles.

Sometimes books are ghost-written, which means a well-known figure like Roger Clemens might be credited as an author of a hyped-up book on pro baseball but the pages are mostly written by a different, lesser known and often unstated writer. Books are also more interested in profit margins than academic journals. The profit factor varies widely for books: self-help volumes from Dr. Phil sell very well whereas the latest biography by historian Doris Kearns Goodwin may have a smaller audience, and a new novel by an upcoming author even smaller.

These production factors play a larger part in determining the pro's and con's of using books in your presentation. The advantages of books are that the material has been reviewed and proofread by a staff of editors, the competitive process of submitting manuscripts means that not everyone can get their book published (so hopefully the best ones win), and that they are easily accessible in your campus library. Some drawbacks to books are that they take a long time to complete the publication process, they can be very long and dense, and there are outside influences that may shape the content of the book, namely profit and politics.

Magazines

Many of you may subscribe to magazines—ones your mom knows about and ones she may not. Magazines are a periodical source, meaning they are published on a regular but not daily basis. *Sports Illustrated*, *Cosmo* and *Vibe* are all popular periodical magazines, *Time* and *Newsweek* are news periodicals, and magazines like *Popular Mechanics*, *National Geographic* or *Harper's* are considered speciality periodicals. These periodicals differ from academic journals because they are created for less specialized audiences, tend to focus on current events, and are seldom peer reviewed.

Many magazines are published on a much more rapid cycle than books or journals. Futhermore, the language used in magazines tends to be more casual and accessible, you will see more photos and graphics, and often these titles will have their own websites with supplemental information that you will not find for books or journals. Keep in mind that this web-only content may not have received the same rigorous editing as the printed articles, and they may be written for a different audience, those likely to log on and read more online. Citing these web-only materials is also different. The printed articles from these periodicals can be found through using Lexis-Nexis or by searching the library catalog for their title, and then following links to find online access to full-text articles in this publication. Web-only content, by contrast, will not appear in your online database searches.

There are three major drawbacks to consider when using magazine sources. The first two are similar to books: most magazines are interested in earning profits (by attracting readers and advertising), so their choice of topics and style of coverage is influenced by this priority. Think of your average grocery store checkout line; every magazine depicts a catastrophe waiting to happen. News and speciality magazines may not be as dramatic as *People* or *OK!*, but the unavoidable need to earn profits will shape magazine content to some extent no matter the content. The second, and related, drawback is the political perspective some magazines may have: *The Nation* offers a more progressive assessment of politics and culture, while *National Review* continues to position itself at the forefront of conservative thought. These sources may be very credible, in terms of their research and fact-checking, but they also may write with a subjective bias, which means they have a stance on the news they are reporting and they want to convey that to the reader. This means you may use these sources but must realize the bias in your sources and handle them appropriately. For an informative presentation you should seek to balance an article from *The Nation* with a *National Review* article. For a persuasive presentation you might want to read further in one magazine or the other. Finally, magazines do not always share their original data, nor do they necessarily give the reader an easy way to double check this data for themselves. This can be problematic for those looking to maximize their ethos and logos.

Newspapers

Newspapers are published on a daily basis, as we all know, which means reporters are working on tight deadlines and are usually limited to a certain amount of space. Most reporters are expected to give a balanced account of an event, which usually means interviewing both sides and providing this information to the reader. Some journalists, however, write editorial columns, or opinion pieces; these can appear on the Editorial Page as well as in individual sections like sports, business, or local news. It is crucial to ask yourself whether your article is a news report or an editorial column. If it is a news report, you can often cite just the newspaper whereas when you use an opinion piece like an editorial you should make sure you highlight that it is an editorial or opinion piece.

The advantages of using newspaper articles are largely based on time: you can find day-to-day coverage of breaking events. Newspapers can provide valuable details and personal commentary from sources or witnesses to help bring your topic to life. Also, you can use newspapers to get a good sense of local reactions to a larger issue, or to focus on local issues that may be of more interest to your audience.

On the drawback side, you are less likely to get broad historical context when using newspaper articles. The articles can often be short and concise. Newspapers rarely have space to include original data. Sometimes papers run special reports or longer weekend features that will include raw data or graphs. Due to the stress of daily reporting, newspapers are also known to make mistakes. Papers often publish corrections to previous reports, some employ ombudsmen on their staff to handle reader complaints, and even the *New York Times* has been guilty of printing stories by a reporter who was basically making them up for several months.[3] As a result, if you use newspaper sources, it is not a bad idea to read a wider range of articles than you think you might need just to safeguard against potential biases and errors.

"When using newspaper articles for your presentation, a major benefit to finding these papers through Lexis-Nexis is that you will have the complete citation information needed for your bibilography, including page and section that this article was printed in. Getting newspaper articles from newspaper websites may seem logical, but you will rarely know the full citation info on these sites. Also, if the news content has been updated between being printed in the paper and posted to the website, the article is now considered an online resource and may not be accepted by your instructor."

Exercise 10.1. Navigating Search Engines.

If you read lots of newspapers and magazines, you are probably aware of the "cycle of information" or the way one event or idea can be discussed in different ways, with different results, in a variety of sources over time. Watching this happen can illuminate the many important distinctions between sources. Pick a topic that has received some public attention. Good examples are political elections or scandals, historical events, natural disasters, notable people, or locations.

Search for this topic in Lexis-Nexis, choosing Major US Newspapers and ordering your search results by date. Find the earliest mention of your topic. What were the important details reported? What is the "spin" on the topic at this point?

_____

_____

_____

_____

Search Lexis-Nexis again for Major Periodicals. Try to find an article within one month of the newspaper article you've already found. What themes or details seem important now? Are they the same or new? How has the perspective on this topic changed due to time passing?

_____

_____

_____

_____

Search Academic Research Complete for your topic. You may have to expand or change your search terms here to the more general themes or topics discussed in you first two articles. For example, the Virginia Tech school shooting might come up under school violence or education AND guns. What type of experts are writing about your topic? What do they bring from their academic fields to the topic? What kind of data are they using in comparison to the first two sources?

_____

_____

_____

_____

Finally, search the Library Catalog for a book on your topic. Do you have to change the search terms again? How much time passed between your first source and this book? What else is on the shelf near your book—do they add to your understanding of the topic or seem unrelated?

_____

_____

_____

_____

Internet

The way information is produced becomes especially crucial when using internet sources. But first, a word on what counts as an online source for your presentation. Reading an article in Lexis-Nexis that appeared in the *Houston Chronicle* does NOT make this an online source. That article existed as a printed article that was deemed good enough and important enough to be seen by millions of readers. Reading an article on www.joe'sblog.com IS an online source because this material has existed exclusively online, and has only been approved by Joe and potentially his roommate. You should ask your instructor, as a result, about their rules for online sources in your presentation—some allow none, some allow a few, but most agree that this type of source must be limited.

Making this claim, however, does not mean that internet sources aren't valuable. In a circumstance where Joe was the only guy who witnessed a police shooting, for example, Joe's information might be very valuable. If there is a newspaper article related to the topic, however, the latter is probably going to be a better source, or at least a complementary addition, for your presentation. That said, when deciding how credible your website source may be, there are five key criteria:[4]

Authority: Open access to the internet is a double-edged sword. It allows anyone to distribute information, but it also allows *anyone* to distribute information. There are two major ways you can assess a website's authority. First, you should check the domain, or last three letters of a websites address (called its URL). Websites with .edu are only published by accredited educational institutions and .gov sites can only be issued to official government agencies (including the military, which has the .mil domain). Sites ending with .org may be run by a nonprofit groups that may have an advocacy interest but not a profit one; and .com or .net sites are commercial sites whose main priority will be economic success.

It is important to investigate beyond the domain name. Only the .edu and .gov sites are closed domains with strict requirements and regulation. This means any group can establish a .org domain even if they are not a neutral source. To fully assess a website's accountability, you should always ask who sponsors the site, or the individuals and groups responsible for its existence and content. A credible site will have some way to learn about and contact the sponsors—often this looks like a "Contact Us" or "Who are We" link somewhere on the sites homepage. Go ahead and Google the authors or check for their names using other online search tools. If a site does not have any contact information, you should be very nervous about using its content in your presentation.

Accuracy: While you may not be an expert on the topic a website addresses, you can cross-reference sources to assess a site's accuracy. Does the website cite sources or provide references for its own claims and data? Can you find that data on your own through Google and/or the library databases? Are the statistics or figures provided by the website precise and professionally presented? Do the links provided by the website also meet your standards for accuracy?

Objectivity: The distinction between authority and objectivity is crucial for determining credibility. For instance, the Democratic National Committee is a highly credible political source for information on candidates or platform issues of the Democratic Party. It is not, however, politically objective; clearly, the DNC would love to see a Democratic President, Congress and Governors across the country. Ask yourself about whose interests are being served by the information on a website. If the answer is anything beside all readers, your site is not objective. Recall, however, that this does not mean the site is not credible or usable for your presentation. Credibility is determined by a combination of factors, not just one.

Currency: Credible websites will tell you, usually on the homepage or on each content page, when the page was last updated. If you do not see this information, read the pages for the most current information—if its most recent news item is the first Gulf War or the Star Wars trilogy, being re-released in theaters, you might want to reconsider using this website in your presentation. Currency can also include whether all the links on a site are still active and functioning. While most websites never die, inactive links or error messages alert you to an outdated, and perhaps unreliable website.

Diversity: A credible website that will improve your presentation should not contain any offensive material that targets and insults any racial, gender, ethnic or sexual preference or disability group. Even a site that articulates contentious opinions or policy recommendations, such as opposing gay marriage or supporting immigration reform, should use respectful, accepted language for these issues. A site that uses slurs, insults or demeaning language should not form the core of your presentation's research; if anything, this kind of site could be used as evidence against your opponents in a persuasive presentation.

Using website sources take some work, it's true. Nevertheless, when used right they can often be valuable sources of information for your presentation. Websites are excellent for keeping up on breaking news; you could even update your presentation the morning of your presentation! Websites are also great for topics and subjects that don't get a lot of news coverage in the mainstream media, or sources that are well-served by open, accessible forms of information like blogs or even Facebook pages. You must evaluate constantly, however, when using these web pages. One excellent strategy is to use a website as a starting place. A good site will point you towards further information, online or off, and even suggest print materials that may confirm the news and views presented on the site. This is a great way to use Wikipedia; browse around and see what catches your attention, then explore the references list to find a variety of types of sources to build your presentation.

Online Libraries vs. Online

Two of the most popular ways to find information on the internet are Google and Wikipedia. These sites should be used wisely and considered good starting points for your research—NOT the sole source of information. In this section, we will give you tips on using these powerful search tools in the most effective, responsible way.

1. *Ga-Ga for Google*: A very common place to start our Web-based research is the search engine Google (www.Google.com). There are three important things to know about using Google:

   ❏ First, when you type in your topic, let's say "social security reform" into the Google search box, the search results you see are ranked based on an algorithm, or mathematical formula, that values both number of hits that site has received, how many sites it links to or link to the site, and how high each of those links rank in this same formula. This means that the most visited, and most interconnected sites will rise to the top of list, not necessarily the most credible or expert ones. (Before Google updated their algorithm, this led to a social movement tactic called "Google-bombing" when activists write computer code to enter a term and select a specific site over and over until it climbs the Google list.)[5]

   ❏ Second, when you enter your search term, usually two or three websites will appear right at the top in a special box often colored blue or some other contrasting color. These are labeled "Sponsored Links," which means those companies or groups have paid Google to list their site at the top of a search for that particular term. So, if Coca-Cola is trying to push its new employee health plan and you type in "universal health care", you might get Coke's webpage right up top due to this fee-based system.

   ❏ Finally, like learning the Library Catalog, Google has an "Advanced Search" option right next to the results box on its basic search page. This page allows you to manipulate your search to find credible sources among the millions of pages that Google can search. Some helpful features on this page include:

     ❏ Entering an exact phrase

     ❏ Adding search terms to refine your search

     ❏ Searching for the terms in a particular "occurrence" like the title of the page, the URL, or the full text

     ❏ Specifying which domain to search in—this allows you to ONLY find .gov sites or .edu sites. Recall that .org sites can be owned by anyone.

You also should always check with your instructor about whether she or he allows websites to count as sources in your presentation.

Exercise 10.3. Understanding Keywords in Online Searches.

Go to Google.com and enter each of these searches. Record the number of results for each search:

1. Cell phones _____

2. Cellular phones _____

3. Cellular phones and brain tumors _____

4. Cellular phones and "brain tumors" _____

5. Cellular phones and "brain tumors" site:gov _____

What happened as you changed the search terms?

_____

_____

_____

_____

What was the effect of adding the .gov requirement?

_____

_____

_____

_____

Does it seem like you generated better sources for search 5? Why or why not?

_____

_____

_____

_____

_____

_____

2. *Wild for Wiki*: Many students, especially at about this point in any discussion on web-based research, will say "What about Wikipedia? That's an okay website, right?" The best rule of thumb for using Wikipedia is to *use it as a starting point, not an endpoint, of your research*. Some 306M instructors will not allow Wikipedia citations in student presentations, some will. You need to ask you instructor, then read this section either way to equip yourself with the skills to use Wikipedia intelligently, critically, and effectively.

Wiki's are a general term for spaces on the internet where the content is shaped and edited by the site's users. Wikipedia combines this wiki software with our old familiar encyclopedia to generate a huge site for basic information on a massive range of topics. And most of the sites are open to editing at any time by anyone! (Some sites are closed to certified Wikipedia editors; often these sites involve sensitive topics like the Holocaust.) To some experts, this open form of knowledge production is suspicious and risky. To others, a site like Wikipedia is the 21st century version of our founding father's original notion of a free and open society.[6] One thing we know is that the info can be incomplete, or partial, or just changing so fast that we have to be careful about using Wikipedia as the only or final step in our research. However, it is generally not a problem to check out Wikipedia early on in your research (like not the night before your presentation . . .) then use the References and External Links sections to find original sources that have appeared in credible print sources to verify and supplement what you find on Wikipedia.

Media Box

How do YOU feel about Wikipedia? Is it a legitimate source for research? Why or why not?

Visit this chapter's folder in your Chapter Media Contents online. Read the articles "A Stand Against Wikipedia" and "Professors Should Embrace Wikipedia."

Discuss the arguments for and against Wikipedia.

Exercise 10.4. Working with Wikipedia.

The following exercise will help you learn about the way information is produced on collaborative sites like Wikipedia. Review the steps below with any Wikipedia entry that you plan on using in your presentation.

1. Search for your term & copy the entry onto this page of paper.

2. Find the "History Tab" and click on it.

    a. How many changes?

    b. How many different authors?

3. Go back far enough in the history to where the information is **significantly** different than the current entry.

4. Copy this entry here.

5. Respond to each of the following questions:

    a. What are the major differences between the old entry and the current one?

    b. What would your presentation sounds like if you'd used the old entry?

    c. Does one entry seem more legitimate than the other? Why?

    d. Does the exercise of looking at the History tab make you feel more or less confident in Wikipedia? Why?

Interviews

A final way to generate information for a presentation is through the process of interviewing. While interviewing has its drawbacks it can oftentimes be one of the best ways to conduct research. Some topics, for example, demand interviewing methods such as: local issues (e.g., smoking ban), topics that involve eye witnesses (e.g., a campus protest), and topics that relate closely to your audience (e.g., student loans). Furthermore, interviews can provide vivid quotations, precise details otherwise unavailable to you, and can add credibility to a speaker by your association to the interview subject. Chapter 5 gives you tips for conducting an interview—be sure to plan your questions appropriately, take good notes or record your conversation, and ask your instructor about how to document that you conducted an interview. Drawbacks to using interviews nevertheless abound and include the time and effort involved in conducting good interviews (waking up your fraternity brothers or sorority sisters the night before your presentation is not a good plan); the risk of getting a biased individual perspective on the problem (what does your grandmother really know about tax reform?); and the time it takes in your presentation to contextualize your interview subject.

Referencing Sources in Your Outline, Bibliography, and Presentation

So far we have discussed the UT library system and the variety of resources it offers for conducting research. Further, we have reviewed some sources you can incorporate in your presentations and offered you methods for evaluating these sources. Now, we want to turn our attention to integrating your sources into your outline, bibliography, and presentation. Knowing how to gather research is very important. But an inability to incorporate such research into your outline, bibliography, and presentation can potentially nullify all your hard work. For this reason, before you go out and begin doing any research, or even worse any writing, we recommend that you begin by familiarizing yourself with a citation style.

What is a citation style?

A citation style is a method of organization that allows you to integrate research into your outline and bibliography in a particular standardized fashion. By offering a number universal guidelines and regulations, citation styles allow for consistency, organization, and professionalism in the context of writing. You may not realize it, but almost every academic text you read uses some type of citation style. Without a citation style, these books would appear disjointed and disorganized and would make it very difficult for you to follow up on the research they rely on.

Different disciplines use different citation styles. In communication studies, for example, three citation styles are most common: APA, MLA, and Chicago Style. While all three styles have their own merits, in 306M we use APA style which, in case you were wondering, stands for the American Psychological Association. To this end, let us provide you with a little background on APA style and how this citation style can allow you to seamlessly interweave research into your outline and bibliography.

APA Style

APA as we noted earlier stands for the American Psychological Association. While its first publication as a style manual did not transpire until1952, the APA style was first invented in 1928 when a number of editors, business managers, and academics, from both psychology and anthropology, met to develop a universal citation style that could be used in a variety of academic journals. Concerned with the inconsistency that characterized psychological and anthropological writing prior to this time, APA sought to infuse uniformity and organization in the context of professional, social scientific, writing. Today APA is the most common citation style in the social sciences and according to the APA Publication Manuel, fifth edition, is the preferred style guide of more than one thousand academic and professional journals!

For purposes of 306M presentations, there are two importance parts of APA style. <u>Parenthetical citations</u> have to do with incorporating research in the body of your outline whereas <u>bibliographic citations</u> have to do with comprehensively referencing this research at the end of your outline.

Parenthetical citations

The chapter on ethics and professional communication discusses a primary concern for students at UT: avoiding plagiarism. Every year numerous students get reprimanded for engaging in plagiarism. While many of these students consciously intended to plagiarize, there are always some who were simply unaware how to incorporate sources into their texts but ended up plagiarizing nonetheless. To avoid being seen as a plagiarist, you should use parenthetical citations. Parenthetical citations attribute authorship to the ideas discussed in your work without significantly disrupting the flow of your writing. Parenthetical citations provide authorship information in the body of your outline that can then be looked up in more detail in the bibliographic section of your essay. Thus, parenthetical citations must contain enough information so that your reader can clearly distinguish one source from the other, but at the same time, they must not contain so much information as to make the bibliographic section of your outline irrelevant.

So how does the APA style recommend incorporating parenthetical citations into your outlines and essay? Generally speaking, APA has two criteria when it comes to parenthetically citing research. First, you must include the name of the author of the material you are referencing and second, you must provide the year that the material was published.

To use an example, let's say you are giving an informative presentation on global warming and you checked out Tim Flannery's book *The Weather Makers* published in 2005. After reading parts of this book, you decide that when writing your outline you want to note, in your first main point, that since 1950 the amount of sea ice in the Artic has decreased by 20%. To make this claim you obviously need to acknowledge Flannery since his book is where you found this information. But how do you do it? According to APA, one way is to simply put Flannery's information in parentheses at the end of your sentence, such as "Since 1950 the amount of sea ice in the Artic has decreased by 20% (Flannery, 2005)." Another alternative is to integrate Flannery's information into your actual sentence. For example you could write "According to Flannery (2005), the amount of sea ice in the Artic has decreased by 20% since 1950."

Referencing sources parenthetically follows the same formula whether you are citing a book, journal article, magazine, newspaper, internet website, or interview. The only time you do not use this formula, is when you come across a body of research that has no primary author attributed to it. Say, for example, in the June 18th 2007 *Austin American Statesman*, you come across an article titled "Austin Ranked Top City" with no author. When you go to mention this source, in the body of your outline, in replace of the author's name you would put the title of the article. In this circumstance you would probably use the former approach toward parenthetical citing as opposed to the latter since there is no authorship. For instance, when composing an informative outline on Austin you might write something like "In a recent paper in the Austin American Statesman, Austin was reportedly considered to be the best city in the nation ("Austin Ranked Top City," 2007)."

On a final note, it is important to recognize that none of the above examples refer to circumstances where you are <u>directly quoting</u> the original author of the text verbatim. Instead, the above examples refer to <u>paraphrasing</u>, where you rearticulate, in your own words, what you learned from consulting an original author. As a result, if you decide to weave a direct quote into your outline you would *also* need to note the page number(s) that you took your information from. For example, if you want to quote Tim Flannery directly saying that 'climate change carries a high price in America' you would probably write, "As Flannery (2005) argues in his book *The Weather Makers* 'climate change carries a high price in America' (p. 315)." Notice that we put the page number at the end of the quote and did not place it after the year it was published? This was our own stylistic choice and either approach works. We will touch on stylistic issues surrounding parenthetical citations a bit more in the final section of this chapter. For now, however, let's turn our attention to bibliographic citations.

Bibliographic citations

APA rules about parenthetical citations are relatively easy to remember insofar as their usage does not vary much depending on the type of source used. So long as you can remember to put the author's last name (or essay title if there is no author) and the year of publication (and page number if directly quoting) you are pretty much set when it comes to citing works parenthetically. With bibliographic citations, however, things get significantly more complicated. Because bibliographic citations are the formal and comprehensive referenced versions of the sources you have incorporated into your outline, you must reference each type of source in a different fashion. For this reason, the best way to explain bibliographic citations is to provide examples of each main type of source. As a result, let us turn, once again, to the six different types of sources showcased earlier in this chapter: books, academic journals, magazines, newspapers, internet websites, and interviews.

Books are probably the easiest sources to reference in your bibliography. When referencing books you want to make sure to include the full name of the author(s) (the first name and middle name [if applicable] will be abbreviated), year of publication, title of book, location of publisher, and name of publisher. To make things more concrete, let's look at an example. Say we were creating a bibliographic citation of Tim Flannery's book *The Weather Makers: How Man is Changing the Climate and What it Means for the Future of Life on Earth* which was published in 2005 by Grove Press in New York City. We would cite this book APA style in the following fashion:

> Flannery, T. (2005). *The weather makers: How man is changing the climate and what it means for the future of life on earth.* NY: Grove.

When looking at this citation there are probably a number of formatting styles that you observed, all of which, we want to make clear, are done intentionally. First, you may see that the second line of the citation is indented five spaces. Second, you may have noticed that the title of the book was not entirely capitalized but that instead only the first letter of the title and the first letter of the subtitle were capitalized. Third, you may have observed that, in the case of books, the title is the only italicized aspect of the bibliographic citation. Fourth, you might have noticed that Tim Flannery's first name is abbreviated (this would also be the case if Flannery had any middle initials). Finally, you may have seen that when discussing the publisher information we did not put New York, New York as the location but instead simply New York. This too is intentional and stems from the fact that APA declares that the 16 largest cities in the US do not need to have their states referenced.

The above information is really all you need to know when referencing a book APA style. However, if you are referencing an article that appears in a book then things are done a bit differently. Indeed, many books these days are what we call edited books, which are made up of various short articles about the same general topic. Let's use a 1999 article by Thomas Farrell titled "Knowledge, consensus, and rhetorical theory" and published by Guilford Press (New York, New York) in the book *Contemporary rhetorical theory* (pages 140-152) edited by Celeste Condit and John Louis Lucaties as an example. In this situation we would cite Farrell's essay bibliographically in the following manner:

> Farrell, T. (1999). Knowledge, consensus, and rhetorical theory. In J. L. Lucaites, C. M. Condit, & S. Caudill (Eds.), *Contemporary rhetorical theory* (pp. 140-152). New York: Guilford.

There are several aspects of this type of bibliographic citing that you might have noticed. First, the essay by Thomas Farrell is itself not italicized but the book *Contemporary rhetorical theory*, which the essay is taken from, is italicized. Second, you may have observed that the page numbers of the essay by Farrell are placed after the title of the book not the essay Farrell wrote (also note that page numbers are abbreviated with "pp."). Third, you may have seen that the phrase "Eds." is placed in parentheses after the names of the authors of the edited volume. All of these details, while perhaps a bit irritating, are placed there intentionally so that it is easy to understand all the pertinent information about the edited book and the article that you are referencing.

Academic journals are a little more complicated to reference than books but it is still relatively easy once you get the hang of how to do it. When referencing journal articles you need to make sure that you include the author(s) of the article, the year the article was published, the title of the article, the name of the journal the article was published in, the issue of the journal, and, finally, the page numbers of the journal the article was published in.

To concretize referencing journal articles, let's look at the following example: imagine you are composing a presentation on neoliberal capitalism and you want to reference an article by Ronald Walter Greene titled "Rhetorical Capital: Communicative Labor, Money/Speech, and Neo-Liberal Governance." The essay is published in 2007 in the journal *Communication and Critical Cultural Studies*, volume 4 and can be found on pages 327 to 333. Here's how you would cite it:

Greene, R. W. (2007). Rhetorical capital: Communicative labor, money/speech, and neo-liberal governance. *Communication and Critical Cultural Studies, 4,* 327–333.

Reflecting back on this citation, there are a few specific details that you will probably notice. First, while the title of the article is not capitalized or italicized, the journal from which the article is taken is both capitalized and italicized. Second, the volume number is also italicized but the page numbers are not.

Magazines are not too dissimilar from academic journal except that with magazines you typically are dealing with more specific date information which makes the bibliographic citation a little more detailed. Other than that, however, magazine articles require much of the same info as books and academic journals. Specifically, when referencing a magazine you should include the author(s), the specific date of the magazine's publication, the title of the article, the magazine's title, the magazine's issue number, and finally the page numbers. Let's look at an example. Suppose we are giving a presentation on real estate and in our outline incorporate an essay found in the June 5th 2005 issue of *Time* (volume 81) titled "America's House Party" authored by James Poniewozik and located on pages 57- 66. We would reference the magazine in the following manner:

Poniewozik, J. (2005, June 5). America's house party. *Time, 81,* 57–66.

Notice how similar this citation looks to the one above from an academic journal. The main difference is that the magazine contains a little more detailed information where the year is located (e.g., in this case it references 2005, June 5 as opposed to just 2005).

Newspaper references diverge a bit from the last three source types. Nevertheless, once you get the hang of them they are equally simple to do. To reference a newspaper you need to include the following information: author name (if available), the specific date of the newspaper's publication (as in the case with magazines), the title of the article, the name of the newspaper, and the page(s) from which the article is located. Let's look at an example to see how this will be done in APA style. Let's say we are giving a persuasive presentation on why Barrak Obama is a great leader and decide to cite a New York Times article written by Ginger Thompson and Eric Loyd on February 12th 2008 titled "Seeking Unity, Obama Feels Pull of Racial Divide," starting on pages C1 and continuing on C19. Here is how the article would be cited APA style:

Thompson, G., & Loyd, E. (2008, February 12). Seeking unity, Obama feels pull of racial divide. *New York Times,* pp. C1, C19.

There are a couple general features and one specific feature that you should notice about this particular citation. Generally speaking, you might have noticed that, in the case of this essay, there are two authors. As a result, the first author has a comma after their first name and the second author has an ampersand (&) prior to their name. Second, you may have noted that Obama's name is capitalized in the article title. While it is true that normally you only capitalize the first word in an article title (and first word in the article subtitle) in the case of proper nouns such as Obama (and, for example, New York Times) you should capitalize them. Specifically, there is one other aspect of this bibliographic citation that likely caught your attention. Instead of referencing the spread of pages that contain the *New York Times* article you have looked up, you note the individual pages that the article appears on (e.g., C1, C19).

One other dimension of citing newspapers sources that you should be informed about is that sometimes you will come across a newspaper article that has no origin of authorship. In these cases you will have to reference the article in a modified way. To demonstrate using the above example of Obama, let's say, hypothetically, there were no clearly apparent authors of the essay. In such a circumstance you would have to reference the article in the following fashion:

Seeking unity, Obama feels pull of racial divide. (2008, February 12). *New York Times*, pp. C1, C19.

Notice how in this circumstance the date that the article was published gets moved to after the article title as opposed to before the article title. This is because the article title takes the role of the author in situations where there is no author apparent.

For an **internet website**: the name of authors (if available), the date the internet website was made available (if information is provided), the title of the webpage or online article, the date that you accessed the website on, and, finally, the website URL. If you are giving a persuasive presentation on the dangers of drunk driving and want to reference the statistics page of the Mothers Against Drunk Driving Web Site originally launched on May 26 2001 located at the URL of http://www.madd.org/Drunk-Driving/Drunk-Driving/Statistics.aspx and accessed by you on the date of September 9th, 2008. You would reference this website in the following manner:

Mothers Against Drunk Driving. (2001, May 26). *Statistics*. Retrieved September 9, 2008, from http://www.madd.org/Drunk-Driving/Drunk-Driving/Statistics.aspx.

Notice how in this example we listed "Mothers Against Drunk Driving" as the author? This is because when there is no personal authorship attributed to a website APA allows you to put the name of the organization that runs the website. Also, observe how we wrote out "Accessed September 9, 2008, from . . . ." This is how you are supposed to reference an internet website (noting, of course, that the date is totally contingent on the day that you access the webpage). You need to mention not only the date that the website was released (if available) but also the date that you came across the website. Why not the day you accessed the website? Well, suppose your professor tries to visit "the stem cell research website" you referenced in your presentation only to notice when she logs on, the information you claimed came from that webpage no longer existed. With books, journals, magazines, and newspapers it is relatively difficult to change the information once the text is printed and in circulation. With websites, however, information can be updated, changed, and deleted constantly.

Like newspaper articles, there is a chance you will come across an internet website that has no name identified with it. If this happens to be the case, you will do the same as you would do with a newspaper article; use the title of the website as your primary form of authorial identification. If the aforementioned website did not have an author, for example, it would be presented in the following manner (as opposed to the version listed above):

Statistics. (2001, May 26). Accessed September 9, 2008, from http://www.madd.org/Drunk-Driving/Drunk-Driving/Statistics.aspx.

Finally, in the event that there is no original launch date posted on the website, you would cite the website as follows:

Statistics. (n.d.). Accessed September 9, 2008, from http://www.madd.org/Drunk-Driving/Drunk-Driving/Statistics.aspx.

Interviews, unlike the other five sources, are not considered recoverable data and therefore are not required by APA to be referenced in your bibliography. Nevertheless, you should still treat interview encounters as a parenthetical citation. Let's say we interviewed Dr. Richard Cherwtiz on August 15, 2001. When referencing our conversation with Cherwitz we would cite the information parenthetically, as follows:

(R. Cherwitz, personal communication, August 15, 2001)

Exercise 10.5. Distinguishing Between Parenthetical and Bibliographic Citations.

Instructions: Please cite the following material in its appropriate APA format. Please do so for both parenthetical citations and bibliographic citation.

A November 19, 2007 *Daily Texan* newspaper article titled "Initiative lets students use strategies to help ailing local businesses," written by Teresa Mioli

Parenthetical citation

_____

Bibliographic citation

_____

_____

A book titled *Rhetorical Dimensions of Popular Culture* written by Barry Brummett published in 1991 by University of Alabama Press (Tuscaloosa, AL)

Parenthetical citation

_____

Bibliographic citation

_____

_____

A magazine article titled "Changing the Face of Power" written by Marie Wilson, Nurit Peled-Elhanan, and Eve Ensler published in the magazine *Ode* (volume 3) on October 1st 2005 and found on pages 42 to 48.

Parenthetical citation

_____

Bibliographic citation

_____

_____

A journal article by Anita Vangelisti and John Daly titled "Gender differences in standards for romantic relationships." Published in 1997 in the journal Personal Relationships, volume 4 (issue 2), pages 203–219 and paginated by year

Parenthetical citation

_____

Bibliographic citation

_____

_____

Exercise 10.5. (Continued).

An article titled "civil rights" written by the National Coalition for Homelessness on September 8th 2004 from the URL http://www.nationalhomeless.org/civilrights/index.html . The website was accessed on June 4th 2007

Parenthetical citation

_____

Bibliographic citation

_____

_____

An interview conducted by you with Sharon Jarvis on July 5th 2007 and then transcribed into a paper on January 3rd 2008

Parenthetical citation

_____

Bibliographic citation

_____

_____

_____

Communicating Research in Your Presentation

You now have a basic understanding of how to reference sources parenthetically and bibliographically. We know that was a lot of information to take in and may have been a bit exhausting, but trust us, taking the time to get the referencing technique down now will save you a lot of headaches down the road! Having come this far, we are ready to look at the final dimension of this chapter which has to do with referencing sources in the delivery of your presentation, a practice we call oral citations.

Fortunately for you, oral citations are much less complicated than citing sources bibliographically and parenthetically. Indeed, to incorporate oral citations into your presentation you really only need to learn the following 3 rules:

Rule 1: Make sure to mention all your sources in your presentation

Many speakers are under the impression that they do not need to reference their sources in their actual presentation. Many audiences expect speakers, particular those with less expertise on the topic at hand, to reference sources in their *actual presentation*. What this means for you, is that all the sources that you integrate into the outlines and bibliographies of your various presentations should be announced verbally in the various presentations that you give. For example, this means that if in your informative presentation you used *three* sources in your outline and bibliography, you should mention *three* sources in your presentation.

Rule 2: Anytime you introduce a new oral citation into your presentation you must provide a rationale as to why the source you have chosen is credible.

If, when giving presentation, you tell your audience that the US budget has an 8 trillion dollar deficit according to Robert Shiller, your audience members are not likely to be very impressed. By contrast, if you tell your audience that the US budget has an 8 trillion dollar deficit according to Robert Shiller, a renowned Yale economist, your audience is more likely to trust the information. While there are some people that are so famous (such as Martin Luther King Jr., Albert Einstein, Bill Gates) they do not need to have their credibility validated when mentioned in presentations, in most circumstances it is necessary to provide some sort of qualifier as to why the source you are using is credible.

Rule 3: After introducing a particular oral citation into your presentation, you do not need to include a rationale the next time you introduce that same oral citation.

"If you want to make it easy to qualify your various sources in your presentation, try to write out such qualifiers in the actual body of your outline. Remember that parenthetical citations (the citations in the actual body of your outline) are flexible in their structure. As long as you include the author name and date of a given source in the sentence, they can be written in a number of ways. Using the previous example of Robert Shiller for instance, if you were referencing his book *Irrational Exuberance* written in 2005 you could write something like this in your outline "The claim that the American economy is fundamentally unstable has been made by Yale economist Robert Shiller (2005), one of the most highly regarded economist in the nation. In his book *Irrational Exuberance*, Shiller demonstrated that much of value placed on stocks is due to theoretical speculation and not actual performance.""

While it is necessary to describe why your sources are credible when referencing them in your presentation the first time around, after doing so once it is not necessary to do it again. For example, if the first time you mention Robert Shiller you note that he is a prominent economist at Yale, the second time you refer to him you only need to say the words "Robert Shiller." This is because everyone should know now who Robert Shiller is and it would be needlessly repetitive to go over his credibility a second time around.

Media Box

Still worried about presenting your research orally in your speech?

Watch a student from the UT Speech Team expertly integrate research into a presentation.

Visit this chapter's folder in your Chapter Media Contents online and watch the presentation "Interstate Commerce Clause."

Endnotes

1 "Nation's Largest Libraries by Volumes Held." *LibrarySpot*. Accessed December 23, 2005. http://www.libraryspot.com/lists/listlargestlibs.htm.

2 For information on the history of the University of Texas at Austin Libraries, see www.utexas.edu/libraries/history.index.

3 Jayson Blair wrote dozens of fabricated news articles for the New York Times before being exposed in the spring of 2003. Two senior editors at the Times lost their job over the scandal. See Kurtz, H. (11 May, 2003) "N.Y. Times Uncovers Dozens Of Faked Stories by Reporter." *The Washington Post*. p. A1.

4 These criteria are adapted from Professional Communication Skills, 2nd Ed (Pearson Custom Publishing) pp. 338–340 and a tutorial on the Widener Library website, accessed at http://www3.widener.edu/Academics/Libraries/Wolfgram_Memorial_Library/Evaluate_Web_Pages/659/.

5 See Langville, A. N, & Meyer, C. D. (2006) *Google's pagerank and beyond: The science of search engine rankings*. Princeton, NJ: University Press.

6 For a recent and comprehensive review of Wikipedia's credibility as an information source, see Luty, B, Aaron, T. C. H, Thian, L. H, & Hong, C. K. (2008). Improving *Wikipedia's* accuracy: Is edit age a solution? *Journal of the American Society for Information Science & Technology, 59*, 318–330.

Notes

CHAPTER 11

Organizing a Successful Presentation

by Patty C. Malone, Ph.D.

Objectives

After studying Chapter 11, you should be able to do the following:

- ☐ Choose a topic, develop a purpose, and clearly organize your ideas for your presentation.
- ☐ Create a strong first and last impression with dynamic introductions and conclusions to your presentation.
- ☐ Develop logical, well-organized formal and delivery outlines.

Key Terms

TERM	DEFINITION
brainstorming	A group problem-solving technique characterized by spontaneous and unrestrained discussion or a written list of free-flowing ideas.
cause-effect	A speech arrangement used to discuss a problem and the causes of the problem (cause-effect), or a problem and the consequences of the problem (effect-cause).
chronological	Arranges speech topic according to the sequential order in which events or steps occurred.
connective	Words or phrases that connect your ideas together and indicate how they are related to each other.
credibility	Your listeners perceive you as qualified to discuss your topic because you are believable, competent, and trustworthy.
delivery outline	A brief outline intended to jog your memory while you deliver your presentation.
final summary	A recap of the main points at the conclusion of the presentation.
formal outline	A detailed and complete outline intended to help you prepare your speech.
general purpose	A broad purpose for your speech, which is usually to inform, persuade, or entertain.
initial preview	A sentence in the introduction that lets the audience know what is coming in the body of the speech.
internal preview	Sentences used in the main body of the speech to indicate what will be covered in the key points.
internal summary	Statements used during the presentation to summarize what you just said.
mindmapping	A method to generate ideas and determine relationships among ideas for presentations before organizing your outline.
primacy	Your audience will remember what they heard first, so present your most important points first.
problem-solution	A speech arrangement that explores either the causes or consequences of a problem, and then offers a solution that addresses the problem.
recency	Your audience will remember what they heard last, so place your most important points last.
signpost	A verbal or nonverbal signal that the speaker is moving from one topic to another.
sorting	An idea-organizing method for speech preparation that uses note cards so that you may re-stack and re-group ideas that go together.
spatial	A speech arrangement that is organized by geographic location or direction.
specific purpose	A single concise aspect of your topic and what you hope to accomplish in your presentation.
topical	A speech arrangement that uses naturally occurring parts, sections, or divisions, which may or may not be arbitrary.
transition	A word, phrase, or nonverbal cue indicating movement from one idea to another.

Introduction

Some speakers have strong delivery. Some have strong content. However, neither of these alone (or even together) succeeds in making a presentation memorable or even understandable if the speaker is disorganized. When you think of organization, you might picture collecting evidence or writing note cards. Organization in this chapter focuses instead on ideas like brainstorming, outlining, and placement of ideas or arguments in an effective presentation. Using the organizational tools described in this chapter will help you achieve your presentation goals.

Audiences react more positively to an organized speaker than to a disorganized one. Think about it. Do you want to listen to a speaker who jumps from one thought to the next with no clear connection between ideas? Strong organization not only keeps the audience's interest and attention, it also affects perceptions of you as a speaker. Audiences view speakers who are well organized as more competent, confident, and credible.[1] Organization also helps you as a speaker to arrange and develop your ideas.

> "Audiences react more positively to an organized speaker than to a disorganized one."

This chapter will focus on the preparation and organization of a presentation. First, it discusses choosing a topic, determining the purpose of your presentation, preparing and organizing your ideas, strategies for ordering your ideas, and methods clearly linking your ideas so they flow in your presentation. Next, the chapter examines the importance and functions of introductions, methods for gaining and keeping the audience's attention, establishing credibility, and previewing your presentation. Then, the chapter focuses on the importance and purpose of conclusions and different ways to conclude. Finally, the chapter examines different types of outlines and how to construct and use them to your best advantage.

First Things First

Even before planning the specific aspects of your presentation, there are a few things you must determine. First you have to choose a topic. Then you must establish the purpose of your presentation. Only then, should you start thinking about how to organize your presentation. In choosing a topic, students usually have some amount of freedom, but can sometimes become overwhelmed by the possibilities. There are several different approaches to help you choose and narrow your topic that we will discuss now.

Choose your topic first.

Choosing a topic is the first step in preparing your presentation. In most situations, you select your own topic rather than having one assigned. Outside of the classroom, the occasion often determines the topic. In the classroom, the *type* of presentation is usually assigned, but the *specific* topic is not. This allows you to talk about subjects that interest you. In spite of this benefit, choosing a topic often creates anxiety. The topic you choose could be something about which you are already very familiar, excited about, or a topic about which you want to learn more.[2] It also should be a topic that is relevant to the audience and one that makes listening to the speech compelling. Sounds like a lot of rules, right? Let's see if we can clarify some options for topic selection.

> "The topic you choose could be something about which you are already very familiar, excited about, or a topic about which you want to learn more."

Choose a familiar topic.

It is frequently easier to speak about something you are already familiar with, so think about any special knowledge or expertise you may have. For instance, if you coached youth soccer in high school, perhaps you want to talk about the importance of daily physical fitness habits in children or how to foster a sense of teamwork in athletics. Certainly, you want to make sure you can relate your topic to your audience; but often, good topics can be something you have personally experienced or studied. One student discussed his experiences growing up in Trinidad and the differences between living in Trinidad and the United States. Another student who was an unusual type of tour guide talked about his experiences conducting boat tours that observed a large colony of bats located under the Congress Street Bridge in Austin, Texas. Another student had a hobby of wine-making and turned it into an interesting presentation. Still another had taken lessons in Kendo sword fighting for a number of years and discussed the origin and practice of the sport.

Courtesy of Ken Karp/Pearson Education

Choose a topic you are interested in.

Aside from being familiar with a topic, it is important to choose something that is interesting to you. You may be interested in how to stain glass, the sport of mountain climbing, or the study of meteorites. Why is it important to be interested in your topic? If you give a presentation on a topic you care nothing about, even if you know a lot about it, you will have little energy in your presentation and your audience likely will be bored. Basically, if you do not care about your topic, why would your audience be interested? This also could be a perfect opportunity for you to learn about something along with your audience. Maybe you have always wanted to explore women's figure skating or the importance of drinking filtered water, but you have not had a chance to research these topics—now is your chance! Finally, you might think about ideas or values about which you are passionate. You may have some strong opinions you would like to express or even to persuade others.[3] You may have ideas about gun control or the lack of on-campus parking. Any of these ideas could be turned into a presentation.

Consider the audience

Make sure that your topic is relevant to your audience. A good topic is one that the audience cares about and finds important. Your presentation will go more smoothly and be better received if your topic is directly relevant to your audience. For instance, if you are choosing between the two topics "College athletes should be paid a salary" and "Strawberry farming is a challenging career path," you would likely be better off going with the first topic because your audience has a stake in whether college athletes are paid. If you are not sure your audience will care about the topic you have chosen, it is your responsibility to deliver a presentation that makes them care. Let's say you are trying to persuade your audience that high school students should take four years of American history, but you are addressing a college audience that is beyond the need for such classes. Your job is to consider how you can link your topic to your audience so that they, too, will care that high school students can pass basic history.

In Chapter 15, "Speaking to Inform," we said that it is important not to select topics that are overly technical or complicated. If your topic requires you to use specialized jargon, either reconsider the topic, or make sure you have time to adequately define terminology. When you can, it is helpful to "translate" technical information into language your audience can easily understand.[4] For example, if you are a medical student, avoid topics such as the latest developments for preventing myocardial infarction. Instead talk about the latest developments that help people prevent heart attacks. Essentially, you always want to have in mind what your audience knows.

> **"Your presentation will go more smoothly and be better received if your topic is directly relevant to your audience."**

Other ways to generate a topic.

You may also want to use brainstorming techniques to come up with a topic if you are having trouble finding a subject. You can discuss your areas of interest, skills, expertise, experiences, hobbies, and beliefs with friends to generate further ideas. One way to brainstorm is to make lists under headings such as "people," "events," "hobbies," and "political problems." Then, see how many different topics you can come up with that interest you under each heading. For example, under your "people" category you may include President Kennedy, your grandfather, Elvis Presley, and Julia Roberts. Under the category labeled "hobbies" you may list such things as skiing, ice-skating, wine tasting, music, and aerobics. You could then make lists under each sub-topic to narrow your idea even further. For example, under the "music" category you may list rock bands, rap music, and guitars. Under the "aerobics" category you may list bench step, floor, body sculpting, and weight lifting.

Other ways you can search for a topic are through a library database or on the Internet. It is also a good idea to browse newspapers and magazines as well as watch television news. Find out what is happening in current events. Keep abreast of issues, debates, and controversies. Also, keep your eyes and ears open in your everyday interactions with friends, family, and others. Somebody may say something that sparks your interest, such as a

debate about a current controversial issue like animal rights. You may find you have an interest in a topic you had not really thought about before.

Defining the purpose for your presentation.

Now that you have selected a topic, you will need to define the purpose of your presentation. Each presentation has a *general purpose* and a *specific purpose*. The general purpose is very broad. The specific purpose is what you hope to accomplish with the audience by the end of your presentation.[5]

General purpose

In the classroom, the general purpose is usually to inform or persuade. When you present to inform, you want to convey the information in an engaging, interesting way. You could be explaining the steps involved in making homemade yogurt, or you could be explaining how Lasik eye surgery works, or the best way to plan a ski trip.

> "You should be able to state your specific purpose in a concise thesis statement about what you hope to accomplish in your presentation."

If your general purpose is persuasive you are attempting to convince your audience of something or change their viewpoint on a particular topic. You may want to get them to believe something or even take action as a result of what you say. Persuasion could include such things as convincing people why cloning is dangerous, why it is imperative to eat correctly to maintain a healthy weight, or why campus administrators should build more parking lots. Your general purpose frequently will be assigned in a classroom situation—whether it is informative or persuasive. After you know your general purpose, then you can narrow your topic and determine your specific purpose.

Specific purpose

Your specific purpose should focus on only one small aspect of your topic. Make sure your specific purpose is narrow enough that you can actually accomplish it during your presentation. You cannot adequately cover exceptionally broad topics like humankind's progress in space exploration, or the history of religion in the United States in a classroom speech. However, broad topics can certainly be narrowed. For example, instead of talking about progress in space exploration you could narrow it by focusing on the Hubble Telescope or how astronauts eat in space. Rather than talking about the history of religion in the United States, you could focus on the growth of religious cults in the past 10 years, or focus on a particular person such as Billy Graham.

> "It is important to focus on the audience when writing your specific purpose statement."

You should be able to state your specific purpose in a concise thesis statement about what you hope to accomplish in your presentation. The thesis tells the audience what they should know, be able to do, or how they should feel when the presentation is over. It is important to focus on the audience when writing your specific purpose statement. Here is an example of a general and specific purpose statement for a presentation on artist Lisa Fittipaldi:

> **Topic:** Blind Artist
>
> **General Purpose:** To inform
>
> **Specific Purpose:** To inform my audience how Lisa Fittipaldi found her artistic talent in painting after going blind.

Writing specific purpose statements.

There are several ideas to keep in mind when writing a specific purpose statement, which include the following:

❑ The specific purpose statement should be written as a complete sentence, not as a fragment.

> **Fragment:** Importance of exercise
>
> **Complete:** The purpose of my presentation is to persuade the audience why a consistent aerobics program is important to maintain a healthy heart.

❑ The purpose statement should be expressed in a declarative statement, not in the form of a question.

> **Question:** Is caffeine bad for you?
>
> **Statement:** The purpose of my presentation is to convince my audience that caffeine is dangerous to their physical, emotional, and mental health.

❑ Purpose statements should contain only one primary idea, not two.

> **Incorrect with two ideas:** The purpose of my presentation is to convince my audience of the need for more stringent gun control *and* what needs to be done about it.
>
> **Correct with one idea:** The purpose of my presentation is to convince my audience of the need for more stringent gun control.

❑ Purpose statements should use specific language, not vague or general language. Vague statements can be confusing.

> **Vague statement:** The purpose of my presentation is to inform my audience about communication.
>
> **Specific statement:** The purpose of my presentation is to inform my audience about effective communication techniques for an applicant in a job interview.

Exercise 11.1. Writing Your Purpose Statement.

Using your topic for your upcoming presentation and the tips you have been given, write a General and a Specific purpose statement.

Topic:

General Purpose:

Specific Purpose:

Exercise 11.2. Improving a Purpose Statement.

Take a look at the specific purpose statements listed below. For each, write an improved version of the specific purpose statement for the same topic.

A. Do you have trouble parking on campus?

   Improved version:

B. I will convince you that Austin needs to implement a light rail system and implement a series of carpool lanes on I-35.

   Improved version:

C. I'm going to tell you about music.

   Improved version:

Preparing and Organizing Your Ideas

After you choose your topic you are ready to begin planning how to organize your presentation. There are many ways to organize your message, but first you want to make sure your ideas are fully developed, inclusive of the most critical ideas, and that you link and explain the relationships among your ideas. We discussed the techniques of *brainstorming* and *nominal group technique* in Chapter 7, "Working with Teams." Mindmapping and sorting are two additional techniques to help you accomplish this goal.

Developing your ideas through mindmapping.

Mindmapping is a technique for generating and organizing your ideas before making your outline.[6] The purpose of mindmapping is to encourage unencumbered and free-flowing ideas and to examine connections among them to maximize all possible useful ideas and then narrow the field. Patterns of categories that naturally occur together will begin to emerge, helping you arrange your outline in a logical order. This method is similar to brainstorming. Write down every idea you can think of that may fit into your presentation. Focus on including every idea you think is important. Then, try grouping ideas that look as if they fit together and label the primary topic areas as your main points. Daly and Engleberg[7] suggest drawing circles around groups of ideas that go together and drawing lines between them to connect them. Then you will have a visual chart to guide your written outline. Once you have your groups or main points, you can arrange them in a logical order. This system is especially helpful if you have numerous ideas on a topic which you want to include, but are not sure where they fit. Figure 11.1 illustrates this system:

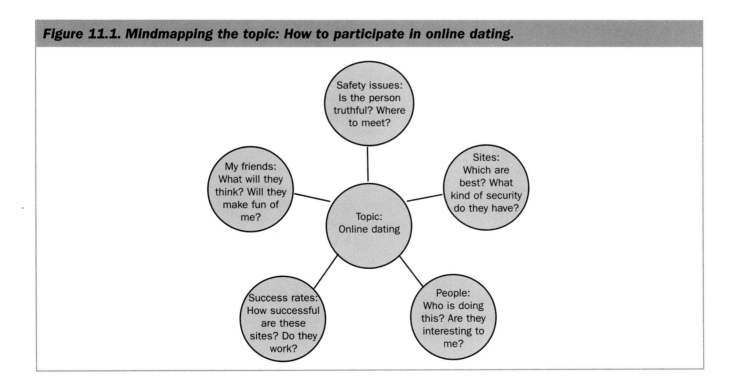

Figure 11.1. Mindmapping the topic: How to participate in online dating.

Exercise 11.3. Creating a Mindmap.

Select a topic and place it in the center circle. Fill in the other circles with any ideas that come to mind. Add more circles if needed. Draw lines between circles if ideas connect. Do not feel like you need to limit yourself.

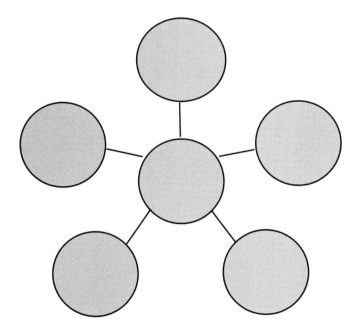

Organize your presentation ideas by sorting.

Sorting is another technique to help you organize your ideas for a presentation. Take a stack of note cards and write down every idea you want to cover. Write down only one idea on each note card. After you have written down every idea you think is important for your topic on a note card, begin grouping the different note cards together based on how the ideas are related. This way you can organize each separate idea into stacks of note cards that seem to go together. Your main points will begin to emerge, depending on how many related ideas you have and how many stacks of note cards that you have created. Then you can decide how to arrange and order your main points.

Ordering your ideas.

How you decide to organize your main points depends on your topic, its purpose, and your audience.[8] Some topics lend themselves to a chronological sequence or a series of steps (e.g. how to create a resume). Others are more spatially oriented (e.g. geographic locations). You also can look for logical divisions that naturally occur in a subject. Another approach is to examine a problem and its solution or the causes and effects of a problem. Some basic patterns for organizing your presentation include the following: chronological, spatial, topical, problem–solution, and cause–effect.[9]

Chronological

Those presentations that are organized chronologically are structured in terms of the order in which they occurred, in a historical sequence. Chronological organization also may be used for presentations that explain how to do something or that describe a particular process that occurs in a definite order. With this arrangement, you explain the steps of a process in the order in which they sequentially occur in time. This pattern is especially effective and frequently used for informative presentations. Examples of chronological organization include such topics as the steps involved in growing your own vegetable garden, examining the history of the women's movement in the South, or the events that led to new security systems currently in place at airports. In any presentation, steps should be grouped into two to five main points. You can clump shorter or smaller steps into larger ones, such as *beginning steps, middle steps,* and *ending steps*.

Spatial

Spatial presentations are organized by geographic location or direction. Descriptions of such things as a department layout or a new factory building utilize spatial arrangements. This arrangement also should follow a logical

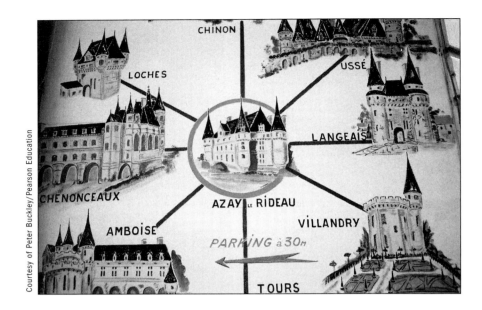

Courtesy of Peter Buckley/Pearson Education

order or the audience will become confused. Other examples might include describing the path the Donner party followed, or the layout of an amusement park such as Disneyland. Spatial arrangements are especially well suited for informative speeches.

Topical

Topical arrangements break down the main topic into subtopics that serve as natural divisions. In topical arrangement, each subtopic is equally important to the overall goal of the presentation. So, if you were to give a presentation on dog breeds, your natural divisions might be: (1) the three most popular breeds for young adults, or (2) apartment dogs, house dogs, and outside dogs, or (3) small, medium and large dogs. Ask yourself: What are the logical divisions of my topic? If your topic does not seem to have logical divisions, you may want to consider another method of ordering your ideas.

> **"Most human beings have terrible memories . . . we are likely to recall the idea that we heard *first* . . . and the idea that we heard *last* . . ."**

For our purposes, let's assume that your topic does break down logically into, ideally, three subtopics. How should you order them? Here you should consider two key terms: primacy and recency. Most human beings have terrible memories; most often, however, we are likely to recall the idea that we heard *first*, or *primacy*, and the idea that we heard *last*, or *recency*. Knowing this, if you have two very strong subtopics and one weaker one, primacy and recency dictate that you should put your weakest point in the middle: STRONG, weak, STRONG. The audience's attention may drift a bit in the middle of the presentation, so it is likely they will not remember your weak point, but may recall your stronger points.

Problem-solution

The problem-solution pattern of organization introduces a problem and then offers listeners a solution. Normally, speakers first discuss the problem, then discuss possible solutions. For example, if your presentation was on the importance of preventing drunk driving fatalities, you probably would want to first provide evidence that drunk driving fatalities are a problem, and then provide possible alternatives to solve the problem. Some solutions maintain the current situation (status quo), others adopt a very different approach than the one currently being used, and some argue for something in the middle.

Cause-Effect

Cause-effect order is precisely what it sounds like: An action results in a reaction. One example would be to argue that driving SUVs contributes to pollution and accelerates the rate of global warming. Cause-effect certainly can be a strong strategy, but it should be used only for persuasive speaking and never for informative speaking simply because you *have* to make an argument for or against something if you use cause-effect ordering. Additionally, you want to ensure the link you are making between two events, such as driving SUVs and accelerated rates of global warming, is indeed factual, logical, and can be supported by evidence. While the SUV/global warming topic is certainly viable considering these standards, if you were to argue that reading causes poor spinal alignment, you may have your work cut out for you!

> "Cause-effect certainly can be a strong strategy, but it should be used only for persuasive speaking . . ."

Media Box

Watch a sample student presentation on the Fru Gene. Which organizational strategy does the speaker use?

Visit this chapter's folder in your Chapter Media Contents online.

Deranged Arrangement

Decide on the organizational pattern that these points would best fit into and then order them appropriately.

1. Pattern_____

___A: The current registration system is unfair.
___B: Registration over the internet or by phone would solve these problems.
___C: The current registration system is inefficient.

2. Pattern_____

___A: A booming economy helps commerce in Texas
___B: A booming economy helps farmers in Travis County.
___C: A booming economy helps the oil industry in the Southwest.

3. Pattern_____

___A: Study abroad will help you meet people with different experiences.
___B: Study abroad will help you experience a different culture.
___C: Study abroad will help you see interesting places.

4. Pattern_____

___A: Fluorocarbons eroded the ozone layer surrounding the earth.
___B: Society has increased the use of aerosol spray cans.
___C: Depletion of the ozone layer exposes people to additional ultraviolet radiation.
___D: Aerosol spray cans release fluorocarbons into the air.

5. Pattern_____

___A: Race relations have improved in the past 40 years.
___B: Race relations were characterized by slavery before the Civil War.
___C: Race relations can still be improved in the future.
___D: Race relations were marked by segregation until the late 1950s.
___E: Race relations saw much improvement in the early 1960s.

Special thanks to Christie B. Ghetian, Communication Arts & Sciences, The Pennsylvania State University

Connecting main points.

Once you have your main points, you need <u>connective</u> thoughts to bridge your points together. Connectives are words or phrases that connect your ideas together and indicate how they are related. Strong connectives are important in good presentations to maintain flow and structure and to serve as a bridge between thoughts. Connectives are also necessary to maintain continuity and keep the presentation from appearing disjointed. Connectives include previews, summaries, signposts, and transitions.[10]

Previews

An <u>initial preview</u> lets the audience know what is coming in the body of the speech. Basically, you tell them what you are going to tell them. The initial preview is used to communicate your central idea and its main points to the audience. It is also the first statement of your main idea, which comes before the body of the presentation. Presented below is an example of an initial preview:

> "Fraternity hazing must be stopped. In order to grasp the extent of this problem, I will first discuss how widespread this problem is across college campuses. Next, I will discuss some of the causes of the problem. Finally, I will offer a solution."

<u>Internal previews</u> are similar to initial previews, but they are used in the main body of the speech to indicate what will be covered in the key points.[11] They work in the same way as an initial preview, except they preview the ideas introduced in the body of the speech as the speech is presented. This can help focus the audience on what they need to listen to. Internal previews describe how you are going to approach a main point. They are especially useful if you have complex ideas with multiple subpoints.[12] Presented below is an example of an internal preview:

> "My next point is to talk about the cause of fraternity hazing."

Summaries

<u>Internal summaries</u> are used during the presentation to summarize what you just said. They also may be used as transitions. An internal summary can help the audience remember the material that you just covered as you move to another main point. The purpose is to summarize the preceding point or points to help reinforce ideas:[13]

> "We have just discussed the cause of fraternity hazing. What can we do to stop it?"

> "An internal summary can help the audience remember the material that you just covered . . ."

<u>Final summaries</u> are often used as a recap of the main points at the conclusion of the presentation. This is the last opportunity to emphasize and reinforce your main points with your audience. A final summary is a great way to help the audience remember your most important points. Here's an example:[14]

> "Let's review what we have covered. First, there is a need for greater education about fraternity hazing rituals. Second, fraternity hazing is personally degrading. Third, fraternity hazing is physically dangerous. Finally, fraternity hazing tarnishes the reputation of the Greek System as a whole."

Transitions

A <u>transition</u> is a word, phrase, or nonverbal cue that indicates movement from one idea to another. Transitions let the audience know that the speaker has just finished one idea, and is moving to the idea or point that is next.

Internal previews are frequently combined with transitions. Examples of transitions include some of the following phrases:

- ❑ *Now we will turn to* the topic of how to increase enrollment.
- ❑ *In addition to* discussing the cause of higher crime rates in urban areas, we will examine some solutions.
- ❑ *Also,* we will explore various methods to alleviate the parking problem.
- ❑ *Besides that,* we will propose a plan to decrease faculty workload.
- ❑ *Next,* we will discuss how to select the best water ski.
- ❑ *Now that we've talked about* the problem of homelessness, we'll discuss some solutions.

Courtesy of Alan Briere /Dorling Kindersley Media Library

Signposts

A signpost is a verbal or nonverbal signal that the speaker is moving to another topic and may include previews, summaries, and transitions.[15] Frequently, a signpost will consist of a brief statement or phrase that focuses attention on where the speaker is in the presentation by emphasizing key ideas. Signposts may include using numbers, questions, or phrases.[16] The following is an example of using numbers as signposts.

- ❑ *The first reason* for the lack of parking is increased student enrollment.
- ❑ *The second reason* for not enough parking is more businesses are opening around the campus.
- ❑ *The final reason* for lack of parking is the university has doubled the size of the faculty in the last five years.

Signposts introduce each new point. Another way to use a signpost is by asking questions to introduce each new main point.

- ❑ Why is drug abuse an increasing problem among today's youth?
- ❑ What can be done to solve the problem of drug abuse?

Another way to use a signpost is with a simple phrase that emphasizes important points.

- ❑ The most important point is. . . .
- ❑ It's important to remember that. . . .
- ❑ The key concept is. . . .
- ❑ Let me repeat that point.

Verbal signposts also may include words and phrases that show relationships among concepts, such as "therefore," "also," "in addition to," and "however." Nonverbal signposts may be used alone to signal a transition or in conjunction with a verbal signpost. Nonverbal signposts include such things as facial expressions, movement, pauses, or a change in vocal pitch or rate. For example, some speakers will raise one finger to signal their first point, then a pair of fingers to indicate a second point.

Outlining Your Presentation

After you have selected a topic for your presentation, you will need to outline your talk so you have direction and structure. There are several benefits to clearly outlining your presentation. An outline helps ensure the ideas are coherent and flow smoothly together, aids you in fully developing your ideas, and serves as a guide for your presentation. If you were heading off on a vacation you would likely not leave without a map and directions, along with a plan as to how best reach your destination. The same is true for an effective presentation. The outline acts as a guide. An outline also acts as a visual aid to show how related items are grouped together, and it helps to build structure. A good outline is also quite helpful for rehearsing your presentation.

There are two primary types of outlines: formal outlines and delivery outlines. The formal outline is far more detailed and complete since its intent is to help you prepare your speech. The delivery outline is very brief and is intended to jog your memory while you deliver your presentation.

> "An outline helps ensure the ideas are coherent and flow smoothly together, aids you in fully developing your ideas, and serves as a guide for your presentation."

Creating a formal outline.

The formal outline helps you decide what to say, how you want your ideas to flow, and how to organize your main points. The formal outline guides the preparation of your presentation. This outline consists of a title, the central idea and a specific purpose statement, and the main sections including the introduction, main points, supporting points, conclusion, and bibliography. Begin with the central idea followed by a statement of your specific purpose as a separate unit that comes before the body of the outline. This will help you ensure that the body of your presentation coincides with your purpose.

The formal outline is the written framework for your presentation and it follows a standard outline format.[17] The formal outline is your written version of the presentation. It ensures that the organization of your presentation is logical and easy for your audience to follow and understand. It helps you know where to insert related supporting material for your main points. Then you can visually review it to see if it is unbalanced in any way. For example, do you have too many statistics or not enough testimony? You also can check each supporting point against its key point and each key point against the central idea to make sure your supporting points actually support your key points and your key points support your central idea.

> "The formal outline is the written framework for your presentation and it follows a standard outline format."

Make sure you label the main sections as "introduction," "body," and "conclusion." The purpose of the outline is to give you a clear visual framework that shows the relationship among ideas.

Guidelines for good formal outlines

Make sure your grammatical style is consistent. Whether you are using a phrase or a complete sentence for each point in your outline, make sure you use the same style all the way through. You may want to check with your instructor as to style preference. Most formal outlines are written out in complete declarative sentences.[18] Stating your main points and supporting points in full sentences helps you fully develop your ideas. Below are points to keep in mind while creating your formal outline:

❑ Use standard numbering and be consistent.
❑ Use Roman numerals to identify main points.
❑ Include two to five main points. More than five points becomes too complex.

❑ Use capital letters to identify subpoints under each main point.

❑ If there are subdivisions, use at least two per point. You cannot divide a point into one subpoint. For every 1, there must be a 2. For every A there must be a B. Divisions must have a minimum of two.

❑ Make sure the Roman numerals, headings for sections, and transitions all line up in the outline correctly and consistently.

Major parts of an outline

The major parts of your formal outline include the introduction, the body, and the conclusion. It is also a good idea to include and label transitions, internal previews, and internal summaries. These are usually not listed as part of the main points or as Roman numerals, but are labeled independently and placed in the outline where they will occur in the presentation.[19] At the end of your formal outline, you should also include a bibliography that lists all the sources of your information. This is where you list the magazines, newspapers, books, journals, websites, and any other source you used for your presentation. Here is a sample formal outline:

Wash Your Hands Before You Eat

  I. Introduction: Look at your hands.

     A. Did you know there are more microbes on your hand than there are people on the planet?

     B. Over one million viruses can fit on the head of a pin.

     C. You will probably eat lunch with those same hands.

  II. My Father is a Pathologist and he has made similar comments many times.

     A. Research from websites of the American Society of Microbiology and the Center of Disease Prevention confirms the importance of washing your hands.

     B. You can do something to prevent germs from causing you to become sick.

 III. Preview: Today I would like to persuade you to help protect yourself from infection and diseases by simply washing your hands before you eat.

Body

  I. First, let's look at what infectious agents may be on your hands.

     A. You may wash your hands after using the restroom, but studies indicate not everyone does.

       1. According to a national survey conducted by the American Society for Microbiology nearly one third of Americans do not wash their hands after using a public restroom.

       2. Microbiology Professor Hugh Pennington says. "The next time you meet someone and shake their hand, there's a one in five chance they are one of those people who do not always wash their hands after going to the toilet."

       3. CNN claims that outbreaks of hepatitis A have been attributed to food contamination spread by inadequate hand washing.

       4. Most infectious diseases are spread by hand-to-hand contact, not by coughing or sneezing.

     B. Bacteria is everywhere and results in many types of infections.

       1. Infection is the third leading cause of death in the United States.

       2. Bacteria can be found on any surface including doorknobs, telephones, computer keyboards, and desktops.

   3. These slides show samples of bacteria from the surface of a doorknob.
      a. The surfaces may also contain viruses that cause the flu.
      b. To prevent these bacteria from staying on your hands, it is important to wash your hands before eating or food preparation.

II. Washing your hands is effective in removing bacteria and viruses from your skin before it contaminates your food.
   A. The National Institute of Allergy and Infectious Diseases says that handwashing is the simplest method to prevent infection.
   B. Follow these steps to rinse away microbes.
      1. Use warm running water and soap.
      2. Be sure to scrub between fingers and under fingernails.
      3. Rinse hands thoroughly.
      4. Dry hands with a clean towel or disposable paper towel.
      5. Turn off the faucet with the towel.

III. Look at these pictures of a student's hands.
   A. The glowing areas are where the bacteria are thriving.
   B. The first picture shows the hands before washing and the second picture shows the hands after washing.
   C. About 60% of the bacteria were eliminated.

Conclusion

In conclusion, microbes are everywhere and live on most surfaces.

   I. People you come in contact with may not be as clean as you think, and can transfer disease-causing microbes to your hands and your food.
   II. Next time you prepare to eat, wash your hands in the nearest bathroom.
   III. Which of these hands would you rather have touching your food?

Using a delivery outline.

The delivery outline is a form of notes used during the delivery of an extemporaneous presentation. The exact words are not written out, but key words are used to help you remember the main points. It is a condensed version of the formal outline and does not contain details or complete sentences. You do not want to read word for word from this outline. It is a good idea to use the same visual framework for your delivery outline as in the formal outline. It will be easier to find where you are when you glance down at your notes. A delivery outline should be clear and easy to read. Use large type if it will help you. If you are using note cards, place one main point with supporting subpoints on each card. Be sure to number cards with each card containing a major section. Try to keep your delivery outline as brief as possible. If you have too many notes, you are more likely to rely too heavily on them and have poor eye contact with the audience.[20]

   The delivery outline also includes written notes to yourself to remind you of different delivery ideas at various points in the presentation. These are cues to help improve your delivery. This information is not included in your formal outline. These cues not only remind you of what to say, but how to say it. These directions may include such things as "slow down," "eye contact," "pause," "smile," and "breathe."[21] Use any techniques that help you, such as colored fonts, large type, or smiley faces. Here is an example:

Wash Your Hands Before You Eat

EYE CONTACT

I. Look at hands
   A. More microbes than people
   B. One million viruses
   C. Eat lunch

PAUSE

II. Father
   A. Research: American Society of Microbiology
      Center of Disease Prevention
   B. Prevention

III. Wash your hands

Body:

SLOW DOWN

I. Infectious agents
   A. Not everyone washes
      1. 1/3 don't wash
      2. Pennington quote "one in five chance"
      3. CNN Hepatitis A
      4. Hand-to-hand contact, not sneezing

TAKE A BREATH

   B. Bacteria everywhere
      1. 3rd leading cause of death
      2. Bacteria on surfaces
      3. Slides
         a. flu
         b. wash hands before food

PAUSE

II. Washing hands effective
   A. National Institute of Allergy & Infectious Diseases
   B. Follow Steps
      1. Warm water & soap
      2. Fingernails
      3. Rinse
      4. Clean towel
      5. Faucet with towel

III. Pictures of hands
 A. Glowing bacteria
 B. Before & after washing
 C. 60% eliminated

SLOW DOWN, PAUSE

Conclusion
 I. People may not be clean
 II. Wash hands before eating
 III. Which hands would you rather have?

Exercise 11.4. Creating a Delivery Outline.

Using your own topic for an upcoming presentation, create a Delivery Outline. Include notes to yourself as you saw in the sample such as "Pause," "Breathe," and "Eye Contact."

I. Intro:

    A.

    B.

    C.

II. Body Point 1:

    A.

    B.

    C.

III. Body Point II:

    A.

    B.

    C.

IV. Body Point III:

    A.

    B.

    C.

V. Conclusion:

    A.

    B.

    C.

Introducing Your Presentation

Once you have developed and outlined your central idea and main points, you can turn your attention to how best to introduce and conclude your topic. We recommend writing your introduction and conclusion *after* you write the body of your presentation because once you know your central ideas of your presentation and the structure to develop them, you will be more successful setting it up and ending it strongly. Yet, because the beginning and end of a presentation are shorter than the body, they tend to be overlooked or underdeveloped elements of the presentation. This is a huge mistake! Introductions and conclusions serve as the first and final impressions of *both you and your ideas*. Audiences often make snap decisions about others based on first impressions. Students may decide in the first one-minute of a new class if their professor is going to be boring and put them to sleep or is dynamic and exciting. The same is true of final impressions. Why is it often true "the best is saved for last?" At a rock concert the band may save their number one hit to play last. A Fourth of July celebration may end with a fireworks display. We are back to the ideas of primacy and recency again: First and last impressions count for a lot.

> **"Introductions and conclusions serve as the first and final impressions of *both you and your ideas*."**

Let's start at the top. A strong introduction accomplishes 5 things. It (1) gains the audience's attention; (2) specifically addresses how the topic is relevant to the audience; (3) states a clear thesis or central idea; (4) establishes the speaker's personal credibility on the topic; and (5) provides a preview of the coming presentation. Let's look at each of these in greater detail.

Courtesy of Bill Varie/Corbis Images

Getting the audience's attention.

Great presenters know that audiences are *never* responsible for paying rapt attention to them. Rather, they are responsible for gaining and keeping the audience's attention. There are several strategies for gaining an audience's attention: startling statements, statistics, questions, quotations, and narratives. Each of these strategies, in turn, can also be used to keep an audience's attention. The key is to always relate each and every step of your presentation, from the first words of the introduction to the last sentence of the conclusion, to your audience.

Use a startling statement

Do you ever wonder why car dealerships make those awful television ads where a man dressed in a brightly-colored suit is shouting things like, "I'll beat any used car deal in Texas!" or "You can drive out of here in a brand new car for no money down!" It's because saying something startling is an effective way of getting an audience's attention. Of course, there are ways to use this technique that are far more effective than wearing strange clothing and shouting. Ideally, you want to make sure your "startling statement" is both relevant to your topic *and* to your audience. An example of a way one student startled the audience on the topic of sleep deprivation was by crushing a soda can behind the podium that no one could see, but it was loud enough for everyone to hear. She then went on to explain that the noise was what her car sounded like when it crashed into an aluminum pole when she had fallen asleep at the wheel because of sleep deprivation.

> "There are several strategies for gaining an audience's attention: startling statements, statistics, questions, quotations, and narratives."

Use statistics

We hear statistics all the time: "Four out of 5 dentists agree that flossing is good for you," "Seventy percent of balding men who used our product had more hair in 3 months," "One hundred percent of our proceeds go to charity." If you use statistics as an attention getter, remember two key elements: Understand what the statistic *really means* and make it relevant to your audience. Statistics can be challenging to understand. For example, you often hear that "half of all marriages in the United States end in divorce." What does this actually mean, however? Does it mean that half of all people who get married will get divorced? Or, does it mean of all the marriages in the U.S., half will end in divorce? It actually means the latter because some individuals will be married and divorced multiple times, but you need to make sure you explain this to your audience in a way that crystallizes the notion rather than muddles it. Second, you must make the statistic relevant to your audience. Because we are surrounded by numerical "proof" of all kinds of phenomena, most numbers go in one ear and out the other unless they are used in a way that is relevant to us at the time. So, instead of trying to gain your audience's attention with "half of all marriages in the U.S. end in divorce," a statistic that has been repeated so many times we are no longer interested or shocked, say something like, "because the divorce rate in the U.S. is so high, in this room alone, at least 30% of us have or will have parents who are divorced—even more frightening, as many as half of us will divorce in our lifetime." It is the same information, just stated in a way that is tailored to your audience.

> "Audience members want to know 'Why is this topic relevant to me?'"

Connect to your audience

If your topic directly impacts your audience, you will engage their interest. Audience members want to know "Why is this topic relevant to me?" In answering this question, you can describe practical applications of your topic or tell them what they will learn from your presentation.[22] Also, if you can make a direct personal connection with the audience or if you can share something in common with them, that can gain their attention. You may have personal experience in something that has a direct affect on them.[23] If the topic itself does not directly impact them, find a way to link it to your audience. One example is of a Chippendale's male dancer. Most students probably don't immediately relate to why a young man would want to dance for Chippendale's, but when he put it in terms of financing his way through medical school, it became a more interesting and relevant presentation. Here is a simple example using the topic of insomnia:

> **Less Effective:** Insomnia prevents a lot of people from getting an adequate amount of sleep. It affects 50% of the adult population at least once over the course of a year.

More Effective: Do you have trouble staying awake in class? Is lack of sleep affecting your performance on tests and class work? If you answered yes to these questions, you may be suffering from insomnia.

This is one example of the same topic illustrating the difference between two approaches. The first is a statement of fact and while informative, it is not particularly engaging. The second directly relates the topic to a classroom audience and how it may affect their daily school life. Using a question about something the class can relate to gains the audience's attention.

Ask questions

Have you ever been in an interview where the conversation went something like this:

Interviewer:	So, how are you?
You:	Fine, thanks.
Interviewer:	Hot enough for you, today?
You:	Yes, it is hot.
Interviewer:	Do you like UT?
You:	Love it.

If you and the interviewer manage to stay awake during this exchange, it would be a miracle! Why is this conversation so dull? The interviewer asked solely closed-ended questions that only required a one-word response. Conversely, an open-ended question or series of open-ended questions gets your audience thinking and the proverbial juices flowing. Instead of asking, "Hot enough for you, today?" ask, "What is the weather like in Austin?" It opens up the possibility for real deliberation and an exchange of ideas rather than shutting down the conversation in one fell swoop.

Many beginning presenters are tempted to use a type of question called a *rhetorical question*, which are not asked to collect information or receive a direct answer. Rather, they are used to make a statement in the form of a question—ideally to prompt people to think about something. Here are some examples: Why are politicians so crooked? Aren't you ashamed of yourself? What business is it of yours? Don't you hate it when you have problems parking on campus?

Though there are times when rhetorical questions are both useful and effective, few presenters are able to really master them as a technique for gaining attention. What tends to happen is that most speakers do not ask rhetorical questions that make audience members perk up and listen. Using rhetorical questions is a very risky strategy because if you lose your audience at the beginning, you probably will not get them back. So, until you become a pro, stick to using open-ended questions that oblige the audience to think and engage.

> "Though there are times when rhetorical questions are both useful and effective, few presenters are able to really master them as a technique for gaining attention."

Use a quotation

Quotations are also effective for immediately gaining the audience's attention by setting the emotional tone of your presentation, whether it is humorous or dramatic. There are numerous sources for attention-getting quotations from famous or historical figures, poems or songs, or even friends or family members. There are many sources for famous quotations on the Internet. The power of the quotation matters most. Whatever quotation you choose, it should be short and to the point since long quotations lose impact and your audience's interest. Make sure you give full credit to the source of the quotation. You will also need to practice your quotation for dramatic impact and effective delivery. Here is an example about citizenship from President John F. Kennedy:

"Ask not what your country can do for you; ask what you can do for your country."

Exercise 11.5. Statistical Analysis and Relevance.

Below are several pieces of fictional statistical data. For each, explain what you believe the statistic means and then draft a way to phrase the statistic so it is relevant to your class audience.

A. 17% of residents in this state have a college degree.

B. 2% of NCAA football players go pro.

C. The 3 tallest mountains in the world are located in the Himalayas.

Tell a story

As human beings, we are drawn to stories. When we are little, we beg our moms and dads to read stories to us before we go to sleep, even if we have heard *Goodnight Moon* every night for a year. Why do we love stories? It could be because we identify with the characters, or appreciate the moral; because they make us feel something powerful; because they make us want to go on the same adventures; or simply because it is human nature. Stories help us connect to ideas. There are a number of places to find good stories, but personal stories are generally more effective than third-person or hypothetical stories. Here is an example of an effective story used as an attention-getter:

Courtesy of Don and Pat Valenti/Getty Images USA, Inc.

"Fifteen years ago, my uncle was driving his car down a residential street. My two cousins, ages 7 and 5 were in the car. Suddenly, my uncle fell asleep at the wheel, lost control of the car and they drove up on a sidewalk, slamming into a telephone pole at 30 MPH. My uncle and cousins were terrified, but escaped with their lives and relatively minor injuries. Why? They were wearing their seatbelts. I am here today to convince you that we need to enact laws that require stiffer penalties for not wearing seat belts."

Remember that your story must be relevant to your audience and that you need to actually practice telling it for it to really work. If you think you can just wing it, you may miss some details, get emotional and not be able to control it, or forget some key aspect of the story.

> ## "Stories help us connect to ideas."

Establishing credibility of your message.

You must also establish your credibility in the introduction. Credibility means your listeners consider you qualified to discuss your topic. You must establish that you are competent and trustworthy. For example, a member of the U.S. Olympic marathon team is qualified to talk about the benefits of running for your health and fitness, while a movie star is not (unless they also happen to be a marathon runner). Audiences want to know why they should believe what you say. Good presenters emphasize some aspect of their experience or knowledge that qualifies them to speak authoritatively on the subject they are addressing.

> **Example:** My love for aerobics started eight years ago when I took my first step class. Like most beginners, I was a bit clumsy at the time. Since then, I have drastically improved my coordination. I even became a certified instructor. With my five years of experience as a trained instructor, I would like to explain the proper way to bench step to avoid injury.

The audience is more likely to pay attention when they realize the speaker knows what she is talking about. Even if you do not have direct personal experience, you may have some other type of knowledge that qualifies you on the subject. For example, you may share that you have a strong interest in the Holocaust and you have read numerous books and viewed documentaries on the subject for years. Your personal research into the Holocaust would also give you credibility and qualify you to speak on the subject.

> ## "Credibility means your listeners consider you qualified to discuss your topic."

Just make sure your audience knows that you are qualified to talk about your topic. Remember, you do not have to be an expert to be qualified to speak, but you need to share your interest in the topic upfront.

Using preview statements.

The introduction should also include a sneak preview of what is to come, including how you are going to develop your central idea. *Preview statements* are important because they tell your audience what specifically you will be talking about and on which main points your presentation will focus. The preview helps the audience mentally organize the presentation. Preview statements also serve to provide a transition into the main body of the speech. Preview statements are usually positioned at the end of the introduction.

> **Example:** Today I will discuss the benefits of a heart-healthy diet, how to design an eating plan that will best work for you, and offer some tips on how to stay motivated to eat healthy food.

> **Example:** We're going to examine the steps involved in starting a wine cellar. We'll begin with the environment of the cellar, discuss the wines that age best in a cellar, and finish with placement of the bottles.

Table 11.1. Guidelines for Your Presentation's Introduction.

- Keep the introduction concise and to the point.
- Clearly link the introduction to the topic.
- Select a powerful attention-getter that is appropriate to your topic.
- Write the introduction after you write the body of your presentation. This will make it easier to determine which type of opening works best for your topic.
- Use your introduction to gain attention, establish credibility, and preview your main points.

Concluding Your Presentation

You now have a good grasp on the construction and function of an introduction. Now, let's turn to the most often overlooked, thrown-together-sounding element in most presentations—the conclusion. We cannot tell you how many times we have heard students give a fantastic speech, then get to what should be a strong conclusion, and announce, "that's it!," pack up their notes, shut down their PowerPoint, and run to their seats without making eye contact with anyone. The theory of primacy and recency instructs us that audiences recall what they see and hear first, and what they see and hear last. If your conclusion is non-existent or poorly done, it may not matter that the body of your presentation was eloquent—what your audience will remember is how it fell apart at the end. It is essential to prepare and practice your conclusion. It is the lasting impression you give your audience. Never, never, never assume that your presentation will come together magically at the end—even professional speakers do not go into presentations with the strategy of "winging" the conclusion because it is far too important to the overall success of the presentation.

> **"If your conclusion is non-existent or poorly done . . . what your audience will remember is how it fell apart at the end."**

A strong conclusion accomplishes two main goals: (1) It gives a summary of the main ideas; and (2) provides a sense of closure to the overall presentation. A summary of your presentation should briefly remind listeners of the key elements of the presentation. For instance, a summary of a presentation on "How to Register for Classes at UT" might sound something like this:

> "Remember, registering for classes at UT does not have to be stressful. You need to know three things: your registration time, a list of options from your advisor, and whether you function better as a student in the morning, afternoon, or evening. If you know those three things, you can successfully register each semester."

A sense of closure is accomplished in many of the same ways as an attention-getter. In fact, returning to the technique you used in your attention getter is the ideal way to give the audience a sense that they have arrived full-circle in the presentation. If you start with a quotation, return to explain how that quotation fits in the larger context of your presentation. If you told a story, tell people the lesson from the story in the conclusion.

Ask a question.

Asking a question can stimulate further thinking and leave a lasting impression. A question demonstrates that your presentation topic is so crucial that the five minutes you spent discussing it should not be the "last word" on the subject. Rather, the audience should leave thinking about how they can apply the information in their own lives. It will also make your closing more personal if you ask a question that applies directly to the audience. Leave them with something to think about. A question can remind the audience of your theme and make a lasting impact. Here is an example on the topic of sleep deprivation:

"Would you rather have a night of dreams or a day dreaming of sleep?"

Make a dramatic statement.

Another way to add impact in your conclusion is to make up your own dramatic statement that applies to the topic.[24] Use language that inspires and creates lasting images. A dramatic statement concludes on a strong emotional note. This type of statement may contain an element of surprise or an unexpected twist. Here is an example:

"You may think a lack of sleep is a simple issue easily resolved with some caffeine. However, sleep deprivation is a serious health issue and over time can place you at serious risk for injuries and behavioral problems or worse. Sleep deprivation may seem like a short-term problem, but ultimately, a lack of sleep can actually kill you."

Courtesy of Laime E. Druskis/Pearson Education

Use a quotation.

A closing quotation can add dramatic impact to the end of your presentation and leave the audience with a memorable thought. Look for a brief quotation that directly applies to your topic and your central idea. The words of others may accurately and dramatically sum up the main point of your message. Quotations are sometimes used as dramatic and emotional finales. Here is an example from the Dalai Lama about sleep.

"Sleep is the best meditation."

Tell a story.

As you know from the section on introductions, telling a story is a powerful tool both for gaining an audience's attention as well as keeping it all the way through to the end of a presentation. Return to the story you told at the beginning for closure. If we return the story about seatbelts saving family members' lives, your closing story might be something like this:

> "Remember the story about the car accident involving my uncle and cousins? Because of the lesson my family learned from this potentially fatal accident, we all started wearing seatbelts every single time we drive or ride in cars. We are all safer because of it. We are not alone—if everyone wears a seatbelt every time they are in a car, automotive injuries and fatalities would drop 80%. It takes two seconds to buckle your seatbelt, but those two seconds could save your life."

Table 11.2. Guidelines to Remember for the Conclusion.

- Briefly summarize your main points.
- Conclude with impact and keep it brief.
- Prepare and practice.
- Make a strong lasting impression with a memorable close.

Conclusion

Organization counts. From choosing a topic to ordering your main points to outlining, audiences judge the effectiveness of both speaker and presentation on organization. We have described several methods to help you choose a topic including listing topics you know about, exploring topics you are not familiar with, and brainstorming. Once you select a topic, determining a general purpose and a specific purpose will help you give a more effective and memorable presentation. Some ideas to help you begin preparation for organization include mindmapping and sorting. After you craft purpose statements, your job is to order your points in the most compelling way possible. Useful methods of organizing your main ideas include chronological, spatial, topical, problem-solution, and cause-effect patterns. The concepts of primacy and recency are also important considerations in idea placement. Finally, connect your main points by using initial and internal previews, internal and final summaries, transitions, and signposts.

Outlining is the visual framework and roadmap for your presentation. It is a way to help you clearly organize your ideas and properly link them together. Two types of outlines are required for an effective presentation either a formal outline or a delivery outline. Formal rules for outlining also help ensure your main points are correctly supported. Delivery outlines contain only key words to prompt your thinking but maintain an extemporaneous style. Also, they give you the opportunity to write notes to yourself to breathe, to smile or to pause, all elements we sometimes overlook in order to get through the content smoothly.

Strong introductions and conclusions gain your audience's attention, establish your credibility, build rapport, and preview and wrap up your main points. Useful methods of gaining attention include a startling statement, a statistic, connecting with the audience, asking questions, telling a story, or using a quotation. Different ways to conclude your presentation include asking a rhetorical question, referring back to the introduction, making a dramatic statement, or using a quotation. You may choose to use any of the introductory or concluding strategies alone or in combination with others. Your choice will depend on your topic, your audience, the emotional tone, and you.

Choosing a topic, preparation and organization, introductions and conclusions, and outlines are all foundations for an effective and memorable presentation. They are also tools to help you give the best presentation you can. Experts say that in real estate, it is all about location, location, location. We remind you that in effective presentations, it is all about organization, organization, organization.

Endnotes

1 John Daly & Isa Engelberg. *Presentations in Everyday Life Strategies for Effective Speaking.* Boston: Houghton Mifflin Company, 2001, p. 130.

2 Ibid., p. 48

3 Stephen E. Lucas. *The Art of Public Speaking,* 7th ed. New York: McGraw-Hill, 2001, p. 76.

4 Ibid., p. 355.

5 Ibid., pp. 81–82.

6 Daly & Engleberg, pp. 147–148.

7 Ibid., pp. 147–148.

8 Lucas, p. 196.

9 Ibid., pp. 196–201.

10 Ibid., pp. 204–208.

11 Ibid., pp. 205–206.

12 Ibid., pp. 205–206.

13 Ibid., p. 206.

14 Ibid., pp. 228–229.

15 Ibid., pp. 206–208.

16 Ibid., pp. 206–208.

17 Daly & Engelberg, p. 151.

18 Dan O'Hair & Roberta Stewart. *Public Speaking Challenges and Choices.* Boston, MA: Bedford/St. Martin's, 1998, p. 191.

19 Lucas, pp. 241–242.

20 Ibid., pp. 248–249.

21 Ibid., pp. 248–249.

22 Daly & Engelberg, p. 162.

23 Ibid., p. 164.

24 Lucas, p. 230.

Notes

CHAPTER 12

Supporting Your Claims[1]

Objectives

After studying Chapter 12, you should be able to do the following:

☐ Identify the different types of evidence.
☐ Know how and when to use different types of evidence.
☐ Learn how to prepare evidence to fit your presentation.
☐ Understand the ethical dilemmas concerning the presentation of evidence.
☐ How to detect fallacies in reasoning.

Key Terms

TERM	DEFINITION
causal reasoning	Assumes that the one event influences or controls other events.
causal relationship	Arising from a cause.
connotative meaning	Suggestive or indirect meaning.
deductive reasoning	The deriving of a conclusion by reasoning; inference in which the conclusion about particulars follows necessarily from general or universal premises; a conclusion reached by logical deduction.
denotative meaning	Standard or literal meaning.
explanation	Something that is made plain and understandable.
emotive terms	Of or relating to the emotions.
evidence	An outward sign or something that furnishes proof.
fallacies	An often plausible argument using false or invalid inference; a false or mistaken idea.
generalization	A general statement, law, principle, or proposition. The act or process whereby a response is made to a stimulus similar to but not identical with a reference stimulus.
inference	The act of passing from one proposition, statement, or judgment considered as true to another whose truth is believed to follow from that of the former; the act of passing from statistical sample data to generalizations.
probative value	Serving to prove something or test it.
tautological reasoning	Needless repetition of an idea or statement.
testimony	Firsthand authentication of a fact or evidence.

Introduction

As Sir Arthur Conan Doyle wrote, "Circumstantial evidence is a very tricky thing . . . It may seem to point very straight to one thing, but if you shift your own point of view a little, you may find it pointing in an equally uncompromising manner to something entirely different."

Evidence is information that you gather from your research and present to an audience in your speech to support your claim. Evidence can perform a variety of functions in a speech: It can help you explore your subject's main qualities and characteristics; it can give you a means to discuss your subject's purpose and significance; it can elucidate your subject's history and its influence on society; and it can provide you with the support needed to make a claim about your subject.

Types of Evidence

There are eight main types of evidence, along with subtypes. Although every form of evidence has its strengths, they each also have their weaknesses. As you do your research, you will need to judge the merits of each piece of evidence that you gather and determine whether or not you should use it in your speech or presentation to support your claims. Once this decision is made, you need to determine how and when you will use it. By studying the definitions, explanations, and strategies that accompany each type of evidence, you can learn powerful strategies for assessing and presenting evidence.

> "Although every form of evidence has its strengths, they each also have their weaknesses."

Remember that your case/speech/presentation is only as strong as your evidence and support for your topic.

Using explanatory evidence.

An explanation is a statement or group of statements that addresses how or why something occurs. Explanatory evidence can clarify your subject by analyzing such things as its historical evolution, its main components and their functions, or its primary causes and effects. The length of your explanation will depend on the degree to which you need to explore your subject. You can organize your whole speech around a series of explanations, as in the case of examining many areas of the brain, or you can simply formulate one specific point, such as a major influence on an author's writing. Either way, your explanation should not just state your point, but should explicate it by offering an analysis of its main characteristics or component parts. For example, when discussing a religious ritual, do not simply state what each step of the ceremony is, but explain how its various symbols, ornaments, and procedures give meaning to rituals.

Regardless of what you are explaining, you should always focus on the main issues or parts of your claim, and avoid getting bogged down in discussing minor points or characteristics that may have less importance or take too long to explain. If your explanation is very abstract and complicated, you can illustrate it with a concrete example, or use an analogy to compare it to something more familiar. You can also clarify a point by stating it in very practical terms. For example, you could explain how virtual reality allows architects to change a building's design and compute its structural needs more easily than would an actual model.

There are three types of explanation: comparison, division, and interpretation.

Comparison

A comparative explanation identifies the similarities and differences between two ideas or objects. Comparative explanations are usually made when you compare something new to something old, something unique to something more typical, or two ideas or objects that are not obviously different. Other forms of comparison are metaphors, similes, and analogies. When making a comparison, first look at general similarities and differences between two entities, and then focus on comparing and contrasting some of their more specific characteristics. For instance, you could make a general comparison between how Caucasians and African Americans view race relations differently in the United States, and then give more specific comparisons between how each group views the police, the legal system, and the mass media.

Division

An explanation by division is made by breaking down a subject and analyzing its various parts or types. When distinguishing your subject's main parts, you need to explain how each part functions individually and then in combination so that the whole can be understood more fully. If you are exploring various types of the same thing, such as different forms of communication on the Internet, first explain what they have in common, and then make clear the characteristics that make each type unique. You also can reverse the process of division by presenting the different elements of your subject first and then combining or assimilating them into a whole. Consider explaining by division when exploring a complex social issue, a large government agency, or a complicated scientific reaction.

> **"When distinguishing your subject's main parts, you need to explain how each part functions individually and then in combination . . ."**

Interpretation

An interpretation moves beyond the simple assertion of facts and offers a substantive analysis of the important issues and themes relating to a subject. When interpreting your subject, do not just state what your subject's main elements are, but tell your audience what they mean, represent, or signify. For instance, do not simply say the symbol of the Tao represents the changing universe, but explain how its use of color, circles, and other design elements exemplifies various opposing forms that create our changing universe. Another strategy of interpretation is to first explain each of the passage's main words, clauses, or sentences separately, and then combine these parts to explain what the passage means as a whole.

> **"Often, your interpretation compares your explanation of a subject to other people's explanations."**

Often, your interpretation compares your explanation of a subject to other people's explanations. Usually, this type of interpretation begins by stating the relevant facts and issues associated with the subject. You can then offer a critical analysis of other interpretations that you deem inadequate or faulty. (In this way, an interpretation is often considered an argument.) Finally, you should give a series of explanations, examples, and arguments that advance your interpretation.

Using definition statements.

A definition is a statement or group of statements that establishes the meaning of a term or phrase by clarifying the main ideas, objects, or characteristics the term refers to. When creating a definition, clearly state the essential characteristics of the object or idea to which the term refers, and then show how these characteristics distinguish it from other similar objects or ideas.

You can create a definition by analyzing a term's linguistic parts, explaining its essential causes and effects, or showing why one meaning of the term is preferable to another. You also can refer to synonyms or give a term's denotative meaning (i.e., standard or literal) and its connotative meaning (i.e., suggestive or indirect). For instance, the denotative definition of a politician is "someone seeking a position in representative government through the election process," whereas the connotative definition might be "someone who would do anything to gain political power and control over the government's purse strings."

When defining a term, do not rely solely on standard dictionary definitions, which may sound overly simplistic or vague. Rather, consult encyclopedias and discipline-specific dictionaries that offer more elaborate and refined definitions. However, as with any type of evidence, avoid using overly technical language when defining the term; it is always better to simplify.

There are three types of definitions: etymological, categorical, and oppositional.

> **"When defining a term, do not rely solely on standard dictionary definitions, which may sound overly simplistic or vague."**

Etymological definition

This type shows how a term's meaning has developed through time, which can help you interpret if the term is used correctly, as well as differentiate it from other terms that have a similar meaning. There are three common ways to define a term etymologically: 1) By analyzing its root, prefix, and suffix; 2) By exploring how its usage differs within various languages, historical periods, geographical locations, or social groups; and 3) By comparing its parts and origins to those of other similar terms. Try to weave these definitions together, so that your audience comprehends the whole better.

> **Example**: Biases against the left hand appear in many different languages. In French, left is *gauche*, meaning ugly or uncouth. In Anglo-Saxon, left is *lyft*, meaning weak or useless. In Latin, *zona-sinistrata*, is a disaster area. In Russian, *nalyevo*, is a black market operator. The *Random House College Edition Dictionary* defines left-handed as "clumsy and awkward."

Categorical definition

This type explains how a term is either similar or different from other members of its class or subclass, or put more simply, distinguishes a term from other terms from which it differs, or associates it with similar terms. Categorical definitions show how a term embodies characteristics of a larger class; contrast a term to other terms within the same class; or describe similarities between a term and other members of its subclass.

> **Example**: There are two standard terms for describing a vegetarian; *vegan* and *lacto-ovo vegetarian*. Lacto-ovo vegetarians eat no meat products but do eat dairy products such as cheese, milk, and eggs. Vegans do not eat any animal products whatsoever. Most vegetarians are lato-ovo vegetarians because dairy products provide a rich source of calcium, protein, and other vitamins.

Oppositional definition

Oppositional defines a term by indicating what it is not. The actual meaning is not stated directly, but is inferred from how it differs from the oppositional definition. These definitions are commonly used when a term is difficult to define or when you want to contrast a term with another that has a clearly negative connotation.

> **Example**: A typical example of a Connecticut Yankee is its former governor Lowell Weicker. Weicker ran for governor as an independent because he realized that the people of Connecticut wanted a governor who was not conservative enough to be a Republican but not liberal enough to be a Democrat.

Using descriptive statements.

A description is a statement or series of statements that creates a vivid picture of your subject's main characteristics and qualities. When introducing your subject, do not give just its name, but describe its main properties so that your audience gains a clearer understanding of its main attributes.

A description also can explore important facts relating to your subject. One strategy for using a description is to combine it with an explanation of the main functions of a subject's various parts. So, when giving a speech on

> " . . . try to get your audience
> to visualize, understand, and
> experience the object you are
> describing."

tennis, describe how each part of a new type of tennis racket is designed and then explain how each of these parts can enhance a player's power or control. You also can combine a description with an analogy. For example, create a series of analogies that illustrate the similarities and differences among the stance, grip, and swing used in tennis, golf, and baseball. Descriptions can be either pictorial or objective.

Pictorial description

A pictorial description is what you normally give when you want to describe something, and it creates a mental picture of your subject. When constructing a pictorial definition, try to get your audience to visualize, understand, and experience the object you are describing. Use graphic language to bring out the look, feel, taste, sound, and smell of your subject, as well as emotive terms to evoke certain feelings from your audience.

In addition, describe elements peculiar to your subject rather than those it has in common with other similar things; emphasize qualities and actions that have immediate and strong effects, rather than those that are inconsequential and develop slowly; and use clear, contrasting terms such as "vibrant" and "dull" or "rigid" and "supple."

> **Example**: Located on the north wing's first floor, the Old Supreme Court Chamber sits next to the Senate wing of the Capitol. The Chamber's classical European design represents enduring, historical values. Its columns, archways, and frescoes reflect the ideals of European republican tradition, while its deep maroon carpet and royal blue accents fill the room with an aura of respect for our nation's highest court.

Objective description

An objective description offers a litany of facts relating to your subject. This description may entail such factual evidence as your subject's size and scope, as well as other forms of statistical information. Objective descriptions can present a brief account of your subject's evolution, depict your subject's main qualities, or portray the different characteristics of its main subtypes.

The main difference between a pictorial and an objective description is that the latter attempts to provide an impartial and unbiased description of the concrete facts relating to your subject. So, consider using an objective description when you want to rid your audience of any preconceived notions or emotional attachment to your subject, or when you want to establish your own objectivity. Once your audience has accepted this description as factual, you can then go on to construct an argument or appeal to their emotions.

> **Example**: According to the U.S. Justice Department, domestic violence is the leading cause of injury to women, more so than muggings, stranger rapes, and car accidents combined. While an act of domestic violence occurs every seven seconds in the United States, officials believe that only one-tenth of actual cases are reported.

Exercise 12.1. Pictorial and Objective Descriptions.

Write a pictorial description of your bedroom. Then, write an objective description of the same room. Compare the two. Which works better for this kind of evidence?

Pictorial Description:

_____

_____

_____

_____

_____

_____

_____

_____

_____

Objective Description:

_____

_____

_____

_____

_____

_____

_____

_____

_____

Using statistics as evidence.

Statistics are any measurement or set of measurements that explains or describes a subject or its main properties. A statistic can be an aggregate, average, ratio, percentage, correlation, or any other form of quantitative information.

Because statistics represent your subject in very clear and concrete ways, they are considered to be a form of evidence. However, given the vast array of statistical information available, you must determine which statistics provide the most relevant information on your subject. You also need to find the best way to state the information. Three highly effective ways to present statistics include (1) showing the rate at which an entity changes over time; (2) representing an entity's aggregate total and then dividing it into its per capita or individual rate; and (3) comparing statistical data on two entities that are literally or figuratively alike.

Thus, when discussing the cost of presidential campaigns, you could first show the increasing amount of money spent on campaigns in the last four elections; second, state how much total money was spent by a candidate in the last election and the average amount spent on each vote; and third, compare the amount of money spent on political television advertisements to the amount spent on laundry soap commercials in the same year.

> **"While statistics have their advantages, they also have their disadvantages. Statistics may sound objective and scientific, but they can also make you appear cold and impersonal."**

Statistics can backfire. While statistics have their advantages, they also have their disadvantages. Statistics may sound objective and scientific, but they can also make you appear cold and impersonal. Additionally, audiences find it difficult to distinguish and remember a large amount of data. Unless your intent is to achieve a strong effect by overwhelming your audience with statistical data that support your point (rather than having them remember and assess the data critically), limit the number of statistics you present at any one time. Also, state clearly what the data mean, rather than having the audience figure out what the data imply.

Descriptive statistics

Like a description of a person or place, descriptive statistics present a picture of your subject by representing it in quantitative terms. For instance, they provide various measurements that illustrate a subject's (or population's) most significant qualities, such as its size or frequency, or they allow your audience to recognize how something has changed over time. Aggregate amounts, ratios, percentages, and averages are all types of descriptive statistics.

Inferential statistics

Inferential statistics provide support that leads to a claim that goes beyond the evidence collected. Statistics can be used in two ways to infer a claim. The first is a soft inference, which offers a measurement of statistical calculation pertaining to one population, as the basis about another. In this case, your claim does not rest on a thoroughly scientific analysis of statistical data. This means that you do not perform an analysis on the statistics themselves, but use the data about one population to infer a claim about another. The most common type of soft inference is a survey or poll that asks questions about a subject to a sample population and then draws conclusions with reference to future actions.

The second type of statistical inference is a scientific inference, which entails more scientific methods of analyzing data. Although there are many different methods for collecting and analyzing inferential statistics, two methods are most often cited:

❑ The first method is a *correlative study*, which measures the relationship between two variables and tells you whether two variables are related and the direction of the relationship. For example, this type of study could investigate whether a relationship exists between the scores made on the Scholastic Aptitude Test (SAT) and scores on the Intelligence Quotient (IQ).

❑ The second method, the *experimental method*, studies the effect of a variable on one group in comparison to the normal reactions of a control group in which the variable has not been introduced or has been introduced at a different level. A test that studies the effectiveness of a new medicine exemplifies this method.

Using examples as evidence.

An example illustrates a particular instance of your subject, and it can make the subject more vivid and clear. It can clarify your claim by providing compelling supplementary details to an abstract explanation, complicated definition, or large statistic. A well-described example also allows your audience to visualize your subject more vividly and, through use of impassioned language, may lend your speech strong emotive appeal. To be effective, an example must clearly relate to the point you are making and portray the main characteristics that you are trying to illustrate.

> **"When choosing an example, make sure that it is relatively current and distinct, yet typical so that your audience readily associates it with other, more common examples."**

When choosing an example, make sure that it is relatively current and distinct, yet typical so that your audience readily associates it with other, more common examples. Describe the example in sufficient detail so that your point is clear. Beware of using an overly simplistic example that offers little insight into your point or a stereotypical one that relies on a common-sense belief that may be untrue. If a well-known example contradicts your example or refutes your claim, explain why it is unusual or an exception to a general rule.

The three main types of examples are factual examples, hypothetical examples, and case studies.

Factual Example

A factual example illustrates a real person, object, or event. It not only confirms the existence of something, but also helps your audience recall or imagine similar instances (for example, empathizing with a real person or reexperiencing a real event).

> **"When using a hypothetical example, make sure it is consistent with the known facts about the subject."**

Hypothetical Example

A hypothetical example creates an imaginary situation that allows your audience to visualize what might happen under similar circumstances. When using a hypothetical example, make sure it is consistent with the known facts about the subject. The best time to use this kind of example is when a factual example is not available and you want your audience to focus on general characteristics of the example rather than the particular people, places, or objects. Always identify the example as hypothetical, so you do not mislead your audience.

Case Study

A case study is a factual example that illustrates a subject in such a characteristic manner that it is worthy of detailed analysis. Case studies take on different forms depending on their field of inquiry. There are three prominent types of case studies: (1) a research study whose findings establish a body of knowledge or a model for conducting further research on a subject; (2) a prototypical example of a successful (or unsuccessful) program that either has been copied or is deemed worthy (or unworthy) of imitation; and (3) a precedent-setting legal case that provides the basis for further rulings.

When discussing a case study, try first to state its subject and intent; second, explain its experimental procedures, programmatic guidelines, or method of interpretation; and third, and most importantly, summarize its main characteristics, findings, and implications.

Narrative

A narrative is a story that illustrates a point through the depiction of the story's various parts. It can be real, as in the case of your own personal story, or fictitious, as in a folktale. A narrative can depict anything from the most grandiose event to an everyday experience.

Narratives serve many different functions. They can represent an abstract value, exemplify a common cultural belief, or simply describe someone's personal experiences. Regardless of the events portrayed, a narrative must allow the audience to experience vicariously the events described, empathize with its characters, and recognize the moral implicit in the story.

A narrative does not provide analytical evidence or necessarily lead to a generalization. It can be an effective form of evidence if it adheres to the principles of narrative rationality. Audiences use this concept to judge the merits of your story. There are three main principles of narrative rationality.

First, a narrative must have structure. It must have a beginning that introduces its setting and characters; a middle where its plot unravels, a conflict emerges, or the character's personality or motive is shown through his or her actions; and an end that depicts how conflict is resolved, describes the consequences of the characters' actions, and reveals the moral of the story.

Second, a narrative must be coherent, which means the various parts must fit together logically. There should be a clear reason why an event took place in a particular setting, why a character has acted in a particular fashion, and why the conflict was inevitable. Moreover, the story should be as concise as possible, although an event that foreshadows what will happen should not be left out.

> **"A narrative does not provide analytical evidence or necessarily lead to a generalization."**

Third, the narrative must be consistent with other stories that your audience has heard and their personal experiences. Unless your intent is to surprise your audience, the story should be plausible and similar to other stories they have encountered.

The three main types of narratives are personal narratives, reports, and anecdotes.

- ❑ A *personal narrative* is a story about an actual experience someone had that is related to your subject or point. A personal narrative should contain an account of the facts that verify what took place, express the sentiments that were brought on by the experience, and explain what insights into your subject were gained as a result of the experience. It can also recount your own experiences.

- ❑ A *report* is a story documenting an event or series of events, such as a newspaper article. It describes concisely what happened, where it took place, and why the event occurred.

- ❑ An *anecdote* is a short story, amusing observation, or engaging comment that relates to your subject or point. It can represent a larger value, principle, or ideal than the point you are making, or it can simply depict a particular incident or offer an observation that relates to your point. Anecdotes are often used in the introduction or conclusion of a speech to stimulate the audience's interest in your topic, add humor, or caution the audience against viewing your subject from a single perspective.

Using the analogy to support your claim.

An analogy is a comparison made between two objects or ideas so that your audience's previous knowledge of the one provides a basis for understanding the other. Like comparative explanations, metaphors, and similes, the intent of an analogy is to lead your audience to infer that the one idea or objects is similar to the other.

Analogies work best when based on something that is well known or directly related to your audience. For example, you could create an analogy by comparing the national percentage of men who suffer from prostate cancer to the number of men in your audience who, by proportion, would potentially acquire the disease.

An analogy can also be an argument when its intent is to prove that two things are similar, and thus will react to an external stimulus in similar ways. When constructing an analogy, make sure that the two entities have more similarities than differences. Otherwise, someone can refute your analogy by pointing out the significant differences between the two entities or by comparing the object or idea being explained to something with more similar traits. Analogies can be either literal or figurative.

> "Analogies work best when based on something that is well known or directly related to your audience."

Literal Analogy

A literal analogy is a comparison of two or more objects or ideas having overtly similar characteristics. For example, you could use a literal analogy to compare two cities or two aerobic activities that share common attributes. When creating a literal analogy, make sure that the two ideas or objects are of equal stature and that you are comparing their main characteristics. Otherwise, your analogy might be considered weak. If necessary, qualify your analogy by accounting for any dissimilar characteristics.

Figurative Analogy

A figurative analogy compares two ideas or objects that have distinctly different, overt characteristics but share similar qualities or act in similar ways. There are two main forms of figurative analogies. In the first form, two common objects or ideas are compared to exemplify some common principle underlying both (for example, comparing a political election to a horse race). In the second form, a complex or unfamiliar entity is compared to one found in nature or everyday life (for instance, comparing how a sculptor works with his unique materials to how a person conducting a small group meeting must be sensitive to each participant's special gifts and weaknesses).

Because the basis for comparing two entities with a figurative analogy is more metaphorical than logical, it is usually considered a weaker form of evidence. Audiences, however, seem to find them interesting and appealing due to the novel way figurative analogies express similarities between unlike things.

Using testimony as evidence.

Testimony is a direct quotation by someone who is either an authority on your subject, a witness whose personal experience provides insight into your subject, or who is considered to be a trusted source of social wisdom. Testimony often provides another person's account of your subject, so it can take the form of evidence or argument. Testimonial statements that show that another person's understanding of a subject is similar to your own can build your credibility. Testimony can be authoritative, lay, or nominal.

> "Testimony often provides another person's account of your subject, so it can take the form of evidence or argument."

Authoritative testimony

Authoritative testimony is a statement or group of statements given by a credible authority or expert. The best time to use authoritative testimony is when explaining a causal relationship, justifying a value or principle, making a prediction, offering a solution to a problem, advocating a policy proposal, or giving an opinion that goes against authority or your audience's prior beliefs. Another effective way to use authoritative testimony is when you find an authority who, on other related issues, takes an opposing view but agrees with you on the issue at hand.

When giving this type of testimony, always provide the expert's credentials first and then summarize or quote his most important statements. Do not quote at length. Be sure you check the statements for accuracy, objectivity, timeliness, and consistency with other evidence.

Lay testimony

Lay testimony states the opinion, expresses the feelings, or recalls the experience of someone who has had some personal involvement with or sentiments about a subject. In cases where an individual expresses how he or she has been positively or negatively affected by the experience, lay testimony can have a strong emotional appeal with your audience. However, that person is not necessarily to be considered an expert in the subject. In fact, the individual may not have studied the subject at all and may have certain positive or negative biases toward your subject that prevent him or her from discussing your subject fairly. So, do not define these statements as authoritative or use them as a basis for explaining or arguing a point.

Nominal testimony

Nominal testimony is a general statement made by a well-known person that can be related to your subject. The person providing the testimony may have no expert knowledge of your subject or any direct experience with it. Instead, nominal testimony relies on the "good name" of the person and the general belief that he or she possesses a unique insight into people and the world. Since nominal testimony relies on general observations made by famous people, it is not always necessary to cite the specific date or other bibliographic information with an oral citation. Nominal testimony is not a reliable form of evidence for backing specific claims because the source lacks authoritative expertise.

An example of nominal testimony would be this famous quote from Albert Einstein, "Imagination is more important than knowledge." Although Einstein is not an authority on art or child development, his famous quote could be used to justify an increased emphasis on the arts in elementary education.

Evidence versus Reasoning

Evidence is a crucial part of developing a clear, compelling argument, and it can be presented in the following forms: explanation, comparison and contrast, illustration, specific instance, statistics, and testimony. As you conduct your search for information, the primary goal is to find supporting materials that are both rationally and motivationally relevant to the claim being advanced.

Using rationally relevant evidence.

The type of evidence you select should reflect the type of claim you advocate. For example, if you are defending the claim that censorship violates the First Amendment guarantee of freedom of speech, then testimony from legal authorities will be useful in supporting your argument. On the other hand, examples, illustrations, and statistics work better if you are arguing that a problem exists or a change in practices is needed. If you argue that shark fishing should be more heavily regulated, you'll find that examples of poor fishing practices and statistical evidence related to over-fishing and potential loss to the ecosystem will be relevant to your purpose. Always ask yourself: "Given this claim, what evidence is naturally suggested by the subject matter? What type of evidence is logically relevant?"

> **"Always ask yourself: 'Given this claim, what evidence is naturally suggested by the subject matter? What type of evidence is logically relevant?'"**

Using motivationally relevant evidence.

Listeners often require more than logically relevant support. Your evidence also must create a compelling desire on their part to be involved, endorse the belief, or undertake a course of action. Why should an audience be concerned about regulating shark fishing? To motivate your listeners, you must answer the "So what?" question. To select motivationally relevant material, consider the following two issues.

Exercise 12.2. Ethical dilemmas with the use of evidence.

The use of evidence generates several potential ethical dilemmas.

- Should you suppress evidence that contradicts a point you are making? If your opponent is not aware of the information, should you mention it?

_____

_____

_____

_____

- What about the use of qualifiers? Should you leave in each "maybe" and "possibly" when you could read or paraphrase a quotation? If you have to submit a written text or outline, you can use ellipses (i.e., the three dots that indicate that something is missing from the original) where the qualifiers once were. Would that be acceptable?

_____

_____

_____

_____

- Does it make any difference if you over-qualify a source? If you've discovered an article by a staff researcher at the National Endowment for the Arts on the issue of funding controversial art, will it hurt to suggest the information is from an associate director of the agency, even if no specific person is cited? If it increases the credibility of the information, should the new (although false) title be used?

_____

_____

_____

_____

- What difference does it make if a poll is conducted by the National Right-to-Life Committee or Planned Parenthood's Pro-Choice Committee? What if each organization asks polling questions in such a way as to encourage a response favorable to its position? Can you just say that "A recent national poll found that 75 percent of U.S. citizens favor abortion rights?" You haven't really lied in suppressing the polling agency or the actual questions asked, have you? Is this acceptable?

_____

_____

_____

_____

What type of evidence will this audience demand?

To orient your thinking, turn this question around and ask: "As a member of the audience, what would I expect as support for this claim to accept it?" What motivates you to accept the argument may well motivate the audience. Some evidence also seems naturally connected to certain subjects. A claim regarding relative costs of competing plans suggests things like statistical graphs or charts. If the audience is able to say "Yes, but . . ." after hearing your evidence, then you have not motivated them to accept your claim.

What evidence will generate the best response?

You should pose the question about what evidence will generate the best response once you've determined the type of evidence required by your argument. For example, if you've decided to use expert testimony, whom should you quote? If you're using an illustration, should you use a factual example from the local group or develop your own? Will your listeners be moved more by a personal story than by a general illustration? Also, what ethical issues might be involved in decisions to use evidence (refer to Exercise 12.2)?

Forms of reasoning (inference).

You make connections among claims, criteria, and evidence using different forms of reasoning or <u>inferences</u>. Forms of reasoning are the habitual ways in which a culture or society uses inferences to connect the material supporting a claim with the claim itself. In U.S. culture, there are five primary patterns: reasoning from example, generalization, sign, parallel case, and causal relations (see Table 12.1).

Inductive reasoning: reasoning from example

The first pattern, reasoning from example, which is often called inductive reasoning, is the process of examining a series of known occurrences and drawing a general conclusion, or of using a single instance to reason to a future instance of the same kind. The conclusion is probable rather than certain.

> "In every election in our community over the past few years, when a candidate leads in the polls by 10 or more points with a month to go, he or she has won. Thus my candidate will surely win next month."

Maybe so—but, maybe not. The inference in this case can be stated as "What is true of the particular cases is true of the whole class, or more precisely, future instances of the same class." Most reasoning from example uses multiple instances in inferring a conclusion. You can argue, for example, that one death at an intersection supports the need for a traffic light. Using relevant examples will ensure a high degree of probability and provide strong justification for the adoption of a claim.

Reasoning from generalization or axiom

Applying a <u>generalization</u> or basic truism to a specific situation is a form of deductive reasoning. Whereas inductive reasoning is typified by an inferential leap on the basis of the evidence, <u>deductive reasoning</u> produces a conclusion that is true only if the premises are true. For example, you may know that generic drugs are cheaper than brand-name drugs. On the basis of this general truism, you ask your druggist for the generic prescription whenever possible because it will save you money. To the extent the generalization holds true, your experience will hold true, as well.

Reasoning from signs

This pattern uses an observable mark, or symptom, as proof of the existence of a certain state of affairs. Sign reasoning occurs, for example, when you note the appearance of a rash or spots on your skin (evidence) and conclude you have the measles (claim). Signs are not causes: A rash does not cause measles, and an ambulance siren does not result in an accident or crisis to which it responds. What the rash or the siren means remains open to further examination. While it may be the case that the rash is a sign of measles, it also may be a sign of an allergic reaction to medication. The meaning of the siren comes closest to an infallible sign relationship—that is, you would normally infer someone was hurt, but whether from an accident or a sudden illness, you could not say. Hence, the inference that the evidence is a sign of the conclusion you want to draw is not always true.

Table 12.1. Distinguishing and Testing Types of Reasoning.

Form	Description	Example	Tests
Example	Drawing a general conclusion from one or more example.	"I enjoy Bach, Beethoven, and Ravel; I like classical music."	1. Sufficient instances? 2. Fairly selected? 3. Important exceptions?
Generalization or axiom	Applying a general truism to a specific example.	"Bichons are friendly dogs; I'll buy a Bichon."	1. Generally accepted? 2. Applies to this instance?
Sign	Using a symptom or other observable event as proof of a state of affairs.	"The petunias are dead. Someone forgot to water them."	1. Fallible sign? 2. Accurate observation?
Parallel case	Asserting that because two items share similar characteristics, they will share results.	"Tougher enforcement of existing laws reduced drunk driving in Indiana; hence, such laws will work in Iowa.	1. More similarities than differences? 2. Similarities are relevant, important?
Causal relation	Concluding that one event influences the existence of a second, later event.	"The engine won't start; the carburetor is flooded."	1. Causes and effects are separable? 2. Cause sufficient to produce effect? 3. Presence of intervening events? 4. Any other cause possible, important? 5. Cause or correlation?

Reasoning from parallel cases

Another common reasoning pattern involves parallel cases—comparing similar events or things and drawing conclusions based upon that comparison. The claim that your state should adopt a motorcycle helmet law might be supported by noting that a neighboring state with similar characteristics passed one and has experienced lower death rates in cases of head injuries. In essence, you are claiming, "What happened there can happen here."

The political candidate's claim that what she or he has done for a community or state can be repeated in a larger arena, though not precisely parallel, draws strength from this type of argument. As the variables separating the cases grow in size and significance, however, this reasoning pattern will become less forceful.

Reasoning from a causal relation

Causal reasoning assumes that the one event influences or controls other events. You can reason from a specific cause to an effect or set of effects or vice versa. For instance, assume that alcohol abuse on a campus appears to be increasing. Is this increase the result of lax enforcement of existing rules? Do loopholes allow for more abusive situations to develop, despite the best intentions? Are students today more prone to abuse than in previous years? Pointing to one or more of these as the cause sets the stage for an analysis of potential solutions. The key is to point to connections between lax enforcement or loopholes and the resulting effect is increased alcohol abuse. The principle underlying this pattern is one of constancy—that is, every effect has a cause.

Adequacy of forms of reasoning.

Central to thinking critically is testing the reasoning pattern for weaknesses, both as a user and a consumer. Each pattern has its own unique set of criteria for establishing a valid, sound argument. For each pattern, apply the questions in Table 12.1 to your own arguments and that of others.

These patterns of reasoning and their tests are not the only means of evaluating the effectiveness of arguments. Arguments can be flawed in other ways, as well. The following section describes common flaws, or fallacies, in reasoning.

> "Each pattern has its own unique set of criteria for establishing a valid, sound argument."

Detecting fallacies in reasoning.

In general, fallacies interrupt the normal process of connecting claims, criteria, and evidence. Here we will discuss 10 of the most common fallacies; these are argument errors that you already have committed or have experienced as you listen to others provide reasons for their claims.

- ❑ *Hasty generalization* (faulty inductive leap): This fallacy occurs when the conclusion is based on far too little evidence. If the answer to the question "Have enough instances been examined" is no, a flaw in reasoning has occurred. Urging a ban on Boeing 747 airliners because one was involved in an accident or on aerosol sprays because one blew up in a fire is insufficient support for the claim being urged.

- ❑ *Genetic fallacy:* This argument rests on an origin, historical tradition, or sacred practice: "We've always done it this way; therefore, this is the best way." That an idea or an institution or practice has been around a long time may have little bearing on whether it still should be. Times change and new values replace old ones, suggesting that new practices may be more in tune with present values.

- ❑ *Appeal to ignorance:* The expression "You can't prove it won't work" illicitly uses a double negative. Incomplete knowledge also does not mean a claim is or is not true. "We cannot use radio beams to signal extraterrestrials, because we don't know what languages they speak." In countering such claims, use arguments from parallel cases and from examples because they both transcend the unknown in providing support for a claim.

- ❑ *Appeal to popular opinion* (bandwagon fallacy): "Jump on the bandwagon" and "Everyone is going" are appeals to group support. If others support the position, then you're pressured into supporting it, as well. "There are a gazillion people who already think that Ricky Martin is one of the best." As an older advertisement put another appeal: "Eat chicken; 10,000 coyotes can't be wrong." While these may, in truth, have value, such claims have little probative value (proof) with respect to justifying an action. Nonetheless, this is precisely the kind of argument that has potency in changing people's minds. If audience members are receptive to popular opinion, then using that as a form of evidence will make a major difference in whether your idea is accepted. Politicians will use poll data to reflect the support that exists, even though such data, in and of itself, is not proof that the policy should be adopted. These claims may function as evidence of what people believe or value, but they are not, for that reason, true. The world has witnessed hundreds of widely believed but false ideas, from the idea that the night air causes tuberculosis to panic over an invasion of Martians.

- ❑ *Appeal to authority:* Citing someone who is popular but not an expert as the basis for accepting a claim is an appropriate use of appeal to authority. The critical question in using authoritative testimony is: Is the source an expert on this topic? If not, why should you accept the claim?

- ❑ *Sequential fallacy:* This phrase literally translates from the Latin *Post hoc, ergo propter hoc* as "After this; therefore, because of this." This is a primitive kind of causal argument because it is based on the sequence of events in time: "I slept near a draft last night and woke up with a nasty head cold." (The draft did not cause the cold; a virus did.) Although the sequence may be appropriate ("The coach gave an inspirational half-time speech, and the players came out on fire."), there often are other circumstances (for example, the players hate the coach but are motivated by each other) that help produce the effect. Timing alone is not sufficient to draw causal connections.

- ❑ *Begging the question*: This is circular or <u>tautological reasoning</u>. "Abortion is murder because it is taking the life of the unborn" rephrases the claim ("It is murder") to form the reason ("It is taking a life"). Nothing new has been said. In other cases, begging the question occurs in the form of a complex question: "Have you stopped cheating on tests yet?" <u>assumes</u> that you have cheated in the past (when that may not be known). Saying yes admits past cheating; saying no admits to both past and present cheating. You cannot win either way. Evaluative claims are especially prone to this abuse of reasoning.

- ❑ *Ambiguity*: A word may have more than one meaning, or a phrase may be misleading. Using a term without clarifying its specific meaning can result in confusion and inaccurate claims: "Dog for sale: Eats anything and is fond of children." Does "eats anything" include the children? Sure sounds like it. Or "Wanted: Man to take care of cow that does not smoke or drink." When was the last time you saw a cow smoking? Former President Bill Clinton introduced a new phrase into the national lexicon with his explanation of sexual relations: "It depends on what 'is' is."

- ❑ *Persuasive definition*: Value terms and other abstract concepts are open to special or skewed definitions that are unique to the person or group offering them: "Liberty means the right to own military weapons;" "Real men don't wear cologne;" and "A true patriot doesn't protest against this country while on foreign soil." Each of these definitions sets up a particular point of view that is capricious and arbitrary. You could say that persuasive definitions are self-serving because they promote an argument at the expense of more inclusive definitions of the same terms. If you accept the definition, the argument is essentially over. Substituting a definition from a respected, widely accepted source is a way of challenging this fallacy.

- ❑ *Name-calling*: There are several forms of this fallacy; they all involve attacking the person, rather than the argument. You may attack special interests ("Of course you're defending her; she's your cousin.") or personal characteristics ("No wonder you're arguing that way; geeks always think that way."). In these two cases, being related is not proof of defense, and geeks may have ideas as good as anyone else (or better). Claims should be judged on their own terms, not on the basis of the people or ideas with which they may or may not be connected. On the other hand, note the powerful effect of name-calling as used by political candidates—and others. To label someone is also to reject other possible labels for that person. Name-calling, or what is sometimes called *ad hominem* ("to the person") argument, may well be persuasive.

These are some of the fallacies that find their way into causal and formal argumentation. A good, basic logic book can point out additional fallacies. If you know about fallacies, you'll be better able to construct sound arguments and assess the weaknesses in your opponent's arguments. In addition, thinking critically can protect you from being taken in by unscrupulous politicians, sales personnel, and advertisers. The process of protecting yourself from irrelevant appeals can benefit from the model for organizing and evaluating arguments (see Figure 12.1).

Figure 12.1. How to Test Arguments.

Reasoning from Example

1. **Have you looked at enough instances to warrant generalizing?** Just because you passed the last test without studying doesn't mean that not studying is the way to approach all future tests.

2. **Are the instances fairly chosen or representative?** Deciding never again to shop in a store because a clerk was rude isn't exactly working on the basis of a representative, let alone sufficient, sample. You'll want to judge the store in a variety of situations. If you find that rudeness is the norm rather than the exception, your claim may be justified.

3. **Are there important exceptions to the generalization that must be accounted for?** While it is generally true, from presidential election studies, that "As Maine goes, so goes the nation," there have been enough exceptions to this rule to keep candidates who lose in a Maine primary campaigning until the general election.

Reasoning from Generalization or Axiom

1. **Is the generalization accepted?** "Those who go on diets generally gain back the weight lost," and "People who marry young are more likely to divorce." Each of these is a generalization; you need to determine whether sufficient evidence exists to justify the claim, if it is not already accepted as a general truism.

2. **Does the generalization apply to this particular case?** Usually, discount stores offer the best deals, but on occasion, prices are better at sales at local neighborhood stores. While "Birds of a feather flock together" applies to birds, it may not apply to a group of humans.

Reasoning from Sign

1. **Is the sign error proof?** Many signs constitute circumstantial evidence rather than absolute, certain proof. Be especially careful not to confuse sign reasoning with causal reasoning. If sign reasoning were error proof or infallible, weather forecasters would never be wrong.

2. **Is the observation accurate?** Witnesses sometimes testify to things that later prove to be wrong. People differ in their interpretations of events. Be certain that the observation is accurate—that the sign did not exist as described or explained.

Reasoning from Parallel Case

1. **Are there more similarities than differences between the two cases?** Two items may have many features in common, but they also may have significant differences that will weaken your argument. Just because two states appear similar, they may also have many more differences that will weaken the effectiveness of the parallel being drawn.

2. **Are the similarities you've pointed out the relevant and important ones?** Suppose that two students down the hall dress in similar clothes, have the same major, and get similar grades? Does this mean that if one is nice, so is the other? Probably not because the similarities you've noticed are relatively unconnected to niceness. The students' personal values and their relations with others would be more important criteria on which to base a parallel case.

Reasoning from Causal Relations

1. **Can you separate causes and effects?** We often have trouble with "Which came first" kinds of issues. Do higher wages cause higher prices or the reverse? Does a strained home life cause a child to misbehave, or is it the other way around?

2. **Are the causes sufficient to product the effects?** Causes not only must be necessary to produce effects, but they also must be sufficient. While air is necessary for fire to exist, it isn't all that's required, or we would be in a state of constant fire.

3. **Did intervening events or persons prevent a cause from having its normal effect?** Causes do not always produce their expected effects; they may be interrupted by other factors. An empty gun does not shoot. A drought will drive up food prices only if there is insufficient food on hand, the ground was already dry, or cheap alternatives are unavailable.

4. **Could any other cause have produced the effect?** Some effects may be produced by different causes; thus, you need to search for the most likely cause in a given situation. Although crime often increases when communities deteriorate, increased crime rates also can be caused by other changes. Perhaps crime only appears to have risen; in actuality, maybe people are just keeping better records.

5. **Is the cause really a correlation?** Correlations aren't necessarily causally related. Two phenomena may vary together without being related in any way. For example, since Abraham Lincoln's assassination, every president elected in a year divisible by 20 (until President Ronald Reagan) died in office. However, in each case, the year was inconsequential in causing the death.

Conclusion

It's obvious from this chapter that evidence comes in many forms and types. The key is learning how to pick and choose the evidence that will support your argument or theory. A good argument is only as good as its supporting evidence. Evidence must also appeal to an audience and be easily understood. If the evidence is so complex that it is misunderstood or misses the point, the audience will lose interest in your presentation and discount its theories, no matter how prescient or factual they may be. So the message is to construct your case carefully and pay attention to which type of evidence best supports your contentions. Lead your audience down the path you want them to follow and convince them with logic and arguments that you have the solution to the world's problems.

Exercise 12.3. Supporting your claims: The Great Debaters.

Visit this chapter's folder in your Chapter Media Contents online. Select the link for *The Great Debaters,* a movie based on the true story of Melvin B. Tolson, a professor at Wiley College, Texas. Tolson inspired students to form the college's first debate team, which went on to challenge Harvard in the national championship. The scene selected is a debate between students from Wiley College and students from Harvard University. The students are debating whether or not civil disobedience is a moral weapon in the fight for justice. The students from Wiley are arguing the affirmative; the Harvard students the negative.

Watch the scene and answer the following questions.

1. List the types of evidence used by the students at Wiley College. How did they use these types of evidence (provide the examples given by the students for each type of evidence)?

2. List the types of evidence used by the students at Harvard College. How did they use these types of evidence (provide the examples given by the students for each type of evidence)?

3. Did you hear any fallacies? If so, which ones?

Endnote

1   Material in this chapter was taken in part from the following books: *Principles and Types of Public Speaking, Fifteenth Edition,* Raymie E. McKerrow, Bruce E. Gronbeck, Douglas Ehninger, and Alan H. Monroe, Allyn and Bacon: Boston, 2003. *A Handbook of Public Speaking,* Richard Letteri, Allyn and Bacon: Boston, 2002.

Notes

CHAPTER 13

Creating and Using Visual Aids

by Keri K. Stephens, Kristin Stimpson, Lea Ciceraro

Objectives

After studying Chapter 13, you should be able to do the following:

☐ Identify the reasons that both speakers and audiences benefit from visual aids.

☐ Use the guidelines for preparing visual aids.

☐ Understand the visual technology options available for presenting visual aids.

☐ Create an effective PowerPoint® (or other projected slides).

☐ Feel confident about using visual aids strategically.

Key Terms

TERM	DEFINITION
chart	A figure that graphically illustrates relationships between individual parts.
design template	A pre-existing template included in PowerPoint® software that unifies the color, scheme, graphics, and structure of a set of slides.
dual coding	A theory advanced by Allan Paivio and his colleagues that explains how humans cognitively process the simultaneous presentation of visual and verbal stimuli.
Fair Use	Fair Use is part of the US Copyright Act. It provides guidelines for the limited use of copyrighted materials in the case of teaching, research, and scholarship. This is a complex legal document, so be aware that many of these issues are decided in court.
graph	Visual representations of statistics (i.e., numbers).
group items	A technique found in the "Draw" menu that allows the presenter to link two objects together so they appear on a single animation.
high contrast	A situation where combinations of light and dark colors are used such that the eyes can clearly see the distinctions.
LCD (liquid crystal diode) projection system	A projection system designed to interface with the computer to project images stored on the computer.
missed timing	An animation problem that occurs when an image is animated and it is the last item on the slide. Presenters frequently forget about this image while transitioning to the next slide, and then realize they have an out-of-place image that appears.
moving effects	A type of animation where text or graphics physically move as they appear on the screen.
numerical clarifier	A chart or graph used to simplify and explain numerical concepts.
object	Here, objects are broadly defined as graphic elements useful to add interest to text. These include autoshapes, boxes, circles, call outs, and lines.
on-slide animation	A type of animation that controls how objects appear and disappear on slides.

TERM	DEFINITION
over-clicking	A type of animation problem that occurs when a presenter hits the click button too many times and has to go back to reveal the desired content.
remote mouse	A hand-held pointing device that allows a presenter to control slides remotely.
sans serif font	A style of text that lacks hooks (or feet) on the ends of the letters. Most desirable for projection since the text is easier to read.
serif font	A style of text that contains hooks (or feet) on the ends of the letters. Use sparingly if at all for projection.
slide master	A PowerPoint® feature that allows a presenter to make individual changes that will apply to every slide in the show.
slide transitions	A type of animation that controls how one slide is changed and a new slide appears.
stationary effects	A type of animation where the text or graphic does not move around on the screen when it appears.
visual aid	Objects, visual representations, and numerical clarifiers, used to supplement a verbal message, thus enhancing communication goals.
word art	A technique available in all Microsoft products that allows you to type text and then apply a variety of color and shape options to it.

Introduction

So now we have arrived at the part of the semester when you and your classmates give oral presentations—five or six or seven, per day, for days upon days. Today you are an audience member only. You settle in your seat, relaxed, eager, interested, and ready to listen. The first speaker gets up, goes to the front of the room, stands there and talks for four minutes, then sits down. The second speaker does the same. So does the third one. And the fourth and the fifth. And the sixth. . . . Hey, eager audience member! Yeah, you! How are you feeling right now? Wide awake? Engaged? Still happy to be a member of the audience? Looking forward to the next four or five presentations today?

No?

Now imagine that you are one of those speakers, and you know from experience about the audience fatigue that often sets in after too many presentations. Do you really want to use your time talking to a sea of glazed eyes or the tops of slumped-over heads? Do you wish there were something you could do to re-energize your audience and re-gain their interest? There is.

So far you have learned how to analyze the audience you expect to face, invent and organize a presentation designed specifically for that audience, and support the presentation with a variety of appropriate verbal evidence. All this work has been devoted to the verbal part of your presentation, the part that invites your audience to listen and think. But if you stop here in your preparation, you will stop short of utilizing some of the very techniques that help you excite and engage your audience. Using visual aids makes the speaking experience enjoyable for you and engages your audience's senses.

Sensory evidence is a powerful force in professional presentations. People in the business of persuasion commonly use integrated "sensory marketing" or "emotional branding" to engage their customers' visceral responses with a synergistic blend of color, texture, scent, taste, and sound.[1] That is why real estate agents instruct homeowners to put Mozart on the stereo and bake bread or cookies just before potential buyers are due to arrive. That is why automotive companies develop ads that show cars and trucks mastering rugged terrain to the pulsing rhythms of classic rock. And that is why Coca-Cola® includes subtle things like the sounds of opening the can and a slight fizz when the rock star drinks the cola.

For those of us who do not have marketing teams preparing our presentations, though, using multi-sensory evidence can be impractical. For this reason, sensory evidence used in small-scale professional presentations is commonly reduced to the purely visual—hence the general term visual aid. This chapter discusses how to use visual aids to enhance your professional presentations. We begin by exploring how visual aids help both the audience and the speaker. Next, we look at types of visual aids and factors that you, as the speaker, should consider when planning a presentation. Specifically, we cover the types of visual aids used for presentations and the steps you can use to prepare your own visual aids. We then discuss visual technology in its various forms and focus on Microsoft's PowerPoint® presentation creation software, one of today's most popular technologies for creating and presenting visual aids. Finally, the chapter wraps up with tips on how to use visual aids effectively.

Why Use Visual Aids?

Using visual aids to enhance a presentation is not a new concept. In ancient Athens, when Plato famously defined "human being" as a "featherless biped," Diogenes the Cynic plucked a rooster, brought it to Plato's lecture hall, held it up to the assembled audience, and said, "Here is Plato's 'man.'"[2] Fast-forward twenty-five hundred years to *you,* and to your very first grade-school presentation: "Here's what I brought for show and tell," you said, holding up a feather or robin's egg or photograph of you and Big Bird.

Why are visual aids so irresistible? According to psychologist Allan Paivio and his colleagues, humans make separate sense of auditory and visual stimuli in a process called dual coding.[3] Dual coding explains that when streams of information are unrelated (as when you *listen* to a presentation while staring out a window), they interfere with each other. When the streams work together to provide differently coded information about the same topic, they reinforce each other, improving audience interest and recall. For example, dual coding occurs when you listen to a presentation on how to do your taxes while seeing photos of W2s and 1040Es.

Although the idea of using visual aids is nothing new, what *is* new is that now, more than ever, people *expect* multiple streams of simultaneous information. Photography, motion pictures, television, video games, computer graphics, the Internet, DVDs, and streaming video have all accelerated our demand for visual stimuli to complement the verbal. We lose interest very easily if a presentation is "boring," and there is no better way to be boring than to limit your presentations to the mere verbal. In general, listeners can process information much faster than speakers can present it. Most people speak approximately 125 words per minute, but listeners can process over 400 words per minute.[4] When you give your audience nothing to do with the unused portion of their attention, you are likely to lose them to unrelated musings.

Indeed, think about the last few lectures you sat through that used no visual aids at all. What was the content? Can you remember? You may have forgotten what you heard in many of those presentations almost immediately (or never registered it at all) because they failed to compete with what was going on in your life—tests, homework, worries about upcoming projects, text messages, etc. Only the most appealing presentations capture an audience's attention and etch themselves into long-term memory. Your task in creating an effective presentation is to be one of those few—and good visual aids help.

You would be wise to create compelling visual aids for your presentations if your only purpose were to stimulate your audience. But more significantly, well-constructed visual aids stimulate retention of information. In a study comparing presentations with and without visual aids, researchers from 3M Corporation and the University of Minnesota, Douglas Vogel, Gary Dickson, and John Lehan found that for presentations with visual aids, the audience's retention increased about 10 percent, comprehension increased 8.5 percent, attention increased 7.5 percent, and agreement increased 5.5 percent.[5]

Visual aids also can help you as a speaker as much as they help your listeners. You can use visual aids to guide you through your delivery, relieve you of the necessity of memorizing complicated facts, assist you in explaining complex ideas, and improve your professional credibility. That last benefit is particularly significant. In that same study, Vogel and colleagues found that simply using visual aids made the audience view the speaker 11 percent more positively than without visual aids.[6] Use effective visual aids and your reward will be an audience of listeners who pay attention to your words, understand your message, and respond to your goals—rather than doodle in their notebooks and glance at their text messages.

A word of warning before we get into specifics: Notice the word "effective" in the previous sentence. According to Thomas Leech, presentation skills coach for the past 20 years and author of *How to Prepare, Stage, & Deliver Winning Presentations,* poorly prepared or inappropriately used visual aids can actually *reduce* communication effectiveness by 40 to 50 percent, causing audiences to misunderstand a presenter's message.[7] Essentially, he argues that in a presentation there is already enough going on for an audience to understand that when confusing visuals are used, the audience will tune the presenter out. For this reason, we urge you to consider two pieces of advice. First, create your visual aids *after* you outline what you are going to say so that you will use them to aid your presentation, not replace it. Even competently designed visual aids cannot rescue a poorly planned, supported, or delivered presentation. Second, finish outlining your presentation early enough to allow you the time to create, and practice with visual aids that will actually enhance your words. It is humiliating—and damaging to your credibility—to insult your audience with visual aids that are obviously after-thoughts.

Types of Visual Aids

Visual aids allow presenters to explain, simplify, and illustrate complex ideas. Think back to the types of visual aids you have seen presenters use. Do they vary depending on whether the group is large versus small? Have you seen some used very well, and others that left you wondering why they even used the aid? Before you can use visual aids strategically, you need to know about your options. Here, we talk about three types of visual aids that are particularly useful for presentations: objects, visual representations, and numerical clarifiers.

Objects.

The most basic kind of visual aid is a relevant object. Objects are concrete visual aids that can be inanimate (e.g., a baseball) or animate (e.g., a person). For example, if you are giving a speech about your favorite baseball player, you could bring in a personally autographed baseball. You might show this object to the class and tell a story of how you met your idol. You can also use yourself or another person as a visual aid. Perhaps you want to persuade a group to begin taking hip hop classes. You might physically demonstrate several dance moves.

Of course, the objects you use in a presentation can often involve senses other than the visual. Imagine, for example, that you work for Ben & Jerry's as a sales representative. When your company announces a new flavor of ice cream, what better demonstration aid could you use than samples of the ice cream itself? Sure, you will explain that Chunky Monkey has peanuts and bananas, but why not let your audience experience the flavor for themselves?

If you decide to use objects as visual aids, take care to use them judiciously. An object can effectively capture your audience's attention—which is good only to the extent that it engages them in your presentation. When an object is so interesting that it distracts your audience from your presentation, the object becomes a liability. For example, what if you are doing a presentation on the history of Doritos and you decide to pass around small bags of chips to each student? Sure, it is relevant to your presentation and your audience will probably love having a snack during the rest of the presentations. However, think about how loud those bags of chips are when people take one, open it, and then start crunching. Although the audience may be focused, they are not focused on you.

Display the visual aid only when you are discussing it, because curiosity can impede your audience's ability to listen. Imagine, for example, that your instructor walks into class one day, places a large rectangular box on the table at the front of the room, and begins to lecture as usual. The subject for the day is argumentation; the topic being argued is junk food: pro and con. You look at the box and wonder what might be in there, but your instructor does not say. Thirty minutes into class, the faint smell of fried dough permeates the room, but still your instructor lectures on. Finally, just two minutes before class is scheduled to end, he moves to the box and announces that to really bring home the issue, he brought you all doughnuts. Was that an effective use of his visual aid? Only if his intention was to distract you and make your stomachs grumble. (And in that case, he would have been better off opening the box at the beginning of class, letting its aroma loose, displaying its contents for all to see, and taking a bite of a doughnut every once in a while just to torture you.) Your instructor had several other options. He could have passed out doughnuts at the beginning of class, waited for everyone to finish and then begun his lecture. Alternatively, he could have stored the doughnuts outside the classroom, left and returned with the box ready to be distributed. (Yes, and he could also have brought fruit as a positive alternative to doughnuts, and asked each member of the class to make a choice.)

Visual representations.

A second category of visual aids is the visual representation of an object—a photograph, a map, a drawing, a diagram, a blueprint—either enlarged to presentation size or projected onto a screen. Today, photographs offer an excellent alternative to an actual object because they can be easily scanned and imported into formats that are viewable by an audience of any size. Maps are useful when you must show where something is geographically located. Drawings and diagrams offer a simple way to label the specific parts of an object.

The key consideration with visual representations of objects is to make sure that they are clearly relevant—that they display exactly what you are discussing and nothing else. Do not frustrate your audience with visual representations that are too small to be seen or too complicated to be understood. For example, if you show a diagram of the CMA building and you label every single room on every floor, there will be too much information and your message will be lost. If instead you show a diagram of that same building and label only the one room where you need everyone to meet, your message will be much more effective. An additional thing to consider with visual representations is to only display them during your presentation when you are discussing them. If you display them too early, or leave them up after you are finished talking about them, your audience will be distracted and focus on the visual aids not on your message.

Numerical clarifiers.

A third type of visual aid is a numerical clarifier such as a chart or graph, which you can use to simplify and explain complex numerical concepts, particularly numerical data. Charts are figures that graphically illustrate relationships while graphs are visual representations of statistics. In your professional life, you will need to explain numbers for many purposes—to compare profit and loss statistics for a business unit, to contrast specifications of different purchase decisions, and even to justify why you should get a raise. Charts and graphs can help you get your message across. While both the chart and the graph *look* professional, the graph more quickly and clearly illustrates your accomplishments. In general, graphs can be more powerful persuaders than charts because of their visual nature. But as you create graphs, keep in mind that they represent numbers and should be designed logically. Figures 13.1 and 13.2 illustrate two clearly designed graphs. There are several steps to follow when using numerical clarifiers:

1. To enhance readability, size the numerical clarifier to consume the available space.
2. To enhance clarity, limit the amount of information presented.
3. Provide a descriptive title that tells people what to look for in the slide.
4. Label all significant features clearly and in large letters.
5. Present the data logically and accurately.
6. If part of a multi-slide presentation, make the format and color scheme match the other slides in the presentation.

Figure 13.1. Example of a graph.

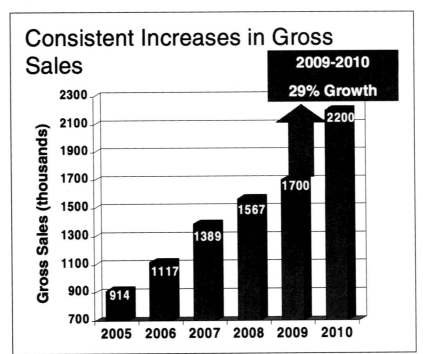

Figure 13.2. Example of a chart.

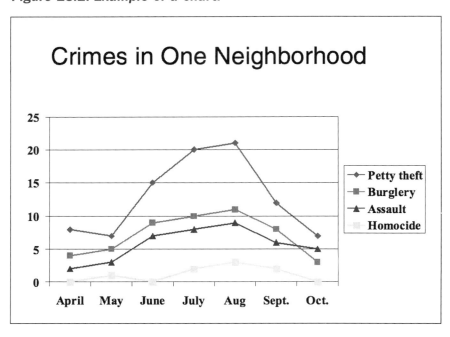

PowerPoint®—Designing Your Presentation for Message Clarity

PowerPoint® is another essential visual aid and often the most popular visual technology used in educational and work settings. Proficiency with PowerPoint® is now a form of "business literacy." Indeed, according to Larry Browning, Organizational Communication Professor at the University of Texas and frequent instructor of the undergraduate communication studies internship course, "Most of our summer interns are tasked with creating technology-assisted presentations—PowerPoint® specifically. Businesses now assume that college graduates are computer literate and know how to create powerful presentations in PowerPoint®." As a potential professional communicator, you need to know how to use it too. This section provides several guidelines for using PowerPoint® to help you design effective visual aids—without a design degree.

Media Box

Watch UT Communication Studies Professor Keri Stephens guide you through some basic PowerPoint® presentation do's and don'ts.

Visit this chapter's folder in your Chapter Media Contents online.

PowerPoint® has transformed the way business people give presentations because the software package makes it possible for ordinary people to create the kind of sophisticated presentation aids that once required the resources of design and production professionals. Although many people forget this fact, PowerPoint® is a tool for creating *visual* aids. While many PowerPoint® reference books have been published, *Save Our Slides,* by scholar and UT graduate Billy Earnest[8], provides a concise set of design guidelines and a series of exercises useful for students and working professionals. See Text Box 1 for a list of his 5 rules for visual design. We will address those rules and several more in this chapter. To begin this process, think about how many times you have seen a slide that looks like Figure 13.3. This slide is not an effective visual aid; in fact, it is barely a visual aid at all—merely text projected on the wall. What would make this visual aid effective?

Figure 13.3. This is not an effective visual aid.

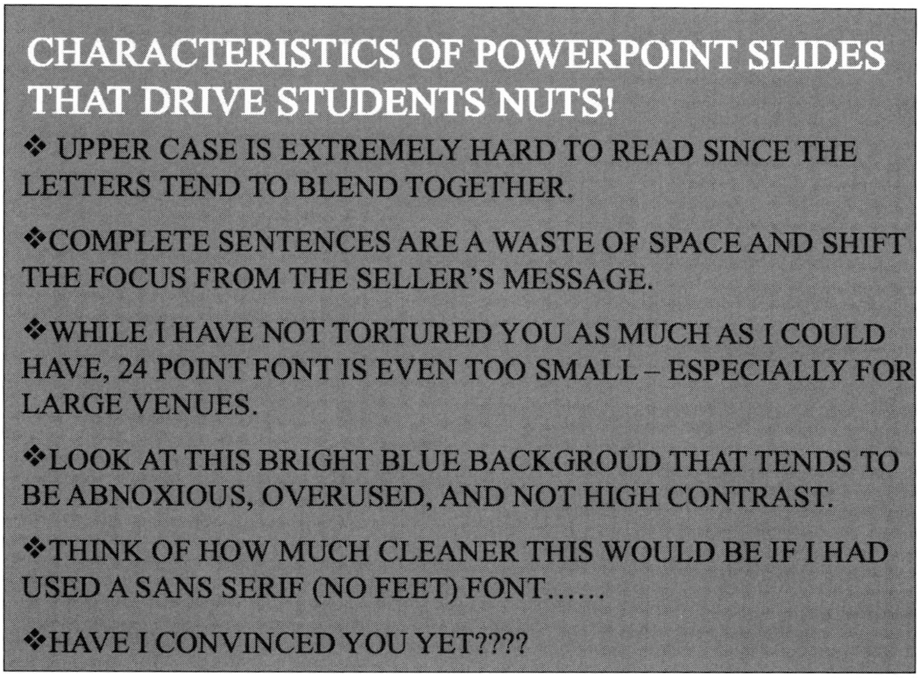

> ## CHARACTERISTICS OF POWERPOINT SLIDES THAT DRIVE STUDENTS NUTS!
>
> ❖ UPPER CASE IS EXTREMELY HARD TO READ SINCE THE LETTERS TEND TO BLEND TOGETHER.
>
> ❖COMPLETE SENTENCES ARE A WASTE OF SPACE AND SHIFT THE FOCUS FROM THE SELLER'S MESSAGE.
>
> ❖WHILE I HAVE NOT TORTURED YOU AS MUCH AS I COULD HAVE, 24 POINT FONT IS EVEN TOO SMALL – ESPECIALLY FOR LARGE VENUES.
>
> ❖LOOK AT THIS BRIGHT BLUE BACKGROUD THAT TENDS TO BE ABNOXIOUS, OVERUSED, AND NOT HIGH CONTRAST.
>
> ❖THINK OF HOW MUCH CLEANER THIS WOULD BE IF I HAD USED A SANS SERIF (NO FEET) FONT……
>
> ❖HAVE I CONVINCED YOU YET????

Create a consistent "look and feel."

Unless the actual point of your presentation has something to do with disjointedness, you should design your visual aids to interrelate. Take for example, the soft drink Coca-Cola®. The words Coca-Cola® were registered as a trademark in 1887[9] and when you see them today, they always appear in the same font and color scheme. This consistent look and feel is important to the Coca-Cola® bottling company because it imprints a recognizable image into the minds of consumers. PowerPoint® has two main tools that help you achieve a consistent look and feel for your presentation: design templates and the slide master.

While you may not have any training in graphic design, Microsoft's designers do, and they have included many design templates that you can use to create a standardized format to contain your content. In some versions of PowerPoint® these are called slide themes. Not only does the software package come with templates, but there are more available on the Microsoft website www.Microsoft.com. When you begin a new PowerPoint® presentation, ask yourself, "What image do I want to project with this presentation? Do I want a nice clean look with simple colored bullets?" Keep in mind that there are many templates and that you can create on your own if you spend a little time. Once you choose a design template and apply it, every slide you create receives the same background color, images, text format, and bullet format. Furthermore, if you find that you want to make design changes to your formatting, simply change the design template and PowerPoint® automatically updates every slide you created with it.

Standard design templates will take you only so far in your presentation design. Imagine that you work for a major company, and you want your company logo to appear on each slide in your presentation. You could choose a design template, create 56 slides from it, and then manually cut and paste your company's logo onto each one, but what a pain. Better to use the slide master to modify or customize the template, place the logo once, and then have it automatically appear on all 56 slides. This is one example of how useful the slide master can be. Slide masters also are helpful for other modifications to design templates. As we will discuss later in this chapter, the style of type embedded in many templates is less than ideal when projected on the wall. The slide master allows you to change the font once and have it apply to all the slides in your file, to place a header at the same location on every slide, to add page numbers to all your slides, and to change the bullet styles.

Design for high contrast.

The fact that Microsoft includes a number of interesting design templates does not mean that all of them provide good results when you use an LCD or DLP projection system to display the image on a big screen. When you select template colors, you should be aware of two issues: color combinations and gradients.

While people have differing opinions about what specific color combinations work the best for PowerPoint® slides, most people agree on a simple guideline: make projection slides high contrast. To create slides that are easy to read, use light-colored text on dark backgrounds and dark-colored text on light backgrounds. The challenge is that *many* color combinations seem high contrast when you view them on your computer screen, but projecting them washes them out, which will make your audience strain to read your words. If you are tempted to try some unique color combinations, make sure to test your presentation on the actual equipment you will use to project it, in the actual room you plan to use. Only through testing can you tell if your color combinations will work.

Color gradients can be described as a background style in which the background hue shifts from dark to light. These are dangerous to use for projected slides, since the color you choose for the text will appear in high contrast on some parts of the slide and low contrast in others as it crosses the gradient. The only sure way to systematically solve this problem is avoid these templates for projected slides and stick with solid colored backgrounds.

Design text for readability.

In all our college courses we are reminded to write our papers using a font like Times New Roman to make it easier for our professors to read and grade our papers. But presentations are different because our readers—our audiences—are located further away from us and they have different expectations. Also, our presentations are typically projected on a screen, not simply read on a piece of paper. In the section that follows, we will talk about the best fonts to use for PowerPoint® presentations including their style, size, and capitalization. We will also discuss how to avoid overusing text and presenting it on slides using appropriate visual balance.

Apart from "novelty" display fonts like puffy clouds and daggers, font styles fall into two categories: serif fonts, which have angled or horizontal "hooks" at the ends of the letters (e.g., Times New Roman and **Garamond**), and sans serif fonts, which do not (e.g., **Arial, Tahoma, Verdana**). Sans serif fonts, which generally have letters of uniform strokes, are clearer to see (although harder to read in large quantities) and are therefore the fonts of choice for small amounts of projected text. While you can use serif fonts for special emphasis or to add interest, do not let them dominate your screen. According to graphic designers, it is better to use a serif font for headings and titles because the pixels on the screen can sometimes have a hard time rendering the serif fonts when the typeface is small. That is why you would use a sans serif for the body copy so the screen does not have to render the serif font, and it is easier to read.

The size of type you use matters considerably. You have probably sat through a presentation where you squinted to read the words on the screen and rolled your eyes in annoyance as the presenter said, "I apologize that this slide is so hard to read..." Follow these guidelines and you will not need to make excuses.

Once you have picked type sizes for your titles, bullet items, etc., use these sizes consistently across all slides. As a general rule, major titles should be at least 44 points in height. Main bullet items should be at least 32 points, and sub-bullets should be 28 points. Again, though, the best way to make sure that your type size is readable when projected is to project a sample to see if audience members in the back of the room you are presenting in can read it.

Capital letters call attention to themselves. That is why when writing we capitalize the first word of a sentence—to make it stand out. However, for whatever psychological reason, many people over-capitalize. Avoid being one of them. To avoid the over-capitalization problem in PowerPoint® presentations, keep these rules in mind:

❑ Use heading capitalization (the first letter of every important word) in main titles only.

❑ Use sentence capitalization (the first letter of the first word, plus proper names) in main bullet items.

❑ Use no capitalization (other than for proper names) in sub-bullet items.

When editing your slides, always double-check to see if you have over-capitalized.

The final step in designing a slide for readability is to judge it for visual balance, then tweak accordingly. You have probably seen slides where all the bullets align on the left-hand side and there is a huge gap of white space on the right-hand side of the slide. Crunching text on only part of the slide, with nothing (e.g., a photo) to balance it, makes the slide look awkward. Use images, photos, and text to help your slides look more visually balanced, and less lopsided.

Your goal is to communicate with your audience; giving more eye contact to an object than to your audience or continually turning your back on your audience to read a screen does not facilitate that process. You should, of course, interact with your visual aids, but not at the expense of interaction with your audience. Merely glance at the screen; use the object purposefully and then put it aside. When you display text on a visual aid, avoid reading it to your audience. They can read it for themselves as you explain it in varying words and with more complexity.

Other creative considerations.

Objects and word art

Occasionally it is appropriate to use objects and word art in your presentations. Objects are graphic elements such as autoshapes, boxes, circles, call outs, and lines, all of which can be used to add interest to text and to organize ideas. Graphic elements can be so creatively used that you might think of them as word-pictures. We say this because they make text considerably more visually interesting.

In addition to graphic elements, WordArt is another option available in PowerPoint®. WordArt allows you to type in text, apply various options to the text (e.g., colors and shapes of the actual text) and end with some interesting effects. While it can be used well, more often the text ends up being hard to read when projected on the wall. As a general rule of thumb, use it sparingly and consider using a textbox or other graphic element before subjecting your audience to this often confusing technique.

Adding effective animation

Animation, as we describe it here, is simply how text or objects appear on the screen over time. Some animation effects look very professional since they help structure ideas by directing the audience's attention to them one idea at a time, or transitioning between slides. Other animation effects like text flying onto the screen make the audience literally move their heads to see what is happening. In this section you will learn how to use the subtle, professional animation necessary to create a solid impression. We will examine the types of animation, how to use it, and how to overcome some common problems.

There are two categories of animation effects: stationary and moving. Stationary effects are those that occur with no text or object movement. For example, "Appear," where the image just pops onto the screen; "Dissolve," where the image fades on of off the screen; "Wipe," where it looks like an invisible window wiper swept off the content; and "Blinds," where it looks like content was hidden behind blinds and as they are opened the content appears. In general, choose a single one of these effects as your primary animation effect throughout your presentation.

Moving effects are those that force the audience's eyes to go from one place to another on the screen, and they often require the presenter to wait until the effect is complete before the slideshow can continue. Examples of moving effects include "Flying," where text and graphics move across the screen until they land in their resting place. Other moving effects include: "Spiral," where content moves around in a spiral format until it rests; "Crawl," where the content moves much like a fly, but does so in a slower, step-by-step way; and "Swivel," where the text looks like it is mounted in the center and is then moved around in a circle. Moving effects should be used sparingly, and only for emphasis, since they can distract from your message when overused.

Animation comes in the form of slide transitions and on-slide animation. A slide transition is simply the way that a slide replaces the one before it. If you use a subtle effect such as "Wipe," and you use it consistently throughout, the transition effect fades into the background and becomes appealing animation. The key is to find an effect that is not overly obvious.

While slide transitions occur between slides, on-slide animation controls the way that objects appear on a given slide. One common type of on-slide animation makes bulleted items appear one at a time. If you are using a remote mouse (a hand-held device that allows you to advance slides), consider making the bullets appear "on mouse click" so you have full control over them. Alternatively, you can time your presentation and have the objects animate after a specified number of seconds. When you plan to speak extemporaneously or interact with your audience, however, avoid automated animation. Remote mice can enhance your professionalism and credibility in a presenting context. These are available for checkout for your 306M presentations at the Instructional Media Center in room 5.110 of the CMA building. You can reserve a remote mouse at their website or by calling 512.471.1199.

A second common type of on-slide animation is animated graphics. You can accomplish this effect by choosing the object to animate and applying an effect. Sometimes, you will want a bulleted item and an image to appear simultaneously. The ability to group items allows a presenter to click once and have all the grouped objects appear simultaneously.

The most common problems with animation are over-clicking (hitting the animation click button too many times) and missed timing (having an image appear at the wrong place in the presentation), both of which are caused by a failure to group items as you animate your visual aids. To avoid over-clicking, you must group objects so that several objects function as a single group. You open yourself up to missed timing in two ways: first, when you line up images to appear *after* the text they accompany, and second, when you forget to click images that you have added to the end of a slide. Bulleted items and their illustrations should be grouped to avoid missed timing. Practicing your speech with your visual aid, and having a printout of your slides so you know how many items are on each slide will always help too.

Adding appropriate sound

As with animation, people tend to over or underuse sound effects in PowerPoint® presentations, creating dead silence or constant, driving noise. While an occasional sound that is relative to the content such as a brief music clip or the sound of an airplane (if relevant and appropriate to your presentation) can create interest and capture the audience's attention, quite often presenters give little thought to how and when to use sound. Use sound effects when they support your goal, which is to add *appropriate* interest to your presentation.

If you decide to use sound in your presentation, keep in mind two technical considerations. First: volume. Make sure to test and adjust the settings on the computer and presentation system before you begin. Second: quality. Quality concerns can arise from the production of the audio file or from problems with the projection system. Make sure to test the sound at actual volume prior to the presentation.

Now that you're equipped with loads of knowledge about PowerPoint® and the most effective and professional ways to present information, look back to Figure 13.3 and ask yourself how the slide could be improved. You may also want to watch the video link that demonstrates the PowerPoint® design tips and walks you through an example of how to correct Figure 13.3.

Copyright considerations of photographs and cartoons

Some concepts need an explanation. As a presenter, one of your jobs is to figure out how you can best explain things. Sometimes a picture, along with your verbal explanation, helps an audience grasp an idea more quickly or more completely. Imagine that you are explaining wakeboarding to a novice. First, are you sure they know what a wakeboard looks like? This is a chance for you to show a photograph, and because wakeboards are large and tough to carry around on campus, a photograph can demonstrate the concept without much hassle.

Today, photographs and cartoons are widely accessible on the World Wide Web and very easy to capture. The fact that you *can* capture a photograph or cartoon from the Web does not mean you have the right to do so, and if you do, you should always be sure to cite where the image came from. While this is not meant to be a legal description of copyright laws, and quite frankly, many of these matters are ultimately decided in court, a basic understanding is important for everyone giving presentations. There are basically two types of images: copyrighted and public domain. Copyrighted images belong to someone and thus, if you want to use them, you must pay a fee. Public domain images also belong to someone, but either their copyright term has expired, or they were produced by an entity, such as the government, that encourages free use. Appropriating a copyrighted image without permission can be construed as stealing, which opens you to liability for copyright infringement and can bring steep legal penalties in certain circumstances. One option you do have when searching for art or photographs and want to use it legally, is to use a stock photography site such as iStock or Getty Images, where photos can be purchased for a minimal fee, and then they are yours to use.

In general, using an image once in a presentation for a class assignment falls under the category of <u>Fair Use</u>.[10] The problem begins when you use a copyrighted image for public uses, especially uses for profit. For example, if you use a Dilbert cartoon in a one-time presentation for class, you are probably fine. However, if you are hired to train groups of workers in PowerPoint® skills and you use the cartoon in your training presentation and copy it into the training packet, you have definitely crossed the line into copyright violation.

Visual Technology

Now that you have a clearer understanding of visual aids, let us turn to how you can disseminate them. Visual technology ranges from the more simple options like handouts and chalkboards, to those requiring electricity and often expensive projection systems like visual media and PowerPoint® Presentations.

Handouts.

The most low-tech of visual aid technologies is the handout—literally, technology that lets you "hand out" text, visual representations, and/or numerical clarifiers to members of your audience. Sometimes you want to make copies of your visual presentation (e.g., the actual slides) and give these directly to the audience. Other times, you want to selectively use more complex visuals as handouts. For example, if your graph is important and possibly a bit complex, you might want to provide a paper copy in addition to showing a simpler version on the screen. Handouts serve two purposes. First, you can keep them in reserve as a backup plan in the case of uncontrollable events such as power failures or computer crashes. Second, you can design them to use during the presentation. People can take notes on the handouts, highlight items they find particularly interesting, or keep them as memory joggers after your presentation. In either case, the handout can duplicate material you present verbally or provide additional material not mentioned during the presentation.

Handouts have a number of advantages. Many people like to have a tangible take-away from any presentation, and handouts accomplish this objective easily. They also free your audience from having to take detailed notes. Finally, they subtly demonstrate that you are organized and prepared. Their most significant disadvantage is their tendency to distract the audience. Under the influence of the handout, audience members may jump ahead in the presentation, ask premature questions, or even leave because they feel that they have gotten all the information they need. To counteract these tendencies, and control your audience's attention, follow these guidelines:

1. If you must distribute a handout during your presentation, design your handout to be simple and easily understood—and therefore less absorbing—and wait to hand it out until you are ready to discuss it.

2. If your presentation is very short—as with many in-class presentations—a handout might be unnecessary.

Visual media.

Visual media can be quite useful during a presentation. Visual media comes in a variety of formats from DVDs, to film montages made on your computer, to clips found on internet sites such as YouTube. Video clips are useful as they show items that you cannot bring with you to a presentation and help engage your audience. With the easy availability of editing equipment, you can edit visual media to your own specifications. Remember, whenever you use visual media make sure that each one is cued and ready to go prior to the presentation. Also, be sure to check the volume level before beginning your presentation if your media requires sound.

Display equipment.

Increasingly, presenters depend on electronic equipment to display the content they create to support a presentation. Available equipment ranges from familiar technology such as overhead projectors and DVD players, to projection cameras and LCD projectors. But no matter what type of display equipment you use, you should learn how to use it, and practice with it in advance. This also includes knowing how to use the two most common types of computer operating systems: Mac and PC. If you are only familiar with one, get to know how to use the other in case that is all you have available to use on presentation day. Unless you are willing to risk the embarrassment of technical failure or lack of knowledge about the equipment you are using, you should double-check every technical detail *before* your presentation begins, and practice using the system that you plan to use on presentation day in advance. In general, two display technologies are most often used: projection cameras and LCD projection systems.

Projection cameras

With projection cameras, you can magnify objects, even tiny ones, for display to a large audience. This comes in handy for people who need to explain the workings of miniature objects. Explaining these concepts can be difficult, and without access to a projection camera, presenters usually fall back on diagrams or enlarged photographs. Projection cameras (sometimes called document cameras) can amplify smaller objects to an audience, which creates a feeling of tangibility since the actual object can be clearly displayed. The biggest disadvantage to using projection cameras is that they can be hard to operate, so make sure to practice using them in advance.

LCD projection systems

When people today speak of "projectors," they generally mean liquid crystal diode (LCD) projection systems or DLP (digital light projectors) which are designed to interface with a computer for content. LCD and DLP projection systems vary significantly from those intended to project huge images to hundreds or thousands of people (think about the JumboTron at the UT football stadium) to portable systems for use in small conference rooms. Larger projection systems are typically mounted to the ceiling. These provide the greatest flexibility for the presenter since they are out of sight and essentially out of mind.

There are five central things to remember in regards to electronic display technology:

1. Always make sure to have paper copies of your material in case the equipment fails.
2. Be careful to avoid tripping on electrical wires.
3. Avoid standing in the way of the projector so as not to block the display.
4. Colors you see on your computer screen are not always the same as those you will see on the LCD screen.
5. Make sure you ask your instructor to turn on the LCD projector unit so it has a chance to warm up!

Presentation pitfalls with PowerPoint®.

Even if your PowerPoint® slides are designed perfectly and you select the ideal visual aid, there are some common presenting pitfalls that you should avoid.

1. Blinded by the light . . . Be sure you do not stand in a location where the projector light blinds you (your audience sees this and you will certainly squint or duck awkwardly). Do not stand in the same place in front of your slides for extended periods of time. Your audience will wiggle and try desperately to see the slides until they get tired, give up, and begin doodling.

2. No face in sight . . . A presenter should know the content so well that only quick glances to the screen are needed. Never turn around and read off your slides because it completely disconnects you from your audience.

3. Is there just a head??? Do not hide behind a podium or a computer keyboard. Move around, work the room, and connect with your audience. That's the value in using a remote mouse. This will help add to both your credibility and your professionalism.

4. This is not the version of PowerPoint® I use on my computer . . . When using a computer (like the ones in classrooms), spend some time getting comfortable with the keyboard and know how to start your presentation and maneuver your slides as needed. Know what version of PowerPoint® is on the computer you will be using for your presentation. This may affect what "version" you save it as. It is usually a good rule-of-thumb to make sure your file is "backwards compatible" if you use a newer version of the program.

5. But I don't know how to use a Mac (or PC . . .)! Know if you will have a Mac or PC available to use on presentation day. This may affect what platform you use to create your presentation, as well as the ease with which you can use the operating system. To be safe, practice using each one so you are comfortable with both!

6. What did that say??? Do not make the mistake of having too many visual aids or slides, so that you only spend a few seconds on each one, leaving your audience no time to fully take in or read what is being projected.

There are also some helpful tips that can make presenting more polished. Try hitting the "B" button or the "W" button on your keyboard in the middle of your slide presentation and you will create a Black or White solid background. If you need to skip ahead slides, you type "14" and the slide that will appear will be number 14 in your presentation.

Summary

This chapter explored several aspects of how you can use visual aids strategically. Hopefully you now realize that both audiences and speakers benefit from visual aids. You should also have a clearer understanding of the three major types of visual aids: objects, visual representations, and numerical clarifiers. When you use aids, technology is often involved and there are both advantages and disadvantages to using presentation software tools like Microsoft PowerPoint®. As you prepare your visuals make sure they are relevant, high quality, and consistent. Finally, be sure that do not use your aid as a crutch, but rather as a way to enhance your strategic communication.

Student exercises.

1. You are planning your first informative presentation and it will be titled, "How to be a college student." List an object, a visual representation, and a numerical clarifier that might be useful during this 5 minute presentation.

2. You have a friend who likes using color in her presentations. Her last speech had five slides and every one used a different color scheme. Which part of preparing visual aids did she miss?

3. Walk into your current classroom, where you will be giving presentations, and make a quick sketch of the room on a sheet a paper. Using the advice in this chapter, what can you do to make using visual aids easier? For example, where is the projector system? Are there any power cord issues?

4. Critique Figure 13.3 (the one with all capital letters on it). Be sure to consider and cite the design considerations found in this chapter.

5. Walk into your current classroom, where you will be giving presentations, and make a quick sketch of the room on a sheet a paper. Where is the projection screen located? What type of computer media does the computer accept? Bring an actual copy of your presentation to class and load it on the computer to verify that it looks OK projected on the wall.

6. In the middle of your PowerPoint® presentation, the screen flickers and goes black. Write out what you plan to do in that situation.

Dr. Billy Earnest's 5 PowerPoint® Rules

Rule 1: Pick a Good Template

Rule 2: Limit the Number of Words

Rule 3: Use Sans Serif Fonts for Better Legibility

Rule 4: Handle Graphic Elements Professionally

Rule 5: Choose High Contrast Color Combinations

Endnotes

1 Katie Weisman, "Brands Turn On to Senses," *International Herald Tribune,* December 4, 2003, http://www.iht.com/articles/120122.html.

2 Diogenes Laertius, *Lives of Eminent Philosophers* (Loeb Classical Library [1925]), vol. 2, sec. VI, line 40.

3 J. M. Clark & Allan Paivio, "Dual Coding Theory and Education," *Educational Psychology Review 3* (1991): 149–210; V. A. Thompson & Allan Paivio, "Memory for Pictures and Sounds: Independence of Auditory and Visual Codes," *Canadian Journal of Experimental Psychology* 48 (1994): 380–98.

4 A. D. Wolven & C. G. Coakley, *Listening* (Dubuque, IA: Wm. C. Brown, 1992).

5 Douglass R. Vogel, Gary W. Dickson, & John A. Lehman, *Persuasion and the Role of Visual Presentation Support: The UM/3M Study,* 1986.

6 Vogel, Dickson, & Lehman, *Persuasion.*

7 Thomas Leech, *How to Prepare, Stage, & Deliver a Winning Presentation* (New York: Amacom, 1993, 2nd edition), p. 128.

8 Earnest, Billy. 2007. *Save Our Slides,* Kendall/Hunt Publishers.

9 http://www2.coca-cola.com/brands/brands_coca-cola.html

10 Zielinski, Dave. 2001. Web Copyright Crackdown. *Presentations Magazine,* July 2001. p. 34–46.

Notes

CHAPTER 14

Delivering a Public Presentation

by J. Kanan Sawyer

Objectives

After studying Chapter 14, you should be able to do the following:

- ☐ Gain a general situational awareness for presentations.
- ☐ Use effective verbal and nonverbal tools for delivery.
- ☐ Explain time-honored delivery techniques.
- ☐ Understand research on delivery.
- ☐ Acquire a toolbox of language skills.

Key Terms

TERM	DEFINITION
articulation	Clearly pronouncing each syllable within each word.
enunciation	Emphasizing one word or group of words within a sentence to highlight an idea.
extemporaneous speaking	Practiced but not memorized speech.
impromptu speaking	Speaking with little to no preparation.
manuscript speaking	Reading verbatim from a prepared document.
memorized speaking	Speaking from rote memorization.
nonverbal delivery	The use of the body, face, and voice during a presentation.
speech voice	An unnatural, forced style of speaking that some adopt thinking it sounds more professional.
verbal delivery	Word choice and language selection during a presentation.

Introduction

A memorable presentation is a well-delivered presentation. How something is said matters as much as what is being said. In this chapter, we will look at what effective presenters do to deliver an outstanding presentation. This chapter will provide the necessary delivery tools to make your message memorable.

You will be given tools in this chapter that will help prepare you to deliver more powerful presentations. These tools include a Do's and Don'ts Delivery List, methods to manage communication apprehension, as well as specific techniques for verbal delivery and nonverbal delivery.

> "How something is said matters as much as what is being said."

Media Box

Do you say "like," "ummm," or "you know" too much when giving presentations? When listeners start tallying these "vocalized pauses," you know you need to make a change . . . you know?

Visit this chapter's folder in your Chapter Media Contents online to watch Caroline Kennedy, Barack Obama, and George W. Bush deal with speaking in the spotlight.

Why Focus on Delivery?

A courageous young sales executive, who had recently failed to gain an important account, called one of the decision-makers to whom she had presented. She asked the manager why her team had failed to retain the account and what they might do to improve in the future. The manager was impressed by her honest inquiry, and was equally as honest when he told her that he had seen her group arguing in the parking lot. He said, simply, that his company did not feel comfortable bringing that sort of tension to his project.

> "Delivery begins long before your presentation starts."

The lesson to be learned from this story: Delivery begins long before your presentation starts. Your professionalism should be clear long before you enter the classroom. Here are some of the do's and don'ts of preparing a presentation (shown in Figure 14.1).

Figure 14.1. Do's and Don'ts Delivery List.

What You **Can** Professionally Do . . .

* Arrive early.
* Use the restroom before your presentation.
* Set up special needs (flip charts, movie clips, etc . . .).
* Be sure that your visual aids work (check your PowerPoint on the machine or be sure that the overhead projector works).
* Turn off cell phones or iPods. Remove head phones.
* Get water before your presentation.
* Move things that might get in your way when speaking.
* Pay attention and be supportive of all other presenters.
* Have a pen and paper available (to take notes for your presentation or on others' presentations).

Figure 14.1. Continued.

What You **Cannot** Professionally Do . . .

- Arrive late.
- Practice your presentation where visible to a potential audience. (Note: It is better not to accept offers to wait outside while others present. Show that you are prepared without the extra time and use the opportunity to scope out the competition.)
- Change or fix attire after arrival (e.g., do not brush your hair while waiting to present).
- Check your PDA or cell phone.
- Play with change or keys in your pockets.
- Chat during others' presentations.
- Chew gum (before, during, or after your presentation. Yes, it happens!)
- Appear to be, or state that you are unprepared.
- Apologize (never tell anyone how tired or unprepared you are or announce a flub).
- Feign knowledge.

Once you are prepared, the following tools will help to set you on the path to an effective message.

Managing Delivery Communication Apprehension

People do get nervous before public presentations. What hurts some people is that they allow this fear to prevent them from presenting or from mastering the communication skills necessary in today's communication-centered world. There are numerous ways to manage communication apprehension both before and during your presentation. Table 14.1 offers you some useful coping strategies for managing your apprehension.

Table 14.1. Coping Strategies for Managing Presentation Apprehension.

Some Common Symptoms . . .	How to Manage Symptoms . . .
Dry Mouth	Try drinking water beforehand. Also, it is fine to bring water.
Shaking Knees	Wear pants or a long skirt. Thick tights can help ladies.
Shaking Hands	Use gestures.
Quivering Voice	Be conversational. Try to explain rather than present.
Poor Volume	Talk to the back of the room.
Blushing	Wear appropriate attire to cover potential areas where you might blush.
Lost Points	Know your key points and have visual aids when possible to help you refocus.
Sweating	Again, attire is the key. Test fabrics to see which fabrics will show perspiration.

Verbal Delivery Tools

Unlike what you may have been led to believe by some speeches or speakers, the oral delivery of a presentation does not require that you adopt a glamorous persona or become anyone other than yourself. Dynamism comes in all shapes and sizes, volumes, accents, and intonations. Your task is to allow your audience to understand your message, to help them remember it, and, perhaps, to embrace that message. The following techniques are time-honored tools for improving the verbal delivery of your message. This section will cover a speech's theses and key points, conversational tone, volume, pauses and pace, articulation and enunciation and, finally, extemporaneous delivery.

> "... choose additional key points to highlight. While we would like our audience to remember everything, they will not."

#1. Have a thesis and key points.

We have all heard a speech (or a lecture) where there was nothing memorable about it. Where the emphasis was no different than Ferris Bueller's teacher calling roll, "Bueller, Bueller . . ." Ask yourself, what *should* stand out? What do I want my audience to remember? Choose a key phrase or question (typically this is your thesis) to ground the speech and then highlight this for the audience (how this is done is covered below in the subsequent "Verbal Delivery Tools" sections). Next, choose additional key points to highlight. While we would like our audience to remember everything, they will not. Instead, we can assist our audience's memory by emphasizing key words and phrases that highlight and clarify the organization, thesis, and the details of our speech.

#2. Use a conversational tone.

People do not want to be presented to or at—they want to be engaged. Novice speakers often believe that this requires a specialized voice. Seasoned public speaking instructors call this "speech voice" and strongly discourage it. Speech voice is an unnatural, typically stiff, and sometimes nasal or throaty version or one's natural voice. While difficult to define, a speech voice is readily recognizable. For fans of the *The Simpsons*, think "Troy McClure;" for nightly news watchers, think of Brian Williams. Presentations in a speech voice do not feel to audiences as if they can be interrupted; they sound pre-prepared or "canned;" they are unnaturally polished; and errors in these speeches are readily recognizable.

> "Presentations in a speech voice do not feel to audiences as if they can be interrupted; they sound pre-prepared or 'canned;'..."

A device to engage your audience is to treat (speak to) them as if you are in a comfortable, interactive conversation. This does not mean that they will interrupt you or participate in your presentation, but your tone should suggest an easy permission to do so. Of course, this is a rather elevated conversation—not just you and the gang getting together to gab. Using a conversational style benefits you tremendously. When using a conversational style, keep the following in mind:

- ❑ Your errors are less noticeable.
- ❑ The audience will feel more engaged.
- ❑ Interruptions do not devastate your presentation.
- ❑ Regular breathing is more natural.
- ❑ Ideas are easier to clarify.

#3: Use an appropriate volume.

The simple fact is that you must be heard for your message to have impact. If you are one of those speakers to whom people always say, "Speak up. I can't hear you," then you need to increase your volume. However, by how much? And, can you be heard without talking at a level that you would consider downright yelling? Yes. Indeed, you should try not to overwhelm either yourself or your audience. Remember to use a conversational style but not a quiet voice.

> "... to engage your audience is to treat (speak to) them as if you are in a comfortable, interactive conversation."

A good rule of thumb is to have your voice "hit the back wall without bowling it over." This means that your volume should be at a comfortable level to be heard well in the back row without having those in the front row feeling blown away. The best method for testing your volume is simply to ask. (For example, "Good morning. I'm so glad to see everyone here today. Before I begin, can everyone in the back row hear me? No? Okay, I'll speak up and just give me a holler if there's a point that isn't clear. People in the front, I'll try not to overwhelm you.") Simple exchanges like this one can facilitate your presentation in a number of ways. First, they help to develop a rapport between you and your audience (the audience is given an opportunity to interact with you). Second, you show the audience that you value their feedback by listening to them and altering your presentation according to their needs. Additionally, these exchanges show that you are prepared to adjust to your environment.

> "The best method for testing your volume is simply to ask."

Volume alteration

Throughout your speech you may wish to raise or lower your volume as a tool for emphasis or to speak over distractions. Often people get a bit louder to stress a point but a softer tone that requires the audience to lean in to listen closely works just as well. Sudden changes in volume are a fun tactic to grab attention when they are not overused. Regardless of your highs and lows, keep in mind that you need to be appropriate to the audience and situation (e.g., not yelling in a church to grab the attention of a reserved congregation or using a whisper when talking to several thousand). Determining what volume is appropriate can be difficult. Feedback is the key. Watch for facial expressions and other nonverbal cues. If you have to yell to wake people up and suddenly the room falls quiet with an uncomfortable air, you should know that your tactic is overdone. Also, keep in mind that what worked well once does not always work a second or third time. Significant changes in volume can get old quickly (keep your

> "Determining what volume is appropriate can be difficult. Feedback is the key."

speech conversational and your volume will likely be effective; consider using volume increases and decreases as you would in telling a story to a friend). (As a note, be sure to read the "Nonverbal Delivery Tools #5 on Movement," which addresses the interdependence between volume and movement.)

#4: Using pauses and pace in your presentation.

The pause is a delicate creature. Use it only when vital and use it wisely. Typically, waiting no more than a beat (the time it takes to blink your eyes or change eye contact) is sufficient to make your point. A longer pause is not wrong, but its use will be very evident. Longer pauses will be considered both highly stylized and dramatized. Use once or twice, at most, in a given talk. Long pauses get attention. However overused, pausing hurts your credibility and the audience's comprehension of your messages.

> "The pause is a delicate creature. Use it only when vital and use it wisely."

Just as with volume, there is no one pace that works for every person or in every situation. Similarly, particular parts of your speech will be delivered more quickly while other parts necessitate a slow, deliberate pace. Audiences can grasp known information delivered at a quick pace but will need more time with new details. For instance, if you are giving a weekly report to your peers on a group project, you should be able to use a quick conversational voice. Alternatively, should you be delivering a sales proposal on a newly developed product to a group that is not familiar with the product, your pace should be on the slower side. The key is to find a balance. Read your audience. Do they look overwhelmed? Slow down. Are they bored or distracted? Pick things up. In order to help clarify your structure and assist your audience's retention, slow down your thesis and key points. Likewise, when using statistics, you should slow your pace. Attention-getters and stories can be delivered more quickly. Here's a good rule of thumb: If the information is known, pick up the pace; if it is new information, slow things down.

#5: Articulation and enunciation in your delivery.

Articulation and enunciation are often used interchangeably. For the purposes of public speaking, consider this fine distinction: Articulation is the clear vocal distinction of each syllable in each word and differentiation between words. Those who articulate have high vocal clarity.

Enunciation occurs when you put stress on individual words or phrases to emphasize or clarify meaning. (For example, "It is important that *you* prepare for the final speech," implies an individual need; whereas, "It is important that you prepared for the *final* speech," implies that the obstacle lies not with the person but rather with the assignment.) Individuals who both articulate and enunciate convey clear messages as well as clear meanings. In addition, if you have a tendency to speak too quickly, learning to articulate and enunciate words will assist you in slowing down.

> "Individuals who both articulate and enunciate convey clear messages as well as clear meanings."

Exercise 14.2. Practicing Articulation and Enunciation.

To help articulation, enunciation and pace, try this simple trick: Bite down on a pen or pencil. Now, try to read a paragraph from this textbook so that a listener would be able to understand you easily. While this exercise teaches you an exaggerated form of articulation and enunciation, it does help you to speak more clearly and avoid mumbling.

#6: Extemporaneous delivery of a presentation.

There are several types of presentational delivery: memorized, manuscript, impromptu, and extemporaneous. Memorized speaking is self-explanatory. Texts are known word for word and do not alter in delivery. Memorized speeches often feel stiff or "canned" to the audience. While many speakers believe this type of speech to be the easiest, it may be the most difficult to prepare given the effort associated with sounding natural. Presenters also run the risk of forgetting lines, phrases, or finding themselves awkwardly pausing while searching for precise wording. Manuscript speaking is similar to memorized speaking because it is also an exact replication of the prepared statement. Speakers read rather than recall the exact text. Manuscript speeches are best used in formal settings. Delivered well, they can be very impactful. However, delivered poorly, they can look and sound awful.

> **"Extemporaneous speaking has the most benefits of any speaking type because it allows the speaker to interact with the audience . . ."**

Impromptu speaking occurs when the speaker is called upon to speak without time to prepare notes, outlines, or research. Those who speak well when using the impromptu style benefit from no required preparation and a highly conversational style. Although popular discourse often equates impromptu speaking with extemporaneous speaking, the two delivery styles are different. Extemporaneous speaking differs from impromptu speaking in the amount of preparation associated with its delivery. Extemporaneous delivery is crafted from a well-developed presentation outline. Although an extemporaneous speech should vary each time it is practiced, the major and minor points are covered in the same sequence. Speakers use the outline as the foundation for the speech but vary the specifics as appropriate to the audience and situation.

Extemporaneous speaking has the most benefits of any speaking type because it allows the speaker to interact with the audience, maintain significant eye contact, move freely, and, most significantly, adapt to audience feedback quickly and consistently. Extemporaneous delivery disadvantages a speaker who may need to insert quotable passages or specific eloquent language, but those phrases or wordings may be added to a presentation outline for ease. In this course, most of your presentations will be extemporaneous.

Nonverbal Delivery Tools

It should be clear to you by now that using your voice in presentational speaking is a skill rather than a talent. It comes from practice and sensitivity. It is also something that can be mastered with time. The key to a skilled verbal delivery is utilizing audience feedback and adapting to meet situational needs. This same philosophy applies to nonverbal delivery tools. This section will provide you with tools for attire, gestures, posture and stance, eye contact, facial expressions, movement, visual aid interaction, and working with groups.

#1: Consider your attire.

What you wear is an element of who you are. Those watching your presentation will glean as much by looking at you as by listening to you. Your attire (what you are wearing) is part of your message. Your attire will begin sending signals even before you speak. These guidelines, therefore, can help you and your audience focus on your message, not your attire:

- ❑ Be clean and groomed. (Do not grab what was on the floor from the day before and do not try to hide a spot on your shirt with a tie instead of getting a clean shirt.)
- ❑ Dress one level above your audience for your presentations. (For example, if they are in jeans, wear slacks, but do not go too far.)
- ❑ Dress appropriately for the audience and situation. (For example, do not wear a tuxedo when everyone is wearing jeans.)

❑ Dress completely ahead of time. (Avoid slipping from tennis shoes into high heels in the hallway just before your presentation. Do not put on your tie as you walk in the room. Have your jacket on in the room so you do not need to fumble for it as you stand and begin your presentation.)

❑ Avoid distractions. (The audience will use any excuse to be pulled from your message.) Here are some basic distracters: 1) the flash of white socks with black pants and shoes, 2) gaudy jewelry, 3) chipped or peeling nail polish pointing to visual aids, 4) tops that are too low or that expose your midriff (put away your midriff until after the meeting), or skirts that are too high or that have slits (not the right message), 5) underarms (presentations are rarely the place for tank-tops).

❑ Never jingle. (Your attire may be the source of distracting noise. Women can wear bracelets or shoes that make noise. Men are worse culprits when they play with change or keys in their pockets.)

#2: Using gestures.

Most people "talk with their hands." Your hands can be used to clarify meaning for an audience or to add emphasis. If a speaker were, for example, to tell you about a large rat in the hallway outside your room, could you guess the weight of this rat? What if the speaker were, instead, to hold out her cupped hand while telling you? Can you provide a more accurate guess now? Suppose that the cupped hand were instead two hands held several inches apart. Would your guess now change? Gestures have the power to add clarity and emphasis to your presentation. Because eyes are drawn to movement, gestures can also engage and excite your audience while adding to your own involvement. Speakers who present without gesture are more likely to hesitate and pause than those who gesture (Frick-Horbury, D. & Guttentag, R. E., 1998). Ineffective gestures, or those that present a closed-body position to the audience, create distance between the speaker and the audience and diminish your rapport. These are called barrier signals. Three barrier signal postures to avoid are hands flat to your sides (the soldier stance), hands clasped behind your back (the hostage stance), and hands hanging down clasped (the Adam stance). Barrier signals can convey that you are nervous or adversarial even when this is not the case. Arm gestures should be open and away from the body, relevant to the verbal text, interactive with visual aids, and natural rather than practiced.

> "Your hands can be used to clarify meaning for an audience or to add emphasis."

Significant debate exists regarding the placement of hands in pockets. Some skilled practitioners claim that this is a natural posture. Speakers should only remember that the audience is engaged by gestures and gestures are hindered when we hide our hands in our pockets. Additionally, because the audience is drawn to movement, it is important to remember what our hands do once they are in a pocket.

When you hold your notes, they can easily become the focus of an audience's attention. Many speakers today use PowerPoint slides as guides. This can be an effective tool if used sparingly because it frees hands to gesture (see "#7: Interacting with visual aids"). However, if your body is oriented entirely toward the projection screen or, worse yet, PowerPoint does not work correctly, your delivery will suffer tremendously. Speakers should consider inconspicuous notes (placed on a nearby table or podium) that are in large, easily readable type.

#3: Consider your posture and stance.

Posture refers to the upper body position (shoulders, back, neck, torso). Stance refers to lower body position (feet placement, legs, hips). Posture and stance help presenters appear professional and confident. Slouching speakers are often, despite actual speaking ease or lack thereof, considered insecure. In order to appear self-assured, speakers should stand with shoulders back and a strong, secure carriage. The lower half of your body will also determine

> "Posture and stance help presenters appear professional and confident."

how you are perceived. Standing with feet shoulder-width apart and facing the majority of the audience is a professional default position.

#4: Eye contact.

A great deal of power rests in your eyes. You should look confidently at the audience. That does not mean you should stare at one person for an extended time. Instead, scan the audience. Look at one person for a reaction, and then move on. Do not stare at the floor, look at the wall, or dwell on an audience member's anatomy. If your audience is small (under 25 people) you should be able to make some eye contact with each member in a moderately lengthy speech of 3 to 5 minutes. If, however, your audience is large or difficult to engage, consider using "anchors," who are a few key individuals with whom to make eye contact who are spread throughout the audience.

#5: Facial expressions.

People often ignore this essential nonverbal communication tool. They should not. Studies show that audiences perceive a relaxed facial expression as an indication of higher legitimacy, expert power, and credibility (Aguinis, Simonsen, and Pierce, 1998). With all our attention to aspects of our speech and other delivery skills, it may be difficult to craft our faces into a particular expression. Indeed, you should *not* create a false image. Facial expressions should be appropriate to the moment and the topic but they should be connected enough with the speech to allow the emotion of the message to appear on your face. This does not mean to just keep smiling. Smiling is a powerful cue that transmits happiness, friendliness, warmth, and liking. If you smile frequently you will be perceived as more approachable; and yet when your topic is somber or difficult to comprehend, it is inappropriate to force a smile. This will actually damage rather than strengthen your presentation. Your face can and will connect to your audience only if it matches your message.

#6: Movement.

Movement in the room or on a stage is part of creating a presence that draws your audience both to you and to your message. Do not hide behind podiums. Instead, move around the room to get the audience's attention. You can certainly manipulate your body movement to communicate. For example, when questions are asked, you can move within a conversational distance. Watch out for nervous movement like pacing or rocking back and forth, but certainly, movement can aid your presentation if it is used effectively.

> **"Do not hide behind podiums. Instead, move around the room to get the audience's attention."**

> **"In a group presentation, do not draw attention away from the speaker."**

#7: Interacting with visual aids.

Too often people only worry about their visual aids before their presentation and not during it. This is a problem. Overheads are put on the projector without attention to placement or prior practice; PowerPoint slides can be flashed on a screen with little correspondence to what the speaker is saying so that visual aids become distractions rather than assistants. Visual aids should only be included when and where they assist your audience in understanding a point in your presentation, following the organization, or picturing an image vital to your message.

#8: Working with groups.

Group presentations add to the pressure of individual presentations, in part, because we must concern ourselves with nonverbal communication both when we are presenting and when we are not. We should not, however, concern ourselves with the delivery elements of our co-presenters during a talk because there is nothing you can do about it; and further, it can distract you from your own message. In a group presentation, do not draw attention away from the speaker. You should not be talking to other members or moving in ways that draw attention away from the presenter. Even the smallest movements will draw attention. If you need to move props or yourself, do so as inconspicuously as possible. It is important to show off your team by knowing when to and when *not* to be the star.

Conclusion

Delivery can either come between an audience and a message or facilitate understanding. It is, therefore, a very important consideration for speakers. This chapter offers you tools to present your message more effectively.

Media Box

Your delivery style can make or break your presentation.

Visit this chapter's folder in your Chapter Media Contents online. Watch students from the UT Speech Team deliver a professional and unprofessional version of a presentation.

Which delivery strategies made the presentation more professional?

Endnotes

1 Aguinis, H., Simonsen, M., & Pierce, C. (1998). *Effects of nonverbal behavior on perceptions of power bases.* Journal of Social Psychology, 138, 455–469.

2 Gronbeck, Bruce E., Kathleen German, Douglas Ehninger, and Alan H. Monroe. *Principles of Speech Communication. Twelfth Brief Edition.* New York: Harper Collins, 1995.

3 Frick-Horbury, D. & Guttentag, R. E. (1998). "The effects of restricting hand gesture production on lexical retrieval and free recall," *American Journal of Psychology,* 45–46.

4 McCroskey, J. C. (2003). *An introduction to rhetorical communication, 8th edition.* Boston: Allyn and Bacon.

5 Morris, D. (1977). *Manwatching: A fieldguide to human behavior.* New York: Harry M. Abrams.

6 Wallechinsky, D., Wallace, I., & Wallace, A. (1977). *The book of lists.* New York: William Morrow and Company.

7 Winans, J. A. (1938). *Speech-making.* New York: D. Appleton Crofts.

Notes

PART 4

Informative and Persuasive Speaking

CHAPTER 15

Speaking to Inform

by San Bolkan

Objectives

After studying Chapter 15, you should be able to do the following:

- ☐ Select an appropriate informative presentation topic.
- ☐ Create both a presentation and delivery outlines.
- ☐ Write a complete and guiding thesis statement.
- ☐ Learn how to open and close a presentation effectively.
- ☐ Use evidence well to support your thesis.

Key Terms

TERM	DEFINITION
audience-focus	To use delivery as a tool to help shape your interaction and involve your audience.
extemporaneous speaking	Presentation style that is practiced.
factual illustration	A detailed accounting that makes several points.
logos	Logical appeals.
message-focus	To focus too much on the message, creating a rift between the speaker and the audience.
pathos	Emotional appeals.
self-focus	To focus too much on what the speaker herself is doing rather than connecting with the audience.
specific instance	An undeveloped example that always follows a factual illustration.

Introduction

Despite how intelligent you are, or how good your ideas may be, and despite how well you have thought out your concepts, the fact remains, if you cannot communicate your message clearly, your ideas may as well not exist. Being able to communicate something to someone in a clear, concise, and engaging way is an ability that can be developed with the right skills, practice, and experience. This ability is important in every facet of your life, from speaking with friends to giving professional presentations. To be able to speak and to communicate using language and symbols is one of the factors that make us unique as humans. As social beings it is of the utmost importance to do this effectively and efficiently.

Informative speaking is not uncommon. The truth is that we both listen to and give informative messages on a regular basis. When you listen to the news, when you tell your significant other how your day went, when your boss describes how to operate a machine, these are all examples of abbreviated informative speeches. The formality and structure may not be the same as you might expect to find in a professional-speaking situation, but the concepts are still there. The basic function of providing information is at the heart of each of these communication interactions and to speak publicly is to simply add a bit of formality to the situation.

The following chapter will go over various concepts of informative speaking and will help you to develop the skills necessary to communicate clearly. First we will go over topic selection. Next we will discuss the importance of evidence and the proper use of supporting material. We will go over effective delivery and then we will examine the informative outline. The chapter will conclude with a few tips on practicing your speech.

Choosing Your Topic

When working on an informative speech, one of the most important aspects to consider is the topic. For many people topic choice can either make or break a speech. After reviewing their own speeches countless students have reported that if they could change one thing about their presentation it would be the topic. So why does this continue to be a problem? The answer lies in five simple reasons. Let's take a look.

#1: Pick a topic that is not over your listeners' heads.

It is important to keep your audience in mind during the creation of the message; while working on the content, make sure that your information will be presented at an appropriate level. To help illustrate this point, consider the following true-life example: When I was an undergraduate, I listened to a speech by an ex-military pilot about Apache attack helicopters and their fighting capabilities. Sounds interesting, right? Wrong. Instead of talking about his experiences flying a sophisticated war machine in combat, the speaker proceeded to explain to a class full of undergraduate Communication majors how a helicopter's rotor system worked, how an engine is built, and several other concepts that were altogether beyond our comprehension. The speech was well delivered; it was just too technical for the listeners. The explanations were far too complicated and necessitated a basic jargon of mechanical terminology that, for many in the class, went undefined. When choosing your topic, be sure that you pick a topic that can be explained at the appropriate level for your audience. If the speaker in this example had given the same speech to a group of helicopter mechanics, it would have been fine. However, because his speech used too much technical jargon, it was ineffective for its target audience.

#2: Pick a topic that is not too personal.

Think back to the last time you met somebody new and they got too personal too soon—maybe it was on the airplane, maybe it was at the bus stop, or perhaps it was at a football game. Again, think back to a point in the conversation when you thought, "Whoa, too much information!" Perhaps you asked someone, "how are you doing?" and instead of responding with the usual

> "It is important to keep your audience in mind during the creation of the message . . ."

"fine" or "great," she looked at you and said, "well, to be honest, I woke up this morning and was out of coffee and then I had to take care of my foot fungus and then. . . ." Although you may be tempted at times to deliver a presentation reliving the time your Uncle Dave fell down after drinking too much at a wedding party, it is necessary that you examine the appropriateness of the presentation in relation to both the audience **and** the speaking situation. Nine times out of ten that sort of story will be best left for the weekend. Select a topic that is classroom appropriate and be sure to disclose only that information which is fitting for that situation.

#3: Pick an intriguing topic.

Look at your audience, put yourself in their shoes, and ask yourself the question, "How would I like to be an audience member for a speech on this topic?" It is important to engage in perspective-taking here. While you may love miniature replicas of Spanish house cats, chances are you are the only one in the crowd who feels that way. Pick a topic that will engage your audience and that will capture their attention. There is little in this world that is worse than an unmotivated audience. Yawning classmates do little for the confidence of any speaker. On the other hand, you need to make sure that you pick a topic that interests you. If you are not excited about the topic, then how can you expect your audience to be engaged and excited? There is a fine line to this. One way to combine the two tips mentioned above is to use what is called a "reason to listen" in your introduction. The reason to listen connects your speech to the interests of your audience. For example, if you really want to give a speech to 20-year olds on the topic of nursing homes, it is important to tie your audience's needs to the content you are about to deliver. To do this, simply tell your listeners how the subject affects them. For example, you might say, "One day, sooner than you think, you may face the decision to relocate your parents to a nursing home because they can no longer care for themselves. When that time comes, the information you learn from my presentation will help you make an informed decision for your parents' best care." A reason to listen provides meaning for the people you are addressing.

#4: Pick topics that are manageable.

In most cases your instructor will set a time limit for your speech that will range anywhere from about 4 to 9 minutes. Understand that it is impossible to give a comprehensive report on the Civil War within this time constraint. The History Channel devotes weeks to the subject, so a 9-minute speech will not do. Instead, choose a portion of the Civil War that is manageable for your time frame. Perhaps a specific battle would work better as a topic, or perhaps a report about the food given to soldiers would be more appropriate. Pick a topic that is rich enough to warrant its selection, but narrow enough to allow an in-depth examination of the subject.

#5: Pick a topic that has substance.

There is nothing worse for a teacher who hears dozens of speeches each day than to sit through a speech on a trivial and unimportant topic. The bottom line is, nobody wants to hear an informative speech on how to take a nap or how to properly take a shower. While there may be some people in the audience that need the extra help, be wise and challenge yourself to think harder. Great informative topics are those that ask the speaker and the audience to do more than simply stay awake; they interest, intrigue and provoke thought in the audience.

> "Pick a topic that will engage your audience and that will capture their attention."

In conclusion, when deciding on a topic for a speech remember the 5 simple rules: Pick topics that are not too technical; pick topics that are not too personal; pick topics that are intriguing; pick a topic that is manageable; and lastly, pick a topic that has substance. Make sure you complete a thorough analysis of your audience and the speaking situation. With these tips in mind, you are on your way to topic success!

Exercise 15.1. Crafting Your Presentation Topic.

Below is a list of topics. Using the 5 rules you have just learned, how can you make these topics well-suited for an informative presentation in CMS 306M?

Original Topic	Improved Topic
How to buy an apple	
The 20th Century	
Technology of the Int'l Space Station	
How I got rid of my head lice	
The World's Largest Ball of Twine	

Evidence

Because informative presentations are based on research, you will need to report to your audience what others have discovered about your topic. To do this you will need to gather and manage outside sources; in short *you will need to present evidence*. Using evidence in speeches is important for a variety of reasons. Evidence not only increases your credibility, but it also gives listeners solid ideas that they can believe and take home, as well as engaging audience members. Good evidence also places what you are saying in a broader context. In the following section you will learn to differentiate between good and bad evidence and what types of evidence are the most effective in various situations. You will next learn how to report evidence and finally how to use it as a tool. This all will be done in the hopes that you use evidence honestly, and not to deceive or mislead. Evidence is complex and, when used well, builds a speaker's credibility. What sorts of evidence are appropriate to presentations?

> "Evidence not only increases your credibility, but it also gives listeners solid ideas that they can believe and take home . . ."

Using statistics.

- ❑ "4 out of 5 doctors recommend brand X over Brand Y."
- ❑ "Nothing is better than Diacticon for relieving foot fungus, fast."
- ❑ "I never used to be able to eat dairy, now I can—in small doses—thanks Bacterion."

Every day we are bombarded with evidence from a variety of sources claiming one thing or another, asking us to believe that some statistics are true while others are false. Most of us are overloaded with this kind of information on a daily basis. For this reason it is essential for us to be critical consumers of statistical evidence to avoid spending money on products we do not need or worrying about illnesses we do not have.

> "Using statistics effectively means understanding exactly what statistics measure."

Take one of the quotes from above for example, "4 out of 5 doctors recommend brand X over Brand Y." Now let's get critical. First of all, ever notice that five people in any ad never seem to agree on anything? There always seems to be that rebel in the ad that does not recommend the brand of toothpaste or cough medicine. Conducting interviews with only five doctors provides a very small sample size. The larger the sample size, the more effective the statistics. If, for example, 1,000 doctors recommended a particular pain reliever, you are far more compelled to believe it is a wise purchase than if only 5 doctors recommend it. Statistics like "4 out of 5 doctors" also can be misleading. It is quite likely that the company making the cough medicine had to ask dozens of groups of five doctors before it reached a group where four agreed on that brand. In other words, there may be many groups of doctors who do not recommend that brand for every one doctor who does. Using statistics effectively means understanding exactly what statistics measure. Eighty percent of doctors do not recommend the cough medicine; 80% of one, isolated group of 5 doctors of some kind recommend it.

Using narrative versus objective evidence.

Narrative and objective evidence are the two basic categories of evidence. Narrative evidence refers to stories that people tell about their own or others' experiences. Stories you tell your friends and personal testimony are both examples of narrative evidence. Objective evidence on the other hand refers to numbers, statistics, and ratios that experts in the field have calculated. The example of the "4 out of 5 doctors" is "objective" evidence.

One of the benefits of narrative evidence is that it can be emotional. This story-telling quality, known as pathos, helps to draw your audience into your speech and makes it real for them. Narrative evidence allows

> "Narrative evidence refers to stories that people tell about their own or others' experiences."

> "Objective evidence, on the other hand, refers to numbers, statistics, and ratios that experts in the field have calculated."

> "While narrative evidence allows your listeners to personally connect with the topic, objective evidence tells listeners that they are not the only ones who identify with the topic."

listeners to connect with the topic in a personal way and helps them to imagine more realistically what you are talking about. Objective evidence, known as logos, on the other hand, helps to paint a global picture of your topic. It shows on a larger scale how much, how many, how long, how often. While narrative evidence allows your listeners to personally connect with the topic, objective evidence tells listeners that they are not the only ones who identify with the topic.

There are drawbacks to both narrative and objective evidence. Narrative evidence often refers to isolated incidents. Just because something happened to one person does not mean it is true for all people. Objective evidence, on the other hand, can often be dry and hard to grasp. For example, the fact that people surf waves 50 feet high does not mean much unless it is presented in a context like, "Some people surf waves upwards of around 50 feet tall. That is the equivalent of surfing a wall of water as tall as a 5-story building."

So, which type of evidence is best? The answer is both. Using narrative evidence in conjunction with objective evidence is really the best way to explain information in an understandable way. For example, in order to explain fully the significance of overpopulation at a university, a student could relate objective evidence that more than five percent of students are unable to graduate in four years because they cannot get into a required class. To make a lasting impression, the student could follow up with narrative evidence, a story about a person who lost a job opportunity because she could not graduate on time.

The Four Types of Evidence

Under the umbrella terms of narrative and objective evidence are four types of evidence that need special consideration. The first is the factual illustration. A factual illustration is a detailed story that makes several points. It is a fully developed example that supports your thesis and helps to create a context for your listeners. A common place for factual illustrations is in the attention getter part of a presentation that is given at the start of the presentation.

Next is the specific instance. A specific instance is an undeveloped example relating to the previous factual illustration. As such, a specific instance should always follow a factual illustration in order to help explain that the first story was not an isolated incident. For example, in my attention getter I could relate a story about a girl who did not graduate on time and how she lost a terrific job opportunity. I would relate all the details of the story and at the end you would feel like you knew her fairly well. Next I would talk *briefly* about another friend who also did not graduate on time. I would report *briefly* how he too lost a job opportunity because of a graduation mishap. Again, a specific instance is an undeveloped example relating to the previous factual illustration that helps to explain that the first story has occurred on more than one occasion to multiple individuals or groups.

The third type of evidence is the *statistic,* which refers to facts or occurrences that are represented numerically. A statistic is a statement using figures and/or numbers that summarizes data and indicates relationships among various phenomena. Statistics enable a person to summarize a large amount of information quickly. You will need to explain your statistics in your presentation. Do not assume that your audience will be able to interpret the numbers on its own.

The final type of evidence is *expert testimony*, which is a claim statement made by an expert in his or her field of expertise. Be sure to use expert testimony competently. For example, it is *not* appropriate to refer to Dr. Hasan Bolkan (PhD in microbiology) as an expert making a claim about 19th-century Victorian literature. His expertise is microbiology and its related subjects, so a literature professor would be more appropriate when referencing classic novels. Also, be sure that the person is actually an expert. Quoting Jason Alexander (a.k.a. George Costanza) about the importance of eating Kentucky Fried Chicken is not using expert testimony well. Alexander no doubt has considerable expertise in a variety of topics, but it would be difficult to convince an audience that he is also a nutritionist or chef.

Reporting your evidence.

One of the biggest mistakes new speakers make is failing to cite their sources. In your presentation it is of the utmost importance that you report the author(s) of your evidence to your audience. You should articulate the sources of your information anytime the ideas you are presenting are (a) not your own, and/or (b) not common knowledge. This needs to be done both thoughtfully and strategically. To do this, you must report the individual or the group who originally gathered and published the evidence, and why that individual or group is credible related to the topic of your speech. For example, when referencing an expert in a speech about kids, you might say, "According to Dr. Bob Ross, an expert on pediatric nutrition at UC Davis, childhood obesity has increased in frequency to the point of being an epidemic." After this initial introduction you can simply say "according to Dr. Ross" for future references in your speech. This may seem tedious at first, but without this source information, speakers both lack credibility and are guilty of plagiarism.

> "... report the source before the evidence if the source is highly credible; report it after the evidence if this is not the case."

Next, it is important that you present your evidence strategically. A good rule to guide you is as follows: report the source before the evidence if the source is highly credible; report it after the evidence if this is not the case. For example, "According to Dr. Bob Ross, expert on pediatric nutrition from the University of California at Davis, "little kids who like to dance lose weight more easily than kids who do not dance." If the source is less credible, you might instead say, "Little kids who like to dance lose weight more easily than kids who do not dance, according to Dr. Mike from an unaccredited medical institution in Appalachia." Maintaining credibility is important in order for the audience to take the information you present seriously, so make sure you are strategic when presenting your evidence.

Lastly, when using evidence, be sure to present your information as a part of an argument rather than simply adding factoids in your presentation. However, it is not enough to simply give a piece of information in your presentation; rather, that information must be used as a tool in an argument towards some end. To ensure this happens, it is necessary to look at the three components of an argument: the claim, the evidence, and the warrant. You will see the ideas of a claim and warrant in the chapters on persuasion and argumentation. Briefly, the claim is a statement of opinion or fact that is the heart of the argument. The evidence refers to data collected in support of the claim. The warrant is supplied as a connective between the claim and the evidence. These three components of an argument are all necessary and important to understand. Arguments can be challenged on any of the three components and without a thorough understanding of an argument's makeup, you will be unable to defend your position. Take for example the statement, "On average, Americans watch four hours of television a day." This is a piece of evidence; notice though that without a claim or warrant it has little meaning and no context—we still need to provide the other two components. My claim may be that Americans watch too much TV. Still this argument is flawed because we have no connection between the claim and why the evidence supports this claim. Once the warrant is supplied, we have context. For example "Americans watch too much TV. On average Americans watch fours hours of television a day. The average hours watched per person around the world is only one hour per day." My warrant helps to place the claim and evidence in a context that makes sense. Notice too that the evidence can be used in a variety of claims which is why the claim and warrant are so important. With the same piece of evidence I could claim that Americans are not exercising enough, or that they are not getting enough of the fine arts anymore. Warrants are still needed and would be as follows: watching television four hours a day takes away from time to exercise; watching television for four hours a day kills the desire to see fine arts, respectively.

Delivery

> "To focus on delivery as an end in itself is a classic mistake of many beginning speakers . . ."

The first thing to think about when delivering an informative presentation is your objective, the goal you want to achieve with this speaking situation. Think what opportunity does this speaking engagement present to me? What sort of relationship am I trying to build with this audience? What do I want to get out of them and what can they gain from me? Set a goal for yourself and work to achieve it through your delivery. Many people concentrate on the delivery as an end in itself, yet this is a mistake. Think of your presentation skills instructor: As an instructor, her goal in many class speaking situations is to inform. At the same time, there is also a relationship she has to develop with the audience that cannot be ignored. She needs to select her delivery style to help achieve her goal. She tries to be friendly when she speaks and addresses her students as she would her friends. She may use personal examples to illustrate various communication concepts and engage her students with lively discussions. She uses a delivery style that helps her students relate to her and by doing so, she attempts to build an atmosphere of friendliness and camaraderie. Because she was able to identify her objective in the speaking situation, she was able to use her delivery skills strategically to reach her goals. If her objectives were different, such as addressing superiors at a board meeting or speaking to professional clients, her delivery strategy would also be different.

Courtesy of Dorling Kindersley Media Library

To focus on delivery as an end in itself is a classic mistake of many beginning speakers; it is what's known as being <u>self-focused</u>. When you are self-focused, your energy is devoted to unengaging aspects of your speech. For example, instead of creating a relationship with your audience by focusing on their needs, you tend to concentrate on what you are doing. How do your words sound? How do your slides look? Is your eye contact good enough? When concentrating on these aspects of your speech, you tend to forget about the audience. In time, they may disengage with you as well.

Once delivery is mastered, many people new to informative speaking get over the self-focused state but move on to another equally problematic method of speaking: <u>message-focused</u>. A message-focused person creates a rift between himself and his audience which makes for a stiff and uninviting speech. People in this stage are often over-prepared on substance yet barely aware of the audience. Instead of interacting and nonverbally engaging their listeners, the message-focused person concentrates on the content and is lost without a written script. Presentations of this sort tend to seem like the speaker is talking *at* the audience rather than *to* them.

> **"A message-focused person creates a rift between himself and his audience which makes for a stiff and uninviting speech. People in this stage are often over-prepared on substance yet barely aware of the audience."**

The place to be in the triad of delivery is what communication experts call <u>audience-focused</u>. When you are audience-focused, you tend to use delivery as a tool to help shape your interaction and involve your audience. You are basically having a sort of "conversation" with your audience and relating your ideas in a simple yet professional manner. This type of delivery helps your audience feel like it is a part of the speech act; instead of being a receptacle of information, it is now a collaborator in the message.

Remember, when working on your delivery, concentrate on the audience and what you want to achieve with them. They may only be classmates at this point who are obligated to listen in order to receive attendance credit, but it does not have to be that way. After your objectives are identified, craft an appropriate message and use your delivery skills to create a communication interaction with your audience that will help you reach your goals. In this book, there is a full chapter on delivery that will expand on this material.

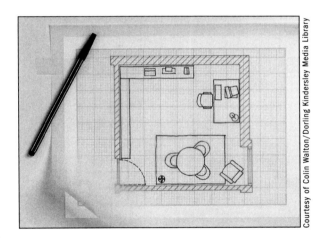

Courtesy of Colin Walton/Dorling Kindersley Media Library

Form

Now that you understand how to pick a topic, how to gather evidence, and how to deliver your speech, all that is left is organization. To do this we now turn to a discussion on outlining.

When creating an informative speech, a good outline is a must. Your outline should be a presentable version of your presentation and should include all the parts required therein. To begin we will go over a few simple rules.

Rule #1: Get organized.

Start by brainstorming all of your ideas to get a feeling of the possible topics you might present. Next begin looking for common themes linking your thoughts. There should be one overarching thesis with several corresponding thought branches. Examine these branches and choose between two and four main points. Organize these points in an appropriate manner (chronologically, topically, etc.). After this step is completed you will have a basic skeletal outline for your speech.

Rule #2. Use complete sentences.

Your outline should be well thought out and a presentable version of your speech; if your professor was to take your outline and read it out loud, it should sound like a well-polished presentation. This type of outline is what is known as the *presentation* outline; it is what you will turn in to your professor for a grade. Your *delivery* outline should look more like what you had after step one. This type of outline aids in the process of <u>extemporaneous speaking</u> but should not be turned in for credit. It is composed of key words that help you to remember the chronology of the speech, key points of evidence, and transition statements.

Exercise 15.2. Brainstorming Topics for Your Presentation.

In informative speaking, topics generally fall into five categories: speeches about objects (digital camera, baseball card collection), speeches about people (Martin Luther King, Jr., John F. Kennedy), speeches about events (Columbine shooting, first day of school), speeches about procedures (how to change a tire, how to join a sorority), and speeches about ideas (evolution, Buddhism). Brainstorm at least 3 topics of interest to you in each category:

A. Speeches about Objects:

B. Speeches about People:

C. Speeches about Events:

D. Speeches about Procedures:

E. Speeches about Ideas:

Exercise 15.3. Write the Thesis and Outline for Your Presenation.

From your brainstorming list above, select one topic with which to work. With this topic, you will write a complete thesis statement as well as create an outline. Fill out the following for a complete presentation outline:

I. Introduction

    a. Attention Getter:

    b. Thesis:

    c. Preview:

    d. Statement for audience interest:

    e. Credibility statement:

Transition statement:
II. Body

    a. Point 1:

        i. Subpoint 1

        ii. Subpoint 2

Transition statement:
    b. Point 2:

        i. Subpoint 1

        ii. Subpoint 2

Transition statement:
    c. Point 3:

        i. Subpoint 1

        ii. Subpoint 2

Transition statement:
III. Conclusion

    a. Review

    b. Parting shot/Sense of closure

Rule #3. Subordinate into outline form.

Many students are tempted to write a narrative version of their informative speeches. Although this is acceptable when attempting to brainstorm, it is unacceptable as an outline. Outlines are designed to be blueprints for presentations and as such, need to be formatted in a subordinated fashion. By this I mean that you should have points and sub-points. Usually each point and sub-point will be composed of only one sentence (see example). Use roman numerals to help accentuate your subordination.

Rule #4. Be efficient.

Your job as a presenter is to communicate your ideas to the audience. Be careful not to cram too much information into a speech in order to fulfill its informative requirement. Furthermore, be sure to pace your information so that your points are equally weighted. This will help the organization of your speech for your audience in that all your information will not be centered on a single main point.

Rule #5. Have a strong introduction.

A strong opening statement makes for a confident start and sets the tone for success. Be sure to think out your introduction and be thoughtful when selecting your ideas. We will use the "First Day of School" as our topic so we can provide specific examples related to the introduction. There are a few components that are necessary for a good introduction:

Attention-gaining device

A good attention-gaining device can justify and limit a topic, provide background information, establish common ground, pique audience interest, and involve your listeners. As such, a strong attention getter is a must. Examples of attention getters are quotations ("It was the first day of school, and Froggy was more than a little nervous," writes Julie Danenberg in her book, *First Day Jitters*); startling statistics (95% of college students admit feeling anxious about starting school); factual illustrations (a study by the University of Illinois Psychology Department demonstrates the adverse effects of school stress on kindergarteners); a demonstration (pretend to be a new student at UT—look around the room anxiously, study a map, try to find the right seat, etc.); and narratives ("I remember it well: My mom had ironed my new shirt and slacks, I asked for help tying my new sneakers, picked up my little green backpack, and headed onto the bus with all the other 6-year-olds. I was terrified."). The attention getter should not distract from your overall message and should relate to your topic. Lastly, if you give a startling statistic, be sure to pause and let the information sink in for the audience. Too often a student will rush through an opening and in doing so, diminish the effect of the attention getter.

Thesis statement

A thesis statement comes next. Here you will tell the audience what you are going to talk about. The thesis statement makes a claim that will be the focus of your speech. For example, the first day of school provokes anxiety in most people, but by following these three simple steps, students of all ages can have a successful first day.

> "A strong opening statement makes for a confident start and sets the tone for success."

> ". . . a strong attention getter is a must."

> "The thesis statement makes a claim that will be the focus of your speech."

Reason to listen

The reason to listen is one of the most important parts of your speech. Without it your listeners will have little motivation to pay attention. The reason to listen makes the topic relevant to your audience. It is your job as the speaker to provide a justification for listening. Explain how the information which is being presented will be useful to *them*. For instance, we have all experienced the anxiety of the first day of school, and soon, as we enter graduate school or the work force, we will have to face this anxiety again.

Credibility

This refers to your right to inform the audience. Why should they listen to what you have to say? Your right as a speaker to inform the audience is based on your knowledge and expertise. This can come from education, experience, and/or research. Be sure to make it clear to your audience that you are an expert on the subject and how you acquired this expertise. An example of a credibility statement might be "I followed these steps to overcome my anxiety as I entered UT as a freshman and I know they can help others do the same."

Preview

It is here that you will whet the appetite of your listeners. Briefly introduce each of the main points that you will cover during your speech. For example, I will be detailing three steps that are invaluable in overcoming first-day jitters; they are, 1) a good night's sleep, 2) exercise, and 3) visualization.

Rule #6: End with strength.

Just as it was important to have a strong opening, it is also important to have a strong conclusion. Use the following guidelines for a successful conclusion.

Restate your thesis

Paraphrase your initial thesis statement to reassert your claim. Make sure that you remind the audience of the focus of your speech. You might say, "In this presentation, I have talked about three steps that can help you overcome first-day jitters."

Review your main points

Continue your conclusion by briefly reviewing each of the main points you discussed during the speech. Remind the audience what you told them in order to ensure a lasting impression. For instance, "I told you that a good night's sleep allows you to be rested, refreshed, and confident; that exercise can reduce the physical effects of first-day anxiety; and that visualization puts your mind in a positive space to begin your journey."

Give your audience a reason to remember

Give your audience something to take home with them. Just like the reason to listen, the reason to remember tells the audience what is in it for them. Tell your listeners what they should do, as individuals, with the information you gave to them. Tell them how the information you covered in your speech will be important in their lives. Take the following statement, for example, "So, whether you are starting at UT as a new student this year or you are about to begin your first 'real' job, remember a good night's sleep, exercise, and visualization can help you overcome your anxiety."

Circle back to the introduction

In order to provide a sense of closure, remind the audience of the attention-gaining device used in your introduction. If you started with a narrative, return to the narrative. Returning to your own story about your first day of school, you might end with, "If I had known these three steps when I was 6, I might not have been terrified—I would have walked into kindergarten like I owned it!"

Rule #7: Use transitions.

Use transitions between your main points. Transitions are phrases that alert your listener that a change in subject is about to occur. These statements help to organize your speech for your listener. They can help the listener to verbally identify your train of thought. Rather than simply jumping from your introduction to your first main point, you should provide a transition such as "No person can overcome the first day of school anxiety without at least adhering to this first step, a good night's sleep."

As a reference, below is another skeleton version of a topical outline. Follow the structural principles of this example in order to create a well-formatted version of your presentation. Included in the example are the specific requirements necessary for an effective introduction and conclusion (also note the transitions). (The following is a recommended for an effective outline. While it is a good resource, be aware that there are many other methods of organization that are just as effective. Ask your professor for specific requirements in your class.)

Exercise 15.4. Use this skeleton outline to create a working version of your presentation.

I. Introduction
   A. Attention Getter: Spark the interest of the audience. This can be done in a variety of ways, just be sure that a) it relates to your speech, and b) it is not distracting.
   B. Thesis Statement: Make a claim that will be the focus of your speech.
   C. Reason to Listen: Tell your audience what's in it for them.
   D. Speaker Credibility: Establish your right to speak intelligently on the subject. This can be done via experience, education, and/or research.
   E. Preview: Identify the main points that will be used to support your thesis.

II. Body
   A. Main Point One.
      1. Sub-point one.
         a. sub sub-point one
         b. sub sub-point two
            i. sub sub sub-point one
            ii. sub sub sub-point two
         c. sub sub-point three.
      2. Sub-point two.
         (Follow the above example for further subordination)

   Transition Sentence: Alert the reader that a change in subject is about to occur.

   B. Main Point Two.
      1. Sub-point one.
         a. sub sub-point one
         b. sub sub-point two
            i. sub sub sub-point one
            ii. sub sub sub-point two
         c. sub sub-point three

   Transition Sentence

   C. Main Point Three.
      1. Sub-point one.
         a. sub sub-point one
         b. sub sub-point two
            i. sub sub sub-point one
            ii. sub sub sub-point two
         c. sub sub-point three

Exercise 15.4. (Continued).

III. Conclusion
    A. Restate Thesis: Paraphrase your initial thesis statement to reassert your claim.
    B. Review: Remind your audience of the main points covered in the speech.
    C. Tie Back: Redirect your speech back to the initial attention getter to alert your audience that your speech is complete and to provide a sense of closure.
    D. Reason to Remember: Give your audience a reason to remember your speech. Focus on why the information was important and what they can do with it in their lives.

Preparing for the Presentation

When preparing to deliver your informative speech, it is imperative that you *practice*. However, memorizing your speech can make you sound robotic rather than natural. Instead, internalize your ideas so that you are comfortable with the concepts and familiar with the information. This flexible approach to practicing and preparing leads to effective extemporaneous speaking. In this kind of speaking, the speaker is rehearsed but does not sound like he is reciting a memorized manuscript. Make sure you practice your presentation in a setting similar to the one where the actual presentation will actually take place. If you are addressing your classmates, get a few friends to listen to a mock presentation. If you are addressing your professors, get your parents to listen to your speech. The point is that you want to become as comfortable and familiar with the speaking situation as possible. Although practicing in front of a mirror may help you become aware of your nonverbal communication, remember that it will not prepare you for the audience interaction that is naturally a part of a public speaking situation.

> **"When preparing to deliver your informative speech, it is imperative that you *practice*."**

Again, practice, practice, and when you are done, practice some more. Even though you may be comfortable with the speech on paper and even though you may consider yourself an

Courtesy of Dorling Kindersley

excellent public speaker, the result of being unprepared can be both noticeable and disastrous. You will tend to become self-focused or message-focused and any hope of audience interaction will be slight at best. Make sure you prepare for the assignment as you would a test and devote the same energy into delivering your material as you did putting it all together.

Conclusion

In this chapter we discussed several aspects of informative speaking from choosing a topic to delivering your message. Remember that informative speaking is a skill that can be developed by virtually anybody. With the right skills and enough practice you can become a polished presenter.

When you start preparing for your informative presentation remember to pick a topic that is appropriate for your audience and the speaking situation. Do not pick topics that are too technical, too personal, too boring, too broad, or too trivial. Be wise in your judgment and pick a topic that will help to ensure your success.

When gathering supporting material be sure that you select unbiased sources and deliver the information in an ethical way. Also, remember your options for the different types of evidence, namely factual illustrations, specific instances, statistics, and expert testimony. Lastly, use evidence as a tool in your argumentation and be sure to supply all the necessary logical components to help your audience understand your assertions.

Next, concentrate on your delivery in order to make a connection with the audience. Your delivery is a tool for enhancing your relationship with listeners and as such it should be seen as a means to an end instead of as an end in itself. Remember to remain audience-focused and try to move away from being self-focused and/or message focused.

Once you have all of your information down and your delivery prepared, concentrate on the form of your presentation. A strong outline is the blueprint for a strong speech. While creating your speech, get organized, use complete sentences, subordinate into outline form, be efficient, have a strong introduction and conclusion, and also use clear transitions.

Once all of the above is complete, make sure you practice in a setting similar to that in which you will present. Practice makes better, and only by practicing in a real life situation can you hope to learn how to speak well. Be serious about the assignment and do not underestimate the stresses of speaking in public.

Media Box

What makes a presentation unprofessional or professional?

Watch two versions of a sample student speech on "Brain Research of the Sexes" and find out!

Visit this chapter's folder in your Chapter Media Contents online.

The chapter you just read was meant to help you gain an understanding about informative speaking; remember, the skills you develop in this class will last you a lifetime and will come in handy both inside and outside the classroom. Hopefully, informative speaking is now a less daunting task.

Informative Presentation

Goal: Your second assignment is an informative speech that tells the audience about a significant issue, who someone is, how something works, or how to do something. See the evaluation form for additional details about how delivery and content will be evaluated.

Written Work: You must turn in a thesis statement, bibliography, and outline of your speech by the deadline set by your instructor.

Research: Your speech must be based on information obtained from **at least 3 current sources.** You must identify each source when you deliver your speech, in the outline of the speech, and on a single-page bibliography. An adequate source citation in a bibliography includes the name of the publication, its author, the date it was published, and the volume, issue, and page numbers. Internet citations should include the name of the web page, the author (or group of authors), and the specific web address.

Topic Selection: Consider your interests, your audience's interests, and available reference materials to select a topic that will engage your audience. A topic is engaging when you are enthusiastic about it and when it interests your audience. Speeches on some topics routinely receive poor grades because students pick them so often; as a result those topics stimulate a low level of interest within the audience. You can avoid this problem by checking your topic with the instructor. Refer to your book for guidance on selecting a topic.

Time Limits: You will have between 3 1/2 to 4 1/2 minutes to deliver your informative presentation. If you speak for less than 3 1/2 minutes, or more than 4 1/2, your grade will be penalized. One point will be deducted for each 15-second interval. For example, a presentation that is 1-14 seconds short, would lose 1 point; a presentation that is 15-29 seconds short, would lose two points, etc. **Please, time your speech when you practice.**

Special Requirements: In this speech you must use **at least 1 visual aid.** It can be an overhead, a poster, Power Point slides, or any other forms of visual aids as described in your book. Be sure that it illustrates a key point of your speech. The images and text must be large enough to read at the back of the room. A transparency made from normal 12-pt type is not acceptable. You may use handouts, but they do not count as visual aids. Your visual aid must be integrated into your speech. It is insufficient to hold it up at the end and say, "Oh yeah, here's my visual aid." Refer to your book for details about visual aids. Due to logistical problems, resource shortages, and the frequent lack of interdepartmental assistance around the university, the presence of a computer projector and other technology in the classroom is not guaranteed.

<u>NOTE:</u> Limit your notes to **<u>your instructor's requirements</u>**. Include only KEY WORDS to prompt your thinking on notes. Do not write out whole sections (or the entire presentation) on your notes. Reading your speech will result in a deduction. An excessive number of notecards will also be penalized. If you choose to ignore this advice, expect to be penalized 5 points.

Submit the following items to your instructor on the day of your presentation:

- ❑ Instructor's Evaluation for the Informative Presentation
- ❑ Presentation notes (place these in the folder following your presentation)
- ❑ Printouts of visual aids (these may be full slides or "handouts")
- ❑ See your instructor to determine if additional items should be included in your folder.

Points Possible	Informative Presentation	60
	Self-Assessment	5
Total Points Possible		65

Content

1. Focus clear - Myers Briggs Pers. Test can be used in all lives + is reliable
   - My thesis was clear
   - I gave main points of speech - Why made, what the prs mean + how to use in life
2. Gave clear explanation of my topic to the aud.

Organiz

1. Very organized - slides conveyed the 3 parts
   - history, test, + personal
   ~~Speech was conversational but stumbled sometimes~~
   ~~tried to talk~~ helped me b/w topics but felt unnatural to me
2. Transitions ~~were natural but sometimes~~

Delivery

1. Speech was conv. but stumbled sometimes b/c tried to talk slowly
   - seems a bit rehearsed but mostly memorized + performed well
2. ~~projected voice well~~, had good eye contacts
   - need imprvmt on face + gestures
3. Volume + inflections were good + effective.
   difficulty when I stumbled + started my sent. over agin
   speed + tone was good! tried to ctrl speed, tone was informative
   pauses b/w topics + in/in diff elements of test   & prof.
4. Delivery made msg. a bit diff to pay attention to
                    - concluding sent was good ending

Overall

sounding natural, being more conf w/ transitions

relax + not be nervous
- seem conf. but vanna test

Practice transitions + reciting to audience
   - make notes of what to improve
   - practice nonverb. gestures

Self-Assessment of Informative Presentation

The purpose of this evaluation is to reflect on the importance of informative speaking and to apply it to your personal experience with this assignment. **You must view the videotape of your presentation before writing this essay.** You are to write a 2-3 page evaluation essay that assesses the performance of your informative presentation. This essay should be typed and double-spaced, using a standard 12 point font (with 1" margins). Please **do not** exceed the 3 page maximum. See your instructor for the due date of this assignment.

2-3 pgs, double-spaced, 12 pt. font

Instructions

❑ Go to the CMA Instructional Media Center. This facility is located in CMA 5-114A and is open Mon–Thurs 7:45–6:30, Fri 7:45–5:00, and Sat & Sun 12:00–6:00. You can reach them at 471-3419.

❑ Once in the lab, ask to view your speech on the tape: Know your instructor's name and the date on which you gave your informative presentation.

❑ Inside the tape case should be a list of speakers to help you find yourself on the tape (if not, refer to the speaking order to find yourself).

❑ Find an available space to view the tape. (The IMC is equipped with several viewing stations. Ask the staff for assistance if necessary.)

❑ Find yourself on the tape (based on the list) and watch the video of yourself speaking.

The essay should include an introduction, body, and conclusion and must include specific examples to support each argument. Answer the questions below. You may need to watch yourself multiple times to fully answer the questions. This assignment is worth **5 points**.

um III

why made, how, what they mean + how to use it

intro - main points ✓ stumbled on last pt
body - kept starting over sent. tried to talk slow but made me mess up seems rehearsed but conversational for most part good transitions, did not read straight off paper
conc. - stopped completely to refer to notes w/ stumbling

Questions To Consider

more up at concl.

1. **Content:** *good ending*

   ❑ Do you think that the focus of your speech was clear to your audience? How did you convey this focus? (e.g., Was your thesis statement clearly identifiable when spoken? Did you preview your main points?)

   ❑ Given that this was an informative speech, did you successfully and clearly convey a sense of your topic to your audience? How so?

2. **Organization:**

   ❑ How well organized was your speech? Was the organization apparent to the audience, or was it only evident to you on paper? Did your speech flow naturally, or was it choppy (e.g., signposts and transitions, or sudden changes between main points)?

3. **Delivery:**

   ❑ How conversational were you? Did it seem like you read, memorized, or performed your speech? How so?

   ❑ What aspects of your nonverbal delivery—gestures, eye contact, facial expressions, etc.—were most effective? What aspects of that delivery need improvement?

   ❑ What aspects of your vocal delivery—speed, tone, pauses, variations in inflection, etc.—made you easily understood and pleasant to listen to? What about your voice impairs your clarity or makes you difficult to listen to?

   ❑ What impact did your delivery have on the content of your message?

4. **Overall:**

   ❑ Based on this viewing, what one thing do you think you need most work on to improve your presentation skills? What will you do to achieve that improvement?

Peer Evaluation Informative

Speaker: _____

Topic: _____

1. **Organization**. How organized was the speaker? Were they easy to follow? Did they transition effectively? Could you detect discrete shifts between Intro and Body, Body and Conclusions?

5	4	3	2	1
extremely				challenge
organized				to follow

What do think were their main points?

2. **Content**. How well did the speaker *develop* their ideas? Did you learn a lot about each of the main ideas they shared?

5	4	3	2	1
well				not
developed				developed

How well did they *support* (illus., facts, stats, defin., examples, opinions, etc.) their main ideas (variety/depth)?

5	4	3	2	1
very				undetectable/
supported				unsure

Name 2 types of support material they used to support their claims? (e.g., facts/stats, narrative, brief/extended illustrations, definitions, descriptions, analogies, hypothetical, etc.) *Ex:* Narrative: Story of brother's battle with autism or Statistic: 70% African American children are born to single mothers.

3. **Introduction**. How *developed* was the introduction? How effectively did the speaker *include each of the intro parts*? Did they have (1) an **engaging opener,** (2) **a clear central idea** (3) **provide relevance** for listeners and (4) **preview body**?

5	4	3	2	1
well				not
developed				developed

What was their central idea/thesis?

Eval Initials

4. **Conclusion**. How well did the speaker close out the speech? Did they (1) *summarize* and did they (2) have *a final, prepared and engaging end*.

5	4	3	2	1
well				not
developed				developed

5. **Delivery**. How effective was the speaker's delivery?

	Excellent				Poor
Eye Contact	5	4	3	2	1
Body Movement/Gesture	5	4	3	2	1
Vocally Delivery/Vocally Interesting	5	4	3	2	1
Interesting speaker/Ability to connect material with the audience	5	4	3	2	1

Comments about delivery: _____

6. **Visual Aid**. How effective was the choice of visual and speaker interaction with visual?

	Excellent				Poor
V/A Choice for topic	5	4	3	2	1
Speaker's Use/Interaction	5	4	3	2	1

Comments about visual: _____

7. **BEST**. What do you think this speaker was most effective at accomplishing? (LIST 2)

8. **NEED TO IMPROVE**. What suggestion(s) for improvement/advice would you offer to make this speaker better? (LIST 2)

a) How much did you know about this topic before the speaker spoke about it?

0	1	2	3	4	5	6	7
knew							Knew a lot prior to speech
nothing							

b) How much did they increase your knowledge as a result of their speech today?

0	1	2	3	4	5	6	7
did not increase							Wow! I know a lot now
knowledge at all							

Peer Evaluation Informative

Speaker: _____

Topic: _____

1. **Organization**. How organized was the speaker? Were they easy to follow? Did they transition effectively? Could you detect discrete shifts between Intro and Body, Body and Conclusions?

5	4	3	2	1
extremely				challenge
organized				to follow

What do think were their main points?

2. **Content**. How well did the speaker *develop* their ideas? Did you learn a lot about each of the main ideas they shared?

5	4	3	2	1
well				not
developed				developed

How well did they *support* (illus., facts, stats, defin., examples, opinions, etc.) their main ideas (variety/depth)?

5	4	3	2	1
very				undetectable/
supported				unsure

Name 2 types of support material they used to support their claims? (e.g., facts/stats, narrative, brief/extended illustrations, definitions, descriptions, analogies, hypothetical, etc.) *Ex:* Narrative: Story of brother's battle with autism or Statistic: 70% African American children are born to single mothers.

3. **Introduction**. How *developed* was the introduction? How effectively did the speaker *include each of the intro parts*? Did they have (1) an **engaging opener,** (2) **a clear central idea** (3) **provide relevance** for listeners and (4) **preview body**?

5	4	3	2	1
well				not
developed				developed

What was their central idea/thesis?

Eval Initials

4. **Conclusion**. How well did the speaker close out the speech? Did they (1) **summarize** and did they (2) have **a final, prepared and engaging end**.

	5	4	3	2	1
	well developed				not developed

5. **Delivery**. How effective was the speaker's delivery?

	Excellent				Poor
Eye Contact	5	4	3	2	1
Body Movement/Gesture	5	4	3	2	1
Vocally Delivery/Vocally Interesting	5	4	3	2	1
Interesting speaker/Ability to connect material with the audience	5	4	3	2	1

Comments about delivery: _____

6. **Visual Aid**. How effective was the choice of visual and speaker interaction with visual?

	Excellent				Poor
V/A Choice for topic	5	4	3	2	1
Speaker's Use/Interaction	5	4	3	2	1

Comments about visual: _____

7. **BEST**. What do you think this speaker was most effective at accomplishing? (LIST 2)

8. **NEED TO IMPROVE**. What suggestion(s) for improvement/advice would you offer to make this speaker better? (LIST 2)

a) How much did you know about this topic before the speaker spoke about it?

	0	1	2	3	4	5	6	7	
	knew nothing								Knew a lot prior to speech

b) How much did they increase your knowledge as a result of their speech today?

	0	1	2	3	4	5	6	7	
	did not increase knowledge at all								Wow! I know a lot now

Peer Evaluation Informative

Speaker: _____

Topic: _____

1. **Organization.** How organized was the speaker? Were they easy to follow? Did they transition effectively? Could you detect discrete shifts between Intro and Body, Body and Conclusions?

5	4	3	2	1
extremely				challenge
organized				to follow

What do think were their main points?

2. **Content.** How well did the speaker *develop* their ideas? Did you learn a lot about each of the main ideas they shared?

5	4	3	2	1
well				not
developed				developed

How well did they *support* (illus., facts, stats, defin., examples, opinions, etc.) their main ideas (variety/depth)?

5	4	3	2	1
very				undetectable/
supported				unsure

Name 2 types of support material they used to support their claims? (e.g., facts/stats, narrative, brief/extended illustrations, definitions, descriptions, analogies, hypothetical, etc.) **Ex:** Narrative: Story of brother's battle with autism or Statistic: 70% African American children are born to single mothers.

3. **Introduction.** How *developed* was the introduction? How effectively did the speaker *include each of the intro parts*? Did they have (1) an **engaging opener,** (2) **a clear central idea** (3) **provide relevance** for listeners and (4) **preview body**?

5	4	3	2	1
well				not
developed				developed

What was their central idea/thesis?

Eval Initials

4. **Conclusion**. How well did the speaker close out the speech? Did they (1) *summarize* and did they (2) have *a final, prepared and engaging end*.

5	4	3	2	1
well				not
developed				developed

5. **Delivery**. How effective was the speaker's delivery?

	Excellent				Poor
Eye Contact	5	4	3	2	1
Body Movement/Gesture	5	4	3	2	1
Vocally Delivery/Vocally Interesting	5	4	3	2	1
Interesting speaker/Ability to connect material with the audience	5	4	3	2	1

Comments about delivery: _____

6. **Visual Aid**. How effective was the choice of visual and speaker interaction with visual?

	Excellent				Poor
V/A Choice for topic	5	4	3	2	1
Speaker's Use/Interaction	5	4	3	2	1

Comments about visual: _____

7. **BEST**. What do you think this speaker was most effective at accomplishing? (LIST 2)

8. **NEED TO IMPROVE**. What suggestion(s) for improvement/advice would you offer to make this speaker better? (LIST 2)

a) How much did you know about this topic before the speaker spoke about it?

0	1	2	3	4	5	6	7
knew							Knew a lot prior to speech
nothing							

b) How much did they increase your knowledge as a result of their speech today?

0	1	2	3	4	5	6	7
did not increase							Wow! I know a lot now
knowledge at all							

Notes

CHAPTER 16

Speaking to Persuade

by Timothy Steffensmeier

Objectives

After studying Chapter 16, you should be able to do the following:

☐ Gain a general understanding of the history of persuasion studies.
☐ Understanding the significance of ethics in persuasion.
☐ Determine the level at which your presentation aims to influence.
☐ Learn how to create a persuasive presentation.
☐ Acquire a toolbox of organizational patterns for propositions of fact, value, and policy.

Key Terms

TERM	DEFINITION
attitude	A learned disposition of feeling toward something.
belief	An understanding that something is true or false.
cognitive dissonance	A state of conflicting thoughts or emotions that produces tension that a person works to reduce.
criteria	Bases on which judgments are made.
Maslow's Hierarchy of Needs	Suggests that there are physiological, safety, social, self-esteem, and self-actualization needs that people desire to have fulfilled.
Monroe's Motivated Sequence	Attention, need, satisfaction, visualization, and action.
persuasion	The process of influence.
question of fact	Determines whether an issue exists (it is real?).
question of policy	Determines whether or not an issue is governed by a policy that should be implemented or changed.
question of value	Determines whether an issue is important or relevant and why.
rhetoric	Discovering the available means of persuasion in any given situation.
Statis theory	From the Greek, "stand," a way of asking questions to determine the main issue of an argument or debate.
target audience	Listeners you most want to influence.
veil of ignorance	Means of "shielding" your eyes from things that might bias you against an argument (e.g., race, gender, religion, etc.).
value	A deeply felt, ethical stance toward something.

Introduction

It has been said, you give a person a fish and she will not starve for a day. Teach a person how to fish and she will not starve for her entire life. A third statement might be added to this maxim: If you convince people to search for alternative food sources, their community will endure when all the fish are gone. At the heart of this dictum is the power of persuasion.

Persuasion provides a tool to create, mold, sustain, and destroy environments and relationships using language. This is a remarkable skill. While you may not be in the habit of thinking of yourself as an agent, a person who can bring about movement, you have been influencing others for years. Since the day you used that shriek to get one more spoon of mashed peas, you have been using a form of persuasion. While people persuade, often without a clue of how or why the process works, an understanding of persuasion provides the tools necessary to create or detect persuasion at work in your everyday life. An understanding of what persuasion is and how it works may better equip you to function and move within your environment—to be an agent.

"To teach is a necessity, to please is a sweetness, to persuade is a victory." This statement, made famous by the ancient Roman statesmen and orator, Cicero, identifies persuasion as the speaker's loftiest goal. While presentations sometimes inform (teach) and other times entertain (please) audiences, those speeches that persuade have been the primary focus of attention for over two millennia. Historically, the study of persuasion (traditionally referred to as rhetoric) has been of particular interest to people involved in political, judicial, and religious arenas. This chapter applies the knowledge from persuasion's rich history and the findings of contemporary research to the presentations you will likely find yourself preparing and delivering throughout your life. Persuasion is at work when addressing your local city council, pitching your ideas in the work place, or asserting your arguments in the classroom. The victory in these presentations is a result of your skill in influencing your audiences, and influencing them in an ethical manner.

> "Persuasion provides a tool to create, mold, sustain, and destroy environments and relationships using language."

This chapter begins by establishing a working definition of persuasion. Special attention is given to the historical and ethical considerations surrounding persuasive presentations. With a definition established, three types of persuasion and various levels of influence are used to make distinctions among persuasive presentations. We focus here on the strategy of using motivation to persuade your audience. From here the chapter concentrates on the invention and arrangement of your presentation.

Defining Persuasion

The study of persuasion has a rich history dating back to the ancient Greeks. Some 2500 years ago the Greeks were working to create, sculpt, and sustain city-states that functioned as democracies. A group of traveling teachers, called Sophists, believed it was important to train people on how to persuade an audience. The idea behind this training was that people needed to understand how to use and assert their voice to sustain a democratic state. These Sophists were teachers of what has come to be known as rhetoric. Today, our understanding of rhetoric has been influenced greatly by the philosopher Aristotle's treatise, *On Rhetoric*. In this text, Aristotle defines rhetoric as "the faculty of observing in any given case the available means of persuasion." In other words, rhetoric works to understand how human beings use language to influence one another. From this perspective, persuasion is defined as "the process of influence."

> ". . . rhetoric works to understand how human beings use language to influence one another."

> ## "The goal of a persuasive message is adoption of some idea by audience members."

During the 20th century, persuasion theories expanded greatly through study and use. The social sciences became interested in how and why attitudes and behaviors change. These researchers work to understand what message variables make a statement persuasive. For example, do statistics persuade audiences better than stories? Do guilt and fear convince people to change their behaviors? By asking these questions, social scientists view persuasion as a campaign. This approach focuses on the effects of a persuasive message. A source (speaker) uses a message in hopes that a receiver (audience) will change their attitude or behavior. The goal of a persuasive message is adoption of some idea by audience members.

Media Box

You hear the term "rhetoric" used in political debates, talk shows and news. What are the connotations of the term in these settings?

The definition of rhetoric has evolved over time. Visit this chapter's folder in your Chapter Media Contents online. Check out the history of "scholarly definitions of rhetoric."

How do you define the term?

Although rhetoric and the social sciences approach persuasion from different angles, they both are interested in the process of influence. Beyond these researchers, many people today are interested in persuasion. And this should be of no surprise to people raised in a mass-mediated culture saturated with advertising, political pundits, and telemarketing pitches. Wallace Fotheringham sums up the significance of the interest in persuasion as "In a sense persuasion is not a field a person might go into, or a "subject" he may decide "to take up" or not. Rather, it is part of living, the most sanctioned means by which one tries to influence others. It is a major means of satisfying a need to deal with one's environment" (1966, p. xi). In line with Fotheringham, you likely will call on persuasion to deal with your community, job, or family members. However, your success in persuasion involves more than delivering a speech that changes the audience's attitudes or behaviors. The primary question to consider is one of judgment: How are you going to judge the value, merit, and usefulness of a persuasive presentation?

Ethical Stances

Ethics are a significant aspect of the debate involving the proper definition, place, and study of persuasion. As you may remember from Chapter 3, ethic refers to those questions, answers, and actions that deal with values or moral conduct. Ethics are an important dimension to consider because of the power associated with persuasion. Persuasion involves the power to influence another. Though much good can result from persuasion, like the Civil Rights movement, the ability to persuade can be employed for inhumane purposes. One only needs a cursory understanding of the past century to realize that persuasion, in the wrong hands or from the wrong mouth, can result in suppression and horrific violence.

> ## "Ethics are an important dimension to consider because of the power associated with persuasion."

Using actions and words to persuade.

Quintilian, a famous Greek rhetorician, is best known for his aphorism on ethical public speaking: "The good man speaking well." A persuasive presentation for Quintilian is ethical if two conditions are met: (1) The speech was appropriate for the occasion; and (2) the speaker lives the actions he or she advocates. Simply, speakers should walk the talk. A "good" speech is impossible without a speaker that lives a "good" life.

Imagine you are presenting at a city council meeting urging council members to establish policies to conserve energy. Using Quintilian's stance, the speech not only needs to be honest and appropriate, your daily actions must reflect the key tenants of your message. Thus, driving a Hummer that gets six miles to the gallon to the energy conservation meeting, and then refusing to examine alternative fuel sources because the research requires funding, contradicts the persuasive message you are advocating. Technically, the speech is sound and appropriate for the occasion, but your actions make this an unethical presentation.

Relationship with the audience

Another ethical position involves the attitude of the speaker toward the audience. A contemporary ethicist, Martin Buber, urges you as the speaker to treat the audience as if you are involved in an "I-Thou" relationship. By this he means developing and delivering your speech with the audience's best interests in mind. The speaker (the "I") develops a relationship with the audience (the "thou"). This is contrary to a speaking model that views the speaker/audience relationship as "I-it." In the "I-it" setting, the speaker is speaking *at* the audience and not *with* them. Buber's ethical stance ("I-Thou") considers the persuasive presentation to be more like a conversation. The conversational approach to presenting is referred to as "dialogic." When persuading, a speaker should enter into a dialogue with the audience. Granted, the audience may not have the chance to verbally respond like one would in a conversation, but you should invent and deliver your speech as if you were involved in a dialogue with members of the audience. Buber's approach shifts the style of public speaking from speaking *at* the masses to speaking *with* other individuals.

This ethical approach seems logical when working to persuade friends that a designated driver should be selected before you head to 6th Street for a late night of club hopping. You approach and deliver the persuasive message like a dialogue that is common among friends with their best interests in mind. Your message might begin by emphasizing how much fun the night will be at the Chuggin' Monkey, move on to state that police are out in droves because it is Saturday night, articulate the dangers of driving under the influence of alcohol, and suggest that a designated driver or a cab would keep everyone safe and out of jail. This example makes the "I-Thou" approach seems obvious. However, think about Buber's approach when developing a persuasive presentation to sell nachos during college football championship game. This is a situation where a target message is developed for the masses. The relationship between the speaker (seller) and audience (target market) is most likely on the level of "I-it." This is not to suggest that the selling of nachos is necessarily unethical. However, it does draw attention to the extent that one engages in persuasion with entirely selfish interests. Buber considers a life lived primarily with "I-It" relationships, as one that ignores our ethical responsibility to communicate with other human beings on an "I-Thou" level.

> "Buber's approach shifts the style of public speaking from speaking *at* the masses to speaking *with* other individuals."

Judging the speaker and audience

One final ethical theory that applies to persuasive presentations involves the judgment that listeners and speakers make of one another. John Rawls is most famous for advocating a "veil of ignorance" between speaker and audience. The veil of ignorance refers to the manner in which people judge speakers and audiences. According to Rawls, if people are to be just in their judgments, they should aim to omit bias and prejudice that may distort their views of speakers and audiences. Rawls suggests that people look through this veil in an effort to obscure or hide traits like race, sex, and social position. The veil allows one to hear people for what they really are saying rather than seeing people as African American or Hispanic, male or female, rich or poor. While people are constantly judging speakers and audiences, Rawls's stance reminds us that for *just* judgments to take place, one must work to suspend preconceptions of a speaker or idea.

Imagine delivering a persuasive presentation to establish a new program that assists homeless people in finding shelter and permanent housing. Though you may see this as a logical and humanitarian gesture, under Rawls' theory, the gesture is not necessarily ethical. To determine a proposal's ethical merit, you would work to ignore your own social standing to see homeless people for who they are. One should take into consideration how homeless people might feel about the new policy. In this process, you might find that certain homeless people do not want to live in more traditional housing arrangements. Approaching the homeless situation with a "veil of ignorance" allows room to produce a persuasive presentation that treats everyone involved in the situation with equal standing.

> **"Indeed, ethics likely are learned and molded best through action. When developing and delivering your persuasive presentation, be critical of your message on an ethical level."**

Quintilian, Buber, and Rawls represent three positions among a variety of competing ethical stances that directly apply to the process of persuasion. Which one of these standards is correct? This answer is primarily left up to you. However, this choice does not mean that all ethical stances are equal in merit. The rock band U2 claims that "some days are better than others;" likewise, some ethical theories are better than others. It is your obligation as a person living within a community to determine the most appropriate way to make value judgments. It is important to remember that persuasion involves the power to influence. When attempting to influence or move other human beings to a particular stance, one should take into consideration the value of that activity. As a speaker, you have an ethical responsibility to the audience. The specific parameters of this responsibility are for you and the culture within which you operate to negotiate. After all this "writing" on ethics, we must acknowledge the aphorist Mason Cooley's statement: "Reading about ethics is about as likely to improve one's behavior as reading about sports is to make one into an athlete." Indeed, ethics likely are learned and molded best through action. When developing and delivering your persuasive presentation, be critical of your message on an ethical level. Furthermore, seek to learn ethical lessons from each of your speaking experiences.

> **"The "victory" in persuasion is when you can influence another person to change their attitudes, beliefs, values, or behaviors."**

> **"Persuasion can be thought of as having a mental dialogue with the audience."**

Persuasion and Cognition

When you engage in persuasion, you are dealing with a psychological process. The necessary ingredient for persuasion is a minimum of two points of view. The "victory" in persuasion is when you can influence another person to change their attitudes, beliefs, values, or behaviors. This general purpose is much more difficult than informing or entertaining. Persuasion is complex because you, the speaker, must constantly anticipate your audience's thoughts. Persuasion can be thought of as having a mental dialogue with the audience. For example, while you are delivering a presentation urging other top managers to adopt a four-day workweek, they might be thinking about decreased customer service or efficiency issues. In order to influence, you must address those questions and counter the arguments sprouting in your audience's mind. In this sense, you are having a dialogue with the audience as you try to answer the concerns they are thinking. Try to recall a speaker that you remember being very persuasive. This speaker most likely addressed your concerns or doubts almost at the very moment you began to counter-argue in your mind. Although it is unrealistic to address everyone's concerns in a given presentation, it is important to carefully construct your speech so that you can attain your primary goal.

In an effort to best address the concerns of the audience you must define the "target audience" of your message. A target audience consists of those listeners you *most* want to influence with your presentation. Earlier in the text, you read about conducting an audience analysis. In most speaking situations you will not have the opportunity to conduct focused research on your audience's attitudes and beliefs toward your topic prior to your presentation. However, you should use any accessible information to determine how you should carve your message. Jamal, treasurer of his fraternity, plans to speak at the next fraternity meeting to urge his brothers to keep costs down over the summer months. The success of this appeal largely will rely on his ability to determine which listeners are most important to persuade. He decides that he will focus on those members who are not working during the summer because they spend the most time in the house. While he does not ignore the other fraternity members, his presentation is primarily geared toward his target audience–the jobless members of the fraternity. In conjunction with establishing a target audience, it is important to determine the level of influence you aim to achieve with your speech.

> **"Persuasion research indicates that attitudes are the easiest to influence, beliefs are harder to influence than attitudes, and values are the most difficult . . ."**

Levels of influence.

Your persuasive presentation will attempt to change or reinforce an audience's attitudes, beliefs, or values. Persuasion research indicates that attitudes are the easiest to influence, beliefs are harder to influence than attitudes, and values are the most difficult to change. The assumption of this approach is that a change in attitude leads to a change in behavior.

Attitudes can be thought of as a learned disposition, manner, or feeling one has toward something. Simply, these are likes and dislikes. "I get so bored reading history," or "snowboarding makes me feel awesome," are both attitudes. While attitudes can be fickle, they are directly related to behaviors.

> **"Values are the most difficult to influence because they represent people's concept of what is right or worthwhile."**

Beliefs are more difficult to influence because they involve our convictions as to what is true or false. Beliefs provide a measure to determine if something is real or probable. Claims like, "studying history will not help me get a job," or "snowboarding is the most challenging winter sport," are primarily beliefs.

Values are the most difficult to influence because they represent people's concept of what is right or worthwhile. You use values to ascertain whether something is fundamentally good or bad. "The study of history is useless," or "snowboarding is a way of life," are both value statements.

Courtesy of Laima Druskis/Pearson Education

Let's consider the following case study, as illustrating influence in action.

Laura, a university student, is working to persuade her audience to support the local theatre scene. Part of the challenge, while analyzing her audience, is to determine if she will be influencing their attitudes, beliefs, or values. The following statements reflect her rationale for choosing to focus on the audience's values and attitudes:

> "From our class discussions, it seems that most students in the class are much more interested in sporting events than live theatre. I will have to do some work to make them think of theatre as entertaining and as exciting as a football game. I need to work on changing their *attitude* toward theatre."

> "Live-theatre is somewhat expensive, and most students I know are on limited budgets. Even if I influence attitudes favorably, will anyone actually pay the money to attend live theatre on a regular basis? Probably not. What I really need to do in this speech is focus on the *value* of attending theatre. When I attend a great theatre performance, I sometimes experience part of the human condition that not only is entertaining but worthwhile. My task is to make the audience value theatre."

> "I can imagine that certain *beliefs* are important to enjoy theatre, but I don't think beliefs are central to being successful with this speech. I will focus primarily on values, while also working to make the audience like theatre."

Laura has taken a significant step toward developing a successful persuasive presentation. Using her knowledge of the audience, she has strategically decided the general focus of her attempt to influence is at the level of values. In other words, Laura will work to persuade her audience that theater is, as Martha Stewart says, "a good thing." All topics have their own idiosyncrasies, but these three levels of influence remain constant for every persuasive presentation. With careful thinking and consideration given to the target audience, a speaker can increase their probability of persuading the audience.

Using motivation to persuade.

An effective and common approach to change someone's values, beliefs, attitudes, or behavior is to use motivation. When you think of great coaches, whether sports, singing, or life, they all share a common skill: They understand how to use motivation to produce a desired effect. Advertisers who make you feel guilty for smoking or hip for buying a certain pair of jeans also understand motivation and persuasion. Furthermore, think about the goal of a "motivational speaker." Chris Farley's character on *Saturday Night Live*, Matt Foley, urged misbehaving teenagers to straighten up and fly right or risk ruining their lives as Matt Foley had and "living in a van down by the river!" All of these people are able to exert influence because they understand a part of the human psyche: People have needs and desires. Tapping into those needs yields tremendous responses in the sense that using motivation to persuade is something of wonder and fear. Much goodness can result in motivating someone to control his or her anger, while much harm can be done in motivating someone to constantly overspend. The following two theories discuss various elements associated with motivation and persuasion.

> **"An effective and common approach to change someone's values, beliefs, attitudes, or behavior is to use motivation."**

Cognitive dissonance

Have you ever wondered why you feel "guilty" when you eat too much dessert? Why you are conflicted because you are dating someone whom your parents would not even let onto the front porch? Maybe you worry that your clothes fail to represent the real you? Dissonance theory would suggest that you, like most people, are troubled by the inconsistency between your values, beliefs, attitudes, and behaviors. Cognitive dissonance is conflicting or inconsistent cognitions which produce a state of psychological tension (dissonance). The theory, proposed by psychologist Leon Festinger (1957), suggests that people will use the simplest solution possible to establish consistency between each of these levels of influence. In an effort to alleviate cognitive dissonance, people tend to do one or a combination of five things: (1) Discredit the source of the information causing the dissonance; (2) reject or deny the new action that caused the inconsistency; (3) seek new information about the source of the inconsistency; (4) stop listening; or (5) alter the values, beliefs, or attitudes causing the dissonance.

Using cognitive dissonance in persuasion is a delicate matter because people desire consistency. When advancing a topic that may be inconsistent with an audience's values, beliefs, or attitudes, you run the risk of listeners performing any of the above five actions instead of being persuaded by your message. For example, if you are trying to convince high school athletes that extended power-lifting damages their joints, you will likely arouse cognitive dissonance. The student athletes might discredit the source ("this speaker looks like she has never even lifted weights"). They might reinterpret the information you are providing ("what we do is not power-lifting but aerobic exercise"). The audience might look for new information to refute your claim ("my fitness magazine says that power-lifting is the only way to be a successful athlete"). They may stop listening altogether ("I wonder what my dad is making for dinner tonight?"). Finally, they might choose to alter their values, beliefs, or attitudes ("Perhaps extended power-lifting will damage my joints.") This scenario illustrates the challenges of using cognitive dissonance to persuade. However, it has been shown to be a very effective strategy of influence. Cognitive dissonance will be discussed further in conjunction with organizational patterns later in the chapter.

Maslow's hierarchy of needs

Abraham Maslow also developed a psychological theory rooted in human motivation. As discussed earlier in your text, Maslow's Hierarchy of Needs theory is based on human beings' unsatisfied needs. The four basic human needs (he called these deficiency needs) are categorized as "physiological," "safety," "social," and "self-esteem." The final need is "self-actualization," unlike the basic needs that are self-serving, self-actualization involves being focused or driven by a cause beyond one's self. Self-actualization is a need that cannot be satisfied; it is the process of growth that expands one's horizons. Essentially, Maslow believes that people are motivated to act because they yearn to fulfill an unsatisfied need. The cycle is endless; once a need has been fulfilled, a new need arises.

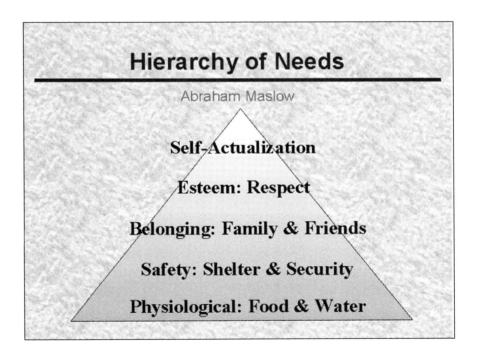

Most interesting to persuasion studies is that people can become fixated on a certain need, and this need becomes the dominating focus of their attention and efforts. For instance, a teenager might neglect their most basic nutritional needs to attain a certain body size. The logic here, faulty or not, is that certain bodies are considered beautiful and allow people to fit in with their peers, fulfilling "social" needs. While Maslow's hierarchy suggests that "physiological" needs are the strongest, the most demanding need for this teenager is "social." You should take into consideration the "need" audience members yearn to satisfy when developing your persuasive presentation. Design your message so the action you are prescribing is directly connected to the "needs" of your audience.

Inventing Your Persuasive Presentation

The first step in developing your presentation involves the creative process of invention. Ancient rhetoricians like Cicero considered "invention" to be one of the five primary areas of speech making. Speakers dedicate considerable amounts of time to create thoughtful presentations with clear purposes that are directed toward specific audiences. Part of the invention process involves determining the level of influence your presentation will address. However, before you reach that step, you first need to develop a specific purpose. An ancient technique still practiced today, especially in the realm of law and policy, is stasis theory.

> **"Part of the invention process involves determining the level of influence your presentation will address."**

Applying stasis theory.

A rhetorician, Hermagoras, made stasis theory popular in the second century B.C.E. by dedicating an entire book to asking questions about the situation surrounding a speech[1]. Stasis theory is a systematic way of asking questions about the issue you are addressing in your persuasive presentation. Stasis originates from the Greek definition meaning "a stand." During the process of invention you are working to determine what "stand" you should take with respect to your topic. Stasis theory offers the following four questions that, when answered in detail, help to locate the disagreement between you and your audience for any given topic:

- ❑ Conjecture—"Is there an act to be considered?" (Is this issue real?)
- ❑ Definition—"How can that act be defined?" (How did it happen?)
- ❑ Quality—"How serious is the act?" (Does this issue have value?)
- ❑ Procedure—"Should the act be submitted to some formal procedure?" (Should this issue be regulated with a policy?)

The above questions should be answered in relation to how the audience might respond. As a speaker you are considering each of the four questions and anticipating your audience's responses. Employing these questions can be very helpful when locating the problem of a given issue. Your success depends on your ability to determine which question needs the most attention for a given audience. Stasis theory provides a system that can be used over and over again to determine the real "issue" in a persuasive presentation.

In the following example, you can see stasis in action:

You have chosen to use the collapse of Enron as your persuasive presentation topic. However, you are uncertain about what is really contested in this complicated matter. This is where stasis becomes useful. The collapse of Enron prompted various legal responses, including extensive questioning by the U.S. Senate Judiciary Committee. Similar to the senators working to discover "what really went wrong" with Enron, you are working to discover what is really at question in this debacle. You start by asking the first question of *conjecture*: Did Enron executives and associates really commit fraud? If you answer "no," then the stance is settled; you persuade your audience that Enron executives and associates are innocent. If your answer is "yes, they committed fraud," you might have to convince your audience this is true, but you also can move to the second question of *definition*: In what specific ways did these people engage in fraud? This answer may reveal that an entire presentation could be aimed at exposing these actions. However, many times the "how" of a certain topic is judged by its *value*. Thus, the third question: How serious was this fraud? This question gets at the value associated with Enron's actions. If the answer to this question is obvious to you and the audience, stasis theory suggests that you should focus on *procedure*. An example of the inquiry of procedure: What action should be taken to punish those involved and reform the corruption? The answers to these four questions of stasis should alleviate the difficulty you might have when working to determine where to "stand" in relation to your topic and situation.

Developing your purpose.

Stasis theory helps you determine the specific purpose of your presentation topic. Part of discovering the "stand" you should take is determining the proposition you are urging the audience to adopt. Persuasive presentations commonly are categorized as propositions of fact, value, or policy. These propositions also can be thought of as the primary question under consideration. What question— whether it be a question of fact, value, or policy—is most appropriate for your presentation topic? The answer to this question will develop into the proposition or specific purpose of your speech.

Questions of fact

A question of fact centers on the reality of a given topic. Presentations posing questions of facts are concerned with whether something is true or false, or if something really exists. There was a time when people were asking the question of fact, "is the world really flat?" In 2001, the 38th Annual National Unidentifiable Flying Objects (UFOs) Conference was held in Austin, Texas. The question in these discussions largely centered on the existence of extraterrestrial life forms. Today, many of our questions of "fact" are settled on scientific grounds. The daytime talk shows use paternity tests to determine the paternity of a child. While some questions can be settled by a simple observation or sound science, other questions of fact take entire persuasive speeches to prove.

The controversy surrounding stem-cell research has recently received a great deal of media attention. The ability of stem-cell research to cure diseases is the primary question surrounding this debate. Michael J. Fox, a vocal advocate of stem-cell research, has delivered persuasive presentations to political elites arguing that this research yields effective results like advances toward a cure for Parkinson's disease. Fox's approach frames the stem-cell debate as one that centers on facts. It is important to note that stem-cell research could also be addressed as a question of value or policy. Yet, in certain circumstances, with a particular audience, the question of fact may be the most important aspect to address.

Questions of value

A question of value involves propositions of rightness, worth, or morality. Presentations working to establish the worth of something are on the level of value. To argue that soccer is the best team sport or that Neil Young is the most insightful songwriter involves questions of value. In both examples, the disagreement involves the relative "worth" of the given topic. Value questions can involve questions of fact, but they are distinct in that these questions call for a value judgment from the audience. The audience is urged to decide if something is right, fair, appropriate, worthy, or good, to name a few judgments. However, questions of value are not the same as those of taste. A speech on "why you like diet soda" is not a value statement until it asks the audience to judge the worth of the claim. So, "I like diet soda" is a question of taste because the audience must simply accept your opinion, but "Diet soda is the

> **"Stasis theory helps you determine the specific purpose of your presentation topic."**

> **"Persuasive presentations commonly are categorized as propositions of fact, value, or policy. These propositions also can be thought of as the primary question under consideration"**

> **"A question of value involves propositions of rightness, worth, or morality."**

Courtesy of Ken Karp/Pearson Education

BEST refreshment drink on the market" is a proposition of value because the audience has to decide if your claim is worthy, fair, or appropriate.

The most heated questions of value tend to explore the space reserved for ethics—the realm of what is right or wrong. A contemporary, highly contested, value question for many churches and state legislatures surrounds the merit of same-sex unions. Although questions of fact and policy are addressed with this topic, the primary area of contestation remains on the level of value. The morality (right or wrong) surrounding homosexuality is the primary issue fueling this debate. As evident in this example, questions of value often are the most difficult to resolve because they involve those deep-rooted convictions that define our sense of right and wrong. However, this should not deter you from presenting on issues of value. The propositions we develop for these most difficult questions serve as the impetus to develop policy.

> "The most heated questions of value tend to explore the space reserved for ethics—the realm of what is right or wrong."

> "Questions of policy can be based on questions of fact or value, but they go one step further by calling the audience to take action."

Questions of policy

Questions of policy are distinct from the previous questions of fact and value because they involve a specific plan of action. Questions of policy can be based on questions of fact or value, but they go one step further by calling the audience to take action. Questions of policy outline a plan of action that should be adopted or followed to alleviate the problem. A question of policy can be as simple as the dirty dish problem that plagues you and your four roommates' two-bedroom apartment. While questions of fact (the dishes are dirty) and value (clean dishes are better than dirty ones) are involved in this situation, the convincing needs to happen on the policy level. A specific course of action (dish duty will be rotated on a weekly basis) must be used to solve the cleanliness issue.

Questions of policy initially start as questions of fact and value. The determinations or judgments made on these levels are the basis for questions of policy. When something is unknown or you are ambivalent toward the topic, the question of policy lacks the impetus to arise. Simply, you cannot design a specific course of action without determining the facts and values supporting a topic. The Supreme Court ruling—mentally retarded people cannot be punished with the death penalty—is a policy question that involves a host of fact and value questions. The breadth of issues from the definition of mental retardation to the just distribution of crime sentences make this policy question extremely complex. However, the defining characteristic of this decision is that a specific policy, a plan of action, was set forth by which all states must abide.

Arranging Your Persuasive Presentation

Now that you have invented your speech by determining the "stand" and "proposition" you are advocating, it is time to begin planning the logical structure of your speech. The second major step in designing your persuasive presentation is the arrangement of the speech. Like invention, arrangement is one of the primary areas of speech making. Even more so than informative presentations, the way in which you organize your main points in a persuasive presentation plays a crucial role in your ability to influence. This is because persuasion depends on your ability to manipulate language to best present your case. You are working to align your thoughts and research, moving from idea to idea in a manner that makes sense to the audience. In addition, you are building arguments through various "appeals," whose strength is built, in part, by their placement within a well-structured speech. (Building arguments with various appeals will be detailed in the next chapter.) What is important to remember is that your organizational pattern needs to follow a logical structure that works to support and prove the specific purpose of your speech.

> "... your organizational pattern needs to follow a logical structure that works to support and prove the specific purpose of your speech."

Arrangement is similar to your body's skeleton. Where the bones provide a frame and structure to support your head, arms and legs, the arrangement of your speech's main points provides the form for your presentation's supporting material. The arrangement of main points should follow a logical progression of thought. This thought progression is the organizational pattern of your persuasive presentation. The following section will discuss various ways to arrange your speech (organizational patterns), whether you are concerned with a question of fact, value, or policy.

Organizational patterns: questions of fact.

Questions of fact are often structured around key assertions that work to prove a given proposition.

Items of logical proof

Like a "topical" organizational pattern, the "items of logical proof" are uniquely related to the topic being discussed. The logical proofs used in this organizational pattern are the key reasons why something is true or exists. As the title of this organizational pattern suggests, these main points should prove your specific purpose using logical appeals. For instance, Oscar's presentation involves the question: Are cell phones harmful to the community's health? From this question of fact, Oscar uses his research to develop three logical proofs to show that cell phone use has an adverse effect on human health. His presentation outline appears below:

General Purpose: To Persuade

Specific Purpose Statement (the proposition derived from your question): To convince the audience that cell phone use is harmful to the body.

Central Idea Statement: Cell phones are harmful to your health because they increase your chances of having an automobile accident; when discarded they produce dangerous toxins; and they have been shown to negatively alter certain brain cells.

Main Points:

I. Driving while talking on a cell phone greatly increases your chances of having an automobile accident.

II. The toxins contained in the growing mountain of discarded cell phones produce harmful pollution.

III. Scientists recently discovered that prolonged cell phone use negatively alters brain cells.

Oscar has structured his speech by using three proofs that support his specific purpose statement. Because this is a controversial topic where the "facts" are being debated, it is important to think about the order of these proofs. The order of these main points is based on the "primacy" structure. The main point moves from the least controversial proof of driving while talking on a cell phone, to the most controversial issue that involves the extended exposure to low levels of radiation. The logic here is that by introducing the audience to information that is generally accepted, they are more likely to consider those points that are more controversial.

Spatial

Like your informative speech, a question of fact can be arranged spatially. You might find that your question of fact involves geographic qualities that can be arranged with space as the defining guide. The following proposition of fact—Austin has a problem with traffic congestion—can be arranged spatially:

General Purpose: To persuade

Specific Purpose Statement: To convince the audience that traffic congestion in Austin, TX is a major problem.

Central Idea Statement: Traffic congestion has caused problems in North Austin, Central Austin, and South Austin.

Main Points:

I. The typical commute from North Austin has increased greatly in just 10 years.

II. Road expansion in Central Austin is not an option because space is at a premium.

III. Rush-hour accidents in South Austin are on the rise.

This speech advances a factual proposition by moving spatially from North to South through the Austin, Texas area. You also can imagine a persuasive speech arranged topically that moves from point to point chronologically.

Questions of value.

Recall that a question of value deals with issues of worth, value, or morality. These persuasive presentations ask the listener to make a judgment. Thus, organizing speeches of value require that you establish a standard by which the audience should judge your speech. These standards are also referred to as criteria. For example, if you are trying to convince your audience that George W. Bush is the best President in United States history, your audience needs to understand what standards you are using to make that value claim. Should one judge the President by his speaking ability, foreign diplomacy, character, or some other criterion? The success of the speech relies on choosing criteria that best support your position. For this reason, value speeches often are arranged with the first main point establishing a criteria or standard.

Familiarity/acceptance

This organizational pattern establishes criteria that are familiar to the audience in the first main point. From this criterion, the second main point shows how the question of value fulfills these standards. Consider the topic above that works to promote George W. Bush as the greatest president in U.S. History. Your first task is to develop standards for the greatest President. Ask yourself these questions: (1) What qualities or character traits would make up the greatest President? (2) Are these criteria familiar to the audience? (3) Are the criteria ethical (this includes those standards you choose to leave out)? The criteria you develop from answering these questions will be used to judge the assertions you make in the second main point. The following outline illustrates how one might structure this speech:

General Purpose: To persuade

Specific Purpose Statement: To convince my audience that George W. Bush is the best President in United States history.

Central Idea Statement: The question surrounding the greatest President in United States history can be answered by focusing on three key elements that are most evident in one recent President.

Main Points:

I. All great Presidents are honest, have excellent support staff, and shine when a crisis calls.

    A. Honest in public disclosures

    B. Excellent supporting staff

    C. Shine in a time of crisis

II. George W. Bush fulfills the above requirements better than any other President

    A. He is honest

    B. He has an excellent support staff.

    C. He rose to the occasion on 9-11-01.

From this example you can see the importance of choosing criteria in order for this speech to be effective. Imagine that one of the criterion were that the president was an eloquent and dynamic public speaker. In the case of George W. Bush, this would be much harder for an audience to accept compared to the criterion of honesty. If President Bill Clinton were inserted into this speech, you might want to replace the honesty criterion with eloquent and dynamic public speaker. However, by not including a criterion that the audience expects, like honesty, you run the risk of the audience dismissing your argument. The familiarity/acceptance model necessitates you use criteria that are familiar to the audience. For the audience to accept that George W. Bush is the best President, they must first be in agreement with what makes a President great. With a limited amount of time, you should spend most of your presentation convincing your audience on the second main point—that is, applying the standards to your proposition. This is only possible if you begin your speech with criteria familiar to the audience.

Justification (Topical)

The justification organizational pattern is another topical approach, but it is distinct from the familiarity/acceptance pattern in that it does not spend the first point establishing criteria by which to judge the second point. The justification approach uses various standards to judge the main points of a question of value. For example, Bryon is working to persuade people that the extensive use of billboards is bad for the neighborhood. Bryon decides that billboard use violates multiple values held by community members. Thus, each main point of his speech proves that billboard use is bad for the community by using a different standard by which the audience judges. The following is an outline of Bryon's speech:

General Purpose: To persuade

Specific Purpose Statement: To persuade my audience that billboards are bad for the community

Central Idea Statement: Billboards are bad for this community because they violate aesthetic and legal codes established by this neighborhood.

Main Points:

I. The size, color, and language of billboards violate this community's aesthetic sensibilities.

II. The placement and size of many billboards violates local building codes established by our development board.

The justification approach used by Bryon judges the main proposition by using two distinct standards. This approach is designed especially for audiences that have diverse standards by which they judge a topic. This strategy is also useful for complex topics, which demand that a listener judge the topic on a variety of levels (e.g., legal, moral, aesthetic, etc.).

Questions of policy.

Arranging persuasive presentations that have at their core questions of policy is more complex than "fact" or "value" questions explained above. Policy issues go a step further by detailing a plan (or solution) to a given problem or pain. There are multiple ways to structure a policy speech. Stasis theory will help you determine which organizational pattern is best suited for your policy presentation. Establishing what is most contested about your topic will determine how you structure your presentation. All policy issues involve a *problem* that has *causes* to which a *solution* works to remedy. Determining the main point that needs the most persuasive work is the challenge of policy presentations. If the "problem" is not evident, you should spend the majority of your work establishing that a real "pain" exists. However, an obvious problem, like the scarcity of energy resources, should be addressed by spending the majority of the presentation evaluating "solutions." The following persuasive organizational patterns can be identified by their unique emphasis on one of the key parts of a policy speech.

> **"Establishing what is most contested about your topic will determine how you structure your presentation. All policy issues involve a *problem* that has *causes* to which a *solution* works to remedy."**

Problem-cause-solution

The most basic persuasive structure follows the logical steps of making sense of tension in our lives. For instance, suppose you are having difficulties sleeping at night.

The *problem*: You are not getting enough sleep at night. At first thought, the *solution*: Get more sleep. However, that solution might not be attainable because you failed to identify the *causes* of your insomnia. After thinking about your sleep patterns, you notice that your sleep is most affected on nights when you talk on the phone with your long-distance partner just before trying to sleep. This is a potential *cause*. Now, the challenge is to convince your partner that late-night phone calls must cease. Your speech can be structured with the following three main points, *problem-cause-solution*. Here is an example of this organizational pattern:

General Purpose: To persuade

Specific Purpose Statement: To convince my partner that late-night phone calls must cease

Central Idea Statement: The insomnia I have developed can be best attributed to our late-night phone calls that need to stop in order for me to maintain a healthy sleeping pattern.

Main Points:

I.   Irregular sleeping patterns are a problem.

II. The insomnia occurs after we have late-night conversations.

III. We must negotiate another time or way to communicate.

This simple example illustrates how problem-cause-solution is best suited for those persuasive speeches where the "cause" of the problem needs to be carefully articulated. The solution outlined above would be quite different if the cause of the problem was "too much late-night spicy food" or "watching countless acts of violence rehashed on the nightly news." (The next chapter will address the logical steps associated with building arguments that operate on the level of cause-effect.)

When using the problem-cause-solution, it is not necessary to have balanced points. Balanced points normally imply equally important material for each point. However, in the problem-cause-solution presentation, the amount of material for each main point depends on the level of contention associated with each aspect of your speech. In the above example, you should spend the most time convincing your long-distance partner about the causes of your insomnia. The problem of sleeping too few hours is an obvious situation that needs remedying. Depending on the situation, the solution might need to be explained in detail, or it can be as simple as arranging to speak on the phone a few hours earlier. The issue here, as was stressed with stasis theory, is to determine the point of most contention, and then dedicate the majority of your speech to making this point clear.

Elimination outline

The elimination outline is best suited for persuasive presentations focused on solutions. When a given problem is generally realized, but the most appropriate way to solve that problem is being contested, the elimination outline can be an effective organizational pattern. The elimination outline involves two main points: The first main point establishes criteria by which to judge alternative solutions; thus, the second main point systematically applies each of the criterion to each solution. The final solution, the one you are advocating, is shown to best meet the criteria established in point one. As indicated in the title, this organizational pattern eliminates solutions so that the audience is encouraged to adopt your proposal. This structure works best when trying to compare and contrast competing solutions.

> **Media Box**
>
> Watch a student use the problem-cause-solution format in a sample persuasive speech. Visit this chapter's folder in your Chapter Media Contents online.

Enrico is working to persuade his audience that wind-generated energy is the solution to the nation's energy problems. The elimination outline is suited for this presentation because there are multiple competing solutions to solve a generally acknowledged problem. On a daily basis, we are reminded that energy is a scarce resource. However, there are a variety of ways to produce energy. Enrico's presentation outline looks something like this:

General Purpose: To persuade

Specific Purpose Statement: To persuade my audience that wind-generated energy is the answer to this country's energy concerns.

Central Idea Statement: Wind-generated energy will solve this country's energy problems because it best meets the necessary energy standards when compared to other energy resources.

Main Points:

I. Energy sources should be safe, efficient, affordable and non-polluting.
II. Wind generated energy meets these needs better than other available energy sources.
    A. Nuclear Power
    B. Fossil Fuels
    C. Solar
    D. Wind

Enrico's success hinges on his ability to show the inadequacies of the first three solutions. He applies each of the criterion—safe, efficient, affordable and non-pollutant—to each of the possible solutions. After the other available solutions have been eliminated, the audience is ready for a solution (wind-generated energy) that meets the standards established in the first main point.

Monroe's Motivated Sequence

Alan Monroe developed the motivated sequence in the 1930s to address those topics wherein the speaker wants the audience to take an immediate action. Monroe's strategy is rooted in the

> "... motivation can be a very effective tool of influence."

Monroe's Motivated Sequence

- **Attention**
- **Need**
- **Satisfaction**
- **Visualization**
- **Action**

psychology of using motivation to persuade. As discussed earlier in this chapter, motivation can be a very effective tool of influence. Monroe's organizational pattern uses cognitive dissonance to motivate an audience to take action. The presentation works to call someone's attention to a "need," and then provide a course of action to ameliorate or solve that need. The five steps of Monroe's Motivated Sequence[6] are described below:

- ❑ **Attention:** You begin your speech by gaining the attention of your audience. This is the same technique described in the "Introduction" and "Conclusion" chapters of this book. The attention device needs to not only attract the interest of the audience, it should adequately represent the issue you are advocating. The most common mistake in this step is using an attention device that results in the audience's thoughts scurrying down the wrong path. Arouse interest down the road, which leads to the proposed call to action.

- ❑ **Need:** This is the step that establishes a certain degree of cognitive dissonance in listeners' minds. You should introduce an issue that is at odds with the audience's current thoughts or actions. You also work to show that there is a "need" to solve a certain problem. The need step should take into consideration the personal interests of the audience. In other words, the need or problem should directly address the "What's in it for me?" question that listeners ask. Remember, the "need" must make the audience realize that something in their life must change. For the motivation sequence to be successful, they must be eager to alleviate the cognitive dissonance.

- ❑ **Satisfaction:** Psychologically, people will do everything possible to avoid living in a state of tension or ambiguity. Your challenge is to provide satisfaction in the form of a solution to the problem you outlined in the "need" step. The satisfaction step should solve each facet of the "need" step to reduce or eliminate cognitive dissonance. You must offer a clear-cut plan that is feasible.

- ❑ **Visualization:** During this step you urge the audience to "visualize" two separate scenarios. You describe (1) what the world will look like if the audience accepts the solution proposed in the satisfaction step; and (2) what the world will look like if audience members fail to adopt the solution proposed in the satisfaction step. It is common for presenters to show the benefits of the plan but omit the consequences of rejecting the satisfaction step. Since people often act to avoid negative consequences, it is important to include both parts of the visualization step.

- ❑ **Action:** In this step, you state exactly what the audience should do with respect to the solution. Furthermore, you tell them precisely how to complete the prescribed action. This "call to action" should be on a very personal and individual level. You need to answer the listener's question: What can I do today to satisfy this need? The call for action occurs during the conclusion of your speech and should be reinforced by your closing remarks.

Monroe's Motivate Sequence in Action

Olivia works part time at the University Counseling Center. She realizes that students are underutilizing the free services offered by the University. Furthermore, she deduces through conversations with friends and other counselors that most students, during their University education, deal with situations themselves that could be better handled by talking with a counselor. In addition, semester finals are two weeks away and stress management is a key issue addressed by the counseling center. Because Olivia wants to call people to action, she decides to use Monroe's Motivated Sequence to organize her speech. Here is the structure she uses to call her audience to action:

General Purpose: To persuade.

Specific Purpose Statement: To convince my audience to take advantage of the University Counseling Center.

Central Idea Statement: Stress is a serious and common problem student's encounter during finals week. Visiting the University Counseling Center, where students can regain their mental health and enhance their exam performance, can alleviate the stress.

Introduction: Gain attention by describing the strain and stress students will be feeling come finals week.

Main Points:

I.   *Need*: College students deal with a variety of psychological problems that often go ignored or untreated because of the negative stereotypes associated with mental health care. When left untreated, these problems can stand in the way of accomplishment and a sense of contentment.

II.   *Satisfaction*: Explain how the University Counseling Center can alleviate the mental health problems students can encounter.

III. *Visualization*: Describe the benefits of being mentally healthy and the increased risks associated with ignoring psychological strain.

Conclusion: *Call to Action* — Encourage people to visit the counseling center if they are in need of services or to learn about their services. Also provide a website to seek further information.

Media Box

Watch a student use Monroe's Motivated Sequence.

Visit this chapter's folder in your Chapter Media Contents online.

Olivia's speech follows Monroe's Motivated Sequence by alerting her student-based audience to a serious problem they may be ignoring. She solves the cognitive dissonance by introducing the audience to the free services offered by the University Counseling Center. The presentation closes by telling the students exactly how to receive services. If you find that your topic calls an audience to immediate action, you may want to consider organizing your speech around Monroe's Motivated Sequence.

Conclusion

This chapter worked to outline the basic definition, theories, and practical ways to develop the framework for a persuasive presentation. The chapter began by defining persuasion as a process of influence. This involves historical and ethical considerations surrounding the study and practice of persuasion. From here, questions of fact, value, and policy were discussed with consideration given to various levels of influence that are used to make distinctions among persuasive presentations. A central element in many persuasive presentations is motivation; both cognitive dissonance and needs can be used to influence people. The remainder of the chapter focused on the

---

Media Box

Watch as a student from the UT Speech Team delivers a professional and an unprofessional version of a presentation. Which strategies did the speaker use to improve content and delivery in the professional version of the presentation?

Visit this chapter's folder in your Chapter Media Contents online. Watch the speech, "Untreated Depression."

---

invention and arrangement of the presentations. Numerous examples were provided to illustrate each of the organizational patterns in action.

Persuasion relies upon the ever-changing thoughts and actions of human beings. The process is too complex and situated to be taught in a paint-by-the-numbers manner; the persuasion cookie-cutter does not exist. However, this chapter provides a basic structure to assist you in attaining the "victory" lauded by Cicero. The charge is for you (the agent) to use this "tool" ethically and productively.

Endnotes

1 Aristotle. (1990). *On rhetoric: A theory of civic discourse* (George Kennedy, Trans.). New York: Oxford University Press.

2 Buber, Martin. (1970). *I and thou* (Walter Kaufmann, Trans.). New York: Scribner.

3 Crowley, Sharon & Debra Hawhee. (1999). *Ancient rhetoric for contemporary students* (2nd ed.). Needham Heights, MA: Allyn and Bacon.

4 Fotheringham, Wallace (1966). *Perspectives on persuasion.* Boston: Allyn and Bacon.

5 Maslow, Abraham, (Lowry Richard ed.). (1998). *Toward a Psychology of Being* (3rd ed.). New York: John Wiley and Sons.

6 Mckerrow, Raymie; Gronbeck, Bruce; Ehninger, Douglas & Alan Monroe. (2000). *Principles and Types of Speech Communication* (14th ed.). New York: Longman.

7 Rawls, John. (1971). *A Theory of Justice.* Cambridge, Mass.

Persuasive Outline Worksheet

Use this worksheet as a guide to <u>separately</u> create your <u>typed, full-sentence outline</u>. You will turn this worksheet into your instructor. <u>A final version of your formal outline is due on your speech day</u>.

Topic: _____

_____

Question of fact, policy or value: _____

_____

_____

Specific purpose statement (a proposition derived from your question):

To_____

_____

What types of evidence will you use (explanatory, definition, descriptive, statistics, examples, analogy, testimony)? _____

_____

_____

_____

How will you motivate your audience (motivationally relevant evidence, cognitive dissonance, Maslow's hierarchy of needs)? _____

_____

_____

_____

What type(s) of reasoning will you use (inductive, deductive, signs, parallel cases, causal relations)?

_____

_____

_____

_____

Your organizational strategy (items of logical proof, spatial, familiarity/acceptance, justification, problem/cause/solution, elimination, refutation, Monroe's motivated sequence): _____

_____

_____

_____

1. **Introduction:**
   a. Attention-getting material: _____

   _____

   b. Benefit of presentation to audience salience): _____

   _____

   c. Establishing speaker credibility: _____

   _____

d. Thematic statement and preview (Part I: A statement based on your proposition. Part II: Your central idea statement.): _____

_____

Transition into body of speech: _____

_____

Body:

2. Item/Topic/Problem/Need or #1 argument to be refuted _____

_____

_____

  a. Subpoint/supporting material/evidence/reasoning _____

_____

  b. Subpoint/supporting material/evidence/reasoning _____

_____

  (Verbal citation, if applicable:_____)

  Transition_____

3. Item/Topic/Cause/Satisfaction or #2 argument to be refuted _____

_____

  a. Subpoint/supporting material/evidence/reasoning _____

  b. Subpoint/supporting material/evidence/reasoning _____

  (Verbal citation, if applicable: _____)

  Transition _____

4. Item/Topic/Solution/Visualization or #3 argument to be refuted _____

_____

  a. Subpoint/supporting material/evidence/reasoning _____

_____

  b. Subpoint/supporting material/evidence/reasoning _____

_____

  (Verbal citation, if applicable: _____)

  Transition _____

Conclusion:

5. **Summary:** _____

_____

  Strong closing thought/call to action: _____

_____

Bibliography of four highly credible sources (in MLA or APA style):

Persuasive Presentation About A Question of Value and/or Policy

Goal: Your third assignment is a persuasive speech concerning values and/or actions. You will try to convince your audience that something is good, bad, or better than another; and you may convince your audience to act on their changed values. Your persuasion involves an attempt to change some of the audience's beliefs, attitudes, and actions. See your book for more details on the different forms of persuasion. Refer to the evaluation form for additional details about how delivery and content will be evaluated.

Written Work: You must turn in a thesis statement, bibliography, and outline of your speech by the deadline set by your instructor.

Research: Your speech must be based on information obtained from **at least 4 current sources**. As before, you must identify each source when you deliver your speech, in the outline of the speech, and on a single page bibliography.

Topic Selection: The most important criteria for selecting a topic for this speech is that it be controversial or debatable. If there is no debate about the topic or if the arguments on one side are very weak, then there is only one side to the topic and you will not be able to effectively argue about it. In addition, successful persuasion always involves addressing counter arguments and refuting them in the course of the speech. If there are no counter arguments, you have likely found a poor topic for this speech. Remember, persuasion is extremely difficult. Take small bites. The wisest approach is to choose a topic where some audience movement is possible, focus your speech on the most negotiable values within that topic, and seek to move your audience within that narrowly defined ground.

Time Limits: You will have between 4 minutes 30 seconds to 5 minutes 30 seconds for your persuasive presentation. If you speak for less than 4 minutes 30 seconds, or more than 5 minutes 30 seconds your grade will be penalized. One point will be deducted for each 15-second interval. For example, a presentation that is 1–14 seconds short, would lose 1 point; a presentation that is 15–29 seconds short, would lose two points, etc. **Please, time your speech when you practice.**

Special Requirements: You must use some type of **computer generated slide(s)** for this speech. This can be in addition to other visual aids. Ensure that your slides meet the previously established criteria for visual aids. Due to logistical problems, resource shortages, and the frequent lack of interdepartmental assistance around the university, the presence of a computer projector and other technology in the classroom is not guaranteed.

NOTE: Limit your notes to **your instructor's requirements**. Include only KEY WORDS to prompt your thinking on notes. Do not write out whole sections (or the entire presentation) on your notes. If you choose to ignore this advice, expect to be penalized 5 points.

Submit the following items to your instructor <u>on the day</u> of your presentation:

- ❑ Instructor's Evaluation for the Informative Presentation
- ❑ Presentation notes (place these in the folder following your presentation)
- ❑ Printouts of visual aids (these may be full slides or "handouts")
- ❑ *See your instructor to determine if additional items should be included in your folder.*

Points Possible	Informative Presentation	60
	Self-Assessment	5
Total Points Possible		65

Content

1. Focus clear? Yes
   how convey? thesis stmt, main points
   visit. hrs in dorms should be extended
   discussed the issue and a realistic solution
2. How choose evidence? Evidence that supported change
   intro was common example

Persuasive Appeal?

Rationally & Motivationally Relevant?

LOGOS? (logic) ~~were~~ expensive living, other schools have it, survey/poll
PATHOS? (emotion) college is freedom

ways evid. more convincing?

B. Organization

How well organized? very; presented the issue and its inconvenience
then explained possible solution

Apparent to audience? PPT helped show problem / soln

Speech Flow? natural w/ transitions + pauses
~~choppy~~

Org. strategy help persuasive quality? displayed problem
that made students aware of the issue.
then the solution was realistic but agreeable

Delivery

Conversational? awkward bc tried to avoid fillers
(read, mem, performed) a bit memorized + kept referring to notes

Nonverbal? Effective — eye contact
Need improvement — body kept moving, no hand motions

Vocal Delivery? Pleasant — speed, tone assertive
Impaired — not as much variation as normally have

Impact on content of msg?

Overall — Persuaded the aud? Yes because most students + R.A's
agree with the reasons to ~~change~~ guest hours.

Self-Assessment of Persuasive Presentation

The purpose of this evaluation is to reflect on the importance of informative speaking and to apply it to your personal experience with this assignment. **You must view the videotape of your presentation before writing this essay.** You are to write a 2–3 page evaluation essay that assesses the performance of your informative presentation. This essay should be typed and double-spaced, using a standard 12 point font (with 1" margins). Please **do not** exceed the 3 page maximum. See your instructor for the due date of this assignment.

Instructions

- ❏ Go to the CMA Instructional Media Center. This facility is located in CMA 5-114A and is open Mon–Thurs 7:45–6:30, Fri 7:45–5:00, and Sat & Sun 12:00–6:00. You can reach them at 471-3419.
- ❏ Once in the lab, ask to view your speech on the tape: Know your instructor's name and the date on which you gave your informative presentation.
- ❏ Inside the tape case should be a list of speakers to help you find yourself on the tape (if not, refer to the speaking order to find yourself).
- ❏ Find an available space to view the tape. (The IMC is equipped with several viewing stations. Ask the staff for assistance if necessary.)
- ❏ Find yourself on the tape (based on the list) and watch the video of yourself speaking.

The essay should include an introduction, body, and conclusion and must include specific examples to support each argument. Answer the questions below. You may need to watch yourself multiple times to fully answer the questions. This assignment is worth **5 points**. *catchy intro*
nervous in beg. - pertains to everyone
many good reasons - adults, tired RAs, exp living
solution - still guest policy, quiet hrs, roommate, safer, other school have it

Questions To Consider

1. **Content:**
   - ❏ Do you think that the focus of your speech was clear to your audience? How did you convey this focus? (e.g., Was your thesis statement clearly identifiable when spoken? Did you preview your main points?)
   - ❏ Given that this was a persuasive presentation, how did you choose your evidence? Explain its persuasive appeal. Was it rationally and motivationally relevant? How so? In what ways did you appeal to logos *and* to pathos? Are there ways your evidence could have been more convincing?

2. **Organization:**
   - ❏ How well organized was your speech? Was the organization apparent to the audience, or was it only evident to you on paper? Did your speech flow naturally, or was it choppy (e.g., signposts and transitions, or sudden changes between main points)?
   - ❏ In what ways did your organizational strategy contribute to the persuasive quality of your presentation?

3. **Delivery:**
   - ❏ How conversational were you? Did it seem like you read, memorized, or performed your speech? How so?
   - ❏ What aspects of your nonverbal delivery—gestures, eye contact, facial expressions, etc.—were most effective? What aspects of that delivery need improvement?
   - ❏ What aspects of your vocal delivery—speed, tone, pauses, variations in inflection, etc.—made you easily understood and pleasant to listen to? What about your voice impairs your clarity or makes you difficult to listen to?
   - ❏ What impact did your delivery have on the content of your message?

4. **Overall:**
   - ❏ Based on this viewing, do you feel you persuaded your audience? How so?

Review of Preparation Outline and Speaking Outline

Name: _____

Please turn this form, with your instructor evaluation form, final draft of your preparation outline and your bibliography, in to your instructor on the day that you present.

Preparation Outline

_____ Typed

_____ Final draft form (no typos, grammatical usage or mechanical errors)

_____ States specific purpose of the speech on a separate line at the top of the page prior to the outline

_____ Identifies the thesis/central idea on a separate line at the top of the page after the specific purpose and before the outline

_____ Restates the "central idea" again as an integrated portion of the

        _____ introduction

        _____ conclusion

_____ Labels the Introduction, Body and Conclusion

_____ Uses a consistent pattern of symbolization and indentation to demonstrate mastery of logical division of ideas

_____ States main point, sub-points and connectives as complete sentences

        _____ Has appropriate number and arrangement of main points as per assignment

_____ Uses only one sentence per main point, sub-point, or sub-sub-point, etc.

_____ Labels transitions, internal summaries and internal previews

_____ Attaches a bibliography (no bibliography = automatic zero)

        _____ Proper format (MLA, APA, Chicago or other approved form)

        _____ Cites the minimum number of sources required

_____ References sources in the text of the outline

_____ Gives speech a title

Speaking Outline

_____ Key-Word Only (unless otherwise stated by instructor)

_____ Brief (see instructors for details: there may be limits on the number of note cards or pieces of paper you're allowed to use while presenting)

Deficiencies?

_____ (subtract this number from the speech grade)

Peer Evaluation Persuasive

Speaker's Name:_____

Topic:_____

1. **Claim.** What is the speaker's thesis / conclusion / main argument?_____
_____

2. Is their conclusion a Proposition of: FACT   VALUE   POLICY

3. **Organization.** How organized was the speaker? In other words, Were they easy to follow? Did they transition effectively? Could you detect discrete shifts between parts, main and minor ideas?

5	4	3	2	1
extremely				challenge
organized				to follow

   Which one of the persuasive organizational patterns did the speaker use?_____
   (e.g. Topical, Problem-Solution, Problem-Cause-Solution, Cause-Effect, Refutation, Monroe's Motivated Sequence)

   What do you think were their main points?

4. **Content.** How effective was the speaker at convincing you of their claims?

5	4	3	2	1
Strong				Weak
Claims & Ideas				Claims & Ideas

   **How well did they *support their premises* (*evidence/facts-stats-opinion, definitions, illustrations. / examples, etc.*) their main ideas (variety/depth)? Name 2 types of support material they used to support their claims? (e.g. Narrative, definition, statistical evidence, testimonial evidence, data, analogies or brief / extended examples).

5	4	3	2	1
Very				undetectable /
supported				unsure

   What was their best piece of evidence?_____

5. **Introduction.** How *developed* was the introduction? How effectively did the speaker *include each of the intro parts*? Did they have (1) an **engaging opener**, (2) **a clear argument** (3) **provide relevance for a target audience** and (4) **preview body**?

5	4	3	2	1
Well				Not
developed				developed

Eval Initials

6. <u>Conclusion.</u> How well did the speaker close out the speech? Did they (1) *clearly review their argument,* (2) reinforce their goal, (3) provide a strong psychological unity and (4) end have *a final, prepared clinch.*

5	4	3	2	1
Well developed				Not developed

7. How did the speaker create

    a. Ethos?

    b. Logos?

    c. Pathos?

8. <u>Delivery.</u> How effective was the speaker's delivery?

	Excellent				Poor
Eye Contact	5	4	3	2	1
Body Movement / Gesture	5	4	3	2	1
Vocally Delivery / Vocally Interesting	5	4	3	2	1
Interesting speaker / Ability to connect self & material with the audience	5	4	3	2	1

    Comments about delivery: _____

9. *BEST.* What do you think this speaker was most effective at accomplishing?

10. *NEED TO IMPROVE.* What suggestions for improvement/advice would you offer to make this speaker better? (Specifically: a Content/development related concern, Structure/organizationally related, or Delivery related concern) *(e.g., Content: Speaker needs more evidence to support argument, Structure: Isolate argument more and increase transition strength; Delivery: More comfort with speech material . . . too much note reliance creates lack of connection with audience)*

    a) Who do you think was their target audience?_____

    b) What was their goal for this target audience (specific purpose/what do they want from them)?

    _____

    c) How effective was the speaker at achieving *THEIR GOAL* for *THEIR TARGET AUDIENCE*?

0	1	2	3	4	5	6	7
Not Effective						Extremely Effective	

Why or why not?_____

Peer Evaluation Persuasive

Speaker's Name:_____

Topic:_____

1. <u>**Claim.**</u> What is the speaker's thesis / conclusion / main argument?_____

_____

2. Is their conclusion a Proposition of: FACT   VALUE   POLICY

3. <u>**Organization.**</u> How organized was the speaker? In other words, Were they easy to follow? Did they transition effectively? Could you detect discrete shifts between parts, main and minor ideas?

5	4	3	2	1
extremely				challenge
organized				to follow

Which one of the persuasive organizational patterns did the speaker use?_____
(e.g. Topical, Problem-Solution, Problem-Cause-Solution, Cause-Effect, Refutation, Monroe's Motivated Sequence)

What do you think were their main points?

4. <u>**Content.**</u> How effective was the speaker at convincing you of their claims?

5	4	3	2	1
Strong				Weak
Claims & Ideas				Claims & Ideas

<u>**How well did they** *support their premises* (**evidence/facts-stats-opinion, definitions, illustrations. / examples, etc.**</u>*)* their main ideas (variety/depth)? Name 2 types of support material they used to support their claims? (e.g. Narrative, definition, statistical evidence, testimonial evidence, data, analogies or brief / extended examples).

5	4	3	2	1
Very				undetectable /
supported				unsure

What was their best piece of evidence?_____

5. <u>**Introduction.**</u> How *developed* was the introduction? How effectively did the speaker *include each of the intro parts*? Did they have (1) an **engaging opener**, (2) **a clear argument** (3) **provide relevance for a target audience** and (4) **preview body**?

5	4	3	2	1
Well				Not
developed				developed

Eval Initials

6. <u>Conclusion.</u> How well did the speaker close out the speech? Did they (1) *clearly review their argument,* (2) reinforce their goal, (3) provide a strong psychological unity and (4) end have *a final, prepared clinch.*

5	4	3	2	1
Well				Not
developed				developed

7. How did the speaker create

    a. Ethos?

    b. Logos?

    c. Pathos?

8. <u>Delivery.</u> How effective was the speaker's delivery?

	Excellent				Poor
Eye Contact	5	4	3	2	1
Body Movement / Gesture	5	4	3	2	1
Vocally Delivery / Vocally Interesting	5	4	3	2	1
Interesting speaker / Ability to connect					
self & material with the audience	5	4	3	2	1

Comments about delivery: _____

9. *BEST.* What do you think this speaker was most effective at accomplishing?

10. *NEED TO IMPROVE.* What suggestions for improvement/advice would you offer to make this speaker better? (Specifically: a Content/development related concern, Structure/organizationally related, or Delivery related concern) *(e.g., Content: Speaker needs more evidence to support argument, Structure: Isolate argument more and increase transition strength; Delivery: More comfort with speech material . . . too much note reliance creates lack of connection with audience)*

    a) Who do you think was their target audience?_____

    b) What was their goal for this target audience (specific purpose/what do they want from them)?

    _____

    c) How effective was the speaker at achieving *THEIR GOAL* for *THEIR TARGET AUDIENCE*?

0	1	2	3	4	5	6	7
Not							Extremely
Effective							Effective

Why or why not?_____

Peer Evaluation Persuasive

Speaker's Name:_____

Topic:_____

1. **Claim.** What is the speaker's thesis / conclusion / main argument?_____
   _____

2. Is their conclusion a Proposition of: FACT   VALUE   POLICY

3. **Organization.** How organized was the speaker? In other words, Were they easy to follow? Did they transition effectively? Could you detect discrete shifts between parts, main and minor ideas?

5	4	3	2	1
extremely				challenge
organized				to follow

   Which one of the persuasive organizational patterns did the speaker use?_____
   (e.g. Topical, Problem-Solution, Problem-Cause-Solution, Cause-Effect, Refutation, Monroe's Motivated Sequence)
   What do you think were their main points?

4. **Content.** How effective was the speaker at convincing you of their claims?

5	4	3	2	1
Strong				Weak
Claims & Ideas				Claims & Ideas

   How well did they _support their premises_ (*evidence/facts-stats-opinion, definitions, illustrations. / examples, etc.*) their main ideas (variety/depth)? Name 2 types of support material they used to support their claims? (e.g. Narrative, definition, statistical evidence, testimonial evidence, data, analogies or brief / extended examples).

5	4	3	2	1
Very				undetectable /
supported				unsure

   What was their best piece of evidence?_____

5. **Introduction.** How *developed* was the introduction? How effectively did the speaker *include each of the intro parts*? Did they have (1) an **engaging opener**, (2) **a clear argument** (3) **provide relevance for a target audience** and (4) **preview body**?

5	4	3	2	1
Well				Not
developed				developed

Eval Initials

6. <u>Conclusion.</u> How well did the speaker close out the speech? Did they (1) *clearly review their argument,* (2) reinforce their goal, (3) provide a strong psychological unity and (4) end have *a final, prepared clinch.*

5	4	3	2	1
Well				Not
developed				developed

7. How did the speaker create

    a.   Ethos?

    b.   Logos?

    c.   Pathos?

8. <u>Delivery.</u> How effective was the speaker's delivery?

	Excellent				Poor
Eye Contact	5	4	3	2	1
Body Movement / Gesture	5	4	3	2	1
Vocally Delivery / Vocally Interesting	5	4	3	2	1
Interesting speaker / Ability to connect self & material with the audience	5	4	3	2	1

    Comments about delivery: _____

9. *BEST.* What do you think this speaker was most effective at accomplishing?

10. *NEED TO IMPROVE.* What suggestions for improvement/advice would you offer to make this speaker better? (Specifically: a Content/development related concern, Structure/organizationally related, or Delivery related concern) *(e.g., Content: Speaker needs more evidence to support argument, Structure: Isolate argument more and increase transition strength; Delivery: More comfort with speech material . . . too much note reliance creates lack of connection with audience)*

    a)   Who do you think was their target audience?_____

    b)   What was their goal for this target audience (specific purpose/what do they want from them)?

           _____

    c)   How effective was the speaker at achieving *THEIR GOAL* for *THEIR TARGET AUDIENCE*?

0	1	2	3	4	5	6	7
Not							Extremely
Effective							Effective

Why or why not?_____

Notes

CHAPTER 17

Professional Argumentation

by Angela J. Aguayo

Objectives

After studying Chapter 17, you should be able to do the following:

- ☐ Define argumentation as a persuasive strategy.
- ☐ Understand the importance of argument in contemporary culture.
- ☐ Determine the appropriate fit of different argumentation structures.
- ☐ Learn how to use argument in presentation contexts.
- ☐ Acquire several argumentation patterns to structure arguments.

Key Terms

anti-thesis	The "other" side of an argument.
argument	A particular structure of reasoning that mediates differences between opposing forces.
claim	A short summary of the argument/statement that the advocate wishes the audience to believe.
dialectic	Ever-present tension between opposing sides of an argument.
ethymeme	A partial syllogism based on the probable with a missing premise.
grounds	This is the evidence that functions as the foundation and support for the claim.
horos	A question of the key terms in the debate.
narrative	Symbolic action, words, and/or deeds that have a sequence of meaning for those who interpret them.
narrative coherence	The degree to which the story holds together.
narrative fidelity	The degree in which the story matches our own beliefs and experiences in the world.
poites	A question of condensing the debate to the necessary and pertinent information.
reasoning	The means to process differences between opposing forces.
stasis	The core point(s) around which the argument revolves.
stochasmos	A question of undisputed facts in a given situation.
syllogism	A form of rhetorical discourse in which certain premises have been made and a conclusive premise follows.
technique of association	An argument made by example.
technique of dislocation	Comparing two incompatible ideas where one is referred to as an "appearance" and the other is referred to as "reality."
thesis	Your "side" of an argument.
warrant	The inferential leap from the claim to the grounds—the reasoning argument works like an elbow connecting the upper arm (the claim) to lower arm (the grounds).

Introduction

As Dudley Field Malone (a lawyer who defended Scopes, and was an advocate of women's suffrage and academic freedom) once said, "I have never in my life learned anything from any man who agreed with me." We live in a contingent world—a world of probabilities and uncertainties. We also live in a world that cannot always be known.

Effective argumentation can be a mediating force between opposing sides and a knowledge-building activity. What do you think of when you hear the word "argumentation?" Perhaps you think of fighting or yelling matches. While argumentation can bring to mind negative images, this chapter will describe argumentation as a positive force for understanding and, ultimately, for change.

This chapter will establish a working knowledge of argumentation and how it functions in contemporary society and in our daily lives. After exploring the definition of argument, with the functions of argument established, four perspectives on argument will be explored. There are four basic approaches to argumentation outlined in this chapter. First, Aristotle's theory of the enthymeme is explained. Next, Toulmin's components of argument are defined. Third, multiple uses of Perelman's techniques of argument are explored. Finally, Fisher's narrative theory is offered as a comparison point for formal argumentation structure. Lastly, this chapter will provide some strategies for utilizing argumentation in your presentation assignments.

> "**Effective argumentation can be a mediating force between opposing sides and a knowledge-building activity.**"

Courtesy of Steve Gorton/Dorling Kindersley Media Library

Defining Argumentation

While persuasion focuses on influence, argumentation is the mechanics of influence and the structure of reason. Argumentation is present in every part of our lives. You may talk the dealership down $2,000 on a new car, get out of an unnecessary course requirement, or win health benefits from your workplace. In each of these situations, you must structure a case for your position—in other words, make an argument. Persuasion is the outcome, but the work that goes into persuading is argumentation.

Because an integral part of argumentation is making sense of the world around us by deliberating with others, argumentation is about creating meaning. One way this can be done is through stories. In ancient Greece and Rome, people told myths as a way of understanding and giving meaning to their world. We do the same today—we have stories of success, of adventure, and of the culture in which we live. These stories structure our reality; they highlight certain values; and they make arguments about what is important. They give us meaning. We also live in a world that cannot always be known—thus argumentation becomes the vehicle of understanding, if only temporarily. This is why lovers still quarrel about the meaning of love, most religions strive to better know God, and the courts struggle over the definition of a fetus. Thus the argumentation process is all around you and consequently a skill you call upon daily as you navigate through the uncertainties of life.

> **". . . argumentation is the mechanics of influence and the structure of reason."**

> **". . . an integral part of argumentation is making sense of the world around us by deliberating with others, argumentation is about creating meaning."**

> **". . . for the process of argumentation to be successful, its participants must have a high tolerance for disagreement and be risk-takers in the process."**

Throughout the centuries scholars have argued about arguing and found that there are a variety of ways to structure an argument and describe the argumentation process. International argumentation scholar Frans van Eemeren describes argument as a verbal and social activity of reason that relates to a particular standpoint or opinion (2001, p. 2). While American argumentation scholars Richard Rieke and Malcolm Sillars write, "Argumentation is puzzling because people so rarely take time to reflect on what they mean and do under the heading of argument or argumentation . . . The difficult part about studying argumentation is keeping your mind open to new ways of thinking about a familiar process" (2001, p. 1).

In order for the process of argumentation to be successful, its participants must have a high tolerance for disagreement and be risk-takers in the process. Disagreement often has the tendency to be confused with disapproval. Because we are human beings, we often side step conflict to preserve relationships and institutional order because the presence of conflict may communicate disassociation or dislike. However, argumentation, when done with the right spirit, has the potential to create closeness and social change that could have a significant impact for all involved. Engaging in the process of argumentation is a self-risking enterprise. The most successful context for argumentation is those instances where the participants are willing to be open and change their sense of the world around them. Given these assumptions, speakers should work towards creating an environment where these goals can be met.

Rationality and reason in argumentation.

Reason alone cannot cure the human cold or sail a boat. Reason, in fact, cannot wash your car or take care of your younger sibling. However, reason can help us know a dynamic and fluid world in very particular ways. While it cannot do many things, reason is our best chance to avoid violence when conflict arises. Therefore, reasoning is the means to process differences between opposing forces. Argumentation is the structure of that reason. However, argument does more than structure reasoning, it has the potential to open up a way of knowing.

Epistemology

The question of *epistemology*, how we know what we know, has been a significant pre-occupation of Western philosophy for centuries. Many communication scholars believe that the way we come to know things is through language. For example, it is often said that the Eskimo language has a dozen words for the concept "snow." What this means is that Eskimo children come to know that snow is tremendously important to the environment and culture of the Eskimo people because of the sheer number of words for the concept of snow. Understanding argumentation has evoked the same questions about epistemology. In addition to providing a means to resolve conflict, argumentation also can function as a means to create knowledge about the world around us. The process of argumentation functions as a dialectic, or an ever-present tension between opposing sides of an argument. A thesis, or your "side" of an argument, and an anti-thesis, or the "other" side of the same argument, are proposed. In other words, the dialectic could be comprised of a thesis statement such as, "Prayer should not be allowed in school" and the antithesis could be, "Prayer should be allowed in school." Theoretically, people taking these positions will discover new ways to think about the world and how we know it by engaging in the process of argumentation over the "poles" (for and against) of the argument.

> "... reason is our best chance to avoid violence when conflict arises. Therefore, reasoning is the means to process differences between opposing forces. Argumentation is the structure of that reason."

> "In addition to providing a means to resolve conflict, argumentation also can function as a means to create knowledge about the world around us."

The Parts and Structures of Argument

Now that we have discussed the definition and functions of argument, we will now turn to the different ways to conceptualize, organize, and develop arguments.

Where does argument begin? It starts with Stasis Theory.

The first step of rhetorical argument is identifying and understanding the point of stasis. The word *stasis* is a Latin word meaning something close to "standstill" or "conflict." So, stasis is the core point(s) over which the argument must be resolved. According to Quintilian, stasis is the "fixed point around which the controversy revolves . . . the real point . . . on which judgment is given" (Mader, 13). For example, many cities across the United States are adopting city ordinances that prohibit smoking in public restaurants and bars. While pro-ordinance advocates will often argue that smoking in bars and restaurants endangers public health, anti-ordinance advocates will argue that individuals should have the right to smoke where they wish. Inevitably, one person's *right* to smoke will trample over another person's *freedom* to have clean air. One point of stasis in

> "... stasis is the core point(s) over which the argument must be resolved."

the city ordinance debate is the struggle between freedom and rights and how those concepts are interpreted in relation to one another in regards to this argument.

When attempting to resolve a conflict or make an argument, it is best to identify the point of stasis—or contention—among two or more sides. The idea is to find the point of mutual-exclusivity of all sides in the argument—or, to put it another way, at what point are side A and side B mutually exclusive of one another? For example, the death penalty was one of the most contested public moral controversies of the 1990s. While some pro-death penalty advocates labeled the act of state execution as retributive justice, anti-death penalty advocates did not (and do not) distinguish between the act of killing someone as murder and the act of killing someone as payback for a crime—both are considered murder. So the stasis point becomes "Are state executions justice or are they murder?" This is the point of contention—how you define execution.

There are three main questions of stasis that apply to the process of argumentation. The first question is stochasmos, which is a question of undisputed facts in a given situation—that is, "what are the agreed upon facts of the situation?" The next question of stasis is horos, which refers to the key terms in the debate—or rather, "what are the key terms?" The final question of stasis is poites, which is how people condense the debate to the necessary and pertinent information. When listening to an argument, you may be interested in identifying the core issues involved in the debate. One way to get at this question is to ask, "what is agreed upon in the debate and identify the issues that are not resolved." Let us take as an example the situation of issuing driver's licenses to the elderly. In terms of stochasmos, we would lay out the facts: Elderly drivers are defined as those over 65; they are more likely to have problems with vision and reflex; and they are more likely to be on prescription medication. Turning to horos, the key terms of the debate might be night driving, vision screening, and annual testing. Finally, in poites, the condensed, pertinent information surrounding the debate might be how often elderly drivers should be tested by the state to prove their competency on the road. Identifying the point of stasis in a complicated dispute is not an easy task. The previous questions will help move you closer to identifying what Quintilian calls "the fixed point around which controversy revolves."

> **"When attempting to resolve a conflict or make an argument, it is best to identify the point of stasis—or contention—among two or more sides."**

Exercise 17.1. Stochasmos, Horos, Poites.

Look at the following debates, and identify the three elements of Stasis.

A. Stem Cell Research:

    a. Stochasmos:

    b. Horos:

    c. Poites:

B. Ethanol/Alternative Fuels:

    a. Stochasmos:

    b. Horos:

    c. Poites:

C. Cloning:

    a. Stochasmos:

    b. Horos:

    c. Poites:

The four theories of argument

Over the centuries, scholars have theorized about argument and the process of argumentation. The structures of argument can take many forms. The following section will describe four ways argument can be structured or how the process of argumentation can be conceptualized. First, this section will discuss Aristotle's enthymeme and the process of invention. Next, Toulmin's components of argument will be discussed in relation to public moral controversy. Third, Perelman's technique of argument will be applied to the argument process. Finally, Fisher's argumentation theory will be explained in terms of argumentation.

Aristotle's enthymeme

One of the most important elements of argumentation is Aristotle's theory of the enthymeme. An <u>enthymeme</u> is a partial syllogism. A <u>syllogism</u> is a form of rhetorical discourse in which certain premises have been made and a conclusionary premise follows. Those are a lot of fancy words, so let's look at an example. One might say, "All living things move (the premise). Rocks do not move (the implied premise). Therefore, rocks are not living (the conclusionary premise)." In an enthymeme, there is a missing, or implied, premise (rocks do not move) that the audience is required to fill in (or deduce) for the speaker. You do this daily, though you may not think of it as a form of argument. Let us imagine that Samantha is telling her best friend, Manuel, about an incident that occurred in her economics class. Samantha might say, "Dr. Smith lectured on macro economics," and followed the comment with "then Dr. Smith began teaching the class to salsa dance!" The implied premise is that an economics professor does not generally teach salsa dancing in the middle of an economics lecture. Samantha assumes that Manuel (or any other audience with experience in a traditional classroom) will fill in this information without her having to say "and, as we all know, teachers act strangely when they teach salsa dancing in economics class." The speaker gives the primary premise and assumes that the audience will provide the missing knowledge in order to reach a conclusion. For another example, one might say, "All living things move. Thus, mountains are not alive." The audience implicitly assumes from the missing premise that mountains do not move. Person A assumes that Person B will fill in the enthymeme the same way he did. If this does not happen, there is a misunderstanding that often can lead to disagreements. An enthymeme is an everyday occurrence in which listeners "fill in" the argument for the speaker.

The audience is made complicit in completing the rhetorical argument by filling in the missing premise; hence, the speaker does not have to be explicit about certain elements of the argument. This can become problematic in instances when the implicit premise has significant consequences if not interrogated. For example, if President Bush says, "All nations who disagree with the United States are against us. France does not support the United States in the War against Iraq." The audience is left to conclude that France is against the United States because the missing premise assumes that the lack of support for the U.S.-led war in Iraq amounts to aggression rather than, perhaps, a difference in opinion or policy. Therefore, we must use the enthymeme strategically, remaining aware of the implications if the premise is not examined. Although Aristotle's contribution is one way to develop an argument, Stephen Toulmin offers an approach to diagramming an argument into parts.

Exercise 17.2. Finding the Implied Premise.

As we just learned, enthymeme requires that the audience fill in the implied or missing premise from an argument. What is the implied premise in each of the following arguments?

Premise: All people are mortal.

Implied Premise:

Conclusionary Premise: Therefore, Socrates is mortal.

Exercise 17.2. Continued.

Premise: All UT students love the Longhorns

Implied Premise:

Conclusionary Premise: Therefore, Suzanne loves the Longhorns.

Premise: Buy this stereo because it has a powerful amplifier.

Implied Premise:

Conclusionary Premise: Therefore, I will buy this stereo.

Premise: "I wanted to serve as President because I love this country and I love the people of this Nation" (Jimmy Carter, 1980 Concession Speech).

Implied Premise:

Conclusionary Premise: Therefore, I ran for President.

Premise: "If the glove doesn't fit, you must acquit" (Johnny Cochrane, OJ Simpson Trial).

Implied Premise:

Conclusionary Premise: Therefore, you must acquit.

Toulmin's components of argument

One of the most widely taught approaches to argument is the Toulmin model. Stephen Toulmin, a logician and contemporary scholar of rhetoric, proposes that regardless of the topic, arguers will proceed through a series of claims, grounds and warrants in the process of argumentation. The Toulmin model is a useful tool for understanding, approaching, and building arguments. It is a method that involves diagramming the parts of an argument in the same vein as diagramming or parsing the grammar used in a sentence. However, unlike the concise method of diagramming the grammar of a sentence, diagramming the parts of an argument is much more loose and fluid. Most natural speech, like casual conversations and op-ed articles, has missing or unclear parts.

A basic argument is comprised of three parts: the claim, the warrant, and the ground, referred to in Figure 17.1 as "evidence." The claim is a short summary of the argument, which is a statement the advocate wishes the audience to believe. It is usually five to seven words and it identifies for the audience what the speaker is clearly advocating. The grounds is the evidence that functions as the foundation and support for the claim. Evidence can take many forms such as statistics, testimony, and expert opinion. Evidence are the facts upon which the case rests. The final critical element of an argument is the warrant. It is not enough to have a claim and evidence; you also need a warrant, which creates the inferential leap from the claim to the grounds. The warrant is like the implied premise you saw in Aristotle's model—the audience must fill in the information that links the claim to the grounds. Again,

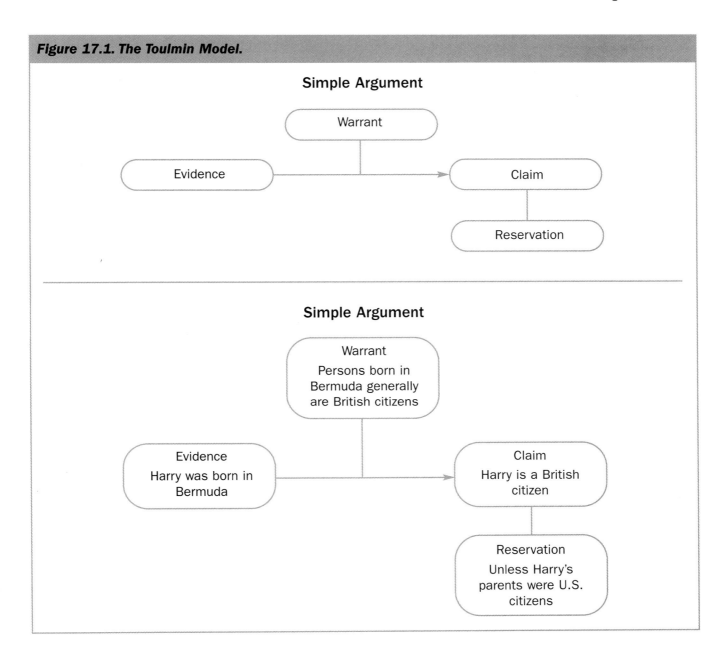

Figure 17.1. The Toulmin Model.

think of the warrant as an elbow to connect the upper arm (the claim) with the lower arm (the grounds), as shown in the following example:

Claim: Despite the tremendous strides women have made in society, they are still treated as lesser human beings than men.

Warrant: We can look at the patterns of labor statistics to see if women earn less money than men for equal work.

Grounds: According to the Bureau of Labor Statistics, women make 75 cents to every one-dollar a man makes with comparable qualifications.

This approach to the argumentation process is useful in developing your own arguments as well as identifying the weakness in others. Much of the time, the warrant is the most contestable part of the argument. It is where the speaker will engage the process of invention and make links that may or may not be true. The second place you

"One of the most effective strategies for developing a convincing persuasive argument is to create coherent and solid reasoning."

should look for a weakness in an argument is the grounds. It is always possible to critique the grounds of an argument. Where does the evidence come from? Is it biased? Is it opinion? Is it outdated?

One of the most effective strategies for developing a convincing persuasive argument is to create coherent and solid reasoning. Toulmin's model of argument provides a method that will organize your ideas effectively. Decide on a persuasive speech topic and read through your research materials. While you are reading, underline key claims, warrants, and grounding. Write down your best arguments on separate note cards. Then develop each argument by providing warrants and grounding. Choose the best arguments to develop the body of your argument. Then create a thesis statement that encompasses the arguments in the body of your argument.

Exercise 17.3. *The Strength of the Argument.*

Using what you know about Toulmin's model, critique the following argument. Is the link made in the warrant true? Is the evidence sound? Why or why not?

Claim: Congress should support stem cell research.

Warrant: The health of millions of people is more important that the ethical concerns of using human embryos for research purposes.

Grounds: Stem cells would be used solely to test therapies and cures for diseases such as Multiple Sclerosis, Parkinson's disease, and Alzheimer's.

_____

_____

_____

_____

_____

_____

_____

_____

_____

_____

_____

_____

_____

_____

_____

_____

_____

_____

_____

Perelman's technique of argument

Another contemporary argumentation scholar is Chaim Perelman. His interest in reason resulted from his work on the nature of justice. Given that Perelman was educated in the theories of formal reasoning, he found that these theories could not account for how speakers reasoned about values. Perelman constructed a new approach that would account for a speaker's practical, rather than formal, reasoning. As a result, he says that argumentation helps speakers come to know the world around them. Upon making an argument, a speaker is confronted with a range of possible ways to persuade the audience. Perelman's approach involves choosing the best possible argument that will gain traction by emphasizing certain elements while de-emphasizing others.

However, Perelman insists that an argument must begin with a premise of agreement, such as a fact, belief, or value. For example, gay adoption has been a highly contested public controversy in the past 10 years. For most of that time, the gay adoption debate has centered around the issue of who does or does not deserve the right to adopt a child. Given an argument based on those terms, the pro-adoption advocates were not successful at opening the doors for gay adoption. However, in the past few years, comedian Rosie O'Donnell and other pro-adoption activists have been able to re-fuel the discussion surrounding gay adoption by changing the terms of the debate. Instead of arguing that gay people have the right to adopt, O'Donnell chose to situate the terms of the debate on mutually agreeable grounds. So the grounds of the debate shifted focus to the lack of parents willing to adopt and concern for the increasing number of children with no families. By beginning with an undisputed fact, that there were huge numbers of children and no one to adopt them, pro-adoption advocates were able to change the grounds of the debate and become more successful at answering anti-adoption advocates.

> **"Perelman constructed a new approach that would account for a speaker's practical, rather than formal, reasoning. As a result, he says that argumentation helps speakers come to know the world around them."**

Perelman identifies several techniques of presentation that are designed to get the audience's agreement. One technique is association, which makes an argument by example. This is a strategy of using examples as a means to create generalizations. This strategy is especially helpful when proving that a problem exists or is significant. We see this principle at work with daily news reports. By accident or by intent, nightly news reports broadcast one crime story after another, leaving the audience to believe that crime is a prevalent and growing problem in communities across America. Though the series of crime stories may have nothing to do with one another, the display of one example after another may lead the audience to make potentially false generalizations about the world around them. A number of cases are provided to construct a pattern and conclusion, thus employing the technique of association.

Another technique used in argumentation is dislocation, which occurs when two incompatible ideas are compared to one another, and then separated. For example, in Michael Moore's documentary *Bowling for Columbine*, he argues that the fear of crime that is perpetuated by the media has developed a society of people that reaches for gun ownership as a deterrent to crime. In his film, Moore uses dislocation to make his argument. Although he recognizes that Americans feel unsafe, he states that the claim is largely unfounded. The manner in which the media constructs the news gives citizens the idea that crime is about to erupt in their backyard. By doing this, Moore separates the "appearance" versus the "reality" of crime.

Imagine you were assigned to construct an informative speech. However, the people in your audience do not know about the specifics of your topic. In order to make your audience aware of the breath and depth of your topic, you might

> **"Fisher argues that reason is best appealed to through stories."**

decide to use Perelman's technique of association. Suppose your topic was an informative speech on racial profiling. You might start by talking about the definition of racial profiling. Using the technique of association, your second point might describe several local racial profiling cases in order to show the audience what it looks like. In this case, think of argument as a solid structure of communicating ideas—even presenting information relies on providing claims and grounding.

Fisher's narrative theory

Walter Fisher, a contemporary rhetoric scholar, believes that we are all storytelling beings. From the beginning of time and in our oldest records of human civilization, stories were communicated to create meaning about the world around us. In fact, Fisher argues that reason is best appealed to through stories. Fisher defines a narrative as a symbolic action, words, and/or deeds that have a sequence of meaning for those who interpret them. Though Fisher believes that everyone has the same ability to interpret the value of stories they hear, he identifies two key components of creating and evaluating a narrative: First, narrative coherence is the degree in which the story holds together, the degree to which the story makes sense. Second, narrative fidelity is the degree to which the story matches our own beliefs and experiences of the world. Therefore, a persuasive narrative appeals strategically to an audience's sense of coherence and fidelity.

> **". . . a persuasive narrative appeals strategically to an audience's sense of coherence and fidelity."**

Narratives are incredibly persuasive strategies that have significant influence in contemporary culture. For example, in 2005, the Gulf Coast region of the United States experienced Hurricane Katrina, the worst hurricane to hit the U.S. in more than a decade. Many were killed, and thousands of people were displaced all over the U.S. For weeks following the Katrina disaster and evacuation, the news media reported the failures of the Federal Emergency Management Administration (FEMA): They knew the storm was coming; they did little to nothing to prepare; they were unavailable for days after the storm hit to help evacuate and rescue; they were not providing people with the necessary resources; and they could not adequately care for evacuated and displaced citizens. These tragic stories of human suffering following Katrina and the angry stories about FEMA's gross mismanagement of the response helped craft the nation's understanding of a bureaucratic government's potential to intervene in disaster. Virtually everyone lost faith in government—people felt that officials did not care about ALL citizens of the U.S., only wealthy, white ones. Continuing stories included topics such as officials have to go through so many layers of bureaucracy to get anything done that little gets accomplished, and the government is unprepared for natural disasters. These stories taught us about issues of race, class, and our system of elected and appointed officials.

Courtesy of Pearson Education

Unlike the theories of argument previously discussed in this chapter, narratives have no formal structure, but are accountable to the standards of fidelity and coherence. In addition, narratives are often more persuasive than other types of argument simply because they are thought of as "just stories." However, stories are tremendously persuasive since we are, as Fisher reminds us, storytelling beings by our very nature.

Everyone struggles with how to begin a speech. A good attention-getter not only intrigues an audience but also makes an argument for what the audience should value and why your audience should listen. Begin your speech with a small narrative that speaks about your topic in some way. As we learned in the chapter on organization, make sure it is short (as an attention-getter should be) and speaks poignantly about your topic.

Conclusion

This chapter outlined the basic framework of argumentation. Although the definition of argument is fluid and evolving, the process serves a significant function in society. Argumentation can be a mediating force between opposing sides and a knowledge building activity. There are four basic approaches to argumentation outlined in this chapter. First, Aristotle's theory of the enthymeme is explained. Next, Toulmin's components of argument are defined. Third, multiple uses of Perelman's techniques of argument are explored. Finally, Fisher's narrative theory is offered as a comparison point for formal argument structure. Most importantly, continue to interrogate arguments—the old adage "if something sounds too good to be true, it probably is," proves wise in this case. We use and are bombarded with arguments daily—our job is to make sure that the argument is sound, based on solid evidence, advances an ethical thesis, and moves people in the right direction. In a world of uncertainty and separation, argumentation is our best hope at moving forward through difference, peaceably.

Endnotes

1 Fisher, W. R. (1989). *Human communication as narration: Toward a philosophy of reason, value, and action.* Columbia, SC: University of South Carolina Press.

2 Mader, T. F. "The inherent need to analyze stasis." *Journal of the American Forensic Association,* 22, 13–20.

3 Perelman, C. (1982). *The realm of rhetoric.* Notre Dame, Indiana: University of Notre Dame Press.

4 Rieke, R.D. and Sillars. M.O. (2001). *Argumentation and critical decision making.* New York: Longman Press.

5 Toulmin, Stephen (1958). *The uses of argument.* Cambridge: Cambridge University Press.

6 Van Eemeren, F.H., Grootendorst, R., Henkemans, F.S. (1996). *Fundamentals of Argument theory: A handbook of historical backgrounds and contemporary developments.* Mahwah, New Jersey: Lawrence Erlbaum.

Notes

CHAPTER 18

The Art of Impromptu Speaking

by Martin R. Cox

Objectives

After studying Chapter 18, you should be able to do the following:

- ☐ Understand some of the historical background of impromptu speaking.
- ☐ Conceptualize methods for developing speeches in an impromptu format.
- ☐ Apply differing structural techniques to the development of impromptu speeches.
- ☐ Generate informal support material for your impromptu claims.
- ☐ Understand and implement techniques for improving impromptu delivery.

Key Terms

TERM	DEFINITION
classification	A structural division that breaks a topic into "classes" of information.
dysfluencies	Interruptions in languages, such as pauses and filler words (e.g., um and uh).
ethos	The Greek word meaning "credibility."
impromptu	A type of speaking wherein the speaker has little to no time to prepare a presentation on a given topic.
logos	From the Greek for "the word;" it is translated as logic.
narrative proof	A story used to support a claim; the story can be personal or hypothetical.
supports	Evidence supporting a claim; the story can be personal or hypothetical.
unification	Structural division in which all main points unify to support the thesis or central idea.

Introduction

You walk into your office. Before you can put sweetener in your coffee, you are called in to provide an immediate overview of the sales situation in the Southwest region. Or, you are presented an award that you were not expecting, and are given some time to speak afterwards. Boston communication consultant Cheryl Wiles recalls the following example:

> In the movie *The Hunt for Red October*, Jack Ryan (played by Alec Baldwin) is summoned to the Pentagon by his boss for a briefing to the Joint Chiefs of Staff on recent Soviet submarine activity. As the two of them sign in to the high-level briefing, Baldwin whispers, "Who is giving the briefing?" His boss calmly says, "You are." The imposing doors swing open and Baldwin is faced with the expectant faces of the Joint Chiefs.[1]

Granted, most situations which demand an on-the-spot presentation will not have far reaching implications for national security. You may be called by name to explain the significance of a historical event in a class, or put on the spot in an interview to explain a detail on your resume, or asked in your public speaking class to deliver a speech on the spot with no preparation time.

All of these situations are real-world possibilities. In the case of the on-the-spot speech in your public speaking class, the situation is a near certainty! All of these examples are scenarios where you would be required to deliver an <u>impromptu</u> presentation—a presentation delivered with very little or no time for advance preparation.

Speaking in an impromptu manner is one of the most challenging situations faced by any public speaker. You have already learned, in previous chapters of this text, about speech anxiety and the challenges of crafting a speech. In the impromptu setting, the anxiety and challenges can be magnified dramatically.

In this chapter, you will learn some of the history of speech that is impromptu in nature, some strategies for organizing the structure and content of an impromptu speech, and some suggestions for developing your skill as an impromptu speaker.

> **"Speaking in an impromptu manner is one of the most challenging situations faced by any public speaker."**

Impromptu and the Oral Tradition

Before the popularization of writing, and long before the advent of the printing press, civilizations flourished under a tradition of orality, which was highly dependent on the skills of impromptu speaking.

Effective impromptu delivery has always relied on variations of formulas and patterns. Indeed, language theorist Walter Ong posits that, "In an oral culture, to think through something in non-formulaic, non-patterned, non-mnemonic terms, even if it were possible, would be a waste of time, for such thought, once worked through, could never be recovered with any effectiveness, as it could be with the aid of writing."[2]

The time of Homer's Greece, for example, was not one in which writing was prevalent. The verses of Homer's *Odyssey* were primarily oral, and were put to parchment later as Greek literacy began to flourish. The tradition of Greek poetry was dependent on a system of narrative devices that were virtually interchangeable. As Greek poets delivered the verses which encapsulated Greek history and myth, they were able to tap into constructions of language and narrative that could be adjusted as the situation demanded change. This strategy is not so different from the methods employed by contemporary rap music artists—certain phrases and rhyming or rhythmic patterns are used and adjusted, depending on the needs of the situation. Because the verse or poetic language forms lent themselves very well to patterning and linguistic formulas, they were extremely valuable as devices of content construction and oral delivery.

Another tradition, more typical of the classical Greek training in argumentation and deliberation known as *forensics*, is explored in the dialogues of Plato and his descriptions of Socrates. Socrates was a teacher of sophistry (argumentation). At the time, it was common practice for well-to-do families to send teenage males to learn the forensic arts from teachers like Plato in preparation for future roles in politics and the courts. If Plato's dialogues are a clear description of the times, it was common practice to engage in spontaneous debates and impromptu explorations of law, society, and philosophy.

A later tradition, developed by scholars of the early Catholic Church during the Middle Ages, emphasized techniques of recalling and delivering vast quantities of information by the employment of "memory theatres."[3] Scholars would begin with a visualization of a mental image, usually a very familiar church or cathedral. Each section of the architectural image would serve a specific purpose (e.g. an entryway as a beginning point, a hallway as a transition, and so forth), and information then would be associated directly with that mental image and rehearsed. Using the method, church scholars could memorize entire religious treatises, and could recall extremely minute details with spontaneity in religious debates and sermons. This kind of memory recall was very important at a time when writing materials were fairly expensive, and where keyword searches of a digital text did not exist. The employment of these memory theatres is a popular technique for organizing information even today. Popular workshops in memory enhancement and information recall make extensive use of visualizations to aid in recall. The body itself becomes a "theatre"—aligning information with digits on the hand or other body parts to help recall information—whether important or trivial.

> "... workshops in memory enhancement and information recall make extensive use of visualizations to aid in recall."

Yet, despite this apparently rich history, very little attention has been given to impromptu speaking as a method itself. In 1985, Randall L. Bytwerk complained that "The impromptu speech, perhaps the type most often given, is also the one most neglected in public speaking courses and textbooks. Many texts give the subject a page or two; a few omit it altogether."[4] His complaint seems equally true over 20 years later. We will try to rectify that in the next sections of this chapter.

Exercise 18.1. Methods for Practicing Impromptu Speaking.

Here are some methods for practicing impromptu speaking. Because impromptu speaking is by definition unpracticed and quickly prepared, practicing with a variety of topics is essential. Try practicing each one, taking no more than three (3) minutes to prepare.

A. **Random Topics:** Write out 10 topics on which you feel comfortable speaking. Choose one randomly and prepare a presentation.

B. **Sell It!:** Reach into your purse, backpack or bag, and pull out an object. Using your powers of persuasion, sell the item to your classmates.

C. **Tap into your anger!** Write out five (5) things that make you angry (for example, a UT policy, a class policy, a pet peeve, a national or world event, and so forth), and prepare to speak on one of your entries.

D. **Taking sides:** Write down 10 current debates (on campus, in Austin, in the nation) and speak for equal times on each side of the issue.

E. **A Toast!** You are the best man/maid/matron of honor at your best friend's wedding. Using a story or stories from your friendship, give a toast honoring your friend on his/her special day.

Impromptu Method

As with writing any good essay, any good impromptu speech begins with the formulation of a thesis, or central idea. Depending on the needs of the situation and the demands of your instructor, the impromptu speech may be of an informative or persuasive nature, or may be humorous or more serious in tone. Be sure that you understand these constraints before presenting your speech.

While an impromptu speech is defined as an off-the-cuff or spur-of-the-moment speech, one where little or no time for formal preparation is given, preparation for an impromptu presentation is an ongoing process. The challenge is to select and organize the materials quickly and efficiently, and to present those materials while at the same time demonstrating your grasp of basic speech mechanics. The classroom impromptu speech will contain structural elements such as a formal introduction (a preview), some kind of division of the body content, and a structural recap and conclusion.

Formulating the thesis, however, is the central task. The following sections will provide some suggestions for attacking different kinds of impromptu speeches. Keep in mind that these are suggested approaches, and they are not all-inclusive. You or your instructor already may have an approach, which better meets the demands of your specific situation.

Types of impromptu speaking.

Earlier you were given an exercise to practice varying types of impromptu speaking. The most common form of impromptu speaking deals with speaking on a particular subject.

TIPS FOR IMPROMPTU SPEAKING

Introduce and conclude. As you learned in the chapter on organization, introductions and conclusions can make or break a presentation. With impromptu speaking, it is particularly important to "bookend" your presentation strongly with a clear introduction and conclusion.

Support. In many impromptu circumstances, you will not be able to specifically cite sources for evidence, but that does not mean you cannot or should not support your main points. In fact, because of the lack of evidence like statistics and exact quotes, your presentation may be less effective if you do not provide any support at all. In impromptu speaking, stories/narratives, opinion, description, explanation, and illustrations are all excellent ways to support your claims in lieu of "hard" data.

Organize. Impromptu speaking is a challenge for most people, but having the basic framework for speaking (parts of the introduction, body and transitions, and parts of the conclusion) in your mind, you can organize any topic in a very short time. Knowing this framework allows you to focus your time on developing the topic rather than deciding what parts go where and delivering a muddled presentation.

Audience Knowledge. A final tip is to assess the level of knowledge your audience may already possess on the topic. For instance, if you are called on in a meeting to provide the sales projections for the third fiscal quarter, you do not have to spend time detailing the history of the company, the product line, the customer set, or the sales territory—these are pieces of information those at the meeting already know. If, however, you are speaking on a topic that seems relatively unfamiliar, you may need to do some work in the way of explanation and definition.

Dealing with subjects

Courtesy of Dorling Kindersley Media Library

The subject-based impromptu speech is usually the easiest with which to deal. In this kind of speech, the student is given a subject of a general nature, and the task of the student is to establish a central claim or argument about that subject.

For example, if given the subject "teachers," the following central claims might be developed to serve as the thesis for the speech: *Teachers are some of the most influential people in our lives*; *teachers are underappreciated*; *teachers get too much credit*; *teachers have a tough job*; and so forth.

Remember to analyze your audience when establishing your central claim about a subject. Given that you will probably be evaluated by your teacher, the central claim that "teachers get too much credit" would need to be treated very carefully!

If the speech is informative in nature, you then might present 2–3 ways in which teachers have a tough job or exert their influence. If the speech is persuasive in nature, you might provide 2–3 reasons *why* teachers are underappreciated or get too much credit.

Dealing with objects

In addition to subjects, you might be asked to speak on an object. Objects are a bit more difficult to deal with, at least on the surface. For example, as you work your way to the front of the room, your instructor hands you a brown bag and tells you to reach in and pull out the contents. The object is a playing card—the queen of hearts.

In almost every instance, an object implies a subject which can be used to establish the thesis. In our example of the playing card, subjects that come to mind include gambling, luck, chance, playtime as opposed to working time, or perhaps even the wildly popular re-emergence of poker as a national pastime. Once you choose your subject, then you can determine the thesis.

Not every object implies an easy subject. For example, in one case a student from the University of Texas reached into a paper bag and withdrew a red pencil—perhaps a touch more difficult than the playing card. In that situation, the student identified the subject as "revisionism"—that we use red pencils and their like to indicate when someone has done something wrong, to highlight the error and to suggest a revision.

The strategy for dealing with objects is similar to the task of association used by psychologists—what subject does the object bring to mind?

Dealing with quotations

The use of the quotation as a prompt is perhaps the most common exercise of impromptu speaking. Quotations are vastly more difficult to attack than simple subjects or objects, and require a very different method. The following guidelines are drawn or adapted from earlier writing on impromptu speaking, particularly from the *Rostrum,* published by the National Forensic League.[5]

The first question that you need to ask yourself in dealing with a quotation is: "What does the quotation mean?" Pinpoint the definitive meaning or relationship suggested by the quotation. Remember that because quotations are proverbial, they usually won't hit you over the head with the meaning. So you need to think about it and decide its clearest meaning. The meaning of the quotation should be clear to you, and you should be able to make it clear to your audience.

> "The use of the quotation as a prompt is perhaps the most common exercise of impromptu speaking."

For example, if you are given the following quotation: "A stitch in time saves nine," by Benjamin Franklin, some possible meanings (or tags) might include: "short-cuts" or "ingenuity" or "foresight."

There are many other possible meanings, but it is very easy to identify the point of this quotation in simple language. Some quotations may be a little more complex and hard to pin down. In these instances, identify the overall relationship.

For example: "Good cheer is something more than faith in the future, it is gratitude for the past and joy in the present."

This quotation says a lot. Were we to tag its meaning as "optimism," we would be neglecting the second half of the quotation which deals with "gratitude for the past and joy in the present." Were we to tag it as "hedonism," we would be focusing on "joy in the present." At the same time, "gratitude for the past" may imply "learning."

Choosing any of these by themselves would demonstrate only a partial analysis of the quotation as a whole. You need to define the *relationship* inherent in the quotation as clearly as possible. An example might be "learned optimism"—that is, we must base our optimism on our learning of the past and our experience of the present.

Division of structure.

Now that we have identified common types of impromptu speeches, let's turn now to detail how you might organize your presentation within the general framework (of the 5-Part Introduction, Body and Transitions, and 2-Part Conclusion) that you already know from this class. There are many variations of organization or structural division.

> "There are many variations of organization or structural division . . . such as topical, chronological, cause-effect, and problem-solution."

> "To say that something is "unified" is to say that separate functions of the speech operate as one organic entity. As a strategy for dividing the structure, unification is most appropriate for more persuasive speeches . . .""

Several of those approaches have been discussed in previous chapters of this text such as topical, chronological, cause-effect, and problem-solution. Once you have mastered these approaches, your task in impromptu speaking is to apply these structures to the on-the-spot mode of delivery.

Impromptu speeches may be structurally divided into more informative or more persuasive formats. We will discuss three types of division: division by classification, division by unification, and division by cause-effect-solution.

Classification

A division by classification subdivides the major topic into separate categories (or *classes*) of thought as they relate to the major subject.

You might think of classification as a method of grouping and taxonomy. For example, if given three bags of candy (one bag of Skittles, one of Reese's Pieces, and one of M&M's), your task would be to classify the broad subject "candy." There are several ways that you might divide the classes of candy to deal with them separately. For example, the candy may be divided by color as one classification. The candy may be divided by size, brand name, or relative sweetness. Finding the *classes* held in common by the three different types of candy enables you to explore the classes deeper.

To go back to our broader subject of "teachers," you might classify your remarks under the following headings: teacher training, teacher development, and teacher accountability. Those three classes can then be discussed as individual concepts related to the broader subject.

Unification

Unification is another strategy for impromptu structuring. To say that something is "unified" is to say that separate functions of the speech operate as one organic entity. As a strategy for dividing the structure, unification is most appropriate for more persuasive speeches in defense of a claim or as an answer to a question.

For example, using the teachers example, you might start with the central claim or argument that "teachers are undervalued." You then might divide the major structure of the speech into two or three reasons why teachers are undervalued.

> **Major claim:** Teachers are undervalued
>
> **Reason 1:** Teachers work long hours for generally low pay.
> **Reason 2:** Teachers are not as respected as members of other professions.
> **Reason 3:** Teachers are viewed with scorn by many students.

This structure would be unified because each reason independently supports the central claim, and each area is directly related to the rationale for the argument.

Cause-Effect-Solution

This approach to the structural division of impromptu speaking applies the major concepts you learned in the chapter on persuasion to impromptu circumstances. This strategy is a much more difficult strategy than the methods described previously, but will give you an idea of how to apply other structures you have learned in an impromptu format.

This presentation depends upon a strong thesis statement which identifies a problem suggested by the broader topic or illuminated by the quotation. The purpose of the presentation is to show why the problem occurs (or why we struggle to make it so), what the potential effects are, and some ways that you can change your thinking or control yourselves or foster a better world.

For an example of this approach, let's take a look at our Benjamin Franklin quotation, "A stitch in time saves nine."

Subject: Foresight

Thesis/Central Claim: Foresight allows us to save ourselves from unnecessary effort later.

Preview: In order to start saving some thread, we need to understand *first*, that our lack of foresight is caused by our focus on the immediate; *next*, that the consequence of that lack of foresight is usually failure; and *finally*, that the best way to get better glasses on the future is to learn how to make educated guesses.

To see the Cause-Effect-Solution approach in action, take a look at the "Example Impromptu Speech" which follows. This speech is the transcribed version of a speech delivered by University of Texas Business student Sandip Gupta in the Fall of 2005.

An Example Impromptu Speech

by Sandip Gupta, University of Texas

In 1978, popular actor Christopher Reeve made the most well-known portrayal of the man in steel, *Superman*. Starring in subsequent *Superman* films, Reeve was an icon of strength. Unfortunately, in 1995, Reeve had a horse-riding accident, paralyzing him from the neck down. The iconic vision that people had made for him was shattered. After putting so much importance in a single vision of himself, suddenly in his later life, it wasn't important at all. Despite the incident, Reeve moved forward with his life in a wheelchair and adapted. He became a director, and even acted in a modern version of *Rear Window*. He learned that life's unpredictability often causes some of the things that you find most important to all of a sudden have no importance at all. It is this attitude of inflating value that is reflected in today's quotation by John Ciardi, "A dollar saved is a quarter earned." What Ciardi is talking about here is inflation, particularly in the way that what we value most tends to fluctuate. Focusing too much on something personally important, our dollars, often causes us to lose out as our belief system changes. To better examine this phenomenon of changing value, and losing things we believe will always be there, we should first, examine our tendency to cling to things that we think have value. Second, we'll see how that clinginess results in inflated importance. Finally we will discover how to have a more flexible open mindset so that our investing of dollars makes some sense.

First, our tendency to save dollars instead of investing them comes from the fact that we often hold too much on to things close to ourselves. We are too caught up in our own efforts to understand that focusing on saving up for a single goal can often leave us high and dry when the market changes. Our dollars become quarters because we are too self-involved. The principle of our goals being self-driven is a concept illustrated in Karl Marx's Labor Theory of value. Marx's social and political reforms were based on a simple observation of human nature. He noted that the value of an object is solely a result of the labor one expended to produce it. The more personally involved an individual is with something, the more likely that they will be stubbornly attached to it. This went so far with Marx that he foresaw a revolution of the proletariat, a class who valued their labor so much that they would invest so many resources with reckless abandon that they would endanger their lives to protect the fruits of their labor. It is this mentality that encourages individuals to not invest in flexibility for the future, but rather to save as many "dollars" of their current value as possible. The attachment created from personal goals is a highly motivating reason for sacrifice. Unfortunately sometimes attachment simply *forces* sacrifice. The dollars just aren't worth that much anymore.

Because we get so involved in ourselves and not open to understanding different interpretations of value, often times a sudden change, or inflation, causes us to miss out. Too much self focus eliminates our ability to perceive the needs of the world around us. We lose the ability to grasp objective perception, a key principle of adapting for inflation. At some point there is a revelation where personally constructed value meets true objective value, causing a disconcerting inflation for the individual. This moment can be found in Franz Kafka's *The Metamorphosis*, in which Gregor Samsa discovers that all of a sudden he is becoming a bug. Throughout his change, he bemoans his inability to fulfill his family's needs, a family who he has always believed was dependent on him. He worries what will become of them once he passes on. His obsession causes him to become increasingly miserable in his bug state. Oddly enough, when he finally passes away, his family feels relief instead of grief and moves on better than ever. Samsa was so focused on his own responsibility and his own misfortune that he could not realize how people perceived him. Instead of adapting to this sudden inflation of his personal values, he was so heavily focused on saving what he had, a past that he could not recapture. Instead of investing in a new future, Samsa ended up stuck trying to save his dollars until they faded slowly away and became quarters.

In order to combat this growing inflation, we must discover that the solution comes not in hoarding our dollars so long that they become quarters, but rather being flexible and investing. Unlike dollars, investments grow as currency grows. Instead of being self-invested, a solution is to be more aware of growing trends in society and constantly adopting different points of view. Adaptation is the key to success. The successful use of this key can be found in the popular brand Tommy Hilfiger. As a corporation, Hilfiger now makes very few of their own products. Instead they outsource a large percentage of their production that they used to do themselves. They give it to smaller clothing companies or contract it overseas. Despite their original business model, maintaining their old means of production would not have been as profitable for them. Their large profit now comes from the markup due to brand name. Hilfiger, upon making a name for himself changed his business model to capitalize on what they had working for it, instead of stubbornly sticking to the traditional manufacturing strategy that got them to where they are. Despite the success, Hilfiger understood that saving those dollars is not as important as investing them to constantly move forward.

When examining the quotation, "A dollar saved is a quarter earned," we understand that a constant struggle should be made to reconcile our personal value with what is an objective value. We've seen first, that we hoard our dollars because we get caught up in ourselves. Second, that we miss out on opportunities as a result, and finally, that we need to be objectively flexible in order to adapt. Reeve placed a lot of hope in his vision of strength. When all of a sudden that lost its value, when his dollars became quarters, he understood, as we all should, that growth comes from adapting instead of giving in.

In this speech, Sandip was given a quote from the film *Rear Window,* "A dollar saved is a quarter earned." Certainly, Sandip demonstrated his grasp of the meaning of the quotation. What is more, he uses the Cause-Effect-Solution structure to discuss the larger significance of the quote to our lives. Sandip took approximately one minute to prepare his remarks, and then delivered the speech. In all fairness, we should realize that Sandip is very practiced at this kind of speaking. Sandip was a two-time Texas State High School champion in public speaking, and not everyone will be able to deliver a speech with this kind of detail and development on such short notice.

Even if we cannot all be as polished and effective as Sandip, the reason the speech serves as an effective model for us is that it shows us how to develop the major structural elements required for formal classroom speaking assignments, while at the same time providing support and illustrations to help develop the ideas. This presentation brings together all the tips we gave you earlier in this chapter: strong introduction and conclusion, support, clear organization, and an understanding of the audience's knowledge.

> "... effective model ... shows us how to develop the major structural elements required for formal classroom speaking assignments, while at the same time providing support and illustrations to help develop the ideas."

> "Develop ... your ability to organize and draw support for your impromptu speech from your personal knowledge and experience ..."

Media Box

What makes an impromptu speech effective?

Watch "professional" and "unprofessional" sample impromptu speeches created by students on UT's Speech Team.

Visit this chapter's folder in your Chapter Media Contents online.

Support in impromptu takes a very different form than in more prepared situations. For longer prepared speeches, you will have had time to investigate your subject and position in advance to include references and sources that validate your claims, and to bolster your credibility and logic with academic research. Impromptu speaking does not allow time for research, yet at the same time it requires support for your claims.

Developing your ability to organize and draw support for your impromptu speech from your personal knowledge and experience will be the subject of the next section.

Exercise 18.2. Getting Better Each Time.

There are those who are decent impromptu speakers, and there are those who are outstanding impromptu speakers. Often, the difference is the knowledge of organizational structure and engaging delivery. Take one impromptu topic of your choosing, prepare (1) an *adequate* impromptu presentation, (2) a *good* impromptu presentation, and (3) an *excellent* impromptu presentation—all on the same topic. What are the differences between the three presentations? How did your presentation go from adequate to excellent? What can you learn from this for future impromptu speaking opportunities?

_____

_____

_____

_____

_____

_____

_____

_____

_____

_____

_____

_____

_____

_____

_____

_____

_____

_____

_____

_____

_____

Preparing for Impromptu Speaking

Certainly, impromptu speaking is a limited preparation activity. This is probably the most nerve-wracking element of impromptu! The very definition of this genre of speech assures us that impromptu speaking allows for little or no time for formal preparation. The ability to generate well-thought and well-illustrated content on the spur of the moment is, perhaps, the single most valuable skill set taught in this course.

Because no formal preparation time is given to the impromptu format, preparation must be an ongoing process—every book that you read, historical anecdote that you memorize, or movie that you watch becomes potential support material for the impromptu speech.

Learn to read deliberately. When you read stories or poems, think about what they say about people. What is the message of the story? What is it telling us to do or not to do? Stories have agendas; think about what they are and under what circumstances you might refer to them. The same is true of poems, paintings, songs, and dramas.

> "The ability to generate well-thought and well-illustrated content on the spur of the moment is, perhaps, the single most valuable skill . . ."

After you have established your central claim and determined how to structure the speech, your next task is to generate examples or supports to help illustrate your ideas.

Supports can be drawn from art, literature, philosophy, music, science, history, or even personal interest stories (just to name a few), which provide narrative proof of your ideas.

For example, "a stitch in time saves nine."

Structural Division: Two classes

Main Subject: Foresight

Thesis/Central Claim: With a bit of foresight, we can save ourselves from unnecessary effort later.

Preview: Foresight allows you to save time in two ways—first, by making you more efficient, and second, by making you more prepared for the unexpected.

Area 1: Explanation of how stitches in time make you more efficient.

Support for Area 1: "When Ben Franklin made his famous statement, his claim was one of common sense—that if you could find the most efficient way to solve a problem now, you could save yourself a ton of time later. That just makes sense. Efficiency is often based on finding shortcuts around obstacles which hold us back from achieving our objectives. Take for example the age-old Founding Father responsible both for writing the Declaration of Independence and for owning slaves, Thomas Jefferson. When Jefferson was deciding whether or not to buy the Louisiana Territory from France, he took it upon himself to find a shortcut around Congress, thereby negotiating a deal with Napoleon to purchase the vast land. The U.S. ended up paying some $15 million dollars for the property, and it has gone down as the best real estate deal in history. France needed the money immediately for its war effort, and had Jefferson waited, the purchase probably would have cost quite a bit more, and it might not have happened at all. By creating a new stitch, and using all of the authority he could muster to buy Louisiana, Jefferson not only saved many more stitches, he saved a lot of money. But TJ wasn't the only one stitching his way to greater efficiency. At the beginning of the twentieth century, Henry Ford saved about 9 billion stitches by formalizing the industrial assembly line."

The second structural area would be developed and supported in a similar way.

This style of "proof" is different from the kinds of proof that come from directed research about a topic. Support, incorporated in this way, relies upon the expertise of the individual speaker. The use of supports in this manner requires great care, however. The potential for misstatement or inaccuracy is very high when drawing material completely from your own recall.

As a result, it is important to be sure that you incorporate materials that you know very well, and that your audience understands that the material is drawn from your own memory. In most impromptu situations, your audience will forgive minor inaccuracies. If major flaws or errors of recall are present in the speech, however, it dramatically undermines the speaker's ethos and logos.

Advice from the Experts: Impromptu Delivery

By Bryan McCann

What I consider to be my biggest breakthrough in impromptu speaking followed the most counterintuitive piece of advice I have ever received from an educator. After I completed a reasonably intelligent but extremely stiff and fast-paced impromptu speech, my coach insisted that I "stop caring so much!" Taken on face value, such advice can send shivers down the spine of a public-speaking educator. Who in their right mind would encourage a student to not care? However, after some critical thought, "not caring" is arguably the most sound advice one can give to an impromptu speaker in order to improve her or his delivery.

Impromptu speaking is something we do all the time. Indeed, our most common public speaking experiences take place when we are called on in class, asked an unexpected question in an interview, or have had to take the lead in a presentation when we were counting on someone else to do it. The commonality of impromptu speaking is where the potential for success truly lies. To be sure, the constant risk of speaking coherently "on the spot" can be a cause for anxiety. However, consider the following "impromptu speaking" scenarios: answering an unexpected call, ordering food at a restaurant, unexpectedly seeing a friend on the street, or talking your way out of a speeding ticket (hopefully you'll never have to deal with that last one).

It is astounding to think about how many situations arise where we find that, in the truest sense of the word, we are engaged in impromptu speaking. Even more impressive is how capable we are when those situations arise! The ability to succeed at impromptu speaking is woven into our very fabric as human communicators. The vast majority of our communicative experiences are unplanned, yet we still find the faculties needed to prevent us from becoming a society of stammering and incoherent social actors.

The key to successful impromptu *public* speaking is to capitalize on those skills and break down that barrier between interpersonal communication and public speaking. To be sure, there are some significant differences between how you talk to friends versus a professional or academic audience, but an ability to relax, "stop caring," and just *talk* to one's audience is what sets a successful impromptu speaker apart from the others. An audience wants to see a speaker who is confident in her or his base of knowledge. Virtually all of the instances in which we find ourselves giving an impromptu speech require us to speak on issues that we are well qualified to talk about. (It's not likely that you will be called on to speak at a meeting you have no business attending in the first place!) The key then becomes unlocking the knowledge you already have and "getting over" the stress of the situation. Getting beyond the stigma of impromptu speaking allows you to focus on the more nuanced dynamics of the event—structure, time allocation, argumentation, and other variables. Delivery is little more than a matter of trusting what you are saying to your audience and allowing them to see a confident and coherent speaker.

Bryan McCann was the 2001 National Forensic Association National Champion in Impromptu Speaking for Illinois State University, and is now a doctoral student in Communication at the University of Texas.

Improving Impromptu Delivery

In general, it is much easier to understand the principles of the impromptu method and structure than to implement those principles in a formal speech. You already have learned from previous chapters in this text about speech anxiety and performance apprehension. The constraints of the actual speaking situation can be stressful—the combination of adrenalin rush, self-consciousness, and the natural defense mechanisms we exhibit when we are on public display can lead to a disruption of the speech, even for the most gifted of speakers.

It is one thing to spot the characteristics of a poor performance when we are sitting in the audience. It is quite another to avoid displaying those characteristics when we are speaking. This fact becomes magnified by the impromptu situation. Controlling nervous anxiety is difficult enough when your speech is fully practiced and prepared; that anxiety is even more difficult to control when you must be focused on developing the content while you are speaking.

The following suggestions are designed to help alleviate the added stress of the impromptu speech, and to help you to gain more control over language and speech fluency. These suggestions are also applicable to more prepared presentations.

Breath support is essential.

When exercising, any fitness guru will tell you that it is important to maintain your breathing. Holding your breath decreases your body's ability to distribute oxygen to the muscles which need that oxygen the most. The same is true while speaking. Maintaining even and full breathing is essential to any presentation. Keep in mind that any use of the voice is an exhalation of air. Complete exhalation requires complete inhalation.

When faced with a moment of panic, many speakers will take incomplete breaths. As a result, the speaker may struggle for breath at inopportune moments, e.g. pausing for breath in the middle of a clause rather than at a natural pausing point. Speakers may also run out of air during a sentence and gasp for air. The results can be compounded by panic—speakers have been known to become light-headed, and even faint. While those situations are rare, avoiding them requires steady and complete breathing.

Keep in mind that posture has an effect on breath support. Hunched or slouched shoulders, for example, decrease your ability to take complete breaths.

Muscle relaxation helps your presentation.

Speech anxiety often manifests itself in muscle tension. Most speakers can feel that tension as a knot in the stomach, though stomach discomfort is just as often caused by an increase in the activity of natural acids in the stomach. The increase is usually a natural result of the increase in adrenalin that typically accompanies any high pressure situation. Impromptu speaking certainly fits that description.

If stomach discomfort manifests itself in very sharp pains or the inability to keep food in its proper place (your stomach, that is), it may be a good idea to speak with a health professional about your symptoms. Please remember, though, that the vast majority of people respond to public speaking with similar levels of anxiety, and that some stress is perfectly natural. Responding to that stress is the key to successful speaking.

We have found that for most of our students, muscle tension during a formal speech assignment is located in three major areas of the body: the triceps, the neck and shoulders, and the knees.

The triceps are the muscles located on the backside of the upper arms, and control the lengthening of the arms. When the triceps are tensed, a speaker's arms may appear rigid and robotic. Tension in the triceps may also be evidenced in speakers who hold their arms out from their sides, or who gesture without bending their arms.

Tension in the neck and shoulders can lead to the hunching described in the previous section, and may affect your breath support. Shoulder tension usually is accompanied by a tensing of the mid- to upper-back muscles, and typically is evidenced by a tendency of the speaker to hold the hands in front or to clasp the hands together. Tension in this body area also dramatically affects gestures, making them either tense and robotic or incomplete.

Tension in the knees usually is evidenced by mild shakes or vibrations. These shakes are relatively minor, and are very seldom noticeable by the audience. They can be very distracting to the speaker, though, and can sometimes make the speaker feel more vulnerable and anxious.

In all of these cases, relaxation is the key. Professional speakers and public figures sometimes hire personal massage therapists to help feel more relaxed prior to delivering a speech. An easier and more affordable approach for the typical public-speaking student is to learn the difference between the way that muscles feel when relaxed or when tensed.

One exercise we teach to students to help define that difference is to stand in a comfortable upright position with the arms resting at the sides. Slowly rotate the upper body from side to side, four to five times, letting the arms trail naturally, then come to a complete stop. Make a mental note of the way that your muscles feel at that moment. Once you become conscious of the difference in feeling, you will recognize tension in the key areas of the body fairly quickly. That muscle memory can help you to identify the locations of tension and learn how to compensate when your body becomes tenser. It is important to identify that distinction prior to delivering the speech.

> "... dysfluencies occur as a result of two circumstances: The speaker loses focus on the construction of language, or the speaker's oral language overtakes the mental development of the language."

Fluency and perfect pace

Pace and fluency is the most difficult skill to master when delivering an impromptu speech. Pace refers to the overall rate of speech, and more technically the number of syllables spoken per unit of time. Fluency is generally a measure of the smoothness of the speech. Fluency also refers to the speaker's correct use of language and grammar. A fluent speech is one devoid of filler words and sounds, minor unintended pauses, and interruptions in the flow of language. These language errors are referred to as dysfluencies.

There is a significant difference, generally, between the impromptu presenting of the spoken word in comparison to its written counterpart. That difference is due mainly to temporality. Writing simply requires more time to construct the language than reading or speaking. As a result, written language tends to be more formal and more precise—writers expend a greater amount of time crafting the language than impromptu speakers, who must devise the language constructions with greater speed and less forethought.

The mental construction of language is very seldom a continuous process. Because language is fluid, different words may have different levels of appropriateness or even meaning at different times and with different audiences. Additionally, speakers are faced with a near limitless array of options for constructing language—that is, there are many ways to explain effectively a single idea.

Usually dysfluencies occur as a result of two circumstances: The speaker loses focus on the construction of language, or the speaker's oral language overtakes the mental development of the language. Losing focus is often the response to distractions. External noise (audible or visual disruptions) or internal noise (nervous anxiety, mental shifts, loss of train of thought) can trigger a loss of focus and disrupt the flow of language.

An equally common and sometimes concurrent phenomenon is overtaking mental formulation. Our brains are not fine-tuned engines that run smoothly once we start them. Thinking tends to be a series of starts and stops. At times, ideas and language seem to form smoothly for a short period of time and then stop. Writers refer to this phenomenon as "writer's block," an inability to form ideas or concepts clearly. Almost all writers and speakers face these mental roadblocks with regularity during the construction of language, but writers have additional time to refocus or to explore alternate options. Because impromptu speakers are faced with temporal constraints, the oral presentation can catch up very quickly to the mental formulation of the language, and often overtake it. These "speaker's blocks" tend to reduce dramatically the effectiveness of the presentation.

To avoid these mental blocks in the impromptu speech, it is essential that the speaker operate at a pace which allows the thought process to operate just ahead of the oral delivery. It is what I refer to as "perfect pace"—the rate of delivery that allows for the mental construction of language enough in advance of oral presentation that the language may be presented devoid of dysfluencies. Perfect pace is subtly different for each individual speaker—some speakers will naturally speak slightly faster or slower than others. Speaking too slowly can lull the audience or make the speaker seem slow thinking. On the other hand, speaking too quickly will almost always result in consistent speaker's blocks.

> "... the attainment of consistent fluency in an impromptu speech is an acquired skill developed through practice."

Some speakers are truly gifted with the ability to deliver an impromptu speech with perfect pace. For the vast majority of people, however, the attainment of consistent fluency in an impromptu speech is an acquired skill developed through practice. The following drills will help you strengthen your impromptu delivery skills while simultaneously refining different aspects of the impromptu methods discussed earlier in this chapter.

Exercise 18.3. Drills to Help Find Your Perfect Pace.

For all of these drills, use a stopwatch to time the length of your drills. Work to increase depth and development, and to lengthen the time of your oral delivery while determining your "perfect pace." The more you practice, the easier it will be to speak comfortably in an impromptu manner.

Fluency Drill. Practice speaking without preparation. Work to construct language effectively at a pace which allows your thought process to work just ahead of your mouth. The simple activity of speaking off-the-cuff is the best way to develop fluency.

Newspaper Drill. Read through a single story in your local or national newspaper from start to finish. After completing the story, restate as much of the story as you can recall. Include details where you can remember them. This drill aids in recall and fluency.

Story Drill. Choose your favorite childhood story. Tell the story three times from start to finish, adding detail and description with each successive telling. This drill helps to improve descriptive language skills, such as the inclusion of useful adjectives and adverbs. The more comfortable you become with added detail, the easier it will be to incorporate similar levels of detail in the impromptu speech.

Movie or Literary Synopsis. Choose a single movie or work of literature. Try to describe the major character, background, and storyline. Explore variations in timeframe—offer a synopsis in 30 seconds; offer the same synopsis in 60 seconds; 120 seconds. This exercise helps to establish the timing of supports to help illustrate your ideas in an impromptu speech, while at the same time developing a sense of timing and appropriate detail.

Exercise 18.3. Drills to Help Find Your Perfect Pace (continued).

Impromptu Advocacy. Select a controversial topic and provide three reasons why you stand against or in favor of the topic. Do not incorporate illustrations. Focus on your ability to subdivide your ideas quickly and to develop the concepts themselves.

Lecture Summary. Recount the major ideas of a classroom lecture from the day. Explain the significance of individual topics of the lecture and predict how you might be tested on those topics. This drill not only aids in recall, but will also help to make you a better student! This exercise is best accomplished at the end of the day, perhaps as you are trying to go to sleep.

Conclusion

Impromptu speaking is a historic art that showcases a speaker's ability to organize and deliver in very little time. This chapter has worked to break impromptu speaking down into manageable parts so that you can feel confident in your ability to use the skills you have learned throughout the semester and throughout the reading of this textbook and bring those techniques together to deliver an excellent impromptu presentation. As important as organization and delivery are, we also have pointed to the critical nature of supporting your argument through proof that does not need to be researched in advance. In addition, relaxation drills can truly make you feel more confident in your abilities as a speaker in impromptu situations, and in other speaking situations as well. Impromptu speaking is a skill you will turn to over and over again in your professional and personal life.

Endnotes

1 "Impromptu Speaking," by Wiles, Cheryl. In Harvard *Management Communication Letter*, Dec. 2001, Vol. 4, Issue 12, pp. 7–8.

2 "Orality, Literacy, and Modern Media," by Ong, Walter. In *Communication and History: Technology, Culture, Society*, by David Crowley and Paul Heyer. White Plains, NY: Longman Publishers, 1995, p. 66.

3 "Communication in the Middle Ages," by Burke, James. In *Communication and History: Technology, Culture, Society*, by David Crowley and Paul Heyer. White Plains, NY: Longman Publishers, 1995, p. 81.

4 "Impromptu Speaking Exercises," by Bytwerk, Randall L. *Communication Education*, Apr. 1985, Vol. 34, Issue 2, pp. 148–149.

5 "Impromptu Speaking," by Cox, Martin R. In *Rostrum*. Vol. 72, Number 9, May, 1998, pp. 11–12.

Impromptu Presentation

Goal: Impromptu speaking is perhaps the most often used delivery style in college and beyond. It is necessary for informal talks, group discussions, question & answer, and argument rebuttals. Impromptu speeches are an effective training aid for numerous important speaking characteristics. In this speech, you will aim to demonstrate sound argumentation, clear organization, and engaged delivery, all with limited preparation time.

Written Work: No written preparation is required for this speech. One note card will be completed during the preparation time given in class. This card will be turned in to your instructor after the completion of your speech.

Procedure: You will have 3 minutes to prepare this speech. At the beginning of your preparation time, your instructor will provide you with a topic. It may range from elaborating on a quote or a noun, selling an item in your backpack, or persuading regarding a social issue. You must generate an organized, but "off the cuff" speech. This speech will need an introduction with a clear thesis statement, a body with two or three main ideas supporting, and a conclusion. You will also need to support your main points with examples or illustrations for each point. You will do 2 of these speeches, and your lower grade will be dropped.

Time Limits: 2–3 minutes. One point will be deducted for every 15 seconds under or over the time limit.

Special Requirements: At the minimum, your speech should include the following:

I. Introduction

    A. Opening Statement

    B. State thesis

    C. Preview of your main points

(Transition to Main Point 1)

II. Main Point 1

    A. Statement of main point

    B. At least one example/illustration

    C. Summary of 1st main point

(Transition to Main Point 2)

III. Main Point 2

    A. Statement of second main point

    B. At least one example/illustration

    C. Summary of 2nd main point

(Transition to Conclusion)

IV. Conclusion

    A. Restate thesis

    B. Review points

    C. Provide closure

Total Points Possible: 30

Instructor Evaluation for the Impromptu Presentation

Name:_____

Topic:_____

Time:_____

EX=excellent   GD=good   AV=meets requirement/loosely   FR=weak   NI=needs improvement

Content

Introduction:

____Captured attention	EX	GD	AV	FR	NI
____Presented a clear thematic statement	EX	GD	AV	FR	NI
____Previewed main points	EX	GD	AV	FR	NI

Body:

____Organized in clear and appropriate manner	EX	GD	AV	FR	NI
____Main points clearly differentiated	EX	GD	AV	FR	NI
____Balance between main points	EX	GD	AV	FR	NI
____Effective use of connectives	EX	GD	AV	FR	NI
____Points are explained & developed well	EX	GD	AV	FR	NI
____Examples were clear and specific	EX	GD	AV	FR	NI

Conclusion:

____Summarized main points	EX	GD	AV	FR	NI
____Restated Thesis	EX	GD	AV	FR	NI
____Provided an effective parting shot/ created a lasting impression	EX	GD	AV	FR	NI

Delivery

____Vocal variety (rate, volume, inflection)	EX	GD	AV	FR	NI
____Strong eye contact with entire audience	EX	GD	AV	FR	NI
____Minimalized vocalized pauses	EX	GD	AV	FR	NI
____Made use of purposeful gestures	EX	GD	AV	FR	NI
____Free of distractions	EX	GD	AV	FR	NI

Comments:

Presentation _____/30

Deductions for Time ____/5

TOTAL POINTS _____/30

Peer Evaluation Form for Impromptu Presentation

In terms of CONTENT, what is:

The STRONGEST element of the presentation?

_____
_____
_____

The WEAKEST element of the presentation?

_____
_____
_____

A piece of CONSTRUCTIVE advice for the speaker?

_____
_____
_____

In terms of DELIVERY, what is:

The STRONGEST element of the presentation?

_____
_____
_____

The WEAKEST element of the presentation?

_____
_____
_____

A piece of CONSTRUCTIVE advice for the speaker?

_____
_____
_____

Peer Evaluation Form for Impromptu Presentation

In terms of CONTENT, what is:

The STRONGEST element of the presentation?

_____

_____

_____

The WEAKEST element of the presentation?

_____

_____

_____

A piece of CONSTRUCTIVE advice for the speaker?

_____

_____

_____

In terms of DELIVERY, what is:

The STRONGEST element of the presentation?

_____

_____

_____

The WEAKEST element of the presentation?

_____

_____

_____

A piece of CONSTRUCTIVE advice for the speaker?

_____

_____

_____

Peer Evaluation Form for Impromptu Presentation

In terms of CONTENT, what is:

The STRONGEST element of the presentation?

_____

_____

_____

The WEAKEST element of the presentation?

_____

_____

_____

A piece of CONSTRUCTIVE advice for the speaker?

_____

_____

_____

In terms of DELIVERY, what is:

The STRONGEST element of the presentation?

_____

_____

_____

The WEAKEST element of the presentation?

_____

_____

_____

A piece of CONSTRUCTIVE advice for the speaker?

_____

_____

_____

Peer Evaluation Form for Impromptu Presentation

In terms of CONTENT, what is:

The STRONGEST element of the presentation?

_____

_____

_____

The WEAKEST element of the presentation?

_____

_____

_____

A piece of CONSTRUCTIVE advice for the speaker?

_____

_____

_____

In terms of DELIVERY, what is:

The STRONGEST element of the presentation?

_____

_____

_____

The WEAKEST element of the presentation?

_____

_____

_____

A piece of CONSTRUCTIVE advice for the speaker?

_____

_____

_____

Peer Evaluation Form for Impromptu Presentation

In terms of CONTENT, what is:

The STRONGEST element of the presentation?

_____

_____

_____

The WEAKEST element of the presentation?

_____

_____

_____

A piece of CONSTRUCTIVE advice for the speaker?

_____

_____

_____

In terms of DELIVERY, what is:

The STRONGEST element of the presentation?

_____

_____

_____

The WEAKEST element of the presentation?

_____

_____

_____

A piece of CONSTRUCTIVE advice for the speaker?

_____

_____

_____

Peer Evaluation Form for Impromptu Presentation

In terms of CONTENT, what is:

The STRONGEST element of the presentation?

_____

_____

_____

The WEAKEST element of the presentation?

_____

_____

_____

A piece of CONSTRUCTIVE advice for the speaker?

_____

_____

_____

In terms of DELIVERY, what is:

The STRONGEST element of the presentation?

_____

_____

_____

The WEAKEST element of the presentation?

_____

_____

_____

A piece of CONSTRUCTIVE advice for the speaker?

_____

_____

_____

Peer Evaluation Form for Impromptu Presentation

In terms of CONTENT, what is:

The STRONGEST element of the presentation?

_____

_____

_____

The WEAKEST element of the presentation?

_____

_____

_____

A piece of CONSTRUCTIVE advice for the speaker?

_____

_____

_____

In terms of DELIVERY, what is:

The STRONGEST element of the presentation?

_____

_____

_____

The WEAKEST element of the presentation?

_____

_____

_____

A piece of CONSTRUCTIVE advice for the speaker?

_____

_____

_____

Notes

CHAPTER 19

Delivering an Elevator Speech

by John McKenzie

Objectives

After studying Chapter 19, you should be able to do the following:

- ☐ Define elevator speech.
- ☐ Organize an effective elevator speech.
- ☐ Recognize opportunities for introducing yourself to professional colleagues using an elevator speech.
- ☐ Recognize three senses of timing relevant to speechmaking.
- ☐ Understand and be able to use specific strategies for establishing a memory in the minds of professional colleagues through speech.
- ☐ Encourage and create opportunities for further communication with professional colleagues you've just met.

Key Terms

TERM	DEFINITION
acronym	A word composed from the beginning letters or syllables of a string of words that form the name of a process, company, product, expression, etc.
buttering query	A question designed to appeal to your listener's ego, which should only be used carefully and judiciously.
conversational tone	A tone of voice a speaker can use to encourage his or her listener to feel welcome to participate in conversation with the speaker, rather than feeling as though he or she is listening to impersonal or disconnected speech.
elevator speech	A very short speech designed to effectively introduce yourself or an idea, given in roughly the amount of time it takes for an elevator to get you from the floor you're on to your destination.
hook	An early part of an elevator speech which answers the question "What makes me a person of interest for my subject in this situation?"
issue query	A question which asks something about an important topic, which should be relevant to your listener's interests or knowledge.
jargon	Obscure and often pretentious language marked by circumlocutions and long words, frequently specific to a particular profession.
kairos	An ancient Greek term for time that means the opportune moment.
krisis	An ancient Greek term for timing that refers to the point in time at which a decision must come to pass on an issue, even if it is to say that no decision can be made, from which the English word crisis is derived.
kronos	An ancient Greek term for time that has a beginning, a middle, and an end, from which the English word chronology is derived.
Mehrabian's Rule	A 1971 research finding that, when listening to a speaker, audiences determined the speaker's likeability based 7% on the words they have spoken, 38% on paralinguistic cues such as tone of voice, and 55% on facial expression and body language.
personal query	A question related to personal concerns rather than professional ones.
reference	A middle part of an elevator speech which gives your listener information about yourself and, ideally, provides a person, organization, or work to which they can turn for additional information about you.
situational query	A question which asks something about the situation or moment you and your listener are in currently.
tag line	A brief phrase that summarizes an idea, much like attaching a title or label to it, which provides an easy reference point for later discussion.
verbal business card	A way to relate much of the same information one would include on a standard business card but made to be more personalized, interactive, conversational, and in speech form.

Introduction

It's 9:00 a.m. You're getting on an elevator in the building you work in. You have been working for this company for two months, and have hopes of working your way up the professional ladder to make a career for yourself. Even if you don't plan on working at this job forever, you know that doing well in this position will help your career prospects for the future. As you enter the elevator, just before the doors close, a person you recognize as the Senior Vice President of the company enters with you. The SVP knows you only vaguely, and you know it would be advantageous for you if they knew you better. You know that impressing this person might help you the next time you're up for promotion, you need a budget approved, or you need to get his or her attention about a business proposal. The SVP nods at you and says, "Hey there! What are you working on right now?" What should you say when you only have a minute or two to answer, but still want to make a lasting impression?

The scenario described here is ideal for what's commonly called an elevator speech. An elevator speech is a very short speech designed to effectively introduce yourself or an idea, given in roughly the amount of time it takes for an elevator to get you from the floor you're on to your destination. The goal of this chapter is to teach you to prepare an effective elevator speech and to recognize opportunities for delivering your elevator speech whenever they may arise. You should think of your elevator speech as a verbal business card to be dispensed when you want yourself or your ideas to be *noticed* and *remembered*. (Remember, though, that in many cases it is still prudent and effective to give the person an actual, physical business card along with your speech.)

You may be asking yourself how much an elevator speech differs from an impromptu speech. While elevator speeches are similar to impromptu speeches insofar as both can take place in unexpected situations, beyond that point the two differ in character dramatically. First, elevator speeches are designed to be given from one person to another, in contrast to impromptu speeches which can be given in front of comparatively larger audiences. Second, choosing to deliver an elevator speech or not is usually up to the speaker's choice, while impromptu speeches are usually given when prompted by another person, audience, or situation in which refusal to speak would be frowned upon. Third, elevator speeches are about professional development and/or the pitching of an idea so as to cement further professional networking opportunities. While there are some similarities between the two types of speech, there are many more differences.

Location and Opportunity

One needs to be able to recognize when an elevator speech is appropriate and could potentially be effective, versus when it is more likely to annoy, irritate, or otherwise disrupt your targeted subject (the person to whom you intend to deliver your speech). It is important to distinguish between interruptions and opportunities. Interruptions arise when:

- ❑ Your potential listener is in deep conversation with someone across the room. If your subject is already involved with someone else, you should not try to interrupt his or her conversation.
- ❑ Your potential listener is obviously angry or upset. You should pay attention to a person's mood or disposition before approaching him or her, as this kind of emotional or psychological noise will negatively affect how your speech will be received.
- ❑ Your potential listener appears to be busy. Interrupting a person who looks especially busy means he or she will likely remember you as an interrupter if anything.

In contrast to interruptions, finding the right opportunity means *recognizing when your subject looks available, approachable, and in the right mood for the kind of conversation you're about to start.* When these conditions are met, you have an opportunity.

Exercise 19.1. A Hypothetical Elevator Speech Scenario (Part 1 of 3).

Jarom Betancourt is an expert in professional communication and has a Bachelor's degree from UT-Austin in Corporate Communications. Nevertheless, he still feels some apprehension from time to time when he's put into certain situations. Jarom works for a small public relations partnership in Austin, and is attending a large business conference with other PR workers from around the country. Jarom will be giving a short presentation on his company's PR work in Austin on the last day of the conference. While at the conference, Jarom recognizes Deanna Surratt, CEO of Surratt Enterprises, the largest public relations firm in Texas, from across the room and watches her enter a room where a presentation is about to be given by another conference attendee. Jarom decides to attend the presentation and, when he enters the room, realizes that the only remaining seat is the one directly next to Surratt. Jarom is nervous and excited, and he decides to take the seat. He knows that he could use this opportunity to make an important connection and advance his career. At this point, though, the presentation is in full swing and he doesn't have the chance to speak with her right away, but he knows he wants to say something to introduce himself and impress this potential new ally. An opportune moment for an elevator speech would be after the presentation. However, in the hustle of the conclusion of the presentation, Jarom loses his opportunity as Surratt quickly moves on and is joined by some other colleagues.

The ancient Greeks used three words to discuss timing in speechmaking, all of which are related to opportunity. The first is <u>kronos</u>, from which the English word chronology comes. Kronos refers to time with a beginning, a middle, and an end. For speechmakers, kronos was important for recognizing that a speech must come at the proper time within a chronology of events to be most effective. For delivering an elevator speech, you should evaluate whether your timing is appropriate within the wider context of a professional chronology: are you prepared to be heard? Is your subject prepared to hear you? If not, perhaps you should consider whether the timing is right for your speech. For example, if today is Susan's first day at her new job and she is unfamiliar with her new setting and colleagues, even if she sees a senior vice president in the elevator she may decide not to give an elevator speech until she is more established, comfortable, and confident in her new position. Instead, she may introduce herself to the vice president, but hold off on delivering her elevator speech until she feels the time is right. She recognizes that, in her case, it is very likely that she will see the vice president at work again, and so she is not losing her only opportunity. By choosing to wait, Susan is paying attention to a professional chronology (or *kronos*) and anticipating a better opportunity in the near future. A particular elevator speech is only effective the *first* time a listener hears it, and by choosing to wait Susan has not lost her opportunity, but recognized her chance to speak at a more effective time.

The second Greek word for timing is <u>krisis</u>, from which comes the English word crisis. Krisis refers to the point in time at which a decision must come to pass on an issue, even if it is to say that no decision can be made. If a *particular* event is close on the horizon, such as an upcoming promotion or budget proposal decision, and your elevator speech may have an impact on a decision that could be made, then consider how best to address this moment of *krisis*. To return to Susan, imagine that it is now six months later. The project she has been working on has been well received, but has been placed in competition with another project within her company. Only one of the projects will be chosen by her superiors to move forward with and be put into further production. Until this point, she has made several presentations to her immediate supervisors, but never has had the opportunity to meet with the upper management team that will make the final decision. This represents a moment of *krisis*: a decision must be made soon, and if Susan's project is accepted it will be a major factor in her company's success and her own professional development. At this point, Susan is looking for a tool that could tip the scales in her favor.

The third, and widely considered to be the most important, Greek term for timing in speechmaking is <u>kairos</u>. Kairos has no direct translation into English, but essentially means "the opportune moment." When considering when to give a speech, or considering when to make specific points, statements, or arguments within a speech, one should attempt to find the opportune moments to do so. Recognizing these opportune moments is a skill you will develop as you gain more and more experience with speechmaking, including the experience you will gain in this class. Let's revisit Susan's case to explain the relationship of *kairos* to *kronos* and *krisis*. If, during the period of *krisis* that Susan identified which we noted in the previous paragraph, she were to find herself entering an elevator with the Senior Vice President of the company again, she would have found the opportune moment (*kairos*) for her elevator speech. Until now, she has not had the opportunity to discuss her project with the management team that will make the final decision, but now is in a room with one important member of that team. By waiting until she was ready and paying attention to the chronology of events unfolding before her (*kronos*), Susan demonstrated a keen sense of rhetorical timing. Susan mentally collects herself, greets her listener, and gives the short elevator speech she has prepared for why her project is important for the company's success. Her pitch, if effective, may become a major reason for management to ultimately choose her project over her competitor's. Throughout this scenario, Susan has demonstrated a careful attention to timing in all three of its senses to identify and take advantage of the best opportunity for giving an effective elevator speech.

A final, important note about location and opportunity with regards to elevator speeches may not be entirely obvious from what we have discussed so far in this chapter: not all elevator speeches take place in elevators. True, the term "elevator speech" originates with the idea of delivering a speech in an elevator, but its primary emphasis is on the brevity of the speech and the *incidental,* rather than planned, nature of meeting someone in an elevator. For an example of an elevator speech scenario that does not take place in an elevator, read the included exercise sections of this chapter, titled A Real Life Elevator Speech Scenario. In general, you should note that one can give an elevator speech in nearly any location. What makes it an elevator speech is not where it takes place, but its extreme brevity, incidental or happenstance occurrence, and that the goal is to introduce yourself and briefly communicate an idea.

Know Your Audience, Know Yourself

When delivering an elevator speech, it is always important that you know something about the person with whom you are speaking. If you are familiar with what the person does, let him or her know it in a way that comes across positively (rather than as obvious or insincere pandering). Knowledge of your subject's background not only gives you something to talk about, it means you can give a much more personalized and effective elevator speech. If you can competently discuss what your listener does, it can make you more interesting to converse with.

On the other hand, you want to do more than just talk about your listener's work and background; your goal with an elevator speech is to get their attention—to get them interested in you and your idea. To give an effective elevator speech, you need to know what you are talking about and be ready to share that information in a meaningful and organized manner. You also need to know what's most valuable or interesting about your idea to the person with whom you're speaking. Knowing your audience is the most effectual way to quickly identify which facts you should share and which you should save for another time.

Organization

Elevator speeches benefit from applying similar organizational strategies to those of longer, more formal presentations, despite the fact that elevator speeches are generally more conversational and informal. Any time one is in a professional communication situation, organization is an important tool to show one's level of expertise and skill to one's audience. Additionally, organization makes one's presentation more understandable, effective, memorable, and, often, more logical. Some advanced organizational strategies are discussed elsewhere in this book; however, it is important that you also understand some of the basics of organizing an effective elevator speech.

A strong elevator speech consists of five basic sections: the *introduction*, the *hook*, the *reference*, the *query*, and the *conclusion* or *farewell*. To introduce yourself, you first need to grab your target's attention. Often, the best way to do this is to call the person by their name: "Professor Campbell?" Next, if the person does not know you or may not remember you, give him or her your name and a way to understand who you are and why you have chosen to talk to them. For example, you could give your name and major. The reason you should give more than just your name is to help your listener to place and remember you.

Once you have identified yourself and initiated the conversation or speech, you should find a way to pique your listener's interest. This is the <u>hook</u>, and should answer the question "what makes you or your idea interesting and important for your listener at this moment?" The more you know about your listener, the more options you have for an effective hook. In general, most people are very busy and already inundated with more information than they can process. This is especially true of professionals who have developed their careers to the point at which you find yourself wanting to present them with an elevator speech. As a result, it takes an effective hook to break through your listener's shell of concern for their other responsibilities and obligations.

While there are many ways of grabbing a person's attention, for an elevator speech you should primarily consider three strategies.

1. **Identify a common associate to your listener.** The first hook strategy is to *identify a common associate*: another professional colleague familiar to you both, and about whom your listener feels positively. If you can build a connection in your listener's mind between that associate and yourself, then you've already introduced yourself with a positive angle. This associate could be your immediate boss, a teammate/coworker, or anyone with whom you have had a professional relationship with in the past. Be careful, however, about who you associate yourself with in these situations so as to maximize the good favor you are trying to build. For example, suppose you work for a well known engineering firm under a well known supervisor who is widely and positively regarded by his or her peers in the business world. Now imagine you are attending a national business conference for engineers and encounter Alay Bhatt, the researcher for Intel Corp that invented the USB drive for personal computers. You happen to know that your own supervisor worked with Mr. Bhatt in the past and the two have a mutual respect for one another. In this scenario, you have the

Exercise 19.2. A Hypothetical Elevator Speech Scenario (Part 2 of 3).

After his encounter with the PR executive Deanna Surratt, Jarom thought a lot about what he could have done differently to take advantage of the opportunity he had been presented with. In particular, he thought about what an effective elevator speech in that scenario would have sounded like. Here is the elevator speech Jarom thinks he should have given to provoke an effective conversation with Mrs. Surratt:

Jarom: "Mrs. Surratt? Hi, my name is Jarom Betancourt; I work at a PR firm in Austin. I wanted to let you know how much I respect the work you've done to make Surratt Enterprises a powerhouse in the industry. Tomorrow I'm giving a talk on some of my company's plans for developing their position in the Austin market, and wanted to invite you to my presentation. I would really value any advice you could share."

Jarom knows that, because of the way he has structured the rest of his speech, Mrs. Surratt will likely ask him for more details about his ideas:

Mrs. Surratt: "It's great to see you. What's your presentation going to be about?"

After giving a brief synopsis of his presentation, Jarom leaves the door open for future contact with Mrs. Surratt:

Jarom: "I hope to see you tomorrow at my presentation."

Mrs. Surratt: "I will try to be there."

perfect setup to use an "associate" hook in an elevator speech by mentioning that you work with his former colleague. By making this connection early, Alay Bhatt will likely be more interested in what you have to say next.

2. **Identify a project of value to your listener.** A second strategy is to identify *something you are working on or a service or expertise you can provide that has value to your listener.* If you are an accountant, mention a recent accounting project you have done and how it is advantageous for your listener or your organization. Anything you can use to imply the potential value of your ideas to the listener can be deployed here as a hooking mechanism. For example, imagine that you run into the CEO for your company and he or she casually asks what you are working on. You explain that you're working on (project X) in a way that entices the CEO to say, "Wow, tell me more about this." The key is to provide enough information to grab your listener's attention, but just little enough to compel them to want to hear more.

   One way to easily manage this "enough information, but not too much" move is to employ what's called a tag line. A tag line is a brief phrase that summarizes an idea, much like attaching a title or label to it. A tag line gives you and your listener an easy reference for later discussion. So, imagine you work for a children's entertainment company that develops and manufactures toys. If you have a chance encounter with your company's CEO, and he or she asks what you are working on, you may want to give a summary rather than all of the full details right away. In reality, you're working on developing a fully-fledged budget for your department for the next fiscal quarter that includes research and development, focus groups, labor, marketing, and manufacturing. But if you want to make all of that sound interesting and memorable for the CEO, you might attach a tag line and simply say, "I'm working on developing the next Furby—the next toy that every parent will have to buy their children." In this statement, "the next Furby" becomes a tag line you and the CEO can use anytime you want to discuss the project in the future. His or her first reaction will likely be to ask you for more information, and by this point the hook has worked. The next day you could send an e-mail with the subject heading "The Next Furby" and the CEO would immediately know what project you mean. Alternately, the next day the CEO could decide to e-mail your department about the project with the same tag line in the header. In both cases, you've established an easily referenced and memorable hook that has had an impact on your listener.

   Tag lines work in a number of communication scenarios beyond elevator speeches as well. For example, consider the impacts of tag lines on the last two presidential elections. During the 2008 presidential campaign, Barack Obama's tag line was "Change." John McCain never had one that stuck. In the 2004 presidential campaign, George W. Bush's tag line was "National Security." John Kerry never had one. Certainly both elections had more to them than these tag lines, but in each case they were heavily relied upon as effective strategies for stirring up voter enthusiasm and support.[1]

3. **Indicate your familiarity with your listener's work.** A third strategy is to *indicate your familiarity with your listener's work.* In general, people like to hear positive feedback about themselves. If you mention something they have recently done or achieved and your own appreciation for that work, your listener is likely to want to hear what you have to say next. This kind of hook both tells your listener why you are interested in talking with them and serves as a bit of an ego function by indicating *his or her* value for you. For example, when John Daly, a professor in the Department of Communication Studies and the faculty coordinator for this course, worked with a nonprofit organization a few years ago, he ran into the CEO. He told her that he had read her recent interview in the news on her research and highlighted the positive response her interview had generated for the company in the media. By mentioning these details and giving genuine praise to his listener, Professor Daly was able to garner her good favor and grab her attention for whatever he wanted to say next.[2]

   Once you have introduced yourself and hooked your listener, the real body of the elevator speech begins. At this point you have your listener's attention and it is time to take advantage of that attention to provide information about your professional credentials and/or the idea you want to emphasize. This third section of your speech is the reference. The reference is the most important part of your elevator speech because it is the part you want your listener to remember most. Think of this section as a short verbal résumé in which you provide some limited but relevant qualifications for yourself and describe your idea in an interesting way. In this section, it is particularly easy to fall into the trap of droning on and giving too much information. You should avoid sounding rehearsed and limit the information you provide to a few critical parts. You should include only one or two key items to give an effective snapshot about you or your idea without sounding overly mechanical as you do so. These snapshot items should be written and delivered so as to entice your listener into asking for additional information.

Once you have provided a reference section, you should attempt to engage your listener in a two-way conversation. Your objective in the elevator speech is to engage your listener in conversation and, ultimately, to get him or her to ask *you* a question. This is the query section.

So then what kind of question should you ask your listener? There are four general types of queries we should discuss for their importance in elevator speeches: *situational* queries, *issue* queries, *buttering* queries, and *personal* queries. With each of these, consider how to formulate questions that invite a question from your listener.

1. **Situational Query.** A *situational query* asks something regarding the context of the moment you and your listener are in. This type of query asks for your listener's input or opinion on the present situation. If you have met at a professional conference, a business meeting, or simply in an elevator in your office building, all have contexts which lend themselves to specific situational questions for which your listener could provide feedback. Imagine that you are attending a large business conference and are engaging in an elevator speech with someone. The business conference is the situation in which the two of you are participating. To ask a situational query that invites a response, you ask "So, which presentations have you seen so far?" Your listener would then likely tell you which presentations he or she has seen, and then return the question to you: "Which presentations have *you* seen?" This question gives you the chance to share more about yourself and your idea and to extend the conversation, giving you more opportunities to build rapport between yourself and your listener.

2. **Issue Query.** An *issue query* asks something about a well-known topic or issue relevant to your listener's expertise or professional knowledge. You should avoid asking a "gotcha" type of question to which your target may not have an answer, but nevertheless your question should demonstrate your own competence in the subject. A well formed issue question is often seen as a reliable indicator of intelligence, focus, and productivity. Remember that the goal of your issue query is to engage your listener in conversation and to prompt your listener to ask a question of you. An example of an issue query might be, "What do you think of the new budget proposal?" Or even better, "What do you think of the new budget proposal? I have some ideas but would like to hear your evaluation before coming to any conclusions myself." In the latter form, the question invites your listener's response to include a question like, "What are your ideas?" Such a question is an invitation for you to share more.

3. **Buttering Query.** A *buttering query* is designed to appeal to your target's sense of ego by highlighting his or her accomplishments. "Buttering" comes from the colloquial expression "to butter someone up," meaning to compliment a person so as to make them more agreeable to a proposal. Buttering queries can work well in conjunction with using familiarity with your listener's work as a hook. An example of a buttering query could be saying to one of your supervisors, "I saw an article about your work in the *Austin-American Statesman* last week; how do you manage to keep getting us such good publicity?" Another example could be asking your listener for some of his or her ideas (the reverse of what your listener may be expecting from an elevator speech scenario): "I've heard you've got some great ideas for the meeting next week; do you mind giving me a bit of a preview so I can prepare?" Buttering appeals can be extremely effective, but should be used cautiously as they can easily backfire if your listener feels you are trying too hard or being insincere. The best and safest time to use a buttering strategy is when you are genuine in your praise. Be sure, also, when using a buttering query that the focus of the exchange flows back to an emphasis on you and your ideas; your goal is to maintain this connection throughout your speech.

4. **Personal Query.** Finally, there are personal queries. A *personal query* is a question directed at private or personal concerns rather than professional matters. For example, asking whether your listener has children

would be a personal query. In general, the circumstances in which one should ask a personal query are (i) if you already know your listener fairly well, (ii) if your listener has asked you a personal question first, or (iii) if your listener seems amenable to establishing personal rapport with you. To decide whether or not you should use a personal query you should consider your listener's openness to answering a personal question and whether you have met or spoken with the person before. The better your interaction on an interpersonal level, the more appropriate and effective a personal query may be. On the other hand, if your interlocutor asks *you* a personal question, it is a good indicator that they are interested in establishing rapport with you. In these cases it is generally acceptable to ask your own personal query in response. If you still feel uncertain about the situation, you can limit your personal query to a similar or related topic. To reverse an earlier example, if your subject asks you if you are a dog person during your conversation, you should feel safe asking your own related question when giving your response: "Yes, I love dogs; I have two golden retrievers. What kinds of dogs do you have?" Personal queries, in general, *can* be (but are not always) limited in their effectiveness in elevator speech scenarios. They often turn professional conversations into private small-talk, but even this can end up as a positive turn depending on the specific circumstance. Establishing positive rapport is an important tool when networking with others. Always use your own careful judgment when evaluating whether to ask a personal query.

The final element of any good elevator speech is the proper way to say goodbye and end the interaction. If you have been well received up to this point, you should attempt to open the possibility of further communication in the future. You should consider which medium for further communication is the most appropriate in your situation. There are a number of interpersonal issues related to asking for further communication that you should seek to avoid. For example, asking for someone's phone number has another common meaning outside of the professional world. On the other hand, asking for a person's *office* phone number doesn't carry the same meaning. In most cases e-mail is a good, neutral medium to which to appeal. Therefore, concluding your conversation by asking if you can e-mail them about work from time to time is an effective strategy for opening a line for further communication while avoiding several potential interpersonal pitfalls. Additionally, when saying goodbye, you should remember to always say "nice to see you" as opposed to "nice to meet you." It is better to train yourself to say "nice to see you" in case you meet the person again in the future and forget that you have met before. By saying "nice to see you," you always leave yourself open for meeting again and again.

Improving Your Delivery

By this point, you should be able to effectively organize your elevator speech. However, another major component to consider is how best to deliver your speech once you have recognized an opportunity and chosen to act upon it.

In most situations, an informal delivery strategy is the most effective. Your elevator speech should not seem like it has been prepared, but is part of a natural flow of comfortable conversation. In general, people are overworked, busy, and not particularly interested in being stopped to take in more information. Using an informal delivery strategy, you can work your way past those reservations by coyly disguising your speech as conversation. The key is in not letting your listener identify your conversation as an elevator speech, as more people are willing to have a conversation than they are to listen to a short, impromptu presentation.

There are two common rules you can follow to improve your effectiveness and appeal. First, you should actively avoid the use of jargon and acronyms. Jargon is obscure and often pretentious language marked by circumlocutions and long words, frequently specific to a particular profession.[3] Jargon is confusing to listen to, reduces comprehension, and is generally unappealing on an interpersonal level. An acronym is a word composed from the beginning letters or syllables of a string of words that form the name of a process, company, product, expression, etc. Acronyms are one form of jargon. Acronyms can be ambiguous because one acronym may refer to many different things, and strings of acronyms are thoroughly unintelligible for most people. For example, ASAP is usually

Exercise 19.3. A Hypothetical Elevator Speech Scenario (Part 3 of 3).

Notice how the organization of Jarom's elevator speech given in the last section can be cleanly split and matched with the organizational strategies described in this section. Here is Jarom's speech again, divided into the recommended organizational sections:

Introduction (Includes a point of reference):

Mrs. Surratt? Hi, my name is Jarom Betancourt; I work at a PR firm in Austin.

The hook (Familiarity with the listener's work):

I wanted to let you know how much I respect the work you've done to make Surratt Enterprises a powerhouse in the industry.

The reference (A current project):

Tomorrow I'm giving a talk on some of my company's plans for developing their position in the Austin market, and wanted to invite you to my presentation.

The query (Issue oriented):

I would really value any advice you or your associates could share.

The farewell (Opens the possibility of further communication):

"It was really nice talking with you, and I hope to see you tomorrow at my presentation."

QUESTIONS FOR DISCUSSION

1. Given what you know about elevator speeches, do you think Jarom's speech would be effective? Why or why not?

_____

_____

_____

_____

2. How could Jarom's elevator speech be improved?

_____

_____

_____

_____

Exercise 19.3. Continued.

3. Could Jarom have included a tag line in his speech? If so, where and how?

_____

_____

_____

_____

4. Could Jarom's query have been improved? What could he have asked instead that would be better?

_____

_____

_____

_____

an acronym meaning "As Soon As Possible," but if you work in air traffic control then ASAP means "Automated Staffing Application Process." So if I were to tell you "An FAA guy from ATC just called and wants you to direct the ATCSCC ASAP," you might have a hard time understanding me. Jargon and acronyms often work to make it impossible for your listener to discover what you actually *do* or are actually talking about. When crafting your elevator speech, if you feel the need to include jargon or acronyms, make sure they are absolutely necessary and kept to a minimum. The use of jargon and/or acronyms may be necessary or helpful in some certain situations, but only when you are certain that your listener shares knowledge of their meanings with you. For example, two doctors may use jargon and acronyms to communicate with one another more quickly or efficiently, but that same language would be incomprehensible if used with their patients.

Second, you should speak in a conversational tone, even if you're using a formal delivery strategy. A conversational tone is a tone of voice a speaker can use to encourage his or her listener to feel welcome to participate in conversation with the speaker, rather than feeling as though he or she is listening to impersonal or disconnected speech. In chapter one you read that every message we communicate includes both content and relationship information. You must consider your appeal as a factor in your elevator speech, and you can manage that appeal through your delivery choices. Your vocal tone should be reserved and professional, but inviting and likeable. In 1971, communication scholar Albert Mehrabian published his finding that, when listening to a speaker, audiences determined the speaker's *likeability* based 7% on the words they have spoken, 38% on paralinguistic cues like tone of voice, and 55% on facial expression and body language.[4] This statistic would later come to be known as Mehrabian's Rule. Before delivering an elevator speech, you should be highly conscious of how to enhance your appeal with your listener. An awareness of Mehrabian's finding can aid you in determining how best to tailor your delivery to develop this appeal.

Conclusion

Developing an effective elevator speech can put you ahead in professional situations where you may otherwise have no way to stand out from the crowd. Remember that while you should prepare your speech in advance, you should always be ready to modify it for the particular moment in which it will be delivered. Every elevator speech is different, and it is this malleability that gives you the ability to choose a target, quickly adapt to your setting, and deliver a lasting impression through carefully considered speech that will advance your professional career.

Exercise 19.4. Elevator Speech Assignment.

For the next class day, you should prepare a short, thirty second to one minute elevator speech designed to introduce yourself to the class. You should imagine a situation in which you might need to use an elevator speech and imagine what kind of person your target for this speech would be, and present your speech as if you were giving it to that person.

This is not a graded assignment, but may count toward overall semester participation grades. You should follow your instructor's specific recommendations for this assignment. You should be motivated to take the assignment seriously by the desire to impress your fellow students, as well as the recognition that the ability to give a good elevator speech is a *really* important skill. You may use the outline on the following page to help you design your elevator speech.

Exercise 19.4. Continued.

OUTLINING YOUR ELEVATOR SPEECH

Instructions: Use this outline to help you design, organize, and write your elevator speech.

Introduction: _____

_____

_____

_____

Hook: _____

_____

_____

_____

Reference: _____

_____

_____

_____

_____

Query: _____

_____

_____

_____

Conclusion: _____

_____

_____

_____

_____

Endnotes

1 Thanks to John Daly and Adria Battaglia for this example.

2 Thanks to John Daly for this example.

3 The first clause of this definition comes from: jargon. 2009. In *Merriam-Webster Online Dictionary.* Retrieved June 2, 2009, from http://www.merriam-webster.com/dictionary/jargon.

4 Mehrabian, Albert. 1971. *Silent Messages.* Belmont, CA: Wadsworth Publishing Company.

Notes

Index

B

I

M